Make the Grade.
Your Atomic Dog Online Edition.

The Atomic Dog Online Edition includes proven study tools that expand and enhance key concepts in your text. Reinforce and review the information you absolutely 'need to know' with features like:

- **Review Quizzes**
- Key term Assessments
- Interactive Animations and Simulations
- Notes and Information from Your Instructor
- Pop-up Glossary Terms
- A Full Text Search Engine

Ensure that you 'make the grade'. Follow your lectures, complete assignments, and take advantage of all your available study resources like the Atomic Dog Online Edition.

How to Access Your Online Edition

- **If you purchased this text directly from Atomic Dog ….**
  Visit atomicdog.com and enter your email address and password in the login box at the top-right corner of the page.

- **If you purchased this text NEW from another source….**
  Visit our Students' Page on atomicdog.com and enter the **activation key located below** to register and access your Online Edition.

- **If you purchased this text USED from another source….**
  Using the Book Activation key below you can access the Online Edition at a discounted rate. Visit our Students' Page on atomicdog.com and enter the **Book Activation Key in** the field provided to register and gain access to the Online Edition.

Be sure to download our *How to Use Your Online Edition* guide located on atomicdog.com to learn about additional features!

This key activates your online edition. Visit atomicdog.com to enter your Book Activation Key and start accessing your online resources. For more information, give us a call at (800) 310-5661 or send us an email at support@atomicdog.com

191HB5PR9

*Some online Editions do not contain all features.

Introduction to Politics

Governments and Nations in the Twenty-First Century

FOURTH EDITION

Martin Slann

Macon State College

THOMSON
™

Introduction to Politics: Governments and Nations in the Twenty-First Century, 4e

Martin Slann

Executive Editors:
Michele Baird, Maureen Staudt, and Michael Stranz

Marketing Manager:
Mikka Baker

Managing Editor:
Kendra Leonard

Sr. Marketing Coordinators:
Lindsay Annett and Sara Mercurio

Production/Manufacturing Manager:
Donna M. Brown

Production Editorial Manager:
Dan Plofchan

Premedia Supervisor:
Becki Walker

Rights and Permissions Specialist:
Bahman Naraghi

Associate Technology Project Manager:
Angela Makowski

Cover Image:
© 2007 Getty

Composition House:
Cadmus/KGL

The Adaptable Courseware Program consists of products and additions to existing Thomson products that are produced from camera-ready copy. Peer review, class testing, and accuracy are primarily the responsibility of the author(s).

Introduction to Politics / Martin Slann – Fourth Edition

BOOK ISBN 0-759-39255-2
PACKAGE ISBN 0-759-39441-5

LCCN 2006908599

International Divisions List

Asia (Including India):
Thomson Learning
(a division of Thomson Asia Pte Ltd)
5 Shenton Way #01-01
UIC Building
Singapore 068808
Tel: (65) 6410-1200
Fax: (65) 6410-1208

Latin America:
Thomson Learning
Seneca 53
Colonia Polano
11560 Mexico, D.F., Mexico
Tel (525) 281-2906
Fax (525) 281-2656

UK/Europe/Middle East/Africa:
Thomson Learning
High Holborn House
50-51 Bedford Row
London, WC1R 4LR
United Kingdom
Tel 44 (020) 7067-2500
Fax 44 (020) 7067-2600

Australia/New Zealand:
Thomson Learning Australia
102 Dodds Street
Southbank, Victoria 3006
Australia

Canada:
Thomson Nelson
1120 Birchmount Road
Toronto, Ontario
Canada M1K 5G4
Tel (416) 752-9100
Fax (416) 752-8102

Spain (Includes Portugal):
Thomson Paraninfo
Calle Magallanes 25
28015 Madrid
España
Tel 34 (0)91 446-3350
Fax 34 (0)91 445-621445-6218

To:
Ruthy, Guy, Tal, Shelley, Liat,
Jacob, Aaron, Lauren, Talia, and Sarah
Oscar, Stella, Homeless, and Dekel

CONTENTS

PART 3:   THE INSTITUTIONS OF GOVERNMENT AND THE POLITICAL PROCESS

PART 4:   INGREDIENTS OF INTERNATIONAL POLITICS

PART 5 THE INTERNATIONAL SITUATION AT THE BEGINNING OF THE CENTURY

Introduction to the Text

This introductory text was written in the hope of making the subject of governments and politics interesting to students and useful for classroom instructors. Hopefully, students who read this book will be alerted to the fact that the world is becoming a more integrated place and eventually desire to become fully aware that what happens in a country thousands of miles away (even one they may not have heard of before) can impact them in a variety of ways—some positively, some negatively, and some downright destructively. Hopefully, instructors using the book will be able to do so in the knowledge that the chapters allow and encourage many opportunities for them to provide selected complementary reading assignments and presentations that focus on preferred issues that reflect their expertise.

The text is also an outcome of many years of teaching introductory politics to students from a variety of disciplines and interests. Through trial and error and a great deal of (sometimes brutally candid) student evaluation, I wrote chapters that were relatively brief and informative. Most of all, I wrote them with the desire that they would be understandable. Most of my students in this course were bright but had little interest in comparative and international politics, let alone political philosophy. In one sense, I couldn't blame them. They have lots of distractions and pressures preparing for a career that could last four or more decades. But this is the challenge of teaching—to get students interested in a subject that really does influence their lives. In fact, the ultimate compliment in such a class was usually along the lines of "Gee, this course was more interesting than I thought it would be." It doesn't take a lot to make me happy.

The accelerating use of communication technology and the globalization of the world economy have made an understanding of different political cultures more useful than ever before. The study of comparative politics enables students to develop an appreciation of societies that are very different from our own—and often in opposition to our values. Remaining aloof from world affairs is no longer an option. Ignorance about other countries is now more of a liability than ever. Students in the United States can especially benefit from the comparative method. American society is ceasing to be monolingual; demographic shifts are producing a population that is unprecedented in its ethnic and religious diversity. Using our own familiar political and social systems as reference points, we must explore the challenges and opportunities provided by the analysis of histories, cultures, religions, political processes and institutions, and cultures distinct from our own.

To get students interested, the topics in an introductory politics textbook, like those in an introductory politics classroom, have to be both current and meaningful. In this text I have focused on essential matters such as how government came to be, different experiments in governmental institutions, the influence of culture on politics, and how geography, demography, and violence create and sustain political outcomes. I try to emphasize the dynamics of terrorism and ethnic conflict as permanent rather than as new phenomena—not to frighten the reader but to get the reader to comprehend them. I have also devoted considerable space to democratization and democracy as well as to the threats to both. In the early years of the twenty-first century, we are still engaged in an evolving international paradigm that is already very different from what is now viewed as the much "cozier" Cold War era. We need to make students aware of the possible outcomes by informing them of the new realities.

Like most comparativists and internationalists, I have traveled extensively. Some of my impressions are almost certainly included in this text. I couldn't help this and do believe that personal impressions can be useful in making a point if done with discretion. However, some holidays in hell probably shouldn't be included. The most pertinent example I can recall has to do with opposing groups in the Middle East (hardliners) telling me that the best thing for the other would be to be thrown off the land they are disputing and never allowed to return.

At the same time, I fully recognize that no text, including this one, offers coverage that satisfies all preferences. Again, my primary concern has been with the needs of the students. Thus, I have included a generous amount of references to American political institutions as a way to get students to do some comparisons. These references also enable the student to be more at ease with handling a lot of unfamiliar material.

The book is divided into five sections into which the chapters naturally seem to fall. Part 1 consists of an introductory chapter that addresses the principal changes that have occurred in political regimes and processes during the decade and a half since the end of the Cold War. Part 2's three chapters develop the theme of politics as a creative and necessary human activity. It includes a review of the features considered as proper ingredients of a political society as well as a review of the impact of history and culture on political outlooks. Part 3 includes four chapters that explain the kind of political institutions and processes that are commonplace, including basic governmental structures that are familiar to most students. Part 4 three chapters explore some current themes of politics such as economics, geography, demography, and violence that we cannot ignore as critical considerations of nearly every country's political life. Finally, the four chapters included in Part 5 review the current international constellation, focusing on characteristics that will continue to affect us all in the coming years.

This print version of this edition contains 16 pages of four-color reproductions of the most important figures. Atomic Dog has provided this additional resource so that students will have no difficulty discerning small portions of graphs, isolated or intricate areas of maps, and the like.

Acknowledgments

Throughout the revision process for this edition, I have been grateful for the encouragement from Kendra Leonard, my developmental editor; and Sheryl Nelson, my copyeditor. Laura Pierson was a constant encouragement, and I am grateful for her expertise. I am grateful to my Production Editorial Manager, Dan Plofchan, who was always there when I needed him. Finally, my division secretary, Debra Slagle, was an invaluable help in preparing the manuscript during the last stages.

My wife Ruthy was, as always, a wonderful companion who really does understand why I'm in the office so much. I will always remain grateful to J. Ben Stalvey, whose recent passing saddened many of his former students, and to Bernard Schechterman, Charles W. Dunn, and William Lasser for their steadfast friendship, helpful advice, and the encouragement of humor.

Finally, I want to thank the reviewers for both compliments and criticism. I incorporated a number of suggestions and was grateful for all of them, even the more candid ones. Because you are a big reason for this text, perhaps you'd be good enough to adopt it.

Donald G. Baker, Long Island University
Baogang Guo, Dalton State University
Keith A. Knutson, Viterbo University
Karen Peterson, Middle Tennessee State University
David Uranga, Pasadena City College
Harald M. Sandstrom, University of Hartford

About Atomic Dog

Atomic Dog is faithfully dedicated to meeting the needs of today's faculty and students, offering a unique and clear alternative to the traditional textbook. Breaking down textbooks and study tools into their basic "atomic parts," we then recombine them and utilize rich digital media to create a "new breed" of textbook.

This blend of online content, interactive multimedia, and print creates unprecedented adaptability to meet different educational settings and individual learning styles. As part of Thomson Custom Solutions, we offer even greater flexibility and resources in creating a learning solution tailor-fit to your course.

Atomic Dog is loyally dedicated to our customers and our environment, adhering to three key tenets:

Focus on essential and quality content: We are proud to work with our authors to deliver a high-quality textbook at a lower cost. We focus on the essential information and resources students need and present them in an efficient but student-friendly format.

Value and choice for students: Our products are a great value and provide students with more choices in "what and how" they buy—often at savings of 30 to 40 percent less than traditional textbooks. Students who choose the Online Edition may see even greater savings compared to a print textbook. Faculty play an important and willing role— working with us to keep costs low for their students by evaluating texts and supplementary materials online.

Reducing our environmental "paw-print": Atomic Dog is working to reduce its impact on our environment in several ways. Our textbooks and marketing materials are all printed on recycled paper. We encourage faculty to review text materials online instead of requesting a print review copy. Students who buy the Online Edition do their part by going "paperless" and eliminating the need for additional packaging or shipping. Atomic Dog will continue to explore new ways that we can reduce our "paw-print" in the environment and hope you will join us in these efforts.

Atomic Dog is dedicated to faithfully serving the needs of faculty and students—providing a learning tool that helps make the connection. We hope that after you try our texts, Atomic Dog—like other great dogs—will become your faithful companion.

Martin Slann

Online Edition

Introduction to Politics is available online as well as in print. The Online Edition demonstrates how the interactive media components of the text enhance presentation and understanding. For example,

- Clickable glossary terms provide immediate definitions of key concepts.
- Highlighting capabilities allow you to emphasize main ideas. You can also add personal notes in the margin.
- The search function allows you to quickly locate discussions of specific topics throughout the text.

Students may choose to use just the Online Edition, or both the online and the print versions together. This gives them the flexibility to choose which combination of resources works best for them. To assist those who use the online and print versions together, the primary heads and subheads in each chapter are numbered the same. For example, the first primary head in Chapter 1 is labeled 1-1, the second primary head in this chapter is labeled 1-2, and so on. The subheads build from the designation of their corresponding primary head: 1-1a, 1-1b, etc. This numbering system is designed to make moving between the Online Edition and print versions as seamless as possible.

Ancillary Materials

Atomic Dog is pleased to offer a competitive suite of supplemental materials for instructors using its textbooks.

For this title, these ancillaries include PowerPoint slides and an Instructors' Manual. Some titles may also have WebCT E-Packs and Blackboard Course Cartridges available. Please contact your Atomic Dog sales representative if you are interested in these products.

A full set of PowerPoint Slides, written by the author, is available for this text. This is designed to provide instructors with comprehensive visual aids for each chapter in the book. These slides include outlines of each chapter, highlighting important terms, concepts, and discussion points.

The Instructor's Manual for this book has also been written by the author and offers suggested syllabi for 10 and 14 week terms; lecture outlines and notes; in-class and take-home assignments; recommendations for multi-media resources such as films and Web sites; and long and short essay questions and their answers, appropriate for use on tests.

Martin Slann has an undergraduate degree in history from the University of Miami, and a master's degree and a doctorate in political science from the University of Connecticut and the University of Georgia, respectively. He is a long-time member of the American Political Science Association and the Midwest Political Science Association. He is a former member and chair of the political science faculty at Clemson University.

Dr. Slann is the author or co-author of several publications on terrorism and ethnic conflict. His most recent work, *Encyclopedia of Terrorism,* 2nd edition, is co-edited with Cindy Combs and published by Facts on File. He has received several awards for advisement excellence at both Clemson and Penn State and has been faculty advisor to Model United Nations student programs at both institutions as well as his current institution, Macon State College. His hobbies include trying to play tennis, reading political history, and amusing his grandchildren.

PART 1

Introduction

The following chapter offers a general perspective on the nature of politics and the reasons for government. Although experiments with different versions of government continue, the belief in democratic processes as the most humane and individually most beneficial kind of governance is growing. The Cold War ended two decades ago, yet the world Americans currently live in is still dangerous and violent. This chapter and several of those that follow help to explain why.

CHAPTER 1
Government and Politics in the Post–Cold War Era

CHAPTER 1

Government and Politics in the Post–Cold War Era

Government is actually a recent innovation whose history goes back about 8,000 years, a very tiny percentage of the time humans have inhabited this planet. Governmental institutions were in large part the result of, and certainly coincided with, the development of agriculture and the establishment of permanent human settlements. The essential purpose of government has not changed since its creation: to achieve and guarantee a degree of social order and individual security that enables society's members to enjoy a maximum degree of physical comfort. This purpose is not easily accomplished. A large proportion of the world's population today remains either under uncertain and frequently incomplete governmental authority, or under governments whose policies toward citizenries are so harsh that they threaten rather than provide either order or security.

Government, whether acting on behalf of people or otherwise, is the result of politics. Politics is often considered a corrupt and debasing profession that no self-respecting person would consider entering. But politics is also a feature common to all human society. It is an activity that "arises from accepting the fact of the simultaneous existence of different groups, hence different interests and different traditions within a territory ruled."[1] Citizens create and participate in politics because they need it. Politics is the imperfect vehicle by which people work out or compromise their differences. Doing so means few if any people will ever get everything they want, but not doing so carries the risk of ideological or religious fanatics insisting, sometimes violently, on getting everything they desire.

Politics is not necessarily a complicated phenomenon. The distinguished political scientist Harold Laswell, for example, has succinctly defined it as a process of determining "who gets what, when, and how." More recently, another respected political scientist David Easton defined politics simply as "the authoritative allocation of values." There is little doubt (although often much disgust) that politics has become an important vehicle in the United States and elsewhere in the world for determining nonmaterial and frequently very intimate and personal values. Decisions on how separate church and state should be, whether homosexuals should be allowed to marry, or even on what language a national or subnational student community will be taught in are dilemmas that have been turned over to the political process.

Politics is far from being an isolated activity that occurs in national capitals such as London, Moscow, Tokyo, Washington, or Kabul. Politics is a common feature of daily human existence that occurs wherever and whenever decisions are made about "who shall get what, when, and how" because the things everyone wants to possess seem to always be scarce. Politics may take a variety of forms, some that may be familiar and desirable to Americans and others that may be neither.

---

[1]Bernard Crick, *In Defense of Politics* (Baltimore, Maryland: Penguin Books, 1964), 18.

This chapter will introduce some of the more current themes in politics as well as activities that continually cause stress in international relations. The chapters that follow will explore all of these topics in more detail.

1-1 Government in the Post–Cold War Era

Politics and government are not the same thing. Politics often occur outside of government. Similarly, politics may (and usually do) involve both governmental and nongovernmental actors. Important political actors may not even hold government posts. In the United States, for instance, the very active role former First Lady Hillary Rodham Clinton took in trying to develop a national health plan in the early 1990s and failing to implement its passage in Congress was apparent from the beginning of the Clinton presidency. Mrs. Clinton is regarded by presidential historians as former President Clinton's closest political advisor and was often his greatest critic. She also put her time as former First Lady to good use, honing her own political skills during her eight years in the White House and becoming the first former First Lady to run for elective office. Mrs. Clinton successfully campaigned for the United States Senate in 2000, taking office in January 2001 as the junior senator from New York, winning re-election in 2006, and, in the opinion of many observers, preparing to run for president in 2008.

Former President Saddam Hussein of Iraq, on the other hand, emphasized the importance of his son Qusay who held no government office, but whose political qualifications consisted mainly of brutalizing anyone who opposed the regime (often by having the critic's tongue cut out). The betting was on Qusay to succeed his father[2] before the second Gulf War in 2003 ended Saddam's regime and Qusay's life. In Syria, Hafez Al-Assad autocratically governed the country between 1970 and 2000 and carefully and successfully planned for his son Bashir to succeed him. In the People's Republic of (North) Korea, Kim Il Sung led one of the most brutal regimes in the world between 1945 and 1993 and was succeeded by his son Kim Jong Il who was just as brutal and also determined to acquire a nuclear weapons arsenal.

Of course, many people don't really care how policy is made as long as it is done in a rational and humane fashion. Government, then, may be defined simply as the formal social instrument that partially or wholly resolves conflicts that arise among individuals or groups. The primary purpose of government is to manage and resolve these conflicts, thereby providing security and continuity for society as a whole and for its individual members. Successful governments do this and more. A successful government is also one that is not itself a source of conflict. Humanitarians, for example, condemned the authoritarian government of Iraq because it was the greatest perpetrator of violence in the country: its most visible accomplishment was the war it conducted against segments of its own population. It will come as no surprise that Saddam Hussein was not a fan of Alexander Hamilton, who argued in *Federalist Paper 51* that

> in framing a government which is to be administered by men over men, the great difficulty lies in this: you must first enable the government to control the governed; and in the next place to oblige it to control itself.[3]

This is a tall order for many of the world's regimes who still insist on either ignoring the people's legitimate needs or who are determined to make life miserable for their people by denying them basic human rights.

In this context, the collapse of the Soviet Union in 1991 is instructive. Its economic system was a disaster that became more blatant during its last years. The

---

[2]Nicholas D. Kristoff, "An Iraqi Man of Letters," *The New York Times*, October 8, 2002, sec A.

[3]James Madison, "The Federalist No. 51," Roy P. Fairfield, ed., *The Federalist Papers: A Collection of Essays Written in Support of the Constitution of the United States* (Garden City, New York: Doubleday & Company, 1966), 158–163.

Soviet population was stunned by the revelation that the Communist regime had avoided economic reforms in order to avoid risking its own political power. To the Soviet communist elite, economic stagnation was a worthwhile price for continued power and privilege. The Soviets had therefore rejected another critical ingredient of successful government by refusing to take the steps necessary to enhance the quality of life for its citizens. During the last two decades of its existence, the Soviet Union became the only industrialized society in history to experience a *decline* in average life expectancy. To the Soviet citizen standing in line for hours to purchase basic foodstuffs, often in subfreezing conditions, it was of little comfort to be told that the Soviet military was achieving parity with the United States. Of more immediate concern was whether meat, bread, and milk would be available when finally reaching the head of the line (after an average wait of two hours).

Another, more timely example is Afghanistan under the Taliban regime during 1996–2001. The Taliban government was composed of radical Islamists whose interpretation of holy writ led to an extreme religious orthodoxy that caused much harm to those on whom it was applied. The Taliban were fanatically intrusive in forbidding men to get haircuts and women to paint their fingernails. Male physicians were forbidden to conduct physical examinations on females who were not their relatives. Women were forbidden to get an education. Many pregnant women did not receive prenatal care. Some experienced severe complications during their pregnancy and a high proportion died needlessly.

Throughout the twentieth century, American government took on an ever-increasing load of responsibility for two main reasons: (1) American citizens want government to do more for them (even though these same citizens are reluctant to pay for additional services with additional taxes) and (2) government is able to do more because of modern technology and increased (if unevenly distributed) economic prosperity. One estimate has it that 85 percent of all scientists who have ever lived are alive today.[4] Hundreds of millions of people in much of the world are the beneficiaries of scientists whose medical and technological breakthroughs are frequently dependent on government funding.

Government in many countries, particularly the more advanced ones in Europe and North America, has unprecedented technological advantages when it comes to delivering services. At the same time, though, government can no longer consider itself the sole monopolizer of information, making pronouncements that the entire citizenry automatically believes. Some governments have a difficult time accepting the fact that satellites, the Internet, and other technological devices have severely lessened any government's ability to monopolize the transmission of information. This reality doesn't prevent some governments from trying anyway. Autocratic regimes have been known to outlaw computers or to restrict their usage in order to discourage their own citizens from acquiring information that detracts from their own control and interpretation of "facts." In North Korea, satellite dishes, modems, and fax machines are banned for ordinary citizens. Hunger is prevalent there, so most citizens are more worried about where their next meal is coming from anyway.[5]

These regimes do this sort of thing at their peril. Whenever a society is sealed off from the outside world, cultural, economic, and technological innovations don't penetrate. The society lags behind any country that accepts and applies new breakthroughs. Some regimes are willing to take the risk because remaining in power is their first and sometimes only priority. Moreover, a dictatorial regime does not usually have a retirement plan for its leadership. Quite frequently, being removed from power is equivalent to exile or possibly death at the hands of the enraged citizens they have brutalized for years.

---

[4]Paul Kennedy, *Preparing for the Twenty-First Century* (New York: Random House, 1993).

[5]*The Wall Street Journal*, October 28, 2003, sec. A.

What does seem to be clear from all of this is the rather impressive fact that government is not going away. Human beings prefer some degree of order and stability in their lives. They must balance this preference with the equally compelling one of a desire for personal freedom. How much government is too much government is a question that can best be answered by each individual society. Dependence upon government is fairly universal, however, and will continue. Bad or ineffective governments remain in power in great part because they control the means of physical force. They fall from power when the military and police themselves become disaffected or refuse to torment their fellow citizens any longer.

An autocratic government usually makes a mess of the national economy. This often occurs because of the rampant corruption that normally accompanies a dictatorial regime. The corruption is characterized by the dictator and family members draining much of the national wealth away from the country into private bank accounts. The regime attempts to blame others for the economic distress of its citizens. Robert Mugabe, president of Zimbabwe, implemented economic policies that by 2002 and beyond were creating large pockets of malnutrition and even starvation in a country that has traditionally been prosperous by nationalizing enterprises and confiscating productive farms.[6] Another technique is to keep the country on a war footing with a propaganda machine that instills the fear of a military invasion from a powerful enemy. The military leadership benefits because resources are diverted from the civilian sector of the economy to purchase new weapon systems.

Government is experiencing both unprecedented assistance in delivering services and unprecedented public scrutiny. The collapse of the Soviet Union suddenly created yet a new challenge. While parts of the former Soviet empire are democratizing, others are suffering breakdowns in governmental authority as ethnic and religious strife reach levels unseen in the modern world for many decades. There has been a mixed amount of success in democratizing countries in Africa, the Middle East, and Asia, in great part because of both ethnic and religious conflict as well as endemic poverty.

While government is ideally the great protector of society, its authority can be overwhelmed, and not simply by other governments. In the early twenty-first century, the scourge of AIDS threatened to destroy any economic progress made by governments in the developing regions. Most of the 15,000 who are infected each day are in poor countries where governments lack adequate resources to combat the epidemic. Other horrifying statistics include the 3 million who die each year from the AIDS virus. In 2006, a total of 60 million people were infected, a larger population than many countries have. Perhaps 80 percent of the AIDS victims are located in Africa and this is one of the most tragic restraints on economic development.[7]

This is not to say that those people who live comfortable lives in the West can relax. Governments all over the world are still reluctant to address the issue in substantial ways. Even worse, governments in rich countries remain reluctant to put aside the necessary sums of money to combat AIDS, in great part because they do not see the epidemic as their problem. Of course, this is a view that is both callous and counterproductive. Humanitarian concerns ought to be apparent to anyone aware of the issue. And the infection spreads easily, continuing to further the epidemic and destroy hopes for economic progress for entire countries.

Estimates of distinct ethnic groups around the world range from 5,000 to 6,000 communities. Some are very small indigenous tribes numbering only a few thousand members; the Han Chinese are the largest ethnic group in the world, with perhaps a billion people. Only a tiny percentage of the world's ethnic groups have their own territorial state and are equipped with the trappings of political

---

[6]Claudia Rosett, "There's Nothing Natural about Zimbabwe's Woes," *The Wall Street Journal,* July 26, 2002, sec. A.

[7]In some places in Africa, infection rates are as much as two-fifths of the adult population. "AIDS: The Long War," *The Economist,* July 13, 2002, 16.

sovereignty, such as a national flag, currency, language, and military. The number of independent states has increased since 1945 from fewer than 60 to nearly 200 by 2000, but 96 percent or more of the ethnic communities in the world do not have their own sovereign system, and most are unlikely to acquire one. The potential challenges stateless communities pose for international political stability are serious and will be covered in more detail in subsequent chapters.

As already suggested, the evolving threat of terrorism with a global reach has added another dimension of government activity. Terrorism respects no national boundaries, statements of neutrality, or international treaties. Nor do terrorists have compunctions about murdering defenseless civilians in huge numbers. During the early years of the twenty-first century, the role of government became severely challenged by well-funded and well-organized terrorist groups prepared for and even desirous of acquiring and using weapons of mass destruction.

1-2 Government and Politics

Democratic governments are more accustomed to dealing with challenges than nondemocratic ones because democratic regimes normally have to either respond to problems or risk being replaced at the next election. Politics is apparent in dictatorial regimes, but it is a politics played out within the confines of a political clique or between competing elements within a political elite. This body only reluctantly, if at all, considers public opinion, even if it knows what public opinion is on a given issue. But this is also why authoritarian government is inherently unstable: the government's lack of interest in and/or knowledge of public concerns is an excellent formula for ensuring that people withdraw both loyalty to and cooperation with the regime. If the public perceives the government as uninterested in or incapable of responding to citizen concerns, there is no point in supporting the regime. With this in mind, it is possible to make some reasonably safe assumptions about the nature of government and politics:

1. *Politics is a natural phenomenon that arises from human diversity.* It should not be replaced by political ideology, a set of comprehensive beliefs about what a government should be doing, and how people should behave. If politics is working right, it will consider but not give way to different and often competing expressions of political ideology. The art of politics involves the selection of the best possible choice from a set of imperfect but workable alternatives. Politicians don't have all the answers. If they are honest, they admit to this. Ideologues brag that they have all the answers without understanding that their answers could easily be wrong or even dangerous.

2. *People create and employ government to help them live more comfortable, secure, and productive lives.* Because it is a human device, government is often a miserable failure when it comes to fulfilling its mission. Governments fail most often when they are guided by either an ideology or a leadership oblivious to and uninterested in what government is all about. To do its job, government must be cognizant of what the citizenry requires and accurate about what it can deliver. Government can do neither if it is uninterested in or intolerant of dissent. Bear in mind, though, that the observation offered by Abraham Lincoln that "government of the people, for the people, and by the people" is less than a century and a half old. It was a radical suggestion when it was first uttered, and it remains so in much of the world today. Most of the history of government is dominated by authoritarian regimes that operate with differing degrees of brutality.

3. *Political stability is enhanced when as much of the citizenry as possible have legitimate and guaranteed access to government.* Historically speaking, governments have been notoriously lax when it comes to accessibility. Many citizenries today still live under severe limitations on freedom of speech and action. Their governments don't want to hear from them. In numerous cases, a government doesn't even

want them around: dozens of countries contain minority ethnic, racial, linguistic, and religious communities that they regard as surly and ill disposed toward "fitting in" with the prevailing majority. Moreover, many such communities are reluctant to accept the legitimacy of the government that has control over them. Many Sikhs in India, some Kurds in Iraq, Muslims in western China, and Tamils in Sri Lanka do not accept the central authority either because they regard the central authority as a detriment to cultural autonomy (as in India) or because the central government is committed to a program of **genocide** against the community (as occurred in Iraq when Saddam Hussein's regime used chemical weapons against its Kurdish citizens during the early 1990s or in the Darfur province of Sudan since 2003).

genocide
The systematic murder, usually planned or at least sponsored by the government, of an entire community or nation of people based on its religion, ethnicity, and/or social status.

4. *Economic prosperity and political democracy are interrelated.* There is no satisfactory way to demonstrate this assumption empirically. However, the most prosperous economies in history have been democratic, and when the Soviet Union collapsed, its demise was at least in part the result of a deteriorating genocide economy that had not only failed to "catch up" with the West but had become altogether inoperable. Indeed, political scientists debate whether it is feasible for every country to establish a combination of political democracy and an economy dominated by the free market.

POLITICAL BIOGRAPHY

Saddam Hussein

Saddam Hussein was born outside of Tikrit, Iraq, in 1936. The whereabouts of his father became uncertain soon after his birth and Saddam was raised during his formative years by his mother's brother. Saddam's uncle was fond of observing that there were three things in the world that should never have been created—flies, Jews, and Persians. Saddam murdered his first political opponent by the time he was twenty. After taking power in the late 1970s, Saddam attacked both Iran, the ancestral home of Persians (during the 1980–1988 conflict), and Israel, a predominantly Jewish state (with Scud missiles in 1991). The conflict with Iran cost a million lives and left both countries economically devastated. Neither country gained any territory at the end of the war.

Saddam terrorized much of the Iraqi population after he took power. In particular, he made life miserable for the Kurds in the northern part of Iraq and the marsh Arabs and Shi'a Muslims in the south because a good many of them opposed his regime. His various secret police agencies spied on the Iraqi citizenry and one another. As a doting father, Saddam took his sons Uday and Qusay when they were in their early teens to inspect his various torture chambers and to learn different techniques of tormenting victims. A favorite method of torture was to dip prisoners into vats of acid. Saddam was also a serial rapist who enjoyed humiliating political personages by seducing their wives, sometimes in front of them. He constructed dozens of palaces and elaborate underground bunkers (that included amenities such as swimming pools) that cost billions of dollars while average Iraqis suffered privations such as food shortages and lack of medical care.

The invasion and occupation of Kuwait in 1990 made an enemy of the United States, a country that had previously supported Saddam during his war with Iran in the belief that Iran was the greater of two evils. Saddam's troops were evicted from Kuwait, but he remained in power despite the stated American desire to see him leave. His desire to acquire weapons of mass destruction and continuing defiance of United Nations resolutions encouraged the United States to drive him from power in 2003. Saddam's regime collapsed in April, but his personal ability to survive remained intact. Months after the American and British occupation of Iraq, Saddam loyalists still attacked U.S. and British soldiers, murdered Iraqis thought to be cooperating with Coalition Forces, and even attacked humanitarian installations in Baghdad such as the Red Cross.

Saddam's hero is Joseph Stalin, another mass murderer. Despite his excesses, Saddam obviously enjoyed some degree of popular support because he operated and planned attacks from his home base in and around Tikrit, the so-called Sunni triangle, an area where Saddam is probably genuinely popular in great part because he is related to many of the local inhabitants. Literally hundreds of Tikritis are blood relatives of Saddam and provided him with some protection. He was captured by Coalition Forces in December 2003. His trial for crimes against humanity began in 2005. Saddam and six other defendants, including a half-brother, from the beginning of the trial demonstrated contempt and disdain for the court even though they may face the death penalty. Saddam also continues to insist that he is the legal president of Iraq and that the current Iraqi government has no authority to place him on trial. He and two co-defendants were sentenced to death on November 4, 2006 by the court.

1-3 The Collapse of the Soviet Union and the End of the Cold War Era

Kremlin
The physical and political center of the Russian government in Moscow through the czarist and communist periods for most of Russian history, except when the capital was located in St. Petersburg during the eighteenth and nineteenth centuries.

command economy
The total control and bureaucratization of a national economy from the political capital, which makes often arbitrary economic decisions without consideration of either need or quality.

Third World
A term traditionally used to denote the 150 or so countries, whose populations include four-fifths of the human race, considered lacking in comprehensive economic modernization.

The Soviet Union officially ceased to exist on December 25, 1991, when its last president, Mikhail Gorbachev, resigned and the Soviet flag flying over the **Kremlin** in Moscow came down for the last time. Months before, the Soviet Union had, for all practical purposes, politically disintegrated as most of its republics seceded and established independent governments and as more and more of its political leadership broke with the Communist party. Boris Yeltsin, for example, became the Russian Republic's first popularly elected president in 1990 after he had turned his back on the party and created his own popular power base. And before then, the Soviet government had begun to wind down its adversarial position with the United States in a remarkable period of international cooperation unseen since World War II that resulted in a build-down of their respective nuclear arsenals.

In retrospect, it was probably inevitable that the Soviet Union would not only lose the Cold War, but also experience an implosion. Its economy had ceased to develop for at least the previous two decades. During this same time, the mostly free markets of Western European, North American, and East Asian countries were expanding to the point that, by the late 1980s, they accounted for nearly four-fifths of the global economy, though their citizenries comprised only about a fifth of the world's population. The Soviet model **command economy** had clearly failed, in not only the Soviet Union but everywhere else it had been tried—Eastern Europe, Southeast Asia, North Korea, Ethiopia, and Cuba. Its economy was lagging so far behind that of the free market democracies, the Soviet Union became increasingly recognized as a **Third World** country, though one that, disconcertingly, possessed thousands of nuclear warheads.

In fact, that was the problem. The Soviet Union was a nuclear power and not much else. It could not even begin to compete economically with the West, and its technology was often woefully inadequate to sustain a modern industrial power. Unless Soviet intentions were to destroy the world (happily, they weren't), there wasn't much use for a nuclear arsenal. It was expensive to build and maintain and severely detracted from chronically urgent consumer needs. Perhaps even worse, the emphasis on centralized control discouraged innovation. In the last years of its existence, the Soviet Union averaged only 400 patents per year—only a few more than Belgium, whose population was about one-twelfth the size.[8]

The Soviet Union has been referred to as the "last colonial empire." This is because only about half of the Soviet population was Russian. Nearly 150 million other people represented perhaps a hundred different nationalities, most of them conquered and occupied by a Russia that had been expanding its territory since the sixteenth century. Thus, the Soviet state was doomed to disintegration in part because the Communist regime had failed to nurture a coherent loyalty of huge sections of its population. Millions of non-Russians retained historical memories of a politically sovereign past free from Moscow's control. The government never eliminated the desire to restore national autonomy. In some cases, the autonomy had never really existed, but that did not detract from the desire to acquire it anyway.

Ironically, the Soviet Union had served an important purpose for Americans. Nearly two generations of Americans had grown up understanding that Soviet communism was an evil but containable global menace. By the 1980s, most of the American population could not remember or even fantasize about what the world was or would be like without a brutal totalitarian regime that was easy to both condemn and accept as a permanent fixture in American lives. Then, rather suddenly, the Soviet Union under Gorbachev, its youngest leader in decades, seemed to mellow politically. The new (and last) Soviet regime understood that the Soviet system had

---

[8]"The New World Order, Based on Share of Leading Patents," *The New York Times,* May 28, 1991.

dismally failed and that drastic reforms were required. The conclusions were based on the increasingly available information that Western Europe, North America, and East Asia contained economies that were consistently growing and the realization that free market economies were simply more prosperous than collectivized ones. But effective reforms could not be successfully undertaken if hostility between the Soviet Union and the United States continued to drain resources from the economy and place them in nonproductive military budgets. Tensions drained away between the two superpowers, and within the Soviet Union, Gorbachev's government tried to reform both the economic and political systems to make them more efficient and more responsive to the citizenry's needs.

The reform attempts, however, only exposed the Soviet system as hopelessly corrupt and inept. After the failure of a coup in August 1991 to restore a more hard-line political elite, no defenders of the Soviet system were left to delay what seemed to be an inevitable demise. The leaders of the coup reflected everything that was wrong with the system—they were not only corrupt, but they revealed an astounding incompetence in planning and activating the overthrow. They had neither popular nor military support for their actions.

1-4 The United States as the First "Universal Nation"

The Cold War era, roughly 1945 to 1990, was over, and the generation of political leadership that had dominated it and whose perspectives had been forged by the trauma of World War II (1939–1945) was now leaving the scene. George Bush, for example, was the last World War II veteran to become president (1989–1993). His successor, Bill Clinton, was elected president in the first post–Cold War American election in 1992. Clinton was born in 1946, just as the Cold War era was beginning, and became president shortly after it ended. George W. Bush, Clinton's successor and the senior Bush's son, is the first president to preside over a global war with international terrorism. He is unlikely to be the last.

But during the four-and-one-half decades of the Cold War, the United States had itself changed in dramatic and often unpredictable ways. The population had increased from about 150 million in the 1950 census to over 250 million in the 1990 census. By 2006, over 300 million people lived in the United States. The nation's demographic composition underwent even more startling change. The United States now counts 110 distinct ethnic groups among its population, making Americans one of the most heterogeneous societies in the world. Hispanic Americans were beginning to replace African Americans as the largest ethnic minority. Figure 1–1 compares demographic data from 1950 to 2050.

The 1950 census revealed that 90 percent of the population was white; by 1990, only 75 percent were in that category (see Figure 1–1). By the middle of the twenty-first century, this proportion is expected to drop to under 50 percent. In short, the American population is growing in both number and complexity, though by mid-century it is expected to level off at around 375 million. At the same time, Americans are becoming an increasingly bilingual society, with currently about 10 percent of the population speaking Spanish as their first language. The Hispanic-American community is the fastest growing in absolute numbers and supplanted African Americans as the largest minority by around 2010. The fastest growing religion in the United States is Islam. American Muslims currently outnumber American Jews and Episcopalians and have become a voting bloc in several states that is now being pursued by both Democrats and Republicans.

The United States is still not completely united, and old ghosts still occasionally haunt American society. For example, the state of South Carolina was recently involved in a controversy over the Confederate battle flag flying over the state's capitol dome. Placed there in 1962, it had long been a source of displeasure, especially

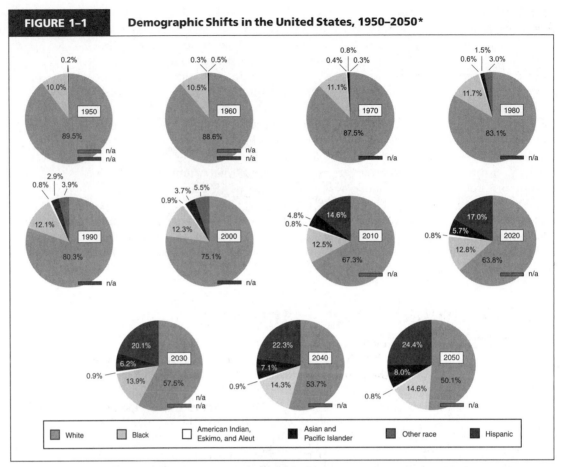

FIGURE 1–1   **Demographic Shifts in the United States, 1950–2050***

*The data indicated in this illustration do not provide proportions for the Hispanic population because the opportunity to identify oneself explicitly as Hispanic or Latino is a recent one. The Bureau of the Census allowed Hispanic or Latino designations but such information was considered a subset of the more traditional categories such as black and white. Future censuses will enable respondents to identify themselves as Hispanic.

for South Carolina's African Americans. This controversy is relatively mild compared to many other gender and ethnic issues that crop up in, but are certainly not confined to, the United States.

The United States is also one of a handful of industrialized democracies whose populations are steadily increasing, in great part because of relatively lenient immigration policies (see Table 1–1) that became an issue in the 2006 Congressional elections. The fear of terrorism, though, is beginning to cause pressure to more stringently limit immigration. Such policies are becoming very restrictive in most of Western Europe and have inspired a resurgence of extreme nationalist political movements, especially in France, Germany, and Italy. Many West European and some of the more prosperous East Asian countries such as Japan have fairly flat population growth rates, meaning that their populations are "aging" faster than the American populace, and that their labor forces are becoming smaller compared to the rapidly growing number of retired people.

Interestingly, while most Americans are generally aware of the legal and illegal immigrants entering the United States from countries in Latin America and the Caribbean, a substantial proportion of immigrants are arriving from East Asia. Most are university students who have come to study at American universities from China, Taiwan, and Japan.[9] A substantial portion will decide to remain in the United States to live and work (usually in well-paid professions such as medicine

---

[9]"Foreign Students in America: Where They Come From—Where They Go," *The New York Times*, November 29, 1989.

TABLE 1–1	Global Migratory Patterns

From	Usual Destination(s)
North Africa (Algeria, Morocco, Tunisia)	France
Turkey, East European countries	Germany
South Asia (Bangladesh, India, Pakistan, Sri Lanka)	United Kingdom and West Indies
Central American countries, Cuba, Haiti,	Canada and United States, Mexico, East Asia

Source: Millions of people are on the move, mostly from less economically developed countries to the more prosperous countries of Western Europe and North America. Most of these immigrants are unwelcome in host countries when unemployment is high. France, for example, experienced mass riots and demonstrations during the early months of 2006 mostly by unemployed Muslim youth whose families emigrated to France from Algeria, Morocco, and Tunisia in the hope of improving their lives. France's Islamic population, around 10 percent of the total, is the largest in Europe.

and engineering). Like previous immigrants, they have found it easy to adapt to the American economic and social systems.

Unprecedented demographic changes are certainly occurring. As they do, the more established elements of the population sometimes feel threatened by or helpless in a society that they increasingly find full of challenging political agendas. During a crucial campaign for the U.S. Senate in 2002 in Texas, for example, changing demographics helped to ensure that a black candidate would have an excellent chance to win the seat. At the same time, a candidate of Hispanic origin ran for governor. Both were candidates on the Democratic ticket in a heavily and traditionally Republican state. Yet by 2002, only 52 percent of the Texan population was white while black and Hispanic communities had increased to more than two-fifths of the total population. Most blacks and Hispanics tend to vote for the Democratic party and by the 2006 elections the white population had slipped to under 50 percent.[10]

In reality, of course, it is a waste of time to live in a multiethnic society and be unappreciative of diversity and the material benefits that it can bring. There is growing evidence, for example, that multiethnic societies more fully understand and can more easily operate in a global economy full of cultural nuances.[11] The United States is about as multiethnic as a country can be, with built-in legal structures to ensure mutual toleration. These don't always work, but it is difficult to argue with the premise that the United States is less race-conscious than it was one or two generations ago. It is thus positioned to continue to be a leading economic and political power. On the other hand, multi-ethnicity has not worked well in other societies where, as in Russia, wars have to be fought to ensure that a political society does not disintegrate. Since 1991, Russia for example has engaged in intermittent conflict with one of its non-Russian communities, Chechnya. These can be never-ending wars that drain resources and national morale. During the early years of the twenty-first century, between twenty and thirty Russian soldiers were dying each week in Chechnya.[12]

At the same time, Americans are also becoming more class-oriented and class-conscious. American society is still a predominantly middle-class society, but the middle class is increasingly fragmented. The American economy has also experienced terrific change. In 1945, because of the devastation of World War II in Europe and Asia as well as growth in America, the United States accounted for

[10]National Public Radio's *Morning Edition*, October 31, 2002.

[11]National Public Radio's *Market Place*, July 6, 1994.

[12]"The Lost Cause of the Caucasus," *The Economist*, November 2, 2002, 25–27.

one-half of the world's economy. Half a century later, that proportion had been cut to around 30 percent of the world's economy. This happened not because Americans were less well off, but because of the recovery and unprecedented economic growth in Western Europe and East Asia. Even with the very serious recession that began in 2000, the nearly $10-trillion-dollar American economy (that continued to grow and was nearly $13 trillion by 2006) was still about as large as the economies of all the countries of Western Europe combined and more than twice the size of Japan's, the second biggest national economy in the world. In fact, the state of California alone had an economy almost the size of the United Kingdom's. If California were an independent country, it would have the seventh biggest economy in the world.

For all of these reasons, the United States will frequently appear in this text as a familiar reference point for purposes of comparison. Its economic, political, and cultural impacts throughout the world are not unlimited, but they are so crucial and pervasive that they cannot be ignored in any assessment of comparative and international politics.

1-5 The New Context of Global Politics

The Cold War era was characterized by a superpower rivalry between the United States and the Soviet Union. This competition consumed trillions of dollars in an arms race and often overshadowed domestic economic concerns and even basic human rights. For nearly half a century, the American-Soviet competition consistently overrode other political considerations. By the time it ended, the Soviet system had disintegrated, but the United States, although clearly the winner, still confronted challenges to international peace, stability, and prosperity from sources that had been submerged until communism's collapse.

As the sole remaining superpower, the United States could naturally be expected to easily get what it wanted: stable, democratic governments with political leaders committed to fostering societies that enhance individual opportunity and welfare. This was a nice prospect, but not very realistic. Former U.S. Secretary of State Henry Kissinger observed that

> ... the United States is actually in no better a position to dictate the global agenda unilaterally than it was at the beginning of the Cold War. America is more preponderant than it was ten years ago, yet, ironically, power has also become more diffuse. Thus, America's ability to employ it to shape the rest of the world has actually decreased.[13]

By the mid-1990s, it was clear that much of the world was adjusting to the winding down of the Cold War. In fact, many governments as well as antigovernment movements felt free to pursue their own agendas, many of which were far from peaceful and several of which were destructive to the point of genocide. Nationalist movements, radical religious fundamentalism, and the expansionist plans of numerous governments have produced what can only be judged as a less peaceful world.

During any given day of the week, as many as three dozen separate conflicts are going on across the globe. Most of these are in Third World countries, but the First World countries of Europe and North America are not immune. In Northern Ireland and the former Yugoslavia, for example, ancient animosities have created—or, perhaps more properly, renewed—such violent phenomena as political terrorism and "ethnic cleansing." Clearly, the beginning of a new era in global politics was no guarantee of worldwide peace. What characteristics mark the new context of world politics? Several stand out, including democratization, westernization, religious fundamentalism, tribalism, and ethnic conflict.

---

[13]Henry Kissinger, *Diplomacy* (New York: Simon & Schuster, 1994), 809.

1-5a Democratization

Democratization should not be confused with democracy. Democratization is a process that, it is hoped, leads a society to create and sustain democracy. Democratization rarely proceeds at an even pace or exhibits identical characteristics everywhere it occurs. Nor is it always the automatic successor of collapsing authoritarian or totalitarian regimes. As can be seen in the aftermath of the Soviet Union's demise, democracy is far from a sure thing. Democratization itself, or reforms toward democracy, while doing fairly well in some of the former Soviet republics such as the **Baltic states**, is found haphazardly, if at all, in other areas.

At the same time, it is important to note that we should not be smug about democracy. We often associate democracy with the Western political process when in reality democracy has appeared in non-Western countries without being imposed by the West's military or political pressures. For example, Nelson Mandela in South Africa during the later twentieth century and Mahatma Gandhi in India during that century's early decades found ways to adapt their cultures to inspire successful democratic efforts.[14]

It is generally acknowledged that to successfully establish a permanent and stable political democracy, the democratization process must achieve certain minimal economic and social conditions. The following list of conditions is not all-inclusive, but it does set forth several basic conditions that tend to foster democratization and that are fairly commonplace wherever democracy occurs:

- *A broad, large, and fairly accessible middle class.* The middle class is often a vague entity (and a complicated one because there are various gradations within the class), but by and large its members enjoy a decent standard of living, have the ability to work realistically toward and access the means for self-improvement, and have at least a modicum of hope that their children will have better lives than they.

- *Literacy.* A well-educated citizenry in itself is no guarantee of democratization, but democracy is probably impossible if the bulk of the citizenry cannot read and write its own language. Literacy enables an electorate to become politically well informed. It's not that literate electorates don't make mistakes. After all, the relatively educated nation of Germany produced, mainly through the electoral process, twelve nightmarish years (1933–1945) of **Nazism**, and Russians, whose reading habits tend to be more sophisticated than those of most Americans, endured more than seven decades of totalitarian communism. Obviously, literacy by itself is far from sufficient to sustain democracy. Some of the other conditions are listed below. In Germany, a literate and comparatively well-educated population was overtaken by the desperation produced by severe economic depression and the seductive message of the megalomaniac Adolf Hitler.

- *Health.* A citizenry must enjoy overall adequate sanitation and proper nutrition to be economically productive, let alone aware of political issues. Chronically sick or undernourished people are unable to build healthy political or economic systems. Some countries still fear outbreaks of famine or disease. Both can be debilitating to the long-term prospects for development. In Egypt, for example, there are literally thousands of villages located along the Nile River in which many if not most adults are lethargic because of a parasitic disease that infects them, sometimes throughout their lives. In such a circumstance, progress is difficult if only because of low energy levels. Thus, millions of Egyptians live no better than their parents or great-grandparents. Some are even worse off than their ancestors were because of greater population density and the government's inability to cope with a population that is doubling every twenty to twenty-five years.

Baltic states
The three small republics (Latvia, Lithuania, and Estonia, with a combined population of about eight million) that were forcibly annexed by the Soviet Union in 1940 and, in 1989, became the first of the Soviet republics to secede, leading to the eventual collapse of the entire Soviet system.

Nazism
The ideology officially expressed in Germany from 1933 to 1945 that practiced racism and genocide.

---

[14]Amartya Sen, "Democracy Isn't 'Western'," *The Wall Street Journal*, March 24, 2006, A10.

- *Modern technology.* The democratization process requires a modern technological as well as cultural infrastructure. The advent over the last quarter century of personal computers, fax machines, and email has enabled and encouraged an unprecedented exchange of information between governments and between people. It is no longer possible for government to monopolize information except in the most tightly controlled dictatorships. The democratization requirements of a free press and free speech have been substantially enhanced by the explosion of accessible and affordable technology.

Perhaps most importantly, though, the democratization process cannot occur until a nation has an overall culture conducive to democracy's success. Ethnic conflict, religious violence, gender discrimination, and severe class divisions are all serious hindrances to democratization, and can even destroy it. This is not to say that undemocratic traditions in a society cannot survive a democratization process and exist in a full democracy. The monarchy in the United Kingdom is an example: It is not a democratically chosen body but rather a monarch assumes her position as the result of inheritance. It survives in a mostly democratic culture because it is politically insignificant.

On the other hand, a society is ill suited for democracy if any segment of its population suffers continual persecution or discrimination. In India—a country making a serious and, in many ways, successful effort to pursue democratization— regular elections occur, an uncensored press informs the people, and civilians control the government. However, India still experiences occasional internal and frequently violent conflicts among Hindus and Islamic and Sikh minority communities. And in China, a dramatic economic surge has occurred since the late 1970s when the economy began to grow at the rate of nearly 10 percent annually. The growth came even while the Chinese political system remained under the exclusive control of the Communist party. The government encouraged (up to a point) a free market economy under the notion that "to get rich is glorious." However, no political challenge or efforts to democratize have been tolerated. The Chinese government made its position very clear during the Tiananmen Square student demonstrations on behalf of democratization of China's political system in Beijing in June 1989. An unknown number of students were arrested and some were never heard from again.

1-5b Westernization

The appearance of European and, even more emphatically, American products and businesses in the East and South Asia, the Middle East, and Latin America suggests that the globe is undergoing a westernization process that includes the adoption of Western value systems as well as Western-style economic and political systems. Millions of Asians, for example, happily consume billions of McDonald's hamburgers and wash them down with either Coca-Cola or Pepsi-Cola. The world's largest Kentucky Fried Chicken outlet is in Beijing, China's capital city (the largest McDonald's is in Moscow, the capital city of Russia). To an appreciable extent, the westernization process is undeniable. But it is possible to overestimate both its influence and non-Western resentment of this influence.

A Western value system usually consists of the features associated with political democracy and free market economics. Both have enabled the West to become globally dominant. Although this may seem a good thing to those who live in the West and enjoy many material benefits, it is important to point out that many non-Westerners do not see it that way. Islamic radicals in Indonesia and theocrats in Iran, for example, resent and fear the West because of what they regard as the West's obsession with materialism, a toleration of alternative lifestyles, gender equality, and individual autonomy. In October 2002, an American official involved with his country's aid program in Jordan was murdered. A group called the Honorable Men of Jordan claimed responsibility and justified the violence based on

American policy against Iraq and in support of Israel as well as Jordan's own close relationship with the United States.[15] In other words, those features regarded by many Americans as virtues are viewed as vices to many outsiders. Religious freedom, for example, is seen as blasphemous, men and women working side by side is immoral, acquiring many possessions is a serious departure from spirituality, and individual actions are selfish distractions from the collective good.

Some critics of Western culture go further. The West is not only devoid of any spiritual values, but its own values threaten to destroy the lifestyle in traditional societies, such as those that are found in much of the Islamic world, with corruption. What Americans, Israelis, and some Europeans refer to as "terrorism" is, in the minds of Islamic radicals, a struggle against a relentless evil. This point is difficult for Americans to understand. They and other Westerners have a difficult time appreciating a mindset that does not enthusiastically embrace material progress and individualism. Among radicals, there is no "live and let live" approach to dealing with those who are beyond the pale of moral respectability. In fact, the West is such a threat that its culture must be destroyed root and branch, a mindset that was applied all too readily on September 11, 2001. This theme will be explored further in later chapters.

It is understandable that some aspects of Western culture are neither desired nor appreciated in non-Western societies. For example, in 1980, the prison population in the United States was 370,000. By 2005, that number had increased to over 2 million, "a higher figure per 100,000 citizens than anywhere in the world."[16] Even many obviously undemocratic societies have a prison population proportionally lower than that in the United States. Non-Western cultures would clearly have to be self-destructive to want to emulate such an element of Western society. For that matter, even within Western society there are communities that question both the political superiority and morality of Western culture. A number of fundamentalist groups, for instance, have turned their backs on the more materialistic characteristics of what they regard as an immoral culture.

Radical and sometimes violent religious fundamentalism, whether Christian, Jewish, Islamic, or Hindu, and vehement expressions of nationalism are in some sense a reaction to westernization. Such expressions oppose a global culture dominated by Western economies, Western language (usually English), and a consumerist mindset.

1-5c Religious Fundamentalism

The term *fundamentalism* may be interpreted various ways. It is often associated with zealots ready to maim and kill at a moment's notice anyone they consider less than adequately enthusiastic about a particular religious viewpoint. Religious radicals do not regard toleration as a virtue, and most treat it as a vice that should be eradicated.

Religion and expressions of nationalism often go together. For example, in sixteenth- and seventeenth-century France, one had to be Catholic to be considered authentically French (both the government and populace regarded Protestants as less than politically loyal), while to be Catholic in England during the same period was almost synonymous with treason.[17] Hostility toward religious minorities can be even more severe.

In the 1930s, to be Jewish (or to have even one Jewish great-grandparent) in Germany was enough to earn expulsion and confiscation of property; by the 1940s, Jews were the targets of outright genocide. With the depressing exception of

---

[15]"Murder, and Its Consequences," *The Economist*, November 2, 2002, 48.

[16]"Bill Bradley, Commonsense Cop," *The Economist*, July 23, 1994, 30. See also http://www.ojp.usdoj.gov/bjs/prisons.htm

[17]Even today, members of the British royal family are discouraged from marrying outside of the Anglican Church. This rule makes sense to the British because the monarch is both head of state and head of the Anglican Church.

Northern Ireland, however, most of Western Europe has stopped equating religion with political loyalty.

Residues of religion in politics, however, are still easy to find in the West. Pro-choice (allowing a woman to decide for herself whether to carry a pregnancy to full term) and pro-life (insisting that it would be immoral to terminate a pregnancy regardless of the woman's wishes) advocates in the United States are vocal and active. Both often decide which congressional candidate to support based simply on the view the candidate holds on abortion, without considering other issues that might be important to the electorate. This exceptionally delicate issue (the death penalty is another) only infrequently leads to physical violence against abortion clinic workers or to the building housing the clinic.[18] While most of those who are against abortion confine their activities to protests, often within several feet of clinics, others have resorted to more extreme methods that have included threats against the persons of physicians who deliver abortion services and the murder of at least three doctors.

Western Europeans and North Americans are exceptions to the general rule that religious violence is rather commonplace. And religious violence is commonplace, often in religions unfamiliar to many Americans. For example, in Assam, a state in northeastern India, much blood has been shed between the Muslims who migrated there and the indigenous and non-Muslim Boro tribe. The Boros would probably attack anyone who was migrating into their ancestral home, but Muslims also represent the largest religious minority in India (and the second largest Islamic community in the world), and to non-Muslims they are a serious menace. India is a country where a great deal of conflict has already arisen between Muslims and Hindus and, occasionally, between Hindus and Sikhs. The problem spills over into foreign relations as well. India and Pakistan have long disputed which of the two countries owns Kashmir, a state in predominantly Hindu India with a Muslim majority. India's mostly Hindu government considers Islamic separatists in Kashmir to be traitors while Pakistan believes them to be patriots.[19] Both countries have a long history of conflict and have fought several wars with one another. They also possess nuclear arsenals and each has theirs aimed at the other.

Religious fanatics often view those who oppose their policies as fanatics themselves. For example, Islamic fundamentalists believe American foreign policy advocates the sort of program that is relentlessly hostile to Islam. They view the Jewish state of Israel as an agent of the Christian West in the midst of the Islamic world. Moreover,

> Christian missionaries . . . loom large for the [Islamic] fundamentalists, who see them as leaders of a systematic assault on Islam. Fundamentalists discern a strong crusading component to U.S. foreign policy. "The U.S. attitude is motivated by several factors, but the most important, in my view," writes Umar al-Talmasani, the Egyptian fundamentalist leader, "[is] religious fanaticism. . . . This attitude is a continuation of the crusader invasion of a thousand years ago."[20]

It gets worse: a popular movie in Turkey during 2005–2006, an Islamic country militarily allied with the United States and on relatively good terms with Israel, entitled "Valley of the Wolves — Iraq," featured a theme that accused American soldiers in Iraq of murdering and dismembering Iraqis to support a Jewish organ-selling scheme.[21]

When religious fundamentalists succeed in taking over a government, that government is usually a good deal less than inspired by democratic values. Even dress

---

[18]Keep in mind, though, that pro-life advocates regard an abortion as an act violent enough to be termed murder. Two Pensacola, Florida, physicians were murdered by pro-life advocates who subscribe to the notion of "justifiable homicide."

[19]"When Religion and Freedom Clash," *The Economist*, October 26, 2002, 41.

[20]Daniel Pipes, "Fundamentalist Muslims between America and Russia," *Foreign Affairs* 64, No. 5 (Summer 1986): 947.

[21]Robert L. Pollock, "After Ataturk," *The Wall Street Journal*, March 18–19, 2006, A8.

codes are strictly enforced. In Iran, for instance, government-sponsored religious police are on the lookout for young women who fail to wear sufficient clothing and for young couples who flaunt their affection for one another by holding hands.[22] The state considers the overall moral conduct of Iranians as an activity that government can legitimately regulate according to religious precepts.

In sum, radical religious fundamentalism normally includes the following characteristics:

1. An absolutist doctrine not open to compromise or change
2. An intolerance of dissent and opposition
3. An insistence on a particular lifestyle and official enforcement of doctrinal values[23]
4. A binding social and familial hierarchy that spells out specific duties by gender, age, and religious status
5. A legal system dependent upon scriptural remedies for crimes and immoral activities and that sees little difference between crime and immorality.

1-5d Tribalism and Ethnic Conflict

As the Soviet Union and communism collapsed in eastern and central Europe, ancient ethnic tensions that had been contained for most of the twentieth century bubbled to the surface. Ethnicity is not the only source of conflict in the post–Cold War era, but it is easily one of the most important. One scholar, for example, has identified in Russia a total of 204 "ethnoterritorial" conflicts.[24] And these are only in one country. Keep in mind that with anywhere between 6,000 and 8,000 distinct ethnic communities crowded into only 200 states worldwide, the possibilities of conflict are virtually endless.

In fact, the existence of states themselves may be a critical reason for ethnic and tribal violence. Many—perhaps most—states are rather unnatural creations. This point is most vivid in the African continent, where Belgian, British, and French colonizers drew boundary lines between their possessions during the nineteenth century for their convenience rather than for the benefit of the indigenous tribes that lived there. Inevitably, tribes were divided and found themselves in the post-colonial era (after 1945) living in different countries with fellow citizens who spoke different languages, practiced different religions, and were often traditionally hostile to one another.

Again, the West is neither immune nor insulated from the conflict responsible for the numerous wars currently underway all over the globe. Some West European countries have been affected by immigration from the North African countries of Algeria and Morocco. The immigrants may already speak the language of their adopted country, especially if they emigrate to France. But the immigrants are encountering varying degrees of hostility from indigenous populations that see serious economic challenges from workers willing to provide labor for lower wages. Perhaps even more gripping is the fear among indigenous groups in France, Germany, and Britain who see immigrants as destructive of and in competition with native cultures. Nativism is evident when the native inhabitants of a country in effect retreat into a nationalist shell to exclude immigrants they consider undesirable.

The southern European countries of Spain, France, and Italy are feeling the brunt of immigration, much of it illegal from northern Africa. Some of the immigrants raise special concerns because they are suspected Islamic extremists.[25]

At the same time that resentment against immigrants is increasing in the West, Western society itself is becoming increasingly multicultural. The United States,

[22]*The Economist*, July 23, 1994, 39; "An Unmarried Couple Caught Holding Hands in Iran are Liable to Prosecution," *The New York Times*, August 3, 1994.

[23]"An Unmarried Couple Caught Holding Hands in Iran are Liable to Prosecution," *The New York Times*, August 3, 1994; *The Economist*, July 23, 1994, 39.

[24]Bogdan Szajkowski, "Will Russia Disintegrate in Bantustans?" *The World Today* (August-September 1993).

[25]"Something New Out of Africa," *The Economist*, July 16, 1993, 41–42.

for example, currently has the fifth-largest Spanish-speaking population in the world; Germany's capital, Berlin, has more Turkish residents than all but two cities in the world; and one out of every five police officers in London is from Africa or the West Indies.[26] Yet despite their numbers, immigrants are usually the first to lose their jobs in hard economic times: in the Netherlands, for example, the unemployment rate around 2001 was 7 percent, significantly more than it was in the United States. But the Netherlands has large ethnic minorities; unemployment among Turks and Moroccans living there that year was five to six times higher.[27]

1-5e Nations and States

nation
A community of people who possess distinctive ethnic, linguistic, religious, geographical, and cultural and historical commonalities. These features do not have to all be simultaneously present.

state
The institutional structure of a political society that contains sovereignty, a governing apparatus, and a population that, while contained within designated geographical boundaries, may or may not be characterized by ethnic, linguistic, or religious homogeneity.

There is an inaccurate tendency to use the term **nation** interchangeably with the term **state**. Most nations are, in fact, stateless, and a great many states can actually count several nations within their borders. A genuine nation-state is an unusual entity. For example, the United Kingdom is a state that consists of the English, Scottish, Welsh, and Irish nations. Collectively, these people are frequently referred to as "Britons." But not among themselves: most prefer to be known as English, Scots, Welsh, or Irish.

When World War II ended in 1945, perhaps five dozen or so sovereign states existed in the world. In the late 1940s, and continuing into the 1950s and 1960s, the British, French, Belgian, and Dutch colonial empires shrank as one colony after another became politically independent. As a result, by the end of the 1980s, there were around 170 sovereign countries. After the collapse of the "last colonial empire," the USSR, more countries emerged as sovereign, while others either dissolved (such as East Germany) or subdivided (as Czechoslovakia and Yugoslavia did). By 2000, over 200 independent countries were in the world, a record number in modern times.

Some experts believe the process is far from over. Some predict that some countries may, in cell-like fashion, continue to divide and redivide. The possibility of a world with 500 or more countries is a serious one, as distinct communities secede and establish their own political structures. This eventuality is not one that most authorities are enthusiastic about, and for good reason:

> There is simply no way in which all the hundreds of peoples who aspire to sovereign independence can be granted a state of their own without loosening fearful anarchy on a planetary scale.... An international system made up of several hundred territorial states cannot be a basis for global security and prosperity.[28]

One of the most important challenges for the early years of the next century is how to contain or at least coordinate the unprecedented explosion of states, many of which are not expected to become economically viable.

1-5f "Nations Against States"[29]

Very few countries in the world have been ethnically, religiously, and linguistically homogeneous. It helps to live in an out-of-the-way place where no one else lives and where no one else wants to live. Anyone deciding to settle in such a place would have to determine to live in an uninhabited land, all settlers would originate from the same place, and thus everyone would share an identical cultural and historical background (as in Iceland).[30] These happy circumstances rarely if ever occur; the

---

[26]David C. Gordon, *Images of the West: Third World Perspectives* (London and New York: Rowman & Littlefield Publishers, 1989), 40–41.

[27]"Europe and the Underclass," *The Economist,* July 30, 1994, 19.

[28]Gidon Gottleib, *Nation Against State: A New Approach to Ethnic Conflict and the Decline of Sovereignty* (New York: Council of Foreign Relations Press, 1994), 26–27.

[29]This phrase is taken from Gidon Gottleib, *ibid.*

[30]Iceland's approximately 300,000 inhabitants are nearly all descendants of Scandinavians who established settlements approximately a millennium ago.

| FIGURE 1–2 | Ethno-Linguistic Boundaries |

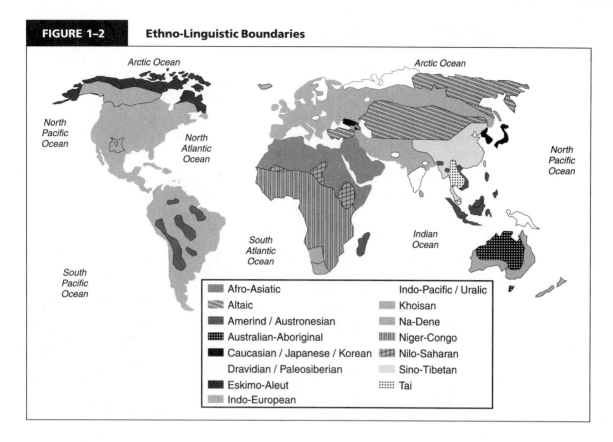

places where they have occurred could probably be counted on the fingers of one or at most two hands.

Most countries are heterogeneous to some extent. A fortunate few find heterogeneity to be a virtue. The diverse population of the United States, although not without some negative aspects (such as ongoing racism and religious bigotry, as well as local disagreements over whether the United States is a mono- or bilingual country) has created an enriching cultural and economic experience.

Even stable democracies have their problems. A fourth of Canada is French-speaking and Catholic, while most of the remaining three-fourths are English-speaking and Protestant. The French and Catholic part of the country, Quebec, may secede from Canada, perhaps causing substantial economic dislocation and hardship to itself as well as to other parts of the country. But at least secession, if it occurs, will most likely be peaceful in Canada. (See Figure 1–2 for a summary of main language groups across the globe.)

Separatism is even more volatile and common in Third World countries. India (with fifteen official languages and several religions), for example, could unravel. Even in Western Europe, separatist movements such as the Basques in Spain and the Lombardy League in Italy (which doesn't want to secede so much as throw the southern and poorest third of the country out) have threatened to separate.

In these and dozens of other cases, nations reside in states they are neither loyal to nor consider their own. Moreover, this isn't simply a case of regime loyalty. For instance, while President Saddam Hussein was an especially unpopular ruler of Iraq, the country itself is a good deal less than a natural entity, anyway. The Kurds in the northern third of the country and the Shiite Muslims in the southern third hardly consider themselves Iraqi and were far from loyal to the central government long before Saddam took power. They understandably desired to escape the genocidal tendencies not only of Hussein, but also of his predecessors.

Countries that unravel are not uncommon. The unraveling of a superpower, however, is somewhat frightening. When the Soviet Union disintegrated in 1991, it

TABLE 1–2	Noncitizens in Selected Middle Eastern Countries (percent of total population)

Country	Approximate Percentage of Noncitizens
Bahrain	37
Kuwait	45
Qatar	40
United Arab Emirates	81

Source: Adopted from *CIA World Factbook*, 2006, Central Intelligence Agency, Reston, Virginia.

was replaced by fifteen successor states, four of them with nuclear arsenals. Several of the fifteen were soon embroiled in internal conflicts, usually based on ethnic rivalries, but also on border disputes.

During the dictatorship of Joseph Stalin (1924–1953), a preferred tactic of the Soviet government was brutally displacing entire national communities hundreds or even thousands of miles from their ancestral homelands. Many who were forcibly moved died in the process from hunger and exposure. They were often dumped in a place with no way to support themselves. Now some of the survivors and their descendants are attempting to move back. Some of the Tatars, for example, are trying to return to the Crimea, even though few have ever seen the region. After they were forced out, their homes were occupied by Russians and Ukrainians who are still there and who show no desire to be replaced.

Perhaps a situation with even greater potential for havoc is found in countries whose citizenries are (sometimes vastly) outnumbered by noncitizenries. Several of the Persian Gulf states are experiencing this political incongruity (see Table 1–2). Very large minorities and often substantial majorities in these countries are simply guest workers who benefit from the jobs generated by the country's oil industry. These people generally are denied access to the political process (as much as one exists) and are not permitted to own businesses of their own. They are often exploited and abused, particularly if they are female house servants. In short, there is no reason for them to demonstrate any loyalty to the regime or to go to the slightest trouble to preserve it.

During the closing years of the twentieth century and the first years of the twenty-first century, the international constellation was punctuated not by conflicts between states as much as by conflicts within them. Several types of governments or states may be subject to such conflict, including:

1. Countries that have sizable ethnic and/or religious minorities who wish to establish their own territorial states (for example, French-speaking Canadians).
2. Countries with noncitizen populations so large that they threaten the political process they are usually denied access to (for example, United Arab Emirates). Noncitizens are usually brought in to perform menial work that no citizen wants to do. They are transient with no reason to cultivate a political loyalty to a regime that exploits them.
3. Countries that are artificially contrived and that have sizable ethnic and/or religious minorities that want to join their brethren across the borders (for example, Kurds in Iraq who desire to establish a Kurdistan state with the Kurds in Iran and Turkey). Countries such as Jordan and Iraq were both created during the 1920s by the British government, at that time trying to create a sphere of influence for itself in the region.

Naturally, most countries consider their territories sacrosanct and will not often see them change in peaceful fashion. Some, though, will probably change one way or another, and this may usher in an era of new and perhaps irresolvable border disputes.

1-6 New Political Formulations

Political scientists often enjoy speculating on political scenarios that usually don't come true. However, such scenarios occasionally correspond to reality. Today, speculation even seems appropriate—Americans are living in a transitional period that began with the end of the Cold War and as yet has no end in sight.

What does seem likely is that as states divide and new countries are created, new territorial disputes will arise. Some may actually be resolved peacefully. When Czechoslovakia dissolved in 1993 into two countries, the Czech Republic and Slovakia, the dissolution was without violence. Peaceful examples of secession, though, seem to be the exception rather than the rule.

Regardless of how state boundaries are drawn, some minorities will always get stranded in countries they have little affection for and whose majority populations have little toleration for nonindigenous populations. One of the most serious examples of this situation involves the 25 million Russians living in the non-Russian former Soviet republics. A large proportion is content where they are and have been more or less accepted by the indigenous population. But many aren't either content or accepted. Hundreds of thousands of Russians are residents of the three small Baltic republics, and they complain of all sorts of discriminatory measures that the Baltic governments have taken against them. In some sense, there is a balance: as many as 35 million non-Russians, more than 20 percent of the total population, live in the Russian Federated Republic, and many of them complain and worry about discrimination by the Russian authorities.[31]

1-6a Possible Alternatives to the Traditional State

As traditional states experience internal conflicts that cause them to splinter, other alternatives may increasingly come into play.

Mini-States. A state small in both population and territory has a certain advantage. If such a country lacks valuable natural resources such as oil, it can usually expect to be left alone. Europe has had mini-states for centuries: Andorra, Liechtenstein, Monaco, San Marino, and Vatican City, to name some. The economies of these countries are based often on a single product that ranges from legalized gambling (Monaco) to banking (Liechtenstein) to religion (Vatican City). A plethora of mini-states has also cropped up in the West Indies and the South Pacific. Most have populations between 10,000 and 100,000 and are dependent upon outside economic assistance. These countries are members of the United Nations (where they have a vote equal in weight to that of the United States in the General Assembly), regularly exchange ambassadors with other countries, print their own currency and stamps, and have all the other trappings of a sovereign state.

Regions with Limited Political Autonomy. Varying degrees of autonomy have become a political fact in several countries that contain diverse linguistic, ethnic, and religious communities. In order to retain political unification, central governments in several countries, from Spain to Russia, have granted substantial degrees of local autonomy to various regions.

The degree is normally dependent upon the deals the central government can work out with the respective regions. Obviously, this is no easy task. The Basque

---

[31]Central Intelligence Agency, *The World Factbook 2004* (Washington D.C.: Brassey's, Inc., 2002) 431–434.

region in Spain has a strong separatist movement that wants complete independence. In Russia, Tatarstan and Chechnya have announced with limited success their departure from the Russian Federated Republic. Tatarstan has had trouble getting the international community as well as the Russians to take its independence seriously because it is completely surrounded by Russian territory. Hence, it is necessary to travel either across or over Russia to get to or from Tatarstan.

Despite such occasional incongruities, experiments in limited autonomy are going forward, sometimes in unlikely places. Israel and the Palestinian Authority (PA), for example, negotiated for several years in a peace process that broke down by the end of 2000. The PA had hoped that Israeli withdrawal from the Gaza Strip and the West Bank would lead to a sovereign state of Palestine. Instead, unilateral withdrawal by Israel from the Gaza Strip and the construction of a security barrier between itself and Palestinian areas has led to conflict between factions within the Palestinian community, especially since the Islamic radical party, Hamas, took control of the government in January 2006. Israel considers Hamas to be a terrorist organization while Hamas considers Israel to be an illegitimate state, not a good basis for fruitful negotiations.

The experimentation with limited political autonomy will no doubt continue as central governments, either voluntarily or by coercion, give up at least partial authority over various regions. It is a delicate matter. To give in too completely to local demands may actually cause the collapse of an entire country; on the other hand, for a government to attempt to retain full control over a disaffected region may incite civil war. Alternatives for providing limited autonomy range from the inhumane to the reasonable:

1. A central government may refuse to grant any local autonomy and may resort without hesitation to genocidal policies to retain control (for example, Iraqi treatment of Kurds and Muslim Shiites during the reign of Saddam Hussein).
2. A central government may grant local cultural autonomy, usually including free use of the local language, control over the educational system, and limited political autonomy, but retain control over foreign policy and military forces (for example, Russia's relationship with Tatarstan and other members of the federated republic).
3. A central government may operate in a fairly democratic and commonsense fashion, addressing needs that are more or less national in scope and making itself available to assist in regional and local matters whenever all sides agree it is desirable (for example, most democracies in Western Europe and the United States).

All of these alternatives will be further discussed.

Chapter Summary

1. While government and politics are not identical, they are inseparable. Politics precedes and usually results in government and remains its driving force.
2. The Soviet Union's political regime is an excellent example of how a governmental structure can completely fail to provide for the needs of its citizenry by adhering to an unworkable ideology and institutionalizing corruption and incompetence.
3. Government that actively seeks to provide for the security and overall welfare of its citizenries tends both to survive and to receive the loyalty of those under its jurisdiction.
4. American society and its political system are good reference points because of the economic and political impact the United States has had in the rest of the world and its status as a "universal nation."
5. The Cold War period (1945–1990) was, in retrospect, a simpler time when the world seemingly could be divided into bad and good governments.
6. The post–Cold War era is much more complex because of the resurgence of ethnic and/or religious conflicts.
7. Democratization is a not-always-successful process that can lead a society to adopt permanently democratic political institutions.

8. Pillars of durable democracy seem to include a citizenry that enjoys a decent standard of living, widespread literacy, universally available modern technology, overall good physical health, and accessibility to self-improvement.

9. Westernization is widespread and popular in some non-Western regions, but deeply resented and feared in others, as expressed through religious fundamentalism.

10. The term *nation-state* does not accurately describe most countries on the map. Many societies are breaking down into tribal and clannish affiliations, and the central government is having a difficult time retaining authority in such regions. In many cases, a central government is having difficulty even establishing control over regions and populations it is considered responsible for.

11. Some new political formulations—including mini-states or areas of limited autonomy—may be implemented to cope with the breakdown of countries into smaller, quasi-independent areas.

Chapter 1 Quiz

1. Politics and government are
   a. not the same thing.
   b. synonymous terms.
   c. only found together in democracies.
   d. contradictory terms.

2. The first former First Lady to become a United States senator was
   a. Hillary Clinton.
   b. Eleanor Roosevelt.
   c. Betty Ford.
   d. Abigail Adams.

3. The first industrialized country in history to experience a decline in longevity rates was
   a. France.
   b. the United States.
   c. the Soviet Union.
   d. Japan.

4. The Taliban government in Afghanistan
   a. introduced political democracy to the country.
   b. encouraged the advancement of females.
   c. adopted a fanatical religious authority as a guide to governance.
   d. required men to have their heads shaved.

5. AIDS is doing the greatest damage to the population of
   a. East Asia.
   b. Northern Europe.
   c. Caribbean basin.
   d. Africa.

6. The Han Chinese
   a. populate most of eastern Siberia.
   b. are the largest ethnic community on the planet.
   c. have mostly converted to Islam.
   d. have spilled over into northern India in overwhelming numbers.

7. Ideology is different from the free play of politics in that ideology
   a. is accepting of diversity.
   b. purports to have all the answers to all problems.
   c. allows for free expression of ideas.
   d. is naturally embracing of the democratic process.

8. Most of the history of government is characterized by
   a. democracy.
   b. authoritarianism.
   c. regular elections.
   d. civilian rule.

9. The most prosperous national economies in history have generally been
   a. totalitarian.
   b. monarchial.
   c. autocratic.
   d. democratic.

10. The term *command economy* is associated primarily with
    a. the European Union.
    b. the Soviet Union.
    c. the United States.
    d. East Asia.

11. The term *last colonial empire* is associated with
    a. American territorial possessions in the Pacific region.
    b. the Soviet Union.
    c. French interests in western Europe.
    d. Puerto Rico.

12. By the 1980s, forms of free market economies were dominant in all of the following except
    a. East Asia.
    b. North America.
    c. West Europe.
    d. the Soviet Union.

13. The Cold War era lasted roughly
    a. during the entirety of the twentieth century.
    b. during 1919–1939.
    c. during 1945–1990.
    d. since the fall of the Soviet Union in 1991.

14. The process of democratization normally includes all except one of the following characteristics:
    a. a broad and large middle class.
    b. educated citizenry.
    c. electorally successful totalitarian political party.
    d. at least some modern technological base.

15. Nations and states
    a. are synonymous.
    b. never combined.
    c. can exist separately.
    d. none of the above.

PART 2

Government and Politics

The following three chapters offer general discussions on such perennial subjects as what politics is and what good it does. As Chapter 2 indicates, politics has been a much-discussed activity for as long as recorded history. An entire discipline, political philosophy, devotes itself to making formulations about what kind of political state is best for most people and how to create it. Chapter 3 reviews the various dimensions and intricacies of political culture. Each country's overall culture heavily influences the society's political culture. The latter both shapes and is shaped by the prevailing political institutions and is guided for better or worse by the country's overall political history. Chapter 4 concentrates on the two primary current forms of political system, democracy and authoritarianism. Each can be broken down into several interpretations and practices. Democracy is a comparatively new political arrangement and is still rather experimental, while authoritarianism has a long, if not always appealing, tradition.

Government, the State, and Political Philosophy

KEY TERMS

dialectical materialism
dictatorship of the proletariat
divine right
elite
ethnocentrism
left
nepotism

polis
proletariat
right
Sharia
social contract
theocracy

Why does the human species prefer to live in a political society regardless of its inherent imperfections? Why do citizens require the state to conduct and guarantee a civilized lifestyle, and why do they expect the state and those in political authority to be friendly and helpful? These preferences, which will be discussed in this chapter, led to the birth of political philosophy at least 2,500 years ago. It is important to briefly review some of the most outstanding theories of the state because theorists have debated political obedience, the rights of the individual versus those of society, and what actually constitutes legitimate government for centuries. These debates are far from resolved and will most likely continue for a long time.

For thousands of years, people have speculated about government: What is the purpose of government? How much government is good for society? How much government is too much? Through what kind of institutions can citizens balance the need for government with the desire for individual freedoms? And, perhaps most importantly, if they don't like their government's policies, how can they change or get rid of them? Two-and-one-half millennia ago, political speculation became more sophisticated in the Greek city-state system as political philosophers began spending considerable amounts of time creating formulas for successful governments. Political speculation has continued ever since, and along the way, society has experimented with a variety of governmental forms.

Some governments have been more successful than others; quite a few have indulged in inhumane practices. Clearly, many governments have caused a great deal more harm than good. Just as clearly, a perfect form of government that guarantees justice and prosperity for every member of society has not yet been achieved. People still debate whether government is supposed to guarantee either, or whether it even has that capability.

This chapter surveys some of the more interesting formulas for government. New communications technologies, unforeseen conflicts among various segments of citizenries, and evolving degrees of cultural autonomy in political jurisdictions will present government with both new opportunities and new challenges. Government and the political processes that determine who governs and through what kinds of institutions will continue to change and undergo refinement; society is far from through developing new forms of government.

2-1 The Classical Sense of Good Government

As mentioned, speculation about the means and ends of government became historically noticeable in a few of the ancient city-states of Greece. Why people began to consider proper governance as a serious profession in Greece is uncertain. A reasonable explanation is that in some of the city-states, the overall culture encouraged inquiry into a wide variety of subjects—physics, biology, mathematics, and philosophy among them. Two-and-one-half millennia ago, Greece experienced an explosion of knowledge, yielding ideas and results so universal that they are still studied, debated, and evaluated.

2-1a Plato

Ironically, one of the first meaningful statements of good government was authored by Plato (427–347 B.C.), a political philosopher who possessed a very substantial dislike of and contempt for politics. Plato did not believe that the free play of politics actually produced useful results or resolved disputes. In politics, he argued, the decision-making process is frequently based less on reason than on what seems to be a good idea at the moment. Moreover, the problem with politics, its give and take, inconclusive ends, and unavoidable passions, has much to do with what politics does ultimately produce—namely unpredictable and therefore dangerous change.

Plato feared and hated change in great part because he was aware that other disciplines, such as mathematics, for example, are quite orderly and predictable. The correct sum of two numbers added together *never* changes. The fact that such a discipline is changeless, orderly, and predictable led Plato to conclude that the same sort of view ought to be applied to human society.[1]

Plato was a reluctant realist, and he preferred a harmonious society that would find no reason to change. He recognized that the creation of such a community would be a massive undertaking, but he firmly believed it was worth the cost. The end result would be an entity in which citizens would have responsibilities that were both necessary and would appeal to their talents. The key was to implement the proper definition of justice.

Justice in Plato's most famous work, *The Republic*, consisted of each citizen doing what he or she does best by natural talent. The health (Plato was fond of using medical terms and analogies) of the Republic was maintained by a citizenry divided into three classes, as Table 2–1 summarizes. The guardians or philosophers of the Republic are analogous to the head of the body, the auxiliaries to the chest, and the rest of the society, the majority, to below the chest (the stomach or abdomen area). Most people, Plato believed, are appetitive—that is, they are motivated by and think more with their stomachs and guts than with their heads and brains. Plato cautions that appetitive people are neither unimportant nor stupid. All three classes perform essential tasks and are interdependent on one another.

Plato is very clear that all three classes are absolutely essential to the well-being of the state. No class would do well or even survive without the others. Guardians are dependent upon auxiliaries to carry out instructions and protect the society, and on the common mass for their very sustenance. Auxiliaries need direction from the guardians. The artisans and craftsmen, who are incapable of providing a just

TABLE 2–1	Classes and Souls in Plato's Republic	
Class	**Area of the Body**	**Soul of Character**
Guardian	Head	Thinks, analyzes, and directs
Auxiliary	Chest	Executes directions from the guardians; thinks less and acts more
Common	Stomach	Is acquisitive and materially productive in a variety of necessary occupations such as agricultural and crafts

[1]This preference for exactitude was carried to its logical conclusion when Plato calculated 5,040 as the perfect number of citizens for a well-adjusted commonwealth.

commonwealth by or for themselves, require the other two classes to resolve their disputes (the guardians) and protect them (the auxiliaries).

The guardians were the class Plato obviously favored and who reflected his own preference that society be in the care of philosophers. Many people would find Plato's requirements for entrance into this class intimidating and unappealing: the guardians were not to own property, establish families, or pursue financially rewarding careers. The craftsmen and artisans would care for the guardians' needs. The guardians would spend their time pursuing knowledge. On occasions that required resolutions of disputes within the Republic, the guardians' accumulated wisdom would ensure the proper application of justice.

The guardians would lead a communist lifestyle. Communism, for Plato, was a privilege meant only for those who don't require material wealth in the first place because they are supposed to be above the need to possess property. Socrates, Plato's teacher, argues in *The Republic* that a guardian should not possess "any property of his own beyond what is absolutely necessary."[2] Should the guardians ever give in to the temptation of becoming like artisans and craftsmen, who prefer money to virtue,

> they will become housekeepers and husbandmen instead of guardians, enemies and tyrants instead of allies of other citizens; hating and being hated, plotting and being plotted against, they will pass their whole life in much greater terror of internal than of external enemies, and the hour of ruin, both to themselves and to the rest of the State, will be at hand.[3]

Once settled into an ascetic existence, these wise men and women would make it unnecessary for the society to establish a legal system or to hold elections. Plato was no democrat and did not believe in the ability and right of the people to govern. Instead, he believed that democracy allowed people without the necessary talent, aptitude, or intelligence to govern badly and to become dangerous to the people who elected them. His argument was basically that someone without expertise would not be allowed to declare him or herself an engineer and build a bridge. Why, then, should a farmer who wants to become a governor be tolerated? Plato also held Athenian democracy responsible for the death of his hero and teacher, Socrates.[4] He took his revenge by bringing Socrates back to life as the leading figure in *The Republic* who carefully maps out the perfect society.

However else *The Republic* may come across to the twenty-first-century reader, certain aspects of it are remarkably modern. In at least two ways, Plato makes the point that he is departing from much that was taken for granted in the ancient world, including its most progressive area, Greece. For one thing, *The Republic* is probably the first description of any society to include mention of gender equality, though its mention was restricted to the guardian class. Female guardians were not meant to simply stay at home and rear families. (In fact, they weren't to have any families to rear.)[5] They would pursue, along with their male counterparts, the very demanding physical and intellectual training that would enable them to become the best possible caretakers of *The Republic*.

There is a certain irony to the Platonic scheme described in *The Republic*. The society of *The Republic* must get its start at some point. It is unlikely that Plato had any knowledge of the Bible, but eight or nine centuries before his own, the Hebrew tribes that had fled Egypt in the Exodus wandered for forty years in the Sinai

---

[2]Plato, *The Republic*, Book III, 305.

[3]Ibid., p. 306.

[4]Socrates was condemned for corrupting the morals of Athenian youths. At seventy years of age, he was given the unhappy choice of exile from the city he loved or death. He chose to drink poison.

[5]By this time, you may be asking yourself how successive generations of guardians would be produced. Plato addresses this issue in *The Republic* by suggesting an annual festival. The children that resulted from the "festivities" would be reared in common. For guardian parents to know who their children were would result in favoritism, a distraction from the pursuit of knowledge Plato thought this class needed to avoid at all costs.

TABLE 2–2	Myth and Structure of Plato's Republic	
Class	**Metal**	**Activities**
Guardians	Gold	Pursuit of ideas and knowledge
Auxiliaries	Silver	Military and administrative activities
Artisans and craftsmen	Bronze	Production of material necessities for all classes

wilderness so that a fresh generation with no memory of slavery could enter the Promised Land.

The *Republic* is Plato's Promised Land, and to enter it requires the elimination of the views of a previous generation. Plato counted on a new, very young (and therefore impressionable) generation (under ten years of age) to realize his goals. What, then, are the under tens supposed to believe? Pure and simple, they are to believe a lie, or, to be less crude about it, a "noble lie." And they *will* believe it. Even ten-year-olds can be skeptical, but Plato reasoned that if a generation grows to adulthood constantly exposed to a particular point of view, the members of that generation will accept the view as their own and will be reluctant to believe anything to the contrary. Plato was an early believer in the power of propaganda.

The noble lie, as summarized in Table 2–2, goes something like this: Each of the three classes is descended from metals that differ in strength and value. In *The Republic*, it is important to know one's place. Only in rare exceptions would a member of one class move to another.

2-1b Aristotle

Early in his most famous work *Politics*, Aristotle wrote that

> Every state is as we see a sort of partnership, and every partnership is formed with a view to some good (since all the actions of all mankind are done with a view to what they think to be good).[6]

Of course Aristotle believed that the state the partnership created would be one in which the population was relatively homogeneous; he did not foresee the ethnic and cultural diversity that characterizes most modern states. But he did fully understand that any state has to be a reflection of common interests and is the natural outcome of human association—and a necessary one, at that.[7]

Aristotle viewed the **polis**, or city-state, as the highest stage of human social and political development, allowing its citizens to find and live the good life.[8] For Aristotle, the polis is the only place where the good life is possible, the only place where the individual can make a good life for her or himself. Because "the city-state is prior in nature to the household and to each of us individually," and because "the whole must necessarily be prior to the part," individuals are "either low in the scale of humanity or above it. . . ."[9] In other words, Aristotle believed no self-respecting member of the human community would consider living anywhere else but within the confines of political society. Aristotle assumed that humans are basically a gregarious species "and so even when men have no need of assistance from each other they nonetheless desire to live together."[10]

polis
The city-state form of government that Plato and Aristotle regarded as the optimal political arrangement for conducting human affairs.

---

[6]Aristotle, *Politics* (Cambridge, Massachusetts: Harvard University Press, 1972), 3.

[7]Ibid., p. 9.

[8]Ibid.

[9]Ibid., pp. 9, and 11.

[10]Ibid., p. 201.

A Note On — THE TERMS *LEFT* AND *RIGHT*

These terms, which apparently originated in the immediate aftermath of the French Revolution of 1789, will come up in other contexts in this text. When the French monarchy was overthrown, some of the more radical revolutionaries, who happened to be sitting on the left side of the newly constituted legislative chamber, advocated such measures as cancellation of all debts, the creation of a classless society, and disenfranchising the Catholic Church, at that time an important factor in French politics and the owner of a third of the national wealth. The more moderate legislators, who happened to be sitting on the right side of the chamber, believed in greater democracy than the monarchy had ever allowed, but still preferred to retain traditional values, free markets, and perhaps the creation of a constitutional monarchy.

The United States also experienced an interesting division as a result of its revolution. The drafters of the Declaration of Independence in 1776 were probably much more radical than those who drafted the Constitution eleven years later. Very few participated at both conventions. After the United States won its independence, the first assemblage, led by Thomas Jefferson, sympathized with the French revolutionaries, while those who supported ratification of the Constitution and a strong central government, led by Alexander Hamilton, leaned toward a more conservative Britain.

Once one is within the confines of the state, the critical question is how the best quality of life can be achieved. Aristotle's formula for political and social success has been imitated by numerous societies through the ages. People and political systems, he argued, enjoy long and productive lives as long as they avoid extremes. And a healthy polis requires healthy constituents. Each individual should know personally how much is too much to be good.

> The man who runs away from everything in fear and never endures anything becomes a coward; the man who fears nothing whatsoever but encounters everything becomes rash.[11]

In other words, neither cowards nor the foolhardy can successfully govern states. It is those who are moderate, who yield to no ideological or political extreme, and who may come across as dull and boring, who are actually best fit to govern and be governed.

Extremes of wealth and poverty, Aristotle believed (and modern societies can attest), are probably inevitable but should be kept minimal. He recommended a large and broadly based middle class as a recipe for political stability. The middle-class society is in place in most of the Western world. It has been instrumental, as Aristotle predicted, in creating successful political democracies that tend to follow moderate and sane economic and social policies. Flirtations with extremes of the political **left** and **right** have more often than not led to disaster. (See the following box for a discussion of the terms *left* and *right*.)

Aristotle further believed that moderation has another value: It is an excellent preservative of the status quo. Aristotle, like Plato, feared change. Unlike Plato, Aristotle understood that some change is inevitable, but he sought to minimize its effects. In particular, he dreaded revolution, the political phenomenon that can completely upset and destroy the status quo. Constant vigilance is required to avoid the destruction that even gradual change brings. Aristotle believed it is dangerous, for example, when a government decides to "give up one of the details of the constitution" because "afterwards they also make another slightly bigger change more readily, until they alter the whole system."[12]

Change, then, is a terrifying if often subtle social and political activity that, Aristotle was convinced, can lead to no good. In this respect he had no argument with Plato, who advocated a society practically frozen in a single time period throughout *The Republic*. In reality, of course, change is impossible to prevent. In advocating a

left
A common reference to ideologies that tend to be liberal or socialist in nature.

right
A common reference to ideologies that tend to be conservative in nature.

---

[11]Aristotle, *Nichomachean Ethics*, 77.

[12]Ibid., p. 19.

totally unchanging society, Aristotle violated his own conviction that extremes are evils to always be avoided.

Aristotle's influence is still vibrant. The founders of the United States, for example, met him halfway. They had not only read his works, but they applied a good many of his political principles. And they also were apprehensive about the prospect of change. They understood that change was inevitable, but also desired to at least control it. They intentionally made it very difficult to amend the United States Constitution. More than two centuries after ratification, the Constitution has been amended only twenty-seven times.

2-1c The Stoics

Aristotle's lifetime coincided with the collapse of the city-state system, an event he seemed oblivious to. He was well acquainted with and in favor of the system and sought to perpetuate its existence, but the city-states could not resist the strength of the empires that gradually absorbed them. By the time the Roman Empire was fully established two to three centuries later, it was becoming increasingly obvious that political philosophy must now take into account a huge political entity, which unlike the polis, might achieve a population in the few hundreds of thousands, including a heterogeneous population numbering in the tens of millions. Making sense of a society that was bigger, more dangerous, and more impersonal (a society that in many ways resembles today's) was a complicated task.

While Stoicism was a philosophy developed by pre-Christian thinkers, it had a great deal in common with early Christianity. Each viewed the universe as a place that was not always friendly. More to the point, each viewed society as dominated by a combination of human stupidity and unjustified and often self-destructive arrogance. Stoics—notably Zeno of Athens, the emperor Marcus Aurelius, and Seneca—viewed the world as torn between virtue and vice;[13] Christianity saw it as torn between salvation and sin. Both considered the world a difficult and disorderly place where personal security and happiness were infrequent and fleeting.

Stoicism offered reason as an escape route out of daily turmoil, whereas Christianity offered faith. Ultimately, the promise of a heavenly and eternal reward after a difficult and often painful life in this world had a greater appeal than a plea to do the best possible without any guarantee of benefits beyond the grave. Even today, the competition between the tradition of reason and the tradition of faith continues: Many Christians write the world off as lost and prepare for the next, while those who cling to reason continue to believe that fools threaten civilization more than sinners do.

Stoics understandably preferred order to disorder, but this preference carried an element of fatalism. Everyone could be essentially equal to everyone else, because social or political rank is arbitrary and temporary, and often even a matter of luck. But this also meant one should accept one's status, whether high or low, and do the best one could in the role one was assigned.

The same principle applies to government and governing. If it is one's destiny to govern, one should do so without complaint, but obviously, it is easier to accept the role of king than of slave. For this reason, Stoicism did not appeal beyond the educated and relatively well-off social classes. Stoicism did provide a prescription for proper governance: A ruler should reject all temptations to pursue or enhance personal glory and wealth. Rather, the purpose of rulership is to provide service for the benefit of the entire society. This was certainly a noble principle of governing, though a frequently ignored one. Yet, the principle itself has been bequeathed to successive generations. Politicians are still allowed to further their own ambitions if people believe they are also serving the public good.

---

[13]Perhaps the best expression of the stoic philosophy is *Meditations*, a work authored by the Roman emperor Marcus Aurelius who reigned during 162–180. *Meditations* was actually a personal journal not intended for anyone else's eyes. In it Aurelius speculates on the universe and the place of humans in it. His conclusions focused on the notion that each of us must accept for what he or she is and make the best of our talents to serve the common good.

For the next millennium, political philosophy was in great part submerged by theology. Then, in the sixteenth century, Nicolo Machiavelli (1469–1522) produced *The Prince*. This slim volume radically departed from traditional political thought. Plato and Aristotle had suggested what they believed political society *should be;* Machiavelli explained what politics really is and how it actually functions. He argued that no leader worth his salt could do well by being morally good. To secure his own leadership, for example, a prince shouldn't hesitate to wipe out both his opponent and his opponent's family, because children who are fond of their parents may seek revenge later. Goodness would be fully exploited by those who aren't good and have no intention of being good.

The Prince, claimed Machiavelli, should uphold the prevailing morality, but not take it too seriously himself. For example, the Prince should attend a house of worship along with family members because it looks good to do so, but he should not take the sermon seriously. Political morality, in other words, is separate from private morality. Machiavelli also believed a prince must be prepared to do what is necessary to uphold both his power and the security of the state. Hesitating to be ruthless when ruthlessness was required would make the prince both politically immoral and a political failure. Successful politicians were already following this advice, which explains why *The Prince* has been continuously in print for nearly five centuries.

2-2 Thomas Hobbes

The expansion of a central government's authority is dependent upon a widespread acceptance of sovereignty. The basic feature of sovereignty is indivisibility: everyone must accept one location where political power is concentrated in any political system. But establishing this type of sovereignty has always been easier said than done. Political philosophers Thomas Hobbes (1588–1679) and John Locke (1632–1704), who were personally close to the political notables of their times, felt compelled to develop prescriptions for the proper place of sovereignty and limitations on sovereigns.

Hobbes began by describing what he referred to as the *state of nature*. In the state of nature, Hobbes argued, each person can do anything he or she wants. Unfortunately, everyone else also has the same right. The state of nature is, in fact, stateless: Every individual is alone and responsible for her or his own physical security in such an arrangement. The world, without order, would be a place of fear where life for everyone is "solitary, poor, nasty, brutish, and short." It would be an unfortunate place where war is perpetual and pits "every man against every man." In his most remembered and quoted work, *Leviathan*, Hobbes observes that the state of nature, in short, is a formula for a decidedly miserable existence that no one would desire or enjoy.

Hobbes proposed an effective if less than pleasant solution in *Leviathan*. He had witnessed the English civil war of the 1640s that culminated in the execution of Charles I. The breakdown of order during this period distressed Hobbes. Not unlike urban Americans watching the steady increase of violent crime degrade their neighborhoods, Hobbes viewed turmoil and chaos as the breakdown not only of the legal system but of civil society itself. Whether criminal behavior or political rebellion poses the threat, Hobbes understood the threat to the maintenance of order was so severe that the end result could only be regression to the state of nature—exactly the place everyone had escaped from and to which no one would wish to return.

Hobbes proposed the creation of a sovereign power that would exercise unquestioned authority. In the dreaded state of nature, people possessed individual liberty. Because everyone had maximum liberty, complete equality prevailed. But in this state, human society could not avoid being violent—with everyone equal to everyone else, no authority could possibly exist. While everyone enjoyed equal liberty and equality, everyone was also equally threatened. For peace and stability to be the norm, inequality must prevail.

Agreeing on a sovereign authority was an act of survival. Hobbes believed that humans are a species at once argumentative and belligerent, both self-motivated and self-serving: "The object of any appetite or desire . . . a man calleth the good; the object of his aversion, evil; for these words . . . are ever used with relation to the person that useth them . . ."[14] The sovereign must be cognizant of this very human characteristic and be both fair and firm in the administration of justice. Civil society could endure and prosper only when the largest number of its members was convinced that by obeying reasonable laws, everyone's self-interest is served. (Deciding which laws are both appealing and reasonable is an issue covered in a later chapter.)

For Hobbes, sovereign authority must be indisputable and unequivocal. A citizenry is first and foremost concerned about the physical security of life and possessions, and a sovereign must take responsibility for these concerns. Hobbes believed that many, perhaps most, people are willing and even eager to cede authority over their lives in exchange for guarantees that safeguard their persons, families, and material possessions. In fact, people do this whenever they pay taxes, accept military conscription, and stop their vehicles at red traffic lights.

The **social contract** Hobbes advocates is not between ruler and ruled. It is a contract between those the sovereign rules. The ruled and their descendants agree "to confer all their power and strength upon one man, or upon one assembly of men."[15] Indeed, Hobbes was not particular what form the sovereign assumed. All that mattered was whether the sovereign was doing the job. Even if the sovereign wasn't performing perfectly, the people would have no recourse. Hobbes was emphatic that even a less than fully competent sovereign was better than the alternative—chaos and violence.

There is no choice in the matter, Hobbes argues. Though he preferred a sovereign that modeled its administration on the basis of justice, Hobbes believed no one should rebel against even inept or tyrannical sovereigns. Revolution is far worse, in this point of view, because it destroys any hope of maintaining the contract that provides for social order.

social contract
An arrangement Thomas Hobbes and John Locke proposed for the establishment of a civil society under a sovereign government.

2-3 John Locke

Like Hobbes, John Locke saw enough civil violence in his time—in 1649, when he was seventeen years old, he personally witnessed the beheading of King Charles I—to attempt a political formula that would ensure domestic peace. Unlike Hobbes, Locke believed there was room for tolerating dissent and occasional justification for revolution. Revolution, though, would be unnecessary if the sovereign never broke the laws that applied to everyone else. Locke's theory of government was published in 1691 as *Treatises on Government*. Nearly a century later, the founders of the United States enthusiastically employed its contents to justify the American Revolution in the Declaration of Independence. A decade after the Revolution began, they incorporated a version of Locke's notion of separation of powers into the United States Constitution.[16]

They did so for good reason. Locke's stateless state of nature was somewhat more benign than Hobbes'. His creation of sovereign authority provided for physical security, but it was mainly formulated for the sake of convenience. Locke's state of nature lacked any authority to make an objective decision when a controversy as

---

[14]Thomas Hobbes, *Leviathan*, XI, p. 23.

[15]Ibid., XVII, p. 89.

[16]Locke considered only the legislature and monarchy in his concept of separation of powers. Americans added the judiciary as another wedge preventing any one branch of government from becoming too powerful.

mundane as a property line dispute arose. In this state of nature, Locke said, people make a contract with one another.

In fact, that is why government was created in the first place—for "the great and chief end"[17] of preserving and protecting private property. Locke argued that most people are fairly reasonable creatures who ask simply to get on with their lives with a minimum of interference. Private property becomes both an incentive and a reward for individual efforts. Government, then, is just and fair as long as it fulfills its primary obligation of protecting property through laws, courts, and, when necessary, military action. In return, government can expect to receive the voluntary obedience of its citizenry.

Society then selects an authority to administer the laws that society imposes on itself. Keep in mind that the seventeenth century was a very autocratic time nearly everywhere. Toleration was not yet a political virtue. In this context, Locke exhibited a remarkably modern and democratic sentiment. The social contract does not give sovereignty to a monarch or anyone else in particular. Rather, the members of society are sovereign. Through voting and/or through legislators (Locke was an early advocate of parliamentary supremacy), citizens select political officers to execute and apply laws.

But governments, like citizens, are obliged to obey laws as well as avoid oppressive legislation. Government cannot appropriate property without just cause or apply unwarranted taxes (which often amounts to the same thing). If it does, "the people are absolved from obedience when illegal attempts are made upon their liberties and properties."[18]

Perhaps the most striking feature of Locke's treatment is his emphasis of the individual over the state. State power is at all times viewed within the context of the individual's chronological and ethical precedence:

> To understand political power aright, and derive from its original, we must consider what state all men are naturally in, and that is a state of perfect freedom to order their actions and dispose of their possessions and person as they see fit, within the bounds of the law of nature, without asking leave, or depending upon the will of any other man. A state also of equality, wherein all the power and jurisdiction is reciprocal, no one having more than another.[19]

This is strong stuff. Locke is arguing very democratically that no member of society who behaves within the boundaries of natural law—showing respect for the property and lives of others, for instance—should have to worry about the state's interference. Locke's views are contrasted with those of earlier philosophers in Figure 2–1.

FIGURE 2–1	**Views of Government, Plato–Locke**				
Plato 427–347 B.C.E.	**Aristotle 384–322 B.C.E.**	**Stoics 50–200 C.E.**	**Machiavelli 1469–1522**	**Hobbes 1588–1679**	**Locke 1632–1704**
Guardians of the state make the big decisions; society is stratified into three classes.	A homogenous population is best; the city-state is the highest form of government.	The role of government and governors is to provide for the greater society without seeking personal aggrandizement.	Amoral ruthlessness is all in succeeding politically.	Sovereign power with absolute, unquestionable authority will protect man from himself.	Government has a protecting role; citizens participate in creating laws.

[17]John Locke, *Second Treatise*, No. 124.

[18]John Locke, *Second Treatise*, No. 28.

[19]John Locke, "An Essay Concerning the True Origin, Extent, and End of Civil Government," in Edwin A. Butt, ed., *The English Philosophers from Bacon to Mill* (New York: Modern Library, 1939), 404.

Locke's goal had been to restrict the powers of the executive branch, the one he considered most prone to regress into tyranny. His influence was persuasive. The British monarchy watched its authority gradually, and, for the most part, peacefully, diminish as it was transformed into its current ceremonial role. The real head of government, the prime minister, can serve only as long as he or she enjoys the support of a parliamentary majority.

Locke helped to create institutionalized distrust of the executive. The distrust was transplanted: In colonial America, colonial assemblies relentlessly watched over governors. Even after independence, states placed term limitations on their executives. Many states still impose one- or two-term limitations on their governors. With the ratification of the Twenty-second Amendment in 1951, a two-term limitation was imposed on presidents.

Locke's influence went beyond his own time and country in other ways as well. Baron de Montesquieu in his *Spirit of the Laws* agreed with Locke that separation of powers offered the best hope of avoiding tyrannical government. Both Locke and Montesquieu envisioned the legislative and executive branches keeping an eye on one another. The American political formulation complemented the formula by adding the judiciary as a co-equal branch of government to fully ensure that no political dictatorship would become practical or likely.

2-4 Conservatism and Liberalism

Probably no other terms in the political lexicon have been as variously interpreted as *conservatism* and *liberalism*. Part of the explanation for this comes from the fact that both ideologies are descended from nineteenth-century *liberalism*, which developed in the aftermath of the French Revolution and Napoleonic wars (1789–1815). Prior to this period, a social order that evolved during the Middle Ages had prevailed in Europe. It was in many respects a simpler time: most of the class structure was based on a predominantly agricultural economy and social system in which a landed aristocracy controlled most of the wealth and all of the political institutions, while a vast and often impoverished peasantry was legally tied to the land.

Rapid urbanization, industrial revolution, relentlessly advancing technology, and the accumulation of unprecedented wealth—events that began in and forever changed the West and are now spreading to East and South Asia, Latin America, and parts of the Middle East—created new roles and opportunities for government. Conservatives and liberals formulated their differences around a debate over the role of government. Conservatives today adhere to the Jeffersonian notion that the less government (and, therefore, the less taxation) the better, while liberals believe that government has a responsibility to provide comfort and security for those who cannot provide for themselves (and to levy taxes to the extent necessary to guarantee adequate social services). Figure 2–2 shows the political spectrum.

There are numerous manifestations of liberalism, including the classical type associated with John Locke. Locke is only one of a multitude of thinkers who could be called or have called themselves liberal. This text does not cover other excellent contributions to nineteenth-century liberal thought, including contributions by thinkers who today would be considered conservative or even libertarian.[20] Generally speaking, liberalism began as an ideology that encouraged the individual realization of human potential unfettered by political and social hindrances. Liberals in the twentieth century increasingly advocated a positive role for government in making the lives of the citizenry better and more secure.

It was the beginnings of the Industrial Revolution that began to undermine the mostly static social system in the sixteenth century as increasing wealth (much of it from gold and silver mines in North and South America) was transferred to

---

[20]For an excellent summary see D. J. Manning, *Liberalism* (New York: St. Martin's Press, 1976).

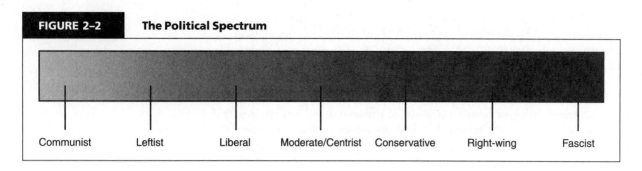

FIGURE 2–2   **The Political Spectrum**

Communist   Leftist   Liberal   Moderate/Centrist   Conservative   Right-wing   Fascist

elite
A privileged minority in society, usually composed of no more than 10 percent of the population, that controls the political decision-making process.

growing urban areas.[21] The Industrial Revolution created for the first time in history opportunities for individuals and governments to amass great wealth. How that wealth would be distributed or accumulated has been debated for the last few centuries. Conservatism has argued against the government determining what to do with wealth or managing its accumulation. Liberalism argued for governmental intervention for the assurance of a basic quality of life regardless of social status or personal gains. Table 2–3 compares contemporary conservativism and liberalism.

The debate between conservatism and liberalism is based on different emphases and on different interpretations of human nature. Conservatives, for example, consider individual liberty an important and natural social condition. Equality for them, on the other hand, is neither natural nor feasible—members of society, in their view, are naturally and inevitably unequal. Conservatives argue that this is nothing to be embarrassed about, but simply a fact. The only way to have equality is to enforce it.

Conservatives assume that in every generation individuals surface as a result of the special talents they possess and that these individuals are obligated to utilize their talents on behalf of the entire community. Talented individuals inevitably assume leadership roles, forming an **elite** within society. Most liberals do not deny that some people are more talented than others. They do believe, however, that talented people who are members of ethnic, racial, or religious minorities may be denied the opportunity to fully realize their talents. Liberals argue that government has the obligation to correct this injustice. The liberal idea is to level the playing field so that each person can maximize individual potential.

The divisions between conservatism and liberalism are serious and complicated in most democratic societies. Conservatives insist that government should leave people alone to pursue their lives as they see fit, but many conservatives also believe that a pregnant woman should not have the option of having an abortion. Liberals argue that government should obligate itself to help people, but they immediately run into the problem of what "help" means: the U.S. welfare system was created with the best of intentions, but even liberals now believe welfare may create more problems than it solves.

Both conservatives and liberals are content to operate within the political boundaries of democratic systems. While their philosophical disagreements are substantial, they also have a great deal in common. American conservatives and liberals both understood by the 1990s, for example, that the national welfare system was expensive, wasteful, and in need of reform. What they could not readily agree upon was how much reform it needed and where budget cuts could be made. Moreover, liberals are often concerned with preserving the dignity of welfare recipients (preferring to provide food stamps rather than set up soup kitchens), while conservatives are more interested in saving money[22] to ensure a responsible political economy and, they hope, a balanced budget. To be sure, both understand that

---

[21]London became the first city in the Western world in modern times to hit the million mark in population; it did so shortly before the year 1800.

[22]See Charles Murray, *In Pursuit of Happiness and Good Government* (New York: Simon & Schuster, 1988).

TABLE 2–3	A Comparison of Liberal and Conservative Beliefs

Topic	Liberal	Conservative
1. Government		
Primary focus	Individual	Community
Preferred government	National	State and local
Direction of sentiment	Internationalist	Nationalist
Method of government influence	Direct	Indirect
Accountability of government	To man	To God
Rate/type of change	Faster/utopian	Slower/prescriptive
Relative importance	Equality	Liberty
Justice achieved by	Governmental reform	Spiritual regeneration
2. Economy		
Source of authority	Central government	Markets
Growth sector	Public	Private
Government function	Regulation	Competition
Tendency	Socialism	Capitalism
3. Cultural and Religious Values		
Ultimate source of knowledge	Reason	Nature/Bible
Biblical interpretation	More symbolic	More literal
Moral standards	Relative/situational	Absolute/orthodox
Relative emphasis	Humanity	God
Moral emphasis	Social	Personal
Relative importance to humanity	Rights	Responsibilities
Origin of evil	Unjust social systems	Original sin

Source: Created from data taken from Charles Dunn and J. David Woodard, *The Conservative Tradition in America* (Lanhurn, Maryland: Rowman & Littlefield Publishers, 1996).

modern welfare systems, while far from perfect, must exist. Both also understand that welfare systems occasionally require a great deal of reform. Conservatives, for example, have suggested that those on welfare rolls be given a precise period of time to get off of them and find work while liberals maintain that young mothers with several children should not be forced to seek work if they are the only available parent.

These characterizations, of course, can be oversimplified. During the Clinton administration (1993–2001), for example, the welfare system underwent substantial changes. Several states increased the requirements necessary to successfully apply for assistance, often with encouragement from some traditional liberals, in an effort to reduce government expenditures and encourage prospective recipients to become part of an economy that was growing.

2-5 Authoritarianism and Totalitarianism

For most of political history, people have enjoyed little access to the formulation of decisions that influence (and in some cases, even threaten) their lives. They lived mainly under dictatorships that were largely aloof from the populations they governed. These dictatorships constituted a special segment of society that maintained a physical or even spiritual distance from the general populace. Dictators themselves were not necessarily evil or insensitive to the needs of the people; some dictators are actually remembered for positive achievements. Four millennia ago, for example, a Babylonian king, Hammurabi, boasted of the prosperity and orderliness his long reign (from 2123 to 2081 B.C.E.) had brought his people:

> I heaped up piles of grain, I provided unfailing water for the lands. . .. The scattered people I gathered; with pasturage and water I provided them; I pastured them with abundance, and settled them in peaceful dwellings.[23]

Hammurabi was a shameless braggart with some reason. His most remembered and enduring accomplishment was the Hammurabi's Code, an arrangement of 285 laws that governed such familiar issues as property rights and marital relationships.[24] Like numerous other leaders in dictatorial regimes, Hammurabi secured his legitimacy through what amounts to **divine right**: He perceived his role as one of selfless devotion to the public good because the gods wanted this for him and for the people.

Unfortunately, Hammurabi is an exception to the rule of mostly brutal tyrants. Most authoritarian dictatorships are completely unconcerned with laws except in using them for personal advantage. The average dictator does not worry much about caring for the people in his or her charge. Most are more concerned with how much money they can store away in Swiss bank accounts before they are abruptly removed from power, usually by someone just as brutal and greedy.

Ferdinand Marcos and his wife Imelda (mis)ruled the Philippines for twenty years, from 1966 to 1986, an ample amount of time to send hundreds of millions (according to some sources, even billions) of dollars to personal overseas investments and banks. The Duvalier family in Haiti did much the same thing around the same time (1959–1986) before being overthrown and forced to live in comfortable exile in Paris. Mrs. Marcos and the former Mrs. Duvalier reputedly spent millions of dollars in exile refurbishing their wardrobes.[25] Many dictators and their families regularly display such greed. Robert Mugabe, the long-serving president of Zimbabwe, is another case in point, apparently shipping a lot of his country's wealth overseas.

Some dictators—the Samozas in Nicaragua (1936–1979), Saddam Hussein in Iraq (1978–2003), the Saud dynasty in Saudi Arabia since at least the 1950s, and the Kims of North Korea (since 1945)—try to ensure their political longevity by placing close relations in key positions and designating their children as their political heirs. **Nepotism** is a basic pillar of authoritarian dictatorship. It is

> patronage within the family circle . . . a natural way for anybody in power, or aspiring to it, to strengthen his support in a society where other institutions are weak or nonexistent, or where the destruction of existing institutions forms part of the power-grabber's intentions.[26]

For obvious reasons, dictators frequently appoint brothers or sons as their (sometimes incompetent) top army commanders. They understandably lack confidence in those who aren't related by blood or marriage. A case study is illustrated in Table 2–4. Saddam Hussein was a firm believer in nepotism and appointed many of his relatives to positions of substantial power. A half-brother, two sons, and a few cousins became wanted fugitives after the regime's overthrow in March 2003. Several relatives were killed while others were jailed and faced trial for murderous activities.

Currently, the most successful and long-running family dictatorship is clearly the one established by North Korean ruler Kim Il Sung. His success is based on both longevity—Kim came to power in 1945 and reigned for nearly a half century until his death in 1994—and relentless ruthlessness. He eliminated all opposition

divine right
A monarch's assumption that he or she has spiritual justification for exercising complete power, with minimal or no constitutional restraints.

nepotism
The practice of appointing one's close relatives to high political office to ensure maximum support and loyalty.

---

[23]Hammurabi, quoted in Will Durant, *The Story of Civilization*, vol. 1: 221.

[24]This is one of the first documents in history that insists on the physical protection of women from abusive husbands. Ibid., 220.

[25]"Not-So-Pampered in Exile," *The Economist*, October 22, 1995, 56.

[26]"Nepotism," *The Economist*, December 24, 1994–January 6, 1995, 47.

TABLE 2–4	Saddam Hussein's Political Family Tree
Minister of Industry	Hussein Kamal al-Majid*, son-in-law
Chief of Party Intelligence (domestic spying)	Ibrahim Sibawi, half-brother
Chief of Military Intelligence	Wadbane Ibrahim, half-brother
Ministers without Portfolio	A cousin and two sons
Governor of Kuwait	Another cousin was selected, but this appointment was short-lived after the Allied coalition led by the United States ousted Iraqi forces from Kuwait in early 1991.

*Hussein Kamal al-Mjid was later murdered after Saddam became convinced of his treasonous tendencies.
Source: Created from data taken from "The House that Saddam Built," *The Economist*, September 29, 1990, p. 43.

quickly and thoroughly after taking power by arranging for the removal of political enemies to concentration camps. By the 1950s, Kim had placed thirty or so relatives in top positions. Their descendants remain in power today. Kim's older son, Kim Jong Il, succeeded his father as president, and Kim Jong Il's younger brother, Kim Yong Ju, became vice president.[27]

Nepotism is regularly practiced in all kinds of political systems. Military as well as communist dictators seem to consider political succession (if they consider it all) the prerogative of their progeny.

2-5a Theocracies

Religious toleration is a recent phenomenon. The assumption that loyal citizenship includes the correct religious affiliation has been in evidence for most of political history. In Western societies, at least, both Catholics and Protestants considered religious toleration a mortal sin for generations after the Reformation. After the Treaty of Westphalia ended the Thirty Years' War in 1648, the modern nation-state system in Europe began to take a form that looks familiar to the late twentieth-century student of political geography. Nationalism began to supplant religion as the primary test of citizen loyalty.

Religious conflict, however, has continued in Europe into modern times. Residues of religious conflict lingered into the closing years of the twentieth century. The "time of troubles" in Northern Ireland erupted between 1969 and the 1990s as Catholics and Protestants resumed murdering one another, a practice they had engaged in off and on for over 300 years. An uneven peace process has been pursued since then and the level of violence after 1997 declined because the British government and elements of the Irish Republican Army (IRA) agreed to discuss terms. In southeastern Europe, Bosnian Catholics, Orthodox Christian, and Muslims still insist on relating political loyalty to religious affiliation.

Religious issues often adopt political features. Debates over abortion, the death penalty, and public school prayers in the United States, divorce in Italy, and contraception in the Republic of Ireland show how strong religious convictions can influence the political and judicial processes and even the outcomes of democratic elections. For the most part, though, political democracies have successfully institutionalized religious toleration. Strong fundamentalist movements, such as the Christian Coalition in the United States, must be prepared to compete with other interest groups to influence public policy.

But religious toleration is still far from assured in a good part of the world. Iran, for example, in the aftermath of the 1979 revolution created a modern

[27]"Nepotism," Ibid., 46.

theocracy
A political system where religious considerations dominate the legal and judicial process.

Sharia
Islamic law that provides a code of rules for correct moral behavior.

theocracy in which both secular law and personal behavior are expected to conform to the Sharia, the Islamic religious law. Its advocates consider the **Sharia** to possess both spiritual and practical qualities. It gives the Islamic faith tangible qualities for the believer and provides guidelines for proper daily behavior. In Islamic societies such as Iran, for example, women are expected to thoroughly veil themselves, allowing only their faces and hands to show in public. The government is expected to support such guidelines and impose penalties on those who flout them.[28]

In this sense, government becomes the primary agent for exemplifying and enforcing a purist form of behavior. The concept of separation of church and state is both alien and immoral. One fundamentalist Muslim put it this way:

> We believe the rules and teachings of Islam to be comprehensive, to include the people's affairs in the world and the hereafter. ... Islam is an ideology and a faith, a home and a nationality, a religion and a state, a spirit and work, a book and a sword.[29]

Muslims are certainly not the only ones to mandate a total lifestyle based on religious precepts with the enforcement of the state available when necessary. A popular movement in India, the Bharatiya Janata Party, combines nationalism with Hinduism. In Israel, Jewish strict Orthodox fundamentalists frequently pressure the largely secularized government to enforce dietary laws and support the establishment of Jewish settlements in the West Bank—a place they refer to by its biblical names, Judea and Samaria.[30]

It is important to realize that no two theological regimes are exactly identical. For example, fundamentalist Islamic regimes govern both Iran and Saudi Arabia. Both countries are indeed administered by regimes that follow Islamic principles. Yet Iran holds regular elections and women exercise the franchise, while neither is true in Saudi Arabia.

Theological regimes do enjoy an overall degree of popular support, and they serve several needs, because they offer security to those who feel overwhelmed by the uncertainties that accompany technological change, the breakdown of the family as a social unit, and urbanization; and they provide the following advantages. They:

1. offer a refuge to those who fear and resent westernization and secularism—the twin representatives of corruption, criminal violence, and lax morality;
2. provide a reassuring and all-encompassing code of personal behavior to those who fear the threat that modernity brings to a traditional way of life;
3. allow countless millions of people whose prospects for a good job, nice home, and overall pleasant lifestyle are remote at best, to have hopes for their children's future in terms of firm morality and minimal violent crime.

Theocracies are not usually short-lived. The Taliban in Afghanistan lasted only five years (1996–2001). Though it took American military might to destroy the regime, the Taliban government did not enjoy widespread popular support. Only a small proportion of the population attempted to defend the Taliban. In Iran the Shiite clergy have been in power since 1979, but an entire generation has grown up increasingly disaffected with the stagnant economy and heavy censorship that the regime has created. One observer has likened the Iranian situation to the one that prevailed in the Soviet Union a short time before communism's collapse.[31] However, this may be wishful thinking because the regime shows no sign of decline.

---

[28]Nora Boustany, "In Iran, the Chador Cloaks a Growing Mood of Unrest," *The Washington Post National Weekly Edition*, November 2–8, 1992, 18.

[29]Abd al-Moneir Said and Manfred W. Wenner, "Modern Islamic Reform Movements: The Muslim Brotherhood in Contemporary Egypt," *Middle East Journal*, vol. 36, no. 3 (Summer 1982): 340.

[30]A valuable analysis of this issue is found in Ian S. Lustick, *For the Land and the Lord: Jewish Fundamentalism in Israel* (New York: Council on Foreign Relations Press, 1988).

[31]R. James Woolsey, "The Coming Revolution in Iran," *The Wall Street Journal*, July 29, 2002, AA 15.

There is no end to attempts to establish theocracies. Al-Qaeda, for example, is attempting to undermine Muslim regimes it considers less than orthodox. Even Saudi Arabia is too liberal for al-Qaeda because of its tolerance of non-Muslims (such as American soldiers) in the birthplace of Islam. High-ranking leaders in Al-Qaeda have adopted the belief that "Islamic society had to be purified, and the only mechanism powerful enough to cleanse it was the ancient and bloody instrument of Jihad."[32]

2-5b Communism

At the end of 1917, communists came to power in Russia. The regime they established endured until the end of 1991. Karl Marx and Friedrich Engels capsulated the theory of communism when they published *The Communist Manifesto* in 1848. For its time, the *Manifesto* was a radical document, calling for such innovations as free public education and ten-hour (rather than longer) work days.

In later writings, Marx and Engels spelled out in detail both the desirability and inevitability of establishing communism. Their motivations were sincere: Both had witnessed the more deplorable elements of the Industrial Revolution in Germany and later in England, where Marx eventually settled. Workers, including women and young children, were inhumanely exploited by a capitalist class that owned the means of economic production, controlled the judicial and political systems, and was motivated only by the lure of ever-increasing profits. The capitalist class was uninterested in the welfare of the workers, or **proletariat**, who, Marx and Engels held, made the profits possible.

Marx viewed the conflict between the proletariat and the capitalist class as a natural consequence of history. He developed a notion referred to as **dialectical materialism**. All history, according to the dialectic, is characterized by a conflict between social and economic classes. Through the ages, the conflict proceeds to more and more advanced economic and technological levels. Table 2–5 illustrates a simplified version of this process.

Marx and Engels were unsure whether a violent revolution would be necessary to establish what they called the **dictatorship of the proletariat**. In this system, social class distinctions would be abolished and all producers would enjoy the fruits of their labor.

Vladimir Ilyich Lenin had no such doubts. Lenin (1870–1924) firmly believed that no entrenched elite ever gives up power peacefully or voluntarily. He led the communist takeover in Russia in 1917 and quickly eliminated all political opposition. His successor, Joseph Stalin (see Stalin's political biography), went further, inaugurating the "great terror" that forced people to relinquish property to the state and eliminated real or imagined opposition through a series of political purges. In a sense, communist ideology was to blame for the excesses of its advocates. The ideology insisted that only the Communist party represented the true interests of workers, and only the workers' class really mattered because they were

proletariat
The class of workers who produce goods and, therefore, profits.

dialectical materialism
The Marxist notion of history as a series of class struggles culminating in a classless society of workers.

dictatorship of the proletariat
In Marxist theory, a condition occurring at the end of history, in which the actual producers in society seize control of the apparatus of the state, abolishing class distinctions and allowing producers to enjoy the fruit of their labors.

TABLE 2–5	Marx's Dialectical Materialism	
Historical Period	**Exploitive Class**	**Exploited Class**
Ancient	Masters	Slaves
Medieval	Landed aristocracy	Serfs
Industrial	Capitalists	Proletariat

[32]Lawrence Wright, "The Man Behind Bin Laden," *The New Yorker*, September 16, 2002.

POLITICAL BIOGRAPHY

Joseph Stalin

Library of Congress, Prints and Photographs Division, LC-USZ62-127379

Joseph Stalin was a man with many natural talents and obvious leadership abilities; during his political career, he was known as the "man of steel". When he was a young man, Stalin's mother tried to influence her son to enter the priesthood. At first he acquiesced. But after studying in a seminary for a period, Stalin left to join the Communist party. Eventually, after taking control of the Soviet Union in the 1920s, he strayed far enough from his religious origins to murder an untold number of Soviet citizens.

Robert Conquest's *The Great Terror* explains why Stalin was ultimately responsible for the deaths of tens of millions of Soviet citizens through execution, starvation, and exposure in Siberian labor camps. Stalin's personality was characterized by a strong streak of paranoia; he was often suspicious of even his closest colleagues and supporters. Most of them ended up in front of firing squads, even though they scrupulously followed Stalin's orders to try to avoid just such an end. Many more people died as a result of Stalin's harsh, oppressive policies.

Not all Russians have bad memories of Stalin, however. Some consider him the architect of the Soviet victory over Germany in World War II. Stalin also led the Soviet Union to become an industrialized country and laid the groundwork for it to become a nuclear power, eventually forging a nation so strong in international politics that the United States felt compelled to treat the Soviets as equals. Many intense Russian nationalists also remember that under Stalin, Russian influence extended into the eastern half of Europe.

Stalin created the first and most durable totalitarian state in modern history. His power was absolute. The territories his armies occupied allowed Russia to realize the age-old Tsarist dream—commanding an empire that included warm water ports, that had expanded into much of Europe and Asia, and that had established itself as a major world power. Yet he also created a collectivized and stagnant economy, and the millions of non-Russians trapped in a modern version of the Russian Empire in the end were too much for the Soviet Union to control. Later Soviet dictators lacked Stalin's ruthlessness and were unable to prevent the implosion that came in 1991, less than four decades after Stalin's death.

the people in society who actually were productive. Managers and owners were parasites who enriched themselves on the backs of laborers and therefore could have no place in a communist society.

The Soviet form of communism was the cornerstone of the most durable totalitarian system in the twentieth century. It ultimately failed because the inherent contradictions in an overcentralized control of a national economy solidly closed all possibility of criticism, innovation, imagination, and experiment. In the end, the Soviet leadership was less interested in the ideals of communism than in retaining power; they were more willing to tolerate economic stagnation than to risk the political uncertainties of reform.

2-5c Fascism

Communists usually believe that their ideology represents the highest form of democracy, establishing complete social and economic equality. In this sense, they could claim to be within the Western political tradition. Fascism, on the other hand, was a candid repudiation of democracy. Fascist movements came to power in Europe during the two decades between the end of World War I in 1918 and the beginning of World War II in 1939, occurring in Italy (1922), Germany (1933), and Spain (1939). The first two of these regimes were destroyed by the end of World War II in 1945. The military-dominated government of Japan in the 1930s and early 1940s has also been referred to as fascist but also did not survive World War II. The Spanish form of fascism dissipated after the passing of its founder, Francisco Franco, in 1976. Since the end of the Franco period, Spain has gradually transformed itself into a democracy.

While Soviet communism basically imploded almost peacefully, fascism was destroyed in a titanic global military effort. Italy, Germany, and Japan were all devastated by the end of World War II, and the Allied occupation forces completely eliminated their fascist regimes. As they were on the rise in the 1920s and 1930s, however, all three countries' governments urged their populations to think of their nations as something special: Benito Mussolini encouraged Italians to restore the Roman Empire throughout the Mediterranean region; Adolf Hitler entreated Germans to assume their natural role as masters of Europe because of their racial superiority; and the Japanese believed their destiny was to build an empire in East and Southeast Asia that would supply the natural resources and cheap labor required to ensure Japan's continued greatness.

European fascism never really developed a systematic ideology. It was a hodge-podge of anti-Semitism, racism, and extreme **ethnocentrism**. Racial destiny was an ideological fixture for fascist regimes. This was bad news for ethnic or religious minorities, whom the majority regarded as an unacceptable alien presence in a society insistent on purifying itself. Even if they weren't living in the midst of the purification effort, they could still be in trouble: one of the main goals of German Nazism, for instance, was to secure more living space by expanding into the territories of other countries whose populations they considered suitable for slavery or extermination.

During the National Socialist (Nazi) era of 1933–1945, Germany instituted the most heinous form of fascism. The Nazis persecuted or systematically murdered at least 12 million people in concentration camps. The Nazi party represented some of the worst elements in German society (one of Hitler's closest aides, Martin Bormann, was a convicted murderer), and it boldly planned extermination programs for European Jews, gypsies, and other "undesirable" minorities under German military control during the occupation of much of Western Europe from 1939 to 1945.

The excesses of fascism completely discredited the movement in world opinion as well as in the countries where fascism surfaced. Within a few years after the destruction of their fascist regimes, Germany, Italy, and Japan became firmly democratic. Unfortunately, many current regimes behave badly enough to exhibit characteristics of fascism. Some, like Syria's, have even committed genocidal acts against ethnic or religious minorities. However, unlike the 1930s and 1940s, no government in any *major* developed nation has adopted foreign or domestic policies that would be considered fascist.

ethnocentrism
A population's almost paranoid aversion to "foreign" minorities and their commitment to a special destiny that justifies maltreatment of other nations.

2-6 Now What?

Democracy has become the most creditable sort of political process. Democracies have defeated fascism and outlasted communism. Of course, plenty of individual fascists and communists remain, but they don't currently pose a serious threat to democracy. Democracy, however, was not the preferred alternative for most political philosophers. Plato and Aristotle distrusted it. Later thinkers, such as John Locke, believed in responsible and legal rulership, but they did not assume that democracy necessarily or exclusively produced it.

Every major political thinker has agreed that people are better off living within a political state, but the state is an unfinished experiment in human social development. Some people need the state more than others; some people want the state to do more, others want it to do less. The debate will continue. Advances in communications and transportation technologies imply new roles for the state, some with no precedent. For thousands of years, the state had no rival when it came to controlling its citizenry. National boundaries now mean less as information is exchanged over thousands of miles instantaneously and almost effortlessly, using the Internet.

Perhaps one reason democracy has survived and has gained so many defenders is that, unlike other governmental forms, it does not seek to avoid or suppress change. Most political philosophers (Plato being a notable exception) recognized the inevitability of change, but few before the late twentieth century understood or foresaw how rapidly change might come. The process of change is challenging more traditional societies, in some cases more severely than democratic ones. In the next chapter, the influence of culture in general and political culture in particular on how well a government responds to social and economic changes will be examined.

Chapter Summary

1. Plato's *The Republic* highlighted the concept that government could be a force for good if wise and unselfish rulers governed. In Plato's view, every citizen would assume only those tasks he or she is suited for by natural talent and intelligence. This would enhance justice and make laws unnecessary.
2. Aristotle understood the political community to be the pinnacle of human social development. For the sake of political and social stability, he argued for moderation in all things, including the establishment of a broad middle class and the avoidance of excessive wealth and poverty.
3. Stoicism offered a philosophy that tried to make sense of a world many believed to be chaotic. Stoics implored people to accept their roles in life and do their best to excel in those roles. This advice was particularly incumbent upon rulers; Stoics called on them to govern on behalf of the entire society and not in their own self-interest.
4. Thomas Hobbes argued that humans began their existence in the stateless state of nature, found its violence unacceptable, and agreed in a social contract to submit to a sovereign power. The primary responsibility of this sovereign is to provide the physical security individuals lack in the state of nature. In exchange for this security, people surrender a substantial proportion of their individual freedom.
5. John Locke adopted a milder view of the state of nature. He agreed it is in the common interest to establish a sovereign power, but he believed the sovereign must also be a party to the social contract and must obey the same generally approved laws as any citizen in the commonwealth.
6. Conservatives and liberals both believe in the intrinsic worth of every individual human being. Conservatives, however, strongly support the traditions and moral foundations of civil society, while liberals argue on behalf of nontraditional social equality and moral relativism.
7. Most governments throughout political history have been authoritarian dictatorships, and most have demonstrated few qualms about employing brutality to remain in power and control the population. Another less violent feature of authoritarianism that helps the dictator to secure power is the practice of nepotism.
8. Theocratic regimes by definition are uninterested in tolerating political dissension. Because theocratic regimes combine church and state, political opponents are also sinners. Legal systems are based on moral codes.
9. Communism is a failed system of government that endured for more than seven decades in the Soviet Union. During that period, the centralized economy created havoc, and the bureaucratization of nearly all social and political behaviors practically destroyed individual innovation and cost millions of lives.
10. Fascism is characterized by strong ingredients of ethnocentrism and racism. The fascist regimes that most seriously threatened Western democracy were destroyed in World War II.

Chapter 2 Quiz

1. Plato viewed change as
   a. always good.
   b. inherently dangerous.
   c. inevitable but manageable.
   d. always orderly.

2. In *The Republic*, Plato portrays the guardian class as
    a. a wealthy elite.
    b. encouraged to intermarry with nonguardians.
    c. without families or property.
    d. the best of the artisans.

3. Aristotle considered the polis to be
    a. always corrupt.
    b. suitable for only the upper classes.
    c. more successful with a heterogeneous population.
    d. the only place for a "good life."

4. The philosophy of Stoicism favored
    a. an illiterate society.
    b. Christianity.
    c. leading a virtuous life.
    d. refusing one's destiny if unhappy with it.

5. Machiavelli believed
    a. in separating political from private morality for political rulers.
    b. that rulers must obey the Ten Commandments.
    c. that democracy is the best kind of political system.
    d. that rulers should be scrupulously ethical in their dealings with the ruled.

6. Thomas Hobbes in the *Leviathan*
    a. applauded the concept of individual liberty.
    b. believed that people are essentially good-natured.
    c. stated that revolutions are sometimes justified.
    d. advocated unquestioned sovereign power.

7. The political philosopher who exerted the greatest influence on the American Revolution was
    a. Thomas Hobbes.
    b. John Locke.
    c. Marcus Aurelius.
    d. Nicolo Machiavelli.

8. Conservatives hold that a proper belief system should include all of the following except
    a. original sin.
    b. reason.
    c. liberty.
    d. capitalism.

9. Nepotism is
    a. often a feature of democracy.
    b. often a feature of dictatorship.
    c. only found in North Korea.
    d. today predominant only in Saudi Arabia.

10. Women are unable to vote in
    a. Iran.
    b. Israel.
    c. Saudi Arabia.
    d. India.

11. All of the following terms are associated with the ideology of communism except
    a. Marx and Engels.
    b. racism.
    c. proletariat.
    d. dialectical materialism.

Political Culture

A country's political culture is rooted in the ways society's members think about and react to government and politics. This thinking, in turn, is based in great part on the country's political and social history. This chapter will review how political culture influences the kind of government a society's members either choose for themselves or have imposed on them. It will also examine how a country's political culture and institutions relate to one another, and what can occur in the absence of consensual political norms and values.

3-1 Political Culture and Political Practices

A great deal of a country's political culture is actually articulated in its constitution, especially in democracies. Although they closely resemble one another in political form, today's democracies have evolved under distinct circumstances. The French, for example, settled on a chief executive with more substantial powers than his or her American counterpart. The French president can assume "emergency powers"[1] that would amount to impeachable offenses if an American president attempted to exercise them. But the French political culture, as reflected in its constitution, sanctions such expansive powers. The French have determined after numerous experiments with other governmental forms that an especially strong but popularly chosen executive is desirable.

In the United Kingdom, the House of Commons (the lower house of Parliament) can call or postpone elections as long as they occur within a five-year statutory limit. In certain situations, that limit may be set aside. Because of the emergency conditions of World War II, for example, the British held no national elections between 1935 and 1945. The United States, in contrast, was constitutionally obligated to hold elections on schedule in 1942 and 1944, even though it was involved in a global conflict. Neither government officials nor rank-and-file citizens seriously contemplated their delay. Elections were also held on schedule in 1862 and 1864 during the Civil War, at least in the states that remained in the Union and in areas that the Union had recovered from the Confederacy. The British could suspend the rules of the political game with public support when an extraordinary situation justified doing so; the U.S. Constitution prohibits such an act.

Political culture is often derived from the overall culture the great majority of a society's members affiliate with. In an overall culture, widely shared and accepted values provide a cohesiveness that helps keep the society intact. Ideally, a political culture does the same thing in the political sphere: contending interests understand and accept the basic political structure and obey the generally agreed-upon rules of the political game. In the United States and other democracies, for example, society regards the principles of free speech, unhindered competition in the marketplace of ideas, and peaceful acceptance of electoral outcomes as necessary for political well-being. Conservatives, liberals, Democrats, Republicans, and Independents agree on these principles, though they differ considerably on the degree

---

[1]Article 16 of the French Constitution.

to which they should be applied. Democratic societies believe that the political process should function in as free and unfettered a manner as practical.

Nondemocratic societies are usually characterized by a conspicuous lack of these same principles. Developing a consensual political culture in such a society usually takes a long time and normally requires generations, if not centuries, to mature. Some countries may never develop one. In fact, their citizenries may not even share a desire to establish one. Worse yet, in attempting to establish a political culture, a society may degenerate into civil war. It is one thing for a society to divide over issues: Americans, for example, are deeply divided over issues such as abortion and the death penalty. But serious division over issues does not in itself threaten the stability of a political system. Democratic societies tend to accept their institutions of government as legitimate and use the legal and political processes available to work out their differences.

In democracies, **legitimacy**, or the perceived right to govern, is conferred by a widely accepted and usually renewable mandate for elected leaders. Authoritarian regimes are frequently devoid of discernible ideology, but some are eager to legitimize their existence with intense nationalism, myths, or a combination of the two. Shah Reza Pahlavi of Iran (1954–1979), who claimed to speak regularly with and be inspired by divine authority, is an instructive example. Desirous of making his country a regional power in the Middle East, the Shah in 1971 proclaimed the twenty-five-hundredth anniversary of the founding of the Persian Empire by Cyrus the Great. This was a futile attempt to link Iran with its glorious ancient past and the Shah with one of the more accomplished empire builders in history. After the collapse of the monarchy in 1979, the Iranian political culture became intimately linked with the theocratic tendencies of a fundamentalist regime. This regime disavowed a good deal of its non-Islamic past and sought political legitimacy in religious orthodoxy.

In Japan an authoritarian fixture, the emperorship, has been preserved even though the country has been a practicing democracy since 1947. The emperor quietly but effectively confers legitimacy on Japan's political process. He is acknowledged as the head of state and is still considered to be divine by much of the country's population. Authoritarian institutions, in other words, can be made compatible with democratic systems as long as they are not powerful. The imperial family provides a link to a 2,500-year-old tradition in Japan and is in many ways inseparable from it.

The development of a political culture is usually a lengthy process for most societies. Many countries never really achieve a coherent political culture because the divisions within the society are so strong and persistent that they preclude its development. It is much easier on a nation's political nervous system to endure ideological divisions and debates over critical issues than to survive a fractious political culture.

legitimacy
The determination through one or more means—by divine right, or through electoral or ideological processes—that a regime has the right to govern for a precise or indefinite period of time.

3-2 Induction into the Political Culture

Every political society inducts each new generation into its political culture. This process is necessary to sustain the political institutions that effectively govern the citizens. Each individual in the political society is required to understand and practice acceptable political habits.

3-2a Political Socialization

Most people take a serious interest in and derive great pleasure from knowing who they are. It makes them feel more comfortable. Similarly, the political culture requires a permanent process of induction; each new generation must learn the particular values and norms of the society it belongs to and, it is hoped, develop a lasting affection for them. This process begins in early childhood. Simply put, political socialization is the process by which each generation transmits its political culture to the next generation. Doing so normally involves familiar agencies such as educational systems, religious organizations, the electronic and print media, and even family members. All of these communicate to children, starting at early ages, the political values and norms held firmly by their elders.

The importance of the process of political socialization should not be underestimated. It is essential to the survival of the political system itself and it would be difficult to even imagine a political process that was not characterized by the primary features of the political culture. The ultimate goal of political socialization is to secure voluntary and widespread support for the norms and values of the political culture. Dictatorships as well as democracies prefer that their policies enjoy popular endorsement, and both prefer it for the same reason: It makes governing much easier. Political socialization, then, enhances and helps to guarantee the legitimacy of political institutions.

Every political system, regardless of its nature and ideology, naturally wants to survive. For this reason, each regime makes an effort to emphasize the socialization process with children. Democracies such as the United States teach values such as individual freedoms and toleration of diversity as early as the primary grades. Schools also extol the more redeeming characteristics of previous political leaders. Presidents George Washington and Abraham Lincoln, for example, are frequently mentioned to young American schoolchildren as models of both personal and political honesty and integrity.

Dictatorships have a serious problem when it comes to political socialization. A typical authoritarian dictatorship revolves around the personality of the dictator. Rank-and-file citizens must be convinced that he is invincible and infallible and that they are really fortunate to have him around. Saddam Hussein, for example, had at different times proclaimed himself a pan-Arab leader, an Islamic fundamentalist, and an intense Iraqi nationalist in efforts to sustain his regime with whatever idea was popular at the moment. His was a typical political socialization process in a dictatorship, where huge pictures of the smiling supreme leader appeared everywhere, especially in every school classroom.

Iraqi schools, like the mosques and the family, were critical agents of political socialization. Whether secular or religious, the school may actually have been the most critical agent of all, because images of the symbol of state authority, Saddam Hussein, were featured in nearly every classroom as well as in other public places. His picture was known to be affixed to the sides of Iraqi refrigerators and sometimes inside of them. Even though foodstuffs were in relative short supply, a hungry Iraqi would be consoled by Saddam's appearance when rummaging for a snack.

In summary, any regime immediately understands that its continuance depends on acquiring the loyalty and confidence of the youngest members of the political society. In a country such as North Korea, of course, the citizen has very few political norms and values to learn: He or she simply adheres to and believes in whatever the leader is quoted as saying at the moment.

This doesn't always work, though. In pluralist and democratic societies *who* a citizen is matters, while in nondemocratic societies *what* a citizen is may matter more than anything else. For example, the political loyalty of a citizen of Bosnia depends on whether one is classified as a Serb, Croat, or Muslim. Based upon a single criterion, ethnicity, one may be judged either a model citizen or someone who richly deserves a bullet in the head.[2]

Political socialization was (or at least seemed) simpler during the Cold War era (1945–1990). During, this time, the political socialization process was clear. One was indoctrinated into the political culture of France, Germany, or the United States. A person would learn that he or she belonged to the French or German or American nation and was a citizen in the French or German or American state. This view, however, may very well be a Western conceit. The same person may also be

---

exposed to the viewpoint that her or his nation is somehow better than others. This is not necessarily a dangerous practice as long as it is not reinforced by military aggression against neighboring states that are considered to be somehow less important.

The nation-state system more or less originated in the West, and it has not caught on substantially in other regions. A political socialization process also exists in some non-Western regions, but not in the sense that most Westerners understand it. Tribal and regional allegiances in Nigeria and Sudan, for example, tend to thwart national unification and the establishment of a pervasive political culture. In the Arab world, for example, there is a widespread notion "that national sovereignty alone was an empty sham" and that it was necessary to turn to fundamentalist Islam and restore "holy law."[3]

Thus, analyzing and understanding political socialization may require more relevant and accurate interpretations. Few states are nation-states in our understanding of the term. Throughout most of modern history and into current times the concept of "nation-state" has been a vague one for many if not most national communities.[4] Citizens in the West find this difficult to understand, but most people in developing regions or Third World countries are socialized to retain only tribal and clannish loyalties and lack a full comprehension of, let alone a loyalty to, the nation-state.

These local loyalties are so durable that they can decisively contribute to the collapse of a superpower. One of the critical reasons usually offered to explain the implosion of the Soviet Union in 1991 relates to the conflicts among the approximately 100 nationalities within the Soviet federation. These nationalities include the Chechens, with whom the central government in Moscow has been militarily engaged with off and on since the nineteenth century. Others include nationalities citizens in the West rarely hear or know about—Moldavians, Ossetians, Ingushetians, and Dagestanis are only a few. Often the conflicts were simultaneously between nationalities and between various nationalities and the central government. Most of them genuinely and correctly felt coerced into the Soviet system and were alienated by a regime they were convinced exploited and brutalized them.

The Soviet regime tried unsuccessfully for decades to create a political culture that emphasized a new economic and political species, the unselfish and hard-working "Soviet man" and "Soviet woman" dedicated to the socialist principles of equality and devoted to "building communism." It is suspected that, in the end, not even the Soviet leadership believed communism was a worthwhile prospect. Most Soviet citizens gradually recognized that the regime was simply a successor state to the Russian Empire that the communists had destroyed in 1917. For the non-Russian half of the population, the Soviet-inspired political culture was, at best, an unrealizable myth and, at worst, a clever device to enable a Russian political elite to continue to oppress non-Russians.

3-2b Liberty Versus Equality: Contradictions in Political Culture

No two political cultures are exactly alike. Even democratic systems, which have a great deal in common, exhibit important differences. The differences are not stark enough to cause conflict between democracies. As a rule, democracies don't fight wars against one another, but they are distinguishable from one another in important ways.

Nor are political cultures static. The countries of Western Europe and North America are stable industrialized democracies, at least for the most part. But like all

---

[3]Bernard Lewis, *Islam and the West* (New York and Oxford: Oxford University Press, 1993), 139. The serious threat to the state system posed by such radical organizations as well as al-Qaeda is more recently explored by George P. Shultz, "An Essential War," *The Wall Street Journal*, March 29, 2004, A18.
[4]Walker Connor, "A Nation Is a Nation, Is a State, Is an Ethnic Group, Is a . . ." *Ethnic and Racial Studies*, I (October, 1978), 86.

other societies, they are undergoing social changes that are the result of or that impact upon political culture. After 1945, the Germans had to reconstruct their political culture to rid it of Nazi influences and create a durable and plausible democratic system. The West Germans in 1949 promulgated their Basic Law (which served as their constitution until East and West Germany reunited in 1989). One of the Basic Law's provisions allowed the federal courts to ban political parties judged to advocate un- or antidemocratic programs and ideologies. The U.S. Constitution contains no such provision; in fact, in view of the Bill of Rights, it cannot do so. More importantly, it doesn't have to. The United States did not lose a world war and did not install and live under a Nazi regime. Therefore, the United States did not find it necessary to rebuild a political culture by stipulating the exclusion of antidemocratic elements.

Immigrants are also responsible for changing political cultures and are most keenly felt in political democracies. Pressures generated by immigration face several democratic societies: The United States now has the fifth-largest and one of the fastest growing Spanish-speaking populations in the world. In fact, by 2006, immigration, both legal and illegal and mostly from Latin America, had become a national political issue and was a substantial feature in that year's congressional campaigns. Moreover, immigrants are desperately needed in some Western countries to replace an aging workforce. In developed countries such as the United States, Canada, Australia, and Austria, foreign-born immigrants form over a tenth of the labor force.[5] Most of the reactions to the newest immigrants have been positive (or at least noncommittal), but some of the reactions (such as neo-Nazi skinheads in Germany beating up immigrant workers) have been unpleasant, even violent, and probably will continue to be until the political culture can adjust by accepting limited numbers of immigrants who desire to become productive and law-abiding citizens.

Democracy is governance by the governed. A democratic political culture involves competition between competing expressions of ideological values. Much of the time citizens are ideological without really noticing. Americans are prone, for example, to label one another as conservative or liberal, pro-life or pro-choice, or affiliates of the "religious right" or the "incompetent left."[6]

As indicated in the previous chapter, the terms *left* and *right* are frequently used to describe the ideological positions of political parties, interest groups, and individuals. Over the years, these terms have undergone substantial modifications and quite a bit of abuse. They have each had some interesting adjectives tacked onto them in recent times: the "loony" left, the "radical" right; and both left and right have been described as "extreme," "totalitarian," or "moderate." In the United States, Americans use these terms rather freely. When they are being politically polite, they tend to label others as liberals or conservatives. Both liberals and conservatives, however, sometimes refer to each other with a sneer of contempt.

3-3 Is Ideology on the Decline?

Ideology probably is on the decline. Certain ideologies appear definitely discredited. By the early 1990s, communism had been swept away in Eastern Europe and the Soviet Union because of the widespread recognition of its economic and political failures. Fascism quickly went out of style after its defeat in World War II. But ideology does not necessarily disappear once it has been discredited. In the case of communism, for example, it simply morphed. To gain respectability and to survive in free elections, Communist parties in both Western and Eastern Europe have in many cases changed their names to drop the term "communist" and reappeared as parties on the democratic left. Some, ironically, have experienced substantial

---

[5]"The Longest Journey," *The Economist*, November 2, 2002, 4.

[6]Senator Arlen Specter used this last set of terms in announcing his candidacy for the Republican nomination for president in 1996. C-SPAN, March 31, 1995.

electoral success. Even revived (but unreformed) fascism has done modestly well in Italian elections.

Nothing changed in places where communism was already a bankrupt ideology. There had never been more than a token amount of support for Communist parties in English-speaking countries and in the former West Germany. The political cultures of these countries had long excluded the communist ideology as politically illegitimate or simply as an unreasonable totalitarian relic in a democratic society. Communism was regarded as a political pariah and an unbeatable formula for permanent economic misery.

Nearly all ideologies by definition try to freeze society into a preferred scenario. Once having established a totalitarian system, Soviet communist leaders had little incentive to tolerate change and attempted to deny its existence. In short, communist leaders confused stagnation with perfection. The communist ideology also legitimized their monopoly on power. In fact, the ideology was the only legitimizer.

With the collapse of communism in most countries with communist-controlled governments,[7] a widespread assumption developed that most of the world was becoming "de-ideologized." Several signs encouraged this point of view. Even in the Middle East, where ideological clashes among Zionists, religious radicals, Arab socialists, and intense nationalists were frequent, optimists appeared for the first time in generations to applaud the progress of a peace process that sprang from a 1993 agreement between Israel and the Palestine Liberation Organization. Pragmatism seemed in this case to replace ideological fanaticism. But it only lasted for a brief time. One of the architects of the peace process, Itzhak Rabin, the Israeli prime minister between 1993 and 1995, was murdered. Extremists on both sides since then have worked hard to destroy hopes for a durable settlement. The complete collapse came in September 2000, when a Palestinian uprising (Intifada) led to a hardening of positions by both the Israeli and Palestinian leaderships.[8]

However, political ideology is going to continue to evolve. An ideology can facilitate the legitimization of both a political regime and political culture. This is especially the case in nondemocratic societies. After all, in the absence of free elections, authoritarian governments must still try to legitimize their presence and provide a rationale for their actions. It is easier to become more aware of the threat an ideology may pose when substantial arsenals reinforce it.

A telling example was the Soviet Union itself. After the communists came to power in Russia in 1917, they immediately singled out the Western, developed, capitalist countries as the "evil" enemy.[9] The United States reciprocated, and by the late 1970s was referring to the Soviet Union as the "evil empire," a label that became especially popular during the early years of the Reagan administration (1981–1989). Each side perceived the other as a mortal threat. By the 1950s, both nations possessed nuclear weapons capable of destroying hundreds of targets. The mutual recognition that each could completely destroy the other (and all life on this planet) certainly helped to contain full ideological expressions.

According to the distinguished historian Arthur Schlesinger, Jr., the reason the Cold War between the United States and the Soviet Union did not become "hot" was the fact that both were very sensibly frightened of using nuclear weapons. Ideology apparently does have its limits: Better to live with "evil" than be utterly destroyed along with it. If nuclear weapons had never been invented, the two sides might well have been tempted to opt for conventional warfare to settle their ideological disputes. Schlesinger supports the suggestion "that the Nobel Peace Prize should have gone to the atomic bomb."[10] However, some Islamic radicals who

---

[7]Communism continues to destroy the economies of North Korea, Cuba, Vietnam, and Cambodia, although even in these hardcore communist states the free market is slowly gaining a foothold.

[8]For a gloomy but not unrealistic view of the difficulties between Israel and Palestine, please see Neal Kozodoy, *The Mideast Peace Process: An Autopsy* (Encounter, 2002).

[9]For an excellent treatment of this perspective, see John Mueller, "Quiet Cataclysm: Some Afterthoughts on World War III," in Michael J. Hogan, ed., *The End of the Cold War: Its Meaning and Implications*, ed. Michael J. Hogan, (New York: Cambridge University Press, 1992), 39–52.

[10]Schlesinger, "Lessons from the Cold War," in Hogan, ed., *The End of the Cold War* (see note 9), 54.

regard the United States and Israel and the West in general as irredeemably evil have resorted to advocating suicide attacks on civilians and military personnel in the belief that dying in a holy cause is worth the sacrifice.

But nuclear destruction is not necessarily an ultimate limitation to the pursuit of ideological goals. Several "rogue" (a term used to describe regimes that tend to avoid abiding by international treaties and/or are in full disregard of the human rights of their own citizens) countries, such as Iran, North Korea, and Libya, are attempting to either purchase or build nuclear weapons. The nuclear quests of at least two, Iran and North Korea, are partially motivated by strong ideological agendas. Of course, deciding to acquire nuclear weapons and deciding to use them are very different processes. It remains to be seen whether ideological inspirations will have their limitations in these countries as well. The quest for nuclear weapons could encourage armed conflict. In 2002, before initiating military action against Iraq, the American government reiterated its desire for a "regime change" before Saddam Hussein acquired a nuclear arsenal, a position that was ultimately supported by a United Nations resolution.[11]

Ideology, of course, isn't everything. The Chinese Communist Party has been in power since 1949. During its first three decades of governance it was effective in collectivizing and in great part destroying the national economy. By the late 1970s, however, the regime, with a new generation at the helm, understood the importance of free markets in economic development and began to selectively create "Special Economic Zones" where private businesses opened and flourished. By the early 2000s China had an annual economic growth rate of 8 to 10 percent. The party remained in complete political control of the country but was enabling the Chinese to pursue economic initiatives that would have been impossible decades earlier.

3-4 The Limits of Toleration

Individual freedoms are most often found and most often enjoy guarantees in political democracies. However, while democracies maximize the toleration of diverse points of view and lifestyles, frequently subtle and occasionally glaring differences exist between them. The United States, for example, probably offers the greatest freedom of the press in the world. It is even more substantial than Britain's, which actually has tougher libel laws on the books and is more protective of personal privacy than the American legal system.[12]

Singapore offers one of the most disciplined democracies. Consider the fact that the city-state has legally banned chewing gum as part of the government's obsessive effort to keep the country as clean as possible. Singapore's citizens have accepted without much reaction a rule most Americans would be outraged over. The other side of this argument, though, suggests that greater social discipline provides greater individual freedom and security. Singapore does provide a good deal less individual freedom than the United States, but Singapore also is a place in which violent crime is rare, the streets are safer as well as cleaner, and drive-by shootings almost never occur.

Toleration ceases to be a civic virtue when it contributes to an uncivil society. Religious fundamentalists not only in theocracies such as Iran but in democracies such as India, Israel, and the United States suggest this. Fundamentalists believe it is morally wrong to tolerate "deviant" lifestyles such as homosexuality or music with lyrics that praise physical violence or satanic cults. A government is only responsible when it is moral as well as effective. Two reputable political scientists have observed

---

[11]"Where the Draft Resolution Stands: 'A Final Opportunity to Comply,'" *The New York Times,* November 8, 2002.

[12]Edwin M. Yoder, Jr., "Why Trash This Symbol of Civility?" *International Herald Tribune,* December 2, 1992.

that "State laws, policies, and institutions must rest on a religious foundation.... Schools and courts must restore moral values to the community."[13] Government institutions

> must cleanse the community of modern vices: premarital sex, pornography, abortion, homosexuality, drug addiction, gambling, and alcoholism. Public schools must conduct orthodox prayers and teach traditional religious values. Courts should enforce religious law based on a literal interpretation of sacred scripture, which contains only one unchanging meaning for all time.[14]

The concern that toleration may not always be desirable is not restricted to religious fundamentalists. As mentioned earlier, democracies are not all the same when it comes to the expression of individual freedoms. The United States is well known for tolerating more violence than other industrial democracies. Japan, on the other hand, is known as the "safest industrialized society in the world."[15] Criminals in Japan are socially ostracized; even their families want nothing to do with them because they have brought great shame and humiliation to their relatives. Criminals who have served prison sentences are shunned after they return to society. Moreover, the National Rifle Association would deplore the fact that only 0.6% of the population owns a legal handgun in Japan in contrast to 40% in the United States.[16]

There is not a single recorded public protest against handgun regulations in Japan. Apparently, the Japanese are far more tolerant of restrictions on individual freedoms than Americans are. Ownership of personal firearms is almost an article of faith among many in the United States; Japan banned personal ownership of weapons in 1588. The ban has retained popular support throughout the last half century of democratization. For a comparative survey of efforts in gun control, see Figure 3–1.

3-5 Political Self-Righteousness

Political self-righteousness is a term that helps describe regimes that refuse to submit their programs to either public criticism or a meaningful election. Dictatorial regimes rarely feel the need or desire to consult the governed about policies. A small, closed political elite controls and manipulates the political culture in such a country for the elite's advantage. The government purports to know what is best for people without asking them and rules over them without their consent.

Several chapters in this text stress the importance of ideology in the political process. This chapter is no exception. Ideology is the cornerstone of political self-righteousness because it firmly adheres to the notion "that everything is relevant to government and that the task of government is to reconstruct society according to the goals of an ideology."[17]

Because an ideology cannot be "wrong" and because it proposes answers to political problems, a government that operates by ideology can justify nearly any act, even the most outrageous and violent. Political self-righteousness is evident in most political settings. It is even occasionally found in democracies, although constitutional restraints limit it.

Every ideology comes equipped with a self-appointed priesthood or "keepers of the faith." They can assure their political legitimacy if they are able to convince the rest of the population of their infallibility. The Communist party functioned this way in a dozen or more countries during the Cold War. The party saw no need

[13]Charles F. Andrain and David E. Apter, *Political Protest and Social Change: Analyzing Politics* (Washington Square, New York: New York University Press, 1995), 52.

[14]Ibid.

[15]Nicholas D. Kristol, "Social Pressure, Gun Laws Keep Crime Down in Japan," *The New York Times*, May 27, 1995.

[16]Coalition for Gun Control, http://www.guncontrol.ca/Content/International.html.

[17]Bernard Crick, *In Defense of Politics* (Baltimore, Maryland: Penguin Books, 1962), 34.

FIGURE 3–1	Gun Control in Selected Countries

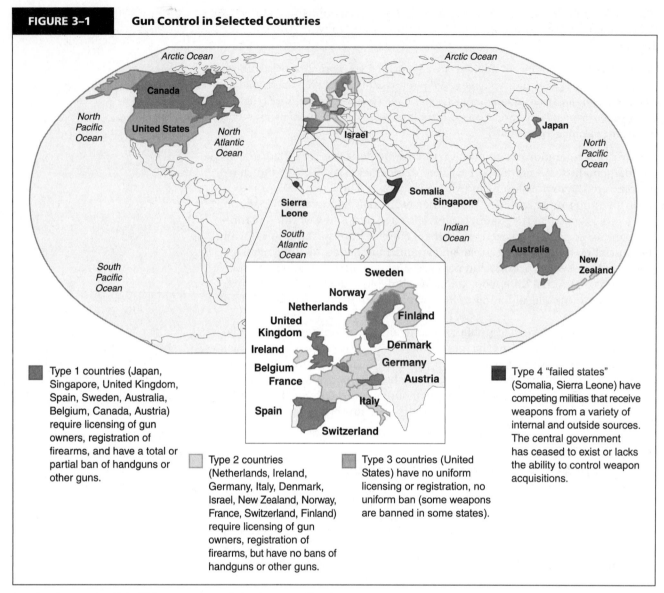

Type 1 countries (Japan, Singapore, United Kingdom, Spain, Sweden, Australia, Belgium, Canada, Austria) require licensing of gun owners, registration of firearms, and have a total or partial ban of handguns or other guns.

Type 2 countries (Netherlands, Ireland, Germany, Italy, Denmark, Israel, New Zealand, Norway, France, Switzerland, Finland) require licensing of gun owners, registration of firearms, but have no bans of handguns or other guns.

Type 3 countries (United States) have no uniform licensing or registration, no uniform ban (some weapons are banned in some states).

Type 4 "failed states" (Somalia, Sierra Leone) have competing militias that receive weapons from a variety of internal and outside sources. The central government has ceased to exist or lacks the ability to control weapon acquisitions.

Imagine the reaction if the U.S. government tried to become a Type 1 country.

to hold free elections, admit dissent, or allow political opposition to function freely because of their monopoly on the "truth." Most ideologies do not allow for or lend themselves to compromise. Ideological self-righteousness means never having to say you're wrong.

3-6 Political Legitimacy

By what right do a few govern—or establish rules of behavior—for the many? In Plato's fictional *Republic*, political legitimacy was vested in a small cadre of philosophers who governed on the basis of their accumulated wisdom. Unfortunately, governance by wisdom has rarely surfaced in any actual political system. Yet the question of political legitimacy is ancient. Nearly every ruler and government, even the most tyrannical, has thought it necessary to somehow justify their power. If a ruler is widely considered legitimate, he or she can exercise power by making important decisions, including those that involve life and death, and expect the people to accept them without question or, at least, without serious resistance.

POLITICAL BIOGRAPHY

Osama bin Laden

Osama bin Mohammad bin Laden was born in 1957, one of fifty or so children in his family. His father was originally from Yemen, but migrated to Saudi Arabia and became a multibillionaire by pursuing construction projects on behalf of the Saudi royal family. Osama studied management and economics. Growing up in Saudi Arabia bin Laden was, of course, heavily exposed to the Wahhabist school of Islam, an especially puritanical and violent religious sect. He gained notoriety during the 1980s by going to Afghanistan to join and then become a leader of the mujahideen in their war against the Soviet occupation that had begun in 1980. The mujahideen were impressed with an extremely wealthy Muslim who was willing to share their struggle and endure a great deal of personal discomfort.

Bin Laden came onto the American intelligence radar screen by the early 1990s. He had offered in 1990 to use his own "Afghan Arab" fighters to protect Saudi Arabia from the Iraqi army that had already occupied Kuwait. His offer was declined and the agreement by the Saudis and the United States to allow American soldiers to be stationed on Arabian soil was considered by bin Laden to be a sacrilege. He never forgave the Saudi royal family and has since worked and called for the elimination of the Saudi control of Arabia.

By this time bin Laden was irrevocably at odds with American policy. He accused the United States of supporting Islamic regimes in and out of the Middle East that were corrupt and heretical. In 1995 he planned terror attacks in Riyadh, the Saudi political capital, and Dhahran. Bin Laden was responsible for the bombings of the American embassies in Nairobi, Kenya, and Dar es Salaam, Tanzania, that killed hundreds of people. He was connected with the first World Trade Center bombing in 1993 By this time bin Laden had organized his al-Qaeda network, sometimes referred to as the Ford Foundation for Terrorism. He financially supported applicants who approached him with plans to slaughter non-Muslims or Muslims considered heretics.

The Clinton administration had two opportunities to apprehend or kill bin Laden, but chose not to do so because of logistical problems and the near certainty of civilian casualties. Since the September 11, 2001, attacks that murdered 3,000 Americans, Bin Laden has been the world's most wanted criminal. He is convinced for his part that he is the leader of a holy war against "Crusaders and Jews," a coalition led by the United States who, bin Laden is convinced, is invading and occupying Islamic lands.

Bin Laden became a fugitive after American and Allied forces overthrew the Taliban regime in Afghanistan in October 2001, which had provided protection to him and his followers. Intelligence experts believe that he is still planning and directing terrorist attacks from hiding places along the Afghanistan and Pakistani border. Whether or not bin Laden is eliminated, there is little doubt that his operations have inspired numerous terrorist acts and will probably continue to do so even if he is no longer free or alive.

In rather rough form, the four most traveled roads toward political legitimacy can be outlined chronologically:

1. The surest road to political legitimacy for rulers thousands of years ago was the divine one. Nearly 6,000 years ago in Egypt, the ruling pharaohs were able to establish the notion that they were gods who had consented for a period of time to live among mere mortals. The will of the pharaoh was therefore a divine commandment that was undeniable and completely enforceable as law. Egyptians by and large believed this notion for millennia—only rarely were insurrections recorded during Egypt's long pharaonic age (about 3,400 to 30 B.C.). Legitimacy in this case was based on the prerogatives of a godhead. As recently mentioned, the Japanese emperor is still considered divine by millions of his subjects even in the early years of the twenty-first century.

2. Later ages produced more modest rulers. From medieval times and well into the eighteenth century, several European monarchs insisted that, while far from divine themselves, they were authorized and supported by **divine right**. This theory was based on the assumption that power is ordained by divine authority. Thus, to rebel against a monarch's rulership was not only an act of political treason, it was a mortal sin. The prophet Samuel, after all, had anointed the first two kings of ancient Israel, according to the Bible. Divine right fell from acceptance as a society became more educated and economically advanced. By 1649 in England and 1793 in France, monarchs who insisted they were accountable to

divine right
A monarch's assumption that he or she has spiritual justification for exercising complete power, with minimal or no constitutional restraints.

no earthly power were overthrown and beheaded by popular movements that did not accept divine right as a viable doctrine or as a practical form of government in modernizing societies.

3. In the twentieth century, legitimacy based on ideology became a crucial cornerstone of totalitarian society. The Nazis in Germany (1933–1945) and the Communists in the Soviet Union (1917–1991) quickly learned how to use ideology to create popular support for their regimes. Nazi leaders consistently told the German people how mentally and physically superior they were to non-Nordic nations. To emphasize the point, government agencies referred to "inferior" peoples (Slavs, Jews, Africans, gypsies, and others) as subhuman. The Soviets stressed the economic and moral superiority of communist society. They taught Soviet citizens that communism represented the most modern form of society, a form that supported human potential more than the corrupt and decadent capitalist societies that encouraged personal greed and selfishness. The Chinese communists under Mao tse-Tung (who ruled China between 1949 and 1976) murdered millions of people for what was considered "counterrevolutionary activities," a euphemism for suspected opposition to the regime. And months before the Chinese Communist government assumed control of Hong Kong in 1997, it announced it would not tolerate political parties or public demonstrations. A totalitarian state sees no reason to tolerate either.

4. In democratic societies, an experiment in electoral political legitimacy began in the nineteenth century and is still in progress. Democracies are distinct from the previously described political models because they base rulership on regular elections, peaceful acceptance of their outcomes, stipulated terms of office, and orderly transfers of power from an incumbent government to the opposition. The next chapter will examine both democracy and democratization in some detail. For now, keep in mind that democracy is still in the experimental stages. Only recently have democracies become a firmly embraced political process in more than a few dozen European and North American countries. Over the last two centuries, democracies have expanded and contracted in number. In the 1990s, they were in an expansionist phase. Because previous expansionist phases have yielded to contractions, a contraction may follow the current expansion.[18] Democracy has yet to fully prevail in a majority of the world's countries.

Even the collapse of totalitarian systems does not necessarily guarantee a bright future for the democratic process. The majority of countries in the world in the early 2000s were still governed by autocratic regimes that exhibited varying degrees of brutality even though much of it was camouflaged by the appearance of democratic institutions. Authoritarianism, a form of government that does not bother to base its power on any form of legitimacy unless one considers brute force legitimate, still limits and challenges the expansion of democracy.

There is a darker side to legitimacy, however. A government, especially one misguidedly following an ideology such as communism or fascism, may regard a portion of its own citizenry as illegitimate. Even worse, the ideology may consider this portion completely beyond redemption. As mentioned previously, Jews in Nazi Germany, Shiite Muslims (a minority sect within Islam but a majority of Iraqis as well as Iranians) in Iraq, or capitalists in the Soviet Union were liable to be executed, worked to death, or bombarded with chemical weapons. Ethnicity, religious identity, and social class origins are critical considerations to ideologically guided regimes. These characteristics can doom an often defenseless minority to punishments ranging from second-class citizenship to wholesale physical extermination.

---

[18]On this subject see the intriguing essay by Samuel Huntington, "Democracy's Third Wave." "A New Era in Democracy: Democracy's Third Wave," *Current*, September, 1990, 27–39. A full treatment of Huntington's concept of democratic phases is provided in his book *The Third Wave: Democratization in the Late Twentieth Century* (Norman, Oklahoma: University of Oklahoma Press, 1991).

3-7 Political Culture and Political Trauma

A political culture is characterized by established norms and values. Americans, for example, take tremendous pride in their individualism and in the opportunities a country with abundant resources makes available. Any country that survives for long must occasionally face drastic cultural and political alterations, which may arise either suddenly or gradually. These episodes can be called **political traumas**. The term *trauma* signifies serious injury. A drastic political trauma such as a war can seriously wound or injure the political system and require extensive "reconstructive surgery." The wound need not be fatal, however, and the healing process can produce a stronger and more durable system.

As fortunate as the United States has been through most of its history, America has not been totally immune to political trauma. In fact, American society has experienced several traumas with lasting effects: the Civil War (1861–1865) and the consequent social readjustments imposed on the South during Reconstruction (1865–1877); the severe economic and social dislocations of the Great Depression of the 1930s and involvement in World War II (1941–1945); and the national division and unrest over U.S. involvement in Vietnam (roughly 1965–1975). Political traumas arise over issues that challenge the viability of a country's political institutions.

Each trauma has impacted the political culture in dramatic ways. A third of the country in 1861, for example, determined that it could no longer work within the political system and that, in fact, the system itself was detrimental to regional interests, leading to the South's secession from the Union. The Civil War and Reconstruction, as difficult as they were, may well have produced both a more unified and more democratic country. The Great Depression helped usher in social programs designed to guarantee Americans some degree of economic security for unemployed workers and for those too old or to ill to work and persuade most of them to accept an expanded role for the national government. And Vietnam made the United States, for better or worse, much more reluctant to become involved in military activities abroad, a reluctance not completely overcome until the September 11, 2001, terrorist attacks; it also made Americans aware that American power is not unlimited.

Other countries, democratic and nondemocratic, have experienced their own traumas, as Table 3–1 summarizes. Some, like Russia, are currently going through a political trauma. Traumas themselves are not always cataclysmic, nor must they be violent. Canada, for example, has discussed for decades whether Quebec should remain a part of the country. If Quebec does decide to secede, Canadians would expect the secession to be peaceful.

Future traumas in many areas of the world will probably redraw national boundary lines and could have implications for international security. New states are regularly appearing as smaller societies secede from older and larger ones. Successful secession is traumatic but not necessarily debilitating in the long term. After the 1989 collapse of communism in Czechoslovakia, the Czechs re-established a democratic form of government. A few years later, however, the Slovak third of the country peacefully seceded. In a separation fondly referred to as a "velvet divorce," Czechoslovakia divided into the Czech Republic and Slovakia.

The concept of states dividing (or even redividing) developed recently but may be around for a while. During the 1990s, twenty new states appeared on world political maps. It is almost certain that more will appear in the twenty-first century. Most will be the offspring of secessions, but it is far from certain that all secessions will be as peaceful as Slovakia's. China, for example, still claims Taiwan as part of the Chinese state and as a "renegade province." It has even warned Taiwan not to consider a unilateral declaration of independence though the Taiwanese have had their own political institutions in place since 1949.

Two important factors may reduce the effects of something as traumatic as a country splitting in two. First, if the split occurs in a democracy, as it might in

political trauma
A severe or devastating shock to a national society as the result of war, unprecedented economic hardship, accelerated and violent civil strife, or a combination of these factors.

TABLE 3–1	Political Culture and Political Trauma	
Country	**Trauma(s)**	**Result**
United States	Great Depression (1930s)	Unprecedented government involvement in and regulation of the economy
Soviet Union (USSR)	World War II invasion (1940s); economic stagnation and hard-line coup; (1991) now Russia and smaller republics	Distrust of the West; breakup of USSR and democratization
Germany	Military occupation after losing World War II	Democratization
Japan	Nuclear bombing and military occupation after losing World War II	Democratization
France	Collapse of colonial empire and near civil war (1946–1958)	Strengthened executive
United Kingdom	Declining economic and political power (about 1945–1970)	Acceptance of United States as replacement world power
Canada	Bifurcation into two national communities, English- and French-speaking (ongoing)	As yet undetermined; possible separatism

Canada and already has in Czechoslovakia, the secession process will most likely be peaceful; and second, the economic integration being achieved in Europe and North America will actually encourage ethnic communities seeking autonomy to secede with a minimum of economic dislocation.[19] Traumas in democratic societies since 1945 seem to be increasingly mild: No democracy has since experienced a life-and-death struggle with a hostile power or an economic setback that threatened extreme solutions.

Sometimes a trauma can be so severe that a regime collapses. Such an event usually means the political culture was not very viable in the first place. A depressing example of a failed culture and a destructive trauma is the violent disintegration of the federated republic of Yugoslavia. The country imploded during the early 1990s, revealing a political culture fragile in the extreme, particularly in Bosnia-Herzegovina, one of the federation's member republics. This region dissolved into three ethnic-religious communities of Orthodox Serbs, Catholic Croatians, and Muslim Bosnians, but not without horrendous violence.

Between 1945 and 1990, constitutional devices and the charisma of Yugoslav leader Josef Broz Tito (born to a Serb father and Croat mother) were able to temporarily neutralize ancient hatreds. However, the ethnic and religious strains within Yugoslav society eventually proved too severe for the country to hold together. After Tito died in 1980, the federation began to unravel, and by the 1990s, it had collapsed into full-scale civil war. Despite the regime's best efforts, it wasn't possible to create a persuasive political culture of mutually accepted norms and values that would retain the loyalty of an extremely divided population.

After the Indian subcontinent was granted political independence by the British in 1947, the huge Hindu and Islamic populations were partitioned because neither wanted to be politically involved with the other. Most Muslims became the nation of Pakistan while the Hindus became the overwhelming majority in India. The partition involved what was probably the largest population of transfer in history as millions of Muslims fled India and millions of Hindus fled what was to become Pakistan. In less than half a century the two countries fought two wars with one another, evidence that the trauma of partition can leave remarkably long residues.

---

[19]"A Wealth of Nations," *The Economist*, April 29, 1995, 90.

Another tragic example is the Korean peninsula. The country was partitioned in 1950 into the Democratic People's Republic of (North) Korea and the Republic of (South) Korea. The south did fine and is today the tenth largest economy in the world with a democratic form of government; the north has a miserably low standard of living, a completely centralized economy that has helped cause widespread food shortages, and a tyrannical form government. North Korea has devoted much of its meager resource base to building a nuclear arsenal, an activity that makes both the south and neighboring China and Japan understandably nervous.

3-8 Secularism Versus Sacralization

Religious values often form the basis of political cultures, especially in traditionalist societies. They exert much less influence in modern societies where secularism prevails. A secular society is one in which

> Individuals gain greater autonomy from community controls. Tolerance for "deviant" lifestyles grows along with the pluralism of worldviews.... Through reason, technology, and the experimental sciences, individuals can understand and control not only the material world but also the social environment.[20]

Sacralization is the opposite of secularization; its advocates want to restore traditional values to a society they believe has misplaced or ignored its spiritual heritage in the pursuit of material goals. Often, they do not reject the benefits of modern technology—many religious fundamentalists in the United States, for example, take full advantage of the electronic media to advertise their message. Instead, sacralizationists view technology as a tool they can use to convince fellow citizens to order their lives in accordance with time-tested social mores. In this sense, toleration, considered a virtue in secular societies, is a vice in sacralized societies. The sacralized society is often modeled on and adheres to a holy writ. Because values are considered divinely inspired, there is no reason to tolerate opinions and lifestyles that don't conform to those spelled out in the holy writ. Even in modern Western societies, not everyone is happy or satisfied with a secularized culture. Religious fundamentalist movements, for example, sometimes react to what they regard as excessive secularization. At best, such deviations are viewed as wrong; at worst, they are sinful. In a sacralized society, either type of deviation may deserve severe punishment. Table 3–2 summarizes the distinctions between a secular and a sacralized society. Religious movements attempt with mixed success to *resacralize* both the political and overall cultures by extolling the virtues of ancient customs and particular religious practices. Orthodox Muslims in Iran, for example, have attempted since 1979 to restore the Sharia, or Islamic sacred law, as a code of conduct for daily behavior. Since September 11, 2001, the Western world in general and the United States in particular have become increasingly familiar with "Bin Ladenism," a doctrine that "explicitly teaches its disciples that the purpose of life is to seek death."[21]

In Somalia, local authorities strictly enforce proper personal conduct, doling out legal punishments for moral infractions most Westerners would find medieval (see Table 3–3). This isn't surprising—the punishments *are* medieval, having been formulated twelve or thirteen centuries ago. Such a "legal system" takes precedence over and often replaces all modern law. The government becomes morally obligated to enforce religious doctrine.

In the United States and many West European countries, crime rates are high and rising. This is the result, say some observers, of too much leniency shown to criminals in the courts and of the breakdown of the family unit—results of secularization.

---

[20] Charles E Andrain and David E. Apter, *Political Protest and Social Change: Analyzing Politics* (Washington Square, New York: New York University Press, 1995), 63.

[21] "Ehud Ya'ari, "Bin Ladenism: The Cult of Death," *The Jerusalem Report*, September 23, 2002, 14.

TABLE 3–2	Characteristics of Secularized and Sacralized Political Cultures	
	Secularized	**Sacralized**
Church and state	Separate	Together and often indistinguishable
Legal system	Mixture of custom and contemporary concepts	Based on holy scripture
Toleration	Maximized on behalf of diverse preferences and lifestyles	Equated with sinful failure to condemn nonscriptural behaviors
Morality	Minimally acknowledged	Strictly enforced
Men and women	Gender equality	Women often considered inferior and subservient to men

TABLE 3–3	Crime, Sin, and Typical Punishments in Some Islamic Countries
Crime/Sin	**Punishment**
Eating in public during Ramadan	Public flogging—35 lashes
Robbery	A hand cut off with a sword
Armed robbery	A hand and a foot cut off with a sword; or gutting in a public square
Murder	Execution; body left outside for three days
Adultery	If married, death by stoning; if unmarried, 100 lashes
Public kissing	30 lashes
Married men caught in a homosexual act	Death by stoning
Unmarried men caught in a homosexual act	100 lashes
Making love to a goat	100 lashes

To be sure, secular societies sometimes reveal rather strong residues of a sacralized sentiment. The perceived breakdown of social order in Western and westernized countries has frightened a great many Christians and Jews. One reaction in the United States is the Christian Coalition; in Israel, the *Gush Emunim* ("block of the faithful") fulfills a similar role, and in India a strong brand of Hindu fundamentalism has gained prominence. In all cases, these religious fundamentalists are thoroughly politicized and exploit the latest technological developments in mass communication to reach as wide an audience as possible. There is little doubt that even political cultures generally considered overwhelmingly secularized will continue to experience serious challenges from sacralizing forces.

3-9 Political and Social Fragmentation

Unfortunately, the subject of political culture is rarely easy to understand. In great part, this is because political culture itself is difficult to create and sustain, and this difficulty may increase rather than diminish over the next few decades. This text has already alluded to the resurgence of the ethnic conflict and religious radicalism

BIOGRAPHY

Irshad Manji

Irshad Manji (b. 1968) is a regular recipient of Islamist death threats who makes her home with her lesbian partner in a Toronto apartment that is equipped with windows made of bulletproof glass. She has been referred to as "Osama bin Laden's worst nightmare."[22] She is also the author of *The Trouble With Islam: A Muslim's Call for Reform in Her Faith*, a best-selling book published in 2002 and translated into several languages that is critical of Islamic radicalism. Ms. Manji has led an interesting life; she remembers her father chasing her around the house with a knife for asking too many questions about the family religion. Her critique of Islam has also earned her criticism from moderate Muslims who consider her to be excessively disdainful of traditional Islamic beliefs.

The most severe criticism she has received has been from Muslims and non-Muslims who condemn her for playing into the hands of Muslim haters and confirming all that they believe is negative about Islam. There is no doubt that Ms. Manji's book and her website (http://www.muslim-refusenik.com/) contain controversial views and that she has been condemned to death for holding them. She does argue vociferously for *ijtihad*, an Islamic tradition that encourages independent thinking.

Manji belongs to a school of thought that some view as the possible salvation of Islam and the most practical way to bring the religion into modernity. The crimes and the punishments for them applied in some Islamic countries (Table 3-3) are what Manji is trying to get people to focus on and to acknowledge that substantial reform is necessary in order for Islam to remain as a faith connected to reality.

that pose challenges for most political systems. Why are such challenges growing in number and severity?

These phenomena are surfacing because the most hospitable habitat for a consensual political culture, a stable society, is no longer taken for granted even in well-established democracies. The notion of "declining governability"[23] is applied to the United States because of the "incapacity of our political institutions to resolve or even mitigate the complex economic and social problems that face us."[24] What this means in a practical sense is uncertain. Apparently, though, the American political culture is changing because the norms and values of the overall culture are changing.

No political culture is static. A political trauma, such as any of those suggested earlier in this chapter, can produce sudden and irrevocable alterations in society. More often than not, though, a political culture changes gradually, sometimes imperceptibly. For example, despite unprecedented economic prosperity in America, a growing number of Americans sense things are not going well; others, especially ethnic minorities, do not feel they belong to the pluralist society American schoolchildren are taught to believe in. Instead, these groups feel a "coercive conformity" to become "Americanized."[25]

Another school of thought holds that tolerance, long an accepted value within the American political culture, has become excessive. Advocates of this point of view argue that tolerance may be desirable, but not at the expense of social discipline. The town of Raritan, New Jersey, for example, passed a city ordinance prohibiting "rude language."[26] Whether government has the legal right to force people to speak courteously is an open matter—one that will probably be argued rather loudly under the auspices of the First Amendment. New York City passed an ordinance in 2006 in an attempt to encourage good health and thinness by banning the use of transfats in restaurants.

---

[22]Clifford Krauss, "An Unlikely Promoter of an Islamic Reformation," *The New York Times*, October 4, 2003.

[23]Bruce D. Porter, "Can American Democracy Survive?" *Commentary*, November 1993, 38.

[24]Ibid.

[25]Benjamin Schwartz, "The Diversity Myth: America's Lending Export," *The Atlantic Monthly*, May 1995, 62.

[26]"In the Front Line of the Politeness War," *The Economist*, February 18, 1995, 22.

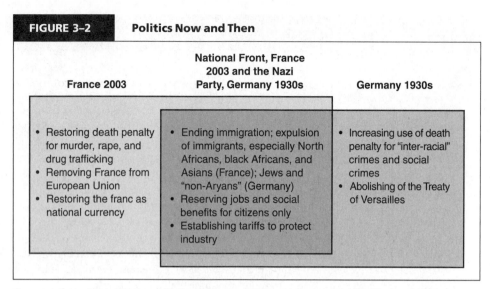

FIGURE 3–2   Politics Now and Then

National Front, France 2003 and the Nazi Party, Germany 1930s

France 2003

- Restoring death penalty for murder, rape, and drug trafficking
- Removing France from European Union
- Restoring the franc as national currency

- Ending immigration; expulsion of immigrants, especially North Africans, black Africans, and Asians (France); Jews and "non-Aryans" (Germany)
- Reserving jobs and social benefits for citizens only
- Establishing tariffs to protect industry

Germany 1930s

- Increasing use of death penalty for "inter-racial" crimes and social crimes
- Abolishing of the Treaty of Versailles

Compare the politics of France's National Front of 2003 and those of the Nazi Party of 1930.

A political culture may also be less substantive than generally thought. Political scientists have long believed the United States to possess a coherent and fairly universal political culture. But how accurate is this perception? The April 19, 1995, bombing of a federal office building in Oklahoma City suggests that a number of people in this country do not accept a political culture that includes any meaningful presence of the national government. Even if only a handful of people are willing to resort to violence, the American political culture is still experiencing severe strain. One credible commentator has gone so far as to suggest that Americans are currently witnessing "a sort of Colombianization of the United States, in which failing political institutions become increasingly marginal in an ungovernable, criminalized, and endemically violent society."[27]

France has long been regarded as a country with a political culture supportive of the democratic process. During France's 2002 presidential election, however, the candidate representing the (decidedly undemocratic) anti-immigrant extremist elements drew the support of almost one out of every five voters. With an unemployment rate of 10 percent and nearly 6 million North African immigrants (to whom many unemployed French workers attribute their problems), voters in a free election demonstrated an interest in supporting extremist and explicitly nondemocratic policies.[28] For an interesting comparison with the Germany totalitarian regime, see Figure 3–2.

France is a major democracy and a West European powerhouse, possessing the second largest economy on the continent (after Germany) and the fourth largest in the world. Even so, the extremist vote in 2002 revealed a political culture not fully developed along democratic lines. France still has a coherent political culture, even with its cleavages. The less-than-democratic elements remain willing to work within the established political process. The riots that occurred in France during the early part of 2006 also revealed a large fissure between the French Islamic community and the rest of the country. There is no doubt that discrimination exists and that it is directed against Muslims whose housing and employment prospects are decidedly lower than non-Muslims. Moreover, the Muslims frequently take their frustrations out on French Jews whose numbers are less than a tenth of those who adhere to Islam, but whose economic prospects are generally better.

[27]John Grey, *The New York Times Review of Books,* January 22, 1995.

[28]For example, the right-wing National Front candidate, Jean Marie Le Pen, got 19 percent of the vote in part by advocating the expulsion of Muslims from France, even if they were French citizens. Expulsion of Muslims would mean an exile of nearly 10 percent of the country's population.

France is hardly alone. In the Netherlands, perhaps the most tolerant country in Europe, democracy is not immune to episodes of horrific violence. Ironically, it is toleration that provoked violence in this case. A filmmaker, Theo van Gogh (great-great-grandnephew of the famous nineteenth-century painter), was murdered by a Dutch citizen who **was** an immigrant from Morocco. He felt compelled "to chop off the head of anyone who insults Allah and the Prophet," something van Gogh had done in a documentary that was severely critical of the ways in which Muslim women are treated.[29] Van Gogh had previously made documentaries critical of Christianity and Judaism but had been left unmolested by those who had found one or both offensive.

In some developing countries, fragmentation rather than cohesion is the rule. Indigenous peoples in the Western hemisphere, for example, still resent the intrusion of white Europeans. For South American Indians, the coca plant possesses religious sanctity, but in North American cities, police and health workers despise and fear it as the source of the addictive and destructive drug cocaine.[30] In Peru, celebrations of the Spanish discovery of America aroused the indigenous peoples to express their desire to end "five hundred years of European dominance."[31] This dominance includes the U.S. threat to eradicate the coca crop, despite the practices of indigenous peoples in Bolivia and Peru. These people consume coca by chewing its leaves, believing it has both religious significance and health benefits. After a half millennium, then, Peru retains an uncertain political culture with a society still fragmented along European and indigenous lines.

Many, perhaps most, states in the world are unable to create a viable political culture. This is primarily because most overall cultures themselves are hardly functioning. Because of primitive communications technologies, the central government is often far removed from the bulk of the population in most developing countries. If it is not far removed, as in North Korea, many wish it was because of its brutality.

In much of the Third World, the centralized structures in many countries are being "replaced by a jagged-glass pattern of city-states, shanty-states, nebulous and anarchic regionalizing."[32] Political cultures now and in the future may increasingly represent simple local subcultures, and the authority of the central government may not remain a part of the political culture. Such authority may actually cease to exist as it withdraws from or simply disintegrates in regions and city neighborhoods within developing countries. Fundamentalist religious organizations are taking on new authority, providing social services—schools, health clinics, even police protection and courts—that the government either can no longer afford or never provided in the first place. Table 3–4 summarizes these changes.

Political scientists have analyzed the theme of political culture rather thoroughly over the last several decades. New analyses may be necessary as national borders become unstable, as governments continue to relinquish control over segments of their populations, and as primary political loyalties embrace clans, tribes, and regions rather than nation-states. In such systems, the values espoused by a religious doctrine or a local warlord supersede other allegiances. This concern is not alarmist—several developing countries have already deteriorated to the point where a national government is mostly ineffective or, in extreme cases such as Somalia, practically nonexistent.

Clearly, political cultures have developed unevenly in different societies. They cannot be taken for granted in even the most stable democracies. In fact, as will be investigated in the following chapter, political culture in democracies is perhaps most subject to challenge and change.

---

[29]For a revealing essay on this incident see Jane Kramer, "The Dutch Model: Multiculturalism and Muslim Immigrants," *The New Yorker*, April 3, 2006, 60–67.

[30]Andrew Weil, "The New Politics of Coca," *The New Yorker*, May 15, 1995, 71.

[31]Ibid.

[32]Robert Kaplan, "The Coming Anarchy," *The Atlantic Monthly*, February 1994, 12–27.

TABLE 3–4	Characteristics of Emerging Localized Political Cultures

1. Central government activities are replaced by local jurisdictions.
2. National political institutions are eliminated or ignored.
3. Social services are either suspended or administered by private (often religious) agencies.
4. Popular perceptions of the central government change; the government is completely discredited, viewed as an enemy, or viewed as incompetent and corrupt.
5. Overall form of *de facto* government develops based either on warlordism or on a clergy extolling a religious value system.

Chapter Summary

1. Political culture is a part of a society's overall culture. It includes the political norms and values generally accepted by the overwhelming part of the citizenry.
2. Political legitimacy is a requirement for effective governance. Every regime must at least appear to be legitimate on the basis of such devices as free elections, ideology, or divine right.
3. Political socialization is the process that inducts each generation of citizens into their political culture. Agents of political socialization include peers, schools, the electronic and print media, and the family.
4. The collapse of fascism in 1945 and Soviet communism in 1991 suggests that extreme ideological convictions and lethal practices are in decline. However, some developing countries such as Iran (with its Islamic fundamentalism) and North Korea (still a Stalinist state) have domestic and foreign policies strongly motivated by ideology.
5. Toleration is not always considered a political virtue. Democracies differ because of the limits each applies to toleration. Some democracies place a greater emphasis on personal security than on maximizing expressions of individual freedom.
6. Political cultures are not engraved in stone; they change over time. Occasionally they change dramatically and suddenly because of a national political trauma.
7. Modern or modernizing societies emphasize secularization, advocating features such as toleration, pluralism, and individual autonomy. The opposite process of sacralization emphasizes a traditional heritage, religious values, and absolute ideals.
8. Very few political societies are completely united. Most constantly experience situations in which certain segments of the population, often ethnic and/or religious minorities, wish to separate or at least distinguish themselves from the rest of society. Subcultures with their own value systems and occasionally their own political agendas frequently result.
9. Many governments, some of them democratic, encourage a preferred political culture through an official or unofficial policy of "coercive conformity."
10. Because of an almost total lack of central authority or cultural cohesion, an increasing number of countries will be characterized by multiple local political cultures.

Chapter 3 Quiz

1. A consensual political culture is usually found in
   a. Middle Eastern societies.
   b. democracies.
   c. totalitarian systems.
   d. all of the above.

2. Political socialization occurs
   a. only in democracies.
   b. in sub-Saharan Africa.
   c. where nationalism is absent.
   d. throughout all political societies.

3. One of the fastest growing Spanish-speaking populations in the world is found in
   a. the United States.
   b. Canada.
   c. France.
   d. Australia.

4. The Soviet Union was referred to as the "evil empire" by the administration of
   a. Bill Clinton.
   b. Ronald Reagan.
   c. Jimmy Carter.
   d. George W. Bush.

5. Handgun ownership was banned in 1588 in
   a. the United Kingdom.
   b. China.
   c. France.
   d. the Empire of Japan.

6. Divine right is a form of political legitimacy found
   a. in present-day England.
   b. several hundred years ago in Europe.
   c. in China.
   d. in a few sub-Saharan African states.

7. The political trauma of defeat in World War II led to
   a. revolution in Russia.
   b. the Great Depression.
   c. democratization in Germany and Japan.
   d. American involvement in Vietnam.

8. The term *velvet divorce* refers to
   a. peaceful secession of Slovakia from Czechoslovakia.
   b. disintegration of the Soviet Union.
   c. disintegration of Yugoslavia.
   d. a proposed dismemberment of Canada.

9. A sacralized political culture usually includes all except which of the following?
   a. holy scripture as law
   b. gender equality
   c. combination of church and state
   d. lack of toleration for nonscriptural authorized behavior patterns

10. The major Western European democracy with a sizeable extremist vote in recent elections is
    a. United Kingdom.
    b. Germany.
    c. France.
    d. Spain.

11. Characteristics of localized political cultures include all except which of the following?
    a. national political influence eliminated or ignored
    b. social services either suspended or administered by private local agencies
    c. central government in popular perception is viewed as corrupt and inept
    d. some local autonomy but firm allegiance to the state

4

Political Democracy and Authoritarian Government

It is important to remember that democracy is far from universally accepted or desired. Tens of millions of Russians have seen their living standards plummet and their jobs and pensions evaporate since democracy was introduced to their country in the early 1990s. A few, however, have become incredibly rich and Russia has its share of billionaires (one of whom is in prison for tax evasion). Hundreds of millions of religious fundamentalists in the developing world as well as within democracies themselves view democratic features such as toleration, the empowerment of women, and individualist expressions as challenges to an absolutist and spiritual authority. And scores of regimes believe, sincerely or otherwise, that enabling their citizenries to make decisions about their own political destinies is impractical and dangerous to social order.

In the established democracies, some raise occasional but very serious concerns over whether individual freedoms can be taken too far and whether social permissiveness equates with a lack of discipline and stability. The process of democracy itself is a mixed blessing. Electoral majorities can be especially unpleasant in their treatment of minorities.[1] Still, it seems safe to conclude that political democracy is a viable process that has survived severe challenges from fascism and communism. Democracy is also a process that is incomplete and continuing to evolve. Democracies tend to survive better than totalitarian regimes because democracies accept and even encourage change. This chapter will examine democracy in terms of its current status, future prospects, and new directions.

Democracy and the process of democratization—both complicated subjects—will be explored. Democracy has been more successful in some places than others, frequently for unanticipated reasons. This chapter will take a detailed look at the cultural, historical, and social motivations that either produce or proscribe democratic political systems.

4-1 Millennia of Political Authoritarianism

The introductory chapter mentioned that institutionalized government is at most about 8000 years old. Government evolved because the permanent human settlements that accompanied the advent of agriculture made order and security necessary. Throughout most of recorded history, government's activities were few but critical to the success of civil society: People needed to be assured that their persons, families, and property would be secure, and government tried to offer this security. It would be difficult in the extreme for individuals to provide security for themselves on their own.

The deal struck between rulers and the ruled seemed Hobbesian: The ruled would receive protection and guarantees of security for themselves, their families, and their property; in return, they would pay taxes (to support the army that protected them) and obey laws that maximized social order. Just one other rule

---

[1] A popular majority can be politically brutal toward individual expressions that the majority considers disagreeable. See the classic treatment of this issue in Jacob Talmon, *The Origins of Totalitarian Democracy* (London: Secker and Warburg, 1952).

prevailed: Keep political thoughts private. Authoritarian regimes apparently believed too much individual speculation and questioning of authority would detract both from social order and from the political power required to maintain it. Plenty of regimes still believe this today.

This arrangement certainly had advantages. Authoritarian government developed first in isolated societies 6,000 to 7,000 years ago. The earliest civilizations in what are today China, India, and the Tigris-Euphrates and Nile river valleys developed impressive cultures and technologies, but their political systems were mainly autocratic. In a world full of predators ready to pounce on defenseless individuals and their possessions at a moment's notice, it was worth almost any price to protect oneself. Even if the government was not interested in individual rights, at least it was effective in providing security. After all, the niceties of human rights would not mean much if society itself was torn asunder by some ruthless invader.

Actually, the means to pursue the goal of security were often brutal—and in many societies still are—but they seemed to have at least tacit popular support, if only because the alternative was violent anarchy. For a long time, the term *democracy* was nearly synonymous with disorder and mob rule. At the Congress of Vienna in 1815, the major European powers agreed to keep the world safe *from* democracy. The Congress took place after the end of the Napoleonic Wars (1799–1814) in which the ideals of the French Revolution were spread throughout much of a Europe that was still very much autocratic. More than a century later, most of these powers and the United States at the Versailles Conference following World War I (1914–1918) vowed to make the world safe *for* democracy.

Yet democracy is not a recent innovation. In its experimental form, it is about 2,500 years old. The first people to try it coined the term itself: *demos* is a Greek word for people and *kratos* is Greek for rule. The most successful early experiment in democracy took place in Athens during the fifth century B.C.E. The democracy was incomplete because it was restricted to only a small portion of the Athenian citizenry and a smaller element of the total population: To fully participate, it was necessary to be a free adult male. Women, resident aliens, and slaves were not part of the political system. In short, the majority of the population enjoyed no more than minimal human rights. These initial rights—such as the sanctity of private property (that then included slaves) and some degree of free speech—were at least a start.[2]

The Athenian democratic experiment and its imitators in some of the smaller Greek cities did not last long. The city-state system gave way, first to the Macedonians and later to the Roman Empire. Some democratic processes appeared from time to time in various locations, but they usually yielded to one form of authoritarianism or another. By the closing decades of the twentieth century, however, authoritarian forms of government appeared increasingly unattractive to growing numbers of people.

This happened not only because authoritarian governments could be extremely brutal, but because so few could claim economic success. South Korea, one of the exceptions, had become an economic success story by the 1980s, as had Chile. Both countries had experienced military governments of long duration, and these governments had not been reluctant to depress political opposition, sometimes violently. But they had also managed to encourage a substantial degree of economic prosperity and a growing middle class.

Ironically, it may have been prosperity that prompted mass demonstrations, particularly in South Korea. Protesters demanded political reform, fair and free elections, and other rights granted by democratic systems. During the 1980s, democracies began to replace authoritarian regimes in much of Latin America and, selectively, in East Asia.

One scholar, Francis Fukuyama, was encouraged by the outbreak of democratic regimes. He suggested that such an outbreak signified "the end of history," when

---

[2]For a readable analysis of the times and the experiment, see Donald Kagan, *Pericles of Athens and the Birth of Democracy* (New York: The Free Press, 1991).

the liberal democracy practiced and endorsed by Western Europe and the United States would undergo "universalization."[3] In the absence of natural enemies, democracy, according to this thesis, is destined at some point to cover the entire globe. The argument on behalf of democratic inevitability seemed to be bolstered by the collapse of totalitarian communism in Eastern Europe and the Soviet Union. Within the span of half a century, democracy had vanquished the two greatest threats to its existence, fascism and communism.

Even better, once democracy was universally established, global peace would prevail. Democracies, after all, tend to refrain from engaging in wars with one another.[4] Of course, Fukuyama's thesis did not foresee the growth and pervasiveness of antidemocratic forces that include nonstate actors such as political terrorists who are prepared to apply weapons of mass destruction against democracies. During the last years of the twentieth century and the first years of the twenty-first, terrorism became the most serious threat to democracy, though whether terrorism is a mortal threat remains unclear. We shall explore this phenomenon in a later chapter.[5]

No one can predict whether worldwide democracy is ultimately feasible. Determining democracy's staying power is of more immediate concern. Optimists enthusiastically embrace Fukuyama's thesis that democracy is inevitable and that terrorism, like communism and fascism, will be eventually overcome. Others suggest that, while democracy has made headway over the last few decades, its final victory is far from certain. Nor is it a given that democracy as a political process will survive, even in the countries where it has recently appeared. It is perfectly possible that non- or antidemocratic governmental forms may outlast even the most significant surge of democracy history has known. Warlordism and **tribalism** in several African countries (both involve primary loyalty to a smaller unit than the nation), the appearance of drug cartels with significant military forces in some Latin American countries, and the complete disintegration of other countries in the Third World suggest that the Western sense of government, let alone of democratic government, remains an alien concept in much of the world.

Some suggest that chaos is more likely to succeed authoritarianism than democracy. Even authoritarian forms of government may be weak or incompetent when it comes to maintaining themselves. As Somalia in the early 1990s suggested, the complete absence of a political infrastructure reduces a society to a situation reminiscent of the Middle Ages. As old political structures break down, local **warlords** replace them. These warlords may be worse for the establishment of political stability than more traditional authoritarianism because the warlords usually control fewer people and less territory, are constantly at war with one another, and provide little if any social stability.[6]

4-2 The Fear of Modernity

It would be almost impossible to imagine living in any society that did not possess a set of widely accepted traditions the overwhelming part of the population subscribes and adheres to. Traditions survive because they make people feel better about who they are and what values they prefer. Traditions help tie people comfortably to the past and provide some basis of hope for the future—or at least, that is what they are supposed to do. Everyone is the product of a culture's traditions whether each individual acknowledges or likes it. For the most part, parents, teachers, siblings, friends, and clergy all see good reasons to preserve traditions that they

tribalism
Refers to a form of political loyalty that is more restricted than the familiar one normally reserved for the state. Tribal political loyalty is often focused on marital and blood ties.

warlords
Political or military leaders who take control of small territories and populations when national order and the central government break down.

---

[3]Francis Fukuyama, "The End of History?" *The National Interest*, no. 16 (Summer 1989): 3–19.

[4]"Democracies and War," *The Economist*, April 1, 1995.

[5]Even after the attacks of September 11, 2001, the American democracy remained unsure about how to develop a strategy for dealing with the threat considered as both real and growing by some observers. See Mark Helprin, "Failing the Test of September 11," *The Wall Street Journal*, September 16, 2002, sec. A.

[6]Robert Kaplan, "The Coming Anarchy," *The Atlantic Monthly*, February, 1994.

received from their own generation. There is a certain comfort and security in knowing from where one came and how one got to be the way one is, which is why people retain certain values and shun others. But not all traditions are desirable: Slavery, for example, is an ancient institution that would shame any society that practiced it today. Some traditions die, most usually because they are gradually seen as morally indefensible, economically stagnant, or both.

Traditions are found in democracies as they are in any other systems. Open and pluralist societies value their traditions as much as any other. But numerous societies view democracy suspiciously, seeing it as a challenge to and perhaps a destroyer of tradition. A lot of countries associate democracy with a social permissiveness destructive of a society's fundamental values. On the other hand, traditional nondemocratic societies do not usually reject modernity per se. There may be a relatively unexplored aspect to rejection of democracy. A society may have been so brutally subjugated by a tyrannical regime or a series of tyrannical regimes that democracy seems a vague and elusive theory. Iraq, for example, has never known a democratic government in its national history, though an infrastructure was formed in 2004. Iraqis could be at the point that their primary concern is simply to survive another day.[7]

Traditionalists understandably enjoy the conveniences electricity and indoor plumbing provide. Islamic, Christian, Jewish, and Hindu radicals may wish society's moral behavior to conform to holy writ, but like most of the rest of us, they don't object to air conditioning and central heating systems. Fear and resentment of modernization is directed mostly toward cultural expressions—"modern" music, fashion, cosmetics, and often gender equality and family planning. Racial integration and the increasing appearance of people of color in positions of responsibility in both the public and private sectors in the United States has caused consternation only among a small minority of Americans. A fringe of this minority, such as the Aryan Nation, has become disconcerted to the extent that it seeks to remove itself from the mainstream by establishing bases in isolated regions of the western United States to preserve racial purity considered threatened by the seemingly relentless advances made by racial minorities.

Of course, societies often use modernization techniques to preserve traditions. Radio, television, email, and fax machines, not to mention sophisticated military weapons systems, have reached an expanded audience of traditionalist movements. Ironically, traditionalists may use modern technology to transmit a message condemning modernized lifestyles.

4-2a Men's and Women's Roles

Perhaps no single social change in history has been as encompassing as the revision of relationships between men and women in both democratic and nondemocratic societies. The Western democracies were the first to recognize and guarantee women's rights. Yet, even the democracies did not pursue these rights until well into the twentieth century, generations after constitutions and laws had been formulated to guarantee human rights.

Women in the United States and in the United Kingdom, for example, gained the vote in the 1920s and 1930s, respectively. It took a few more decades for women to begin appearing in regional and national legislatures. Women didn't start voting in Switzerland (the last democratic holdout) until about 1970.

Many authoritarian societies treat men and women equally in one sense: They systematically oppress both without regard to gender. In other societies where religion is a dominant feature of the regime, discrimination is frequently official and enforced. In Pakistan, women are by law worth only one-half of a man. In Iran, women are discouraged from revealing more than their faces and hands in public

---

[7]Just how brutal Saddam Hussein was during his quarter century of rule is explored by Con Coughlin, *Saddam: King of Terror* (Ecco Press, 2003).

(and their fingernails must not be covered with polish). During the Taliban regime in Afghanistan, even faces were covered and women could only see out of a narrow slit provided in their chadors. In Saudi Arabia, women are forbidden by law to drive any motorized vehicle. Several tried to do so in 1991 after seeing uniformed women in the American military driving jeeps (and even ordering men they outranked around). Government officials arrested the Saudi women and forced their husbands to pay large fines to gain their release. On the other hand, these same regimes, which most Westerners condemn as medieval in their treatment of women, boast that women can venture outside of the home (with a male relative as escort) without fear of harassment or violence, a statement most westernized nations cannot make.

Much of the restrictive policies on women have to do with interpretations of holy writ that imply that women are seductive creatures who lead men away from divine standards. Christianity, Judaism, and Islam all have produced similar interpretations that women must be kept in subjugation or they will inspire all kinds of havoc. Extremist elements continue to maintain that women are morally and, therefore, politically inferior to men and that gender equality is out of the question if only because such a notion is in defiance of divine will.

Ghosts from the past also continue to haunt the progress of women in much of the world. Trials of witches occurred in North America nearly 400 years ago. Nearly all of the witches were women and many were executed because of the belief, entirely unfounded, that they were possessed (and sometimes seduced) by Satan. Sadly, this isn't ancient history. Killing witches is still going on in Africa. In 2001 "at least 1,000 alleged witches were hacked to death in a single 'purge' in the Democratic Republic of the Congo. Far from declining in modern times, fear of witches has intensified."[8]

Even in some democratic settings, women have had a rough time. In India, an uncertain but apparently substantial number of girls killed at birth if their sex disappoints their parents. The tendency for women to outlive men in industrialized democracies is reversed in India; it is more common for women to die before age thirty-five because of exhaustion from child bearing, malnutrition, and a lack of proper health care. Men are strongly favored when it comes to family resources allocated for food, education, and social status.[9]

India is not the only culprit. Infanticide is still widely practiced in many cultures.[10] Female babies in China had a better chance to reach adulthood before the government, in its strenuous efforts to curb population growth, encouraged Chinese couples to restrict their families to one child. Apparently, many couples killed their female babies in order to try again to have a male child. Once it realized this unintended consequence of its population control policy, the government began emphasizing how delightful baby girls can be. By 2006 China's population was approaching 1.3 billion people, one out of every five people on the planet. The government feared that the 15 to 20 million people being added to the population each year would blunt or even wreck the program for economic development. To limit population growth, China has discouraged couples who insisted on having more than one child by refusing to guarantee access to higher education for additional children. Instead of receiving tax breaks for more children, Chinese couples incurred tax penalties. The result has not always been humane. Some pregnant women are forced to undergo abortions. Others, after learning of the fetus's gender, voluntarily have abortions because of the premium placed on male babies. The Chinese government by the early years of the twenty-first century was worried that the emphasis on males had created a shortage of females. The current generation

---

[8]Philip Jenkins, "The Next Christianity," *The Atlantic Monthly*, October 2002, 60.

[9]Jodi Jacobson, "Women's Work," *Foreign Service Journal*, January 1993, 26–29, 31. According to Jacobson, "Male children consistently receive more and better food and health care than their sisters."

[10]"Stark Data on Women: 100 Million Are Missing," *The New York Times*, November 5, 1991, and Jim Yardley, "Dead Bachelors in China Still Find Wives," *The New York Times*, October 5, 2006.

of child-bearing age is vastly disproportional: perhaps as many as 120 boys to every 100 girls. China is fearful that there may in the next decade or so be 45 million bachelors with little or no prospect of finding women to marry. Some young girls have even been kidnapped to be raised in a family not their own in order to guarantee a wife for the eligible male child in the kidnappers' family.

Most countries in Africa are depressingly impoverished, but more women than men are living in complete poverty. Women normally work twice as many hours as men,[11] but earn significantly less—and men's income is barely at subsistence level. In parts of Africa, women are still subjected to genital mutilation, a practice intended to ensure their faithfulness to husbands who may be away from home for days at a time. They are also more likely to contract HIV infections that may then be passed on to their unborn children.

The data about the world's women are not all grisly. In many countries, women have made significant advances in professions such as journalism, business, and medicine. They have also made political gains. In several democracies—including Germany, Canada, Norway, Israel, and the United Kingdom—women are or have been heads of government. They have served as leaders in the democratization process in other countries, including Sri Lanka, Pakistan (although Prime Minister Benazir Bhutto was removed from office in 1996b on charges of corruption), Nicaragua, and the Philippines.

An increasing number of countries are realizing that to disenfranchise and abuse half of the population is to retard both social and economic development. Educated and healthy women, like educated and healthy men, have become firm indicators of economic and technological development.

4-2b The Status of Modern Democracy

As mentioned earlier, democracy as a political system is of recent vintage. In an intriguing essay, Samuel Huntington outlined three waves and two reversals of democracy:[12]

1. The first wave began rather modestly in the 1820s with the expansion of the voting franchise in the United States. The Reform Acts in the United Kingdom swiftly followed, beginning in 1832. The first wave ended in 1926 with a total of twenty-six democracies in the world; between 1922 and 1942, more than half of these democracies succumbed to autocracy or military occupation by totalitarian governments, reducing the number to twelve (the first reversal).
2. The second wave crested about 1945 to 1962, when democratically governed countries advanced in number to thirty-six. This healthy total declined slightly as the result of a second reversal between 1960 and 1975, bringing the number back down to thirty.
3. The third wave of democracy has been in full swing since the early 1980s.

It began in Latin America and expanded to parts of Eastern Europe and East Asia. There are presently a record number of democracies in existence.

As many as 100 countries now have some variant of political democracy. In his essay, Huntington speculates on whether a third reversal is lurking in the future. By the early years of the twenty-first century it was difficult to be sure whether a new reversal was underway or still lurking.

The threat of terrorism and its wholesale application of violence frightened democracies, terrorism's primary target, but did not cause them to erode civil liberties, terrorism's intended casualty.

---

[11]Africa Regional Office of the International Institute of Rural Reconstruction (IIRR), *Sustainable Agriculture Extension Manual for Eastern and Southern Africa* (IRR: 1998) 70, http://www.iirr.org/saem/page70-74.htm# page-70b (accessed Dec. 17, 2003).

[12]Samuel P. Huntington, "A New Era in Democracy: Democracy's Third Wave," *Current*, September, 1990, 27–39. A full treatment of Huntington's concept of democratic phases is provided in *The Third Wave: Democratization in the Late Twentieth Century* (Norman, Oklahoma: University of Oklahoma Press, 1991).

The world is certainly more democratic in the first decade of the twenty-first century than at any previous time in history. But a considerable number of newer democracies are far from secure. Many have had only two or three free elections. Russia has conducted free parliamentary elections since the 1990s. Its fourth presidential election was held in 2004, and according to independent observers, was fairly conducted. Some countries have not yet experienced a peaceful turnover in government: Mexico has conducted free elections since the 1930s, but the same political party, the Institutional Revolutionary Party (PRI), dominated national politics and controlled the federal government for nearly seven decades without interruption, until it lost control of Mexico City and the national legislature in the 1997 elections. Not until 2000 did an opposition party capture the presidency. The PRI, which began as a reform movement three generations ago, is now viewed as an institution that has outlived and even betrayed its usefulness and has fossilized into a corrupt political machine unresponsive to the real needs of the electorate. The Mexican presidential election of 2006 was peaceful despite its closeness and charges of voter fraud.

The 2003 Index of Economic Freedom ranks countries by the amount of economic freedom each has, which is defined in terms of government interference in the economy. Less government interference allows the **free market** to dominate the national economy. The United States, Denmark, and Estonia are tied for sixth place, while Hong Kong is in first place and Singapore is second. There is a direct connection between countries that maximize economic freedom and political democracy. Politically repressed countries such as Iran, Libya, Laos, Cuba, and North Korea have stagnant or declining economies.[13] All of these are governed by an ideological or theological regime that admits no dissent and insists upon government control of daily economic life.

free market
An economic system characterized by minimal government regulation and opportunities for every member of society to acquire material wealth.

It is important to note, however, that the free market, the supposed handmaiden of modern political democracy, does not automatically facilitate the democratic process. The Russian economy is being privatized, but it is also being criminalized as gangsters acquire formerly state-controlled industries. One observer has pointed out, for example, that when Eastern Europeans threw off their communist regimes, both they and Americans believed they would relentlessly seek democracy and that it would prevail. To some extent, that is what happened. The Eastern European revolutions that seemed to arise out of concern for global democratic values quickly deteriorated into a stampede in the general direction of free markets and their ubiquitous, television-promoted shopping malls.[14]

Neither the concept nor the practice of political democracy is interpreted in a uniform fashion. For example, in one of the least hospitable climates for democracy, the Middle East, some advances have been made in the area of individual rights. But these advances are not necessarily democratic and do not necessarily lead to democracy. Here is one scholar's outline of the probable progress of democratization in Arab states:

1. Rulers may allow competitive elections, but they determine who participates in them.
2. Rulers retain control of the media and the agencies that oversee elections.
3. Rulers have no intention of transferring power to anyone outside the political elite, which includes a carefully defined and narrow membership.
4. Maximized democracy allows people to express different points of view without fear of imprisonment.[15]

In Arab societies, stages 1 and 2 above prevail, and stages 3 and 4 are almost nonexistent. Most Western observers don't consider any Middle Eastern country other

---

[13]Mary Anastasia O'Grady, "Liberty = Prosperity," *The Wall Street Journal,* November 12, 2002, sec. A.

[14]Benjamin R. Barber, "Jihad vs. McWorld," *The Atlantic,* March 1992, 61.

[15]Mustapha K. El Sayyid, "The Third Wave of Democratization in the Arab World," in Dan Tschirgi, ed., *The Arab World Today* (Boulder & London: Lynne Rienner Publishers, 1994), 183.

than Israel and possibly Turkey democratic. Israel has regular parliamentary elections and a competitive political party system. So does Turkey, though, on occasion, the Turkish military has intervened to thwart election results it was unhappy with. Turkey is an incomplete democracy. Currently, Islamists are participating in Turkish elections, but there is a fear that they are using democratic processes to "pave the way to theocracy."[16] Yet, both Israel and Turkey are consistent American military and political allies (Turkey is the only Islamic member of North Atlantic Treaty Organization or NATO and desires to join the European Union). In the more politically progressive Arab states, one of the most critical elements of democracy— the peaceful transfer of political power to the opposition after the incumbent government loses an election—is still an unknown and, for many, unacceptable tenet.

Governments willing to conduct free elections are not always willing to accept their results, often because nondemocratic political parties sometimes win. When a fundamentalist Islamic political party won a free election in Algeria and the army intervened and nullified the results, the army's intervention caused substantial violence. And, of course, Germany provides a grim historical reminder of the dangers of free elections when nondemocratic parties prevail; in 1932, the Nazis won the country's last free election until 1949. The Nazis used democratic processes to acquire power. They then ended, often with great brutality, Germany's democratic institutions by outlawing other political parties and, in practice, suspending civil liberties of Jewish citizens and all opponents of the regime.

For the last half of the twentieth century, a dozen countries in Western Europe and North America have been unreservedly democratic with only an infrequent relapse. Nor are democracies necessarily tied to industrial economies.

Costa Rica's economy is mostly agricultural and not nearly as prosperous as those in Western Europe, but the country has been steadfastly democratic since 1948,[17] making it the oldest functioning democracy in Latin America.

Democracy, then, is not the same everywhere. A country's political culture helps to determine whether democracy will flourish or barely survive. In Costa Rica, arguably Latin America's most durable political democracy, the army was dissolved in 1948 in the effort to forestall any future military dictatorship. It also helped that Costa Rica has only two geographically contiguous neighbors, Panama in the south and Nicaragua in the north, not countries that are in a position or mood to threaten Costa Rica's territorial integrity. Often, geography plays an important role in democratic development. Both the United Kingdom and the United States, for instance, were geographically isolated enough to develop their democratic institutions leisurely. They did not have to worry about powerful predators on their borders ready to interrupt or threaten democratic development.

4-3 Where Are the Democracies?

Such a question is difficult to answer, even when looking at a world map and examining the post–Cold War political geography. The established democracies are where one would expect to find them—in North America and Western Europe. Despite the demise of communism, it is still tricky to find other democracies. As Table 4–1 suggests, democracy makes only a rare appearance in most of the Middle East and Africa, is still tentative in much of Eastern Europe, and is only beginning to emerge in East and South Asia. Latin America offers a more optimistic picture because, with the exception of Cuba, civilian rule tends to prevail, and relatively free elections have occurred within the last several years.

But most of Latin America is in the process of democratization rather than in fully functioning democratic systems. Some South American countries, such as

---

[16]Rosemary Righter, "Rally to Turkey," *The Wall Street Journal*, November 12, 2002, sec A.

[17]In 1948, Costa Rica tried to guarantee democratic governance by abolishing its military forces and placing strict term limits on its presidents.

TABLE 4–1   **Status of the World's Nations in Regards to Democracy**

Free	Partially Free	Not Free	Free	Partially Free	Not Free
Andorra	Albania	Afghanistan	Mali	Singapore	Uzbekistan
Argentina	Antigua and	Algeria	Malta	Solomon Islands	Vietnam
	Barbuda		Marshall Islands	Sri Lanka	Yemen
Australia	Armenia	Angola	Mauritius	Tanzania	
Austria	Azerbaijan	Bahrain	Mexico	Togo	
Bahamas	Bangladesh	Belarus	Micronesia	Tonga	
Barbados	Bosnia-Herzegovina	Bhutan	Monaco	Turkey	
Belgium	Brazil	Brunei	Mongolia	Uganda	
Belize	Burkina Faso	Burma	Namibia	Ukraine	
Benin	Central African	Burundi	Nauru	Venezuela	
	Republic		Netherlands	Yugoslavia	
Bolivia	Colombia	Cambodia	New Zealand	Zambia	
Botswana	Comoros	Cameroon	Norway	Zimbabwe	
Bulgaria	Congo (Brazzaville)	Chad	Palau		
Canada	Cote d'Ivoire	China (PRC)	Panama		
Cape Verde	Djibouti Congo	(Kinshasa)	Papua New		
Chile	East Timor	Cuba	Guinea		
Costa Rica	Ecuador	Egypt	Philippines		
Croatia	Ethiopia	Equatorial	Poland		
		Guinea	Portugal		
Cyprus	Fiji	Eritrea	Romania		
Czech Republic	Gabon	The Gambia	St. Nevis and		
Denmark	Georgia	Guinea	St Kitts		
Dominica	Guatemala	Haiti	St. Lucia		
Dominican Republic	Guinea-Bissau	Iran	St. Vincent and		
El Salvador	Indonesia	Iraq	Grenadines		
Estonia	Jordan	Kazakhstan	Samoa		
Finland	South Korea	Kenya	San Marino		
France	Kuwait	North Korea	Sao Tome and		
Germany	Lesotho	Kyrgyz	Principe		
		Republic	Slovakia		
Ghana	Liberia	Laos	Slovenia		
Greece	Macedonia	Lebanon	South Africa		
Grenada	Madagascar	Libya	Spain		
Guyana	Malawi	Maldives	Suriname		
Honduras	Malaysia	Mauritania	Sweden		
Hungary	Moldova	Oman	Switzerland		
Iceland	Morocco	Pakistan	Taiwan (Rep		
India	Mozambique	Qatar	of China)		
Ireland	Nepal	Rwanda	Thailand		
Israel	Nicaragua	Saudi Arabia	Trinidad and		
Italy	Niger	Somalia	Tobago		
Jamaica	Nigeria	Sudan	Tuvalu		
Japan	Paraguay	Swaziland	United Kingdom		
Kiribati	Peru	Syria	(excluding		
Latvia	Russia	Tajikistan	Northern		
Liechtenstein	Senegal	Tunisia	Ireland)		
Lithuania	Seychelles	Turkmenistan	United States		
Luxembourg	Sierra Leone	United Arab	Uruguay		
		Emirates	Vanuatu		

Source: Adapted from Freedom House (www.freedomhouse.org/ratings), 2002.

Colombia, have freely elected governments, but they suffer from rampant corruption as officials regularly succumb to bribes that drug traffickers offer them. The term *narco-democracy* may become more familiar in years to come.

Before placing countries in the democratic category, at least two questions must be asked:

1. How many free elections have been conducted?
2. Has there been at least one peaceful turnover in government?

Peaceful turnovers needn't happen very often for a country to be democratic. Political party control did not change in Britain from 1979 to 1997 or in Germany after 1982. Over a period of forty-three years (from 1949 to 1992), Israel changed party control only twice. Japan was governed by one political party, the Liberal Democrats, for nearly four decades. In the United States, the Democratic party, with rare intervals, controlled both houses of Congress for more than six decades, from 1931 to 1995. The 107th Congress, 1997–1998, marked the first time in seven decades that the Republican party achieved two consecutive congressional majorities. All of these countries, however, conducted national elections when they were constitutionally required to do so. When the incumbents lost, they quietly and peacefully acceded to the election results. The Democrats waited a decade before recapturing both houses in 2006.

Very often, for example, a country's population will include an ethnic or religious minority that does not see itself as an integral part of the citizenry and is unaccepting of the political regime. The government may have a similar view. The three Baltic states, Estonia, Latvia, and Lithuania, provide an interesting case in point. They were the last countries forcibly annexed to the Soviet Union (1940) and the first to declare their independence from it (1989). During the half-century the Baltics were Soviet republics, such a large number of Russians were permanently settled within Baltic borders that the demographics were severely altered. This was particularly true in Estonia and Latvia, where Russians now make up as much as a third or more of the total population. In some regions, such as the northeastern corner of Estonia, Russians actually form the majority. Table 4–2 summarizes the demographic figures for each republic.

Do the large Russian minorities present a problem in the new democracies in the Baltic republics? If democracy means having voting rights, holding political office, and being a part of the overall decision-making process, then ethnic Russians should have all these rights, but the Baltic governments are understandably wary of Russian political power. The Latvian government is disconcerted because its citizens of Russian ancestry prefer to speak the Russian language, indulge in Russian culture, live in Russian neighborhoods, and maintain loyalties to Moscow rather than the Latvian regime in the capital city of Riga. A democracy cannot force an ethnic minority to learn to speak another language or develop a new set of political loyalties unless it wants to cease being a democracy. Either Latvia will have to take its chances and hope that its Russian residents will gradually become integrated or forcibly remove them from Latvian soil. Both choices have risks. In the

TABLE 4–2	Demographic Breakdown of the Three Baltic Republics*		
Country	Indigenous Population(%)	Russian Population(%)	Others(%)
Estonia	68	25	7
Latvia	58	30	12
Lithuania	84	7	9

*Includes both Russian and some Polish residents.
Source: Adapted from *The World Factbook 2006* (www.cia.gov).

former, Russians may be reluctant to become Latvian and in the latter there is a very great risk of universal condemnation and the bankruptcy of Latvian democracy.

4-4 Democracy, Devolution, and Cultural Autonomy

Authoritarian and democratic governments have one thing in common: a political center where the ultimate decision-making authority of the state resides. The two systems quickly part company, however, when it comes to decentralizing authority. Democratic regimes tend to distribute power broadly, keeping a few responsibilities, such as foreign policy and military force, centralized. Activities such as public education and taxation may be shared with or delegated to regional or local jurisdictions. The United States has distributed these powers since its inception.

For some countries, including several well-established democracies, greater democracy may bring more decentralization, or **devolution**. Devolution can be defined as the political process that assigns various regions within a country increasing responsibility for managing their own affairs, to the point of creating regional legislatures. In short, devolution is the decentralization of domestic policy while the central government retains control over foreign policy and national defense. Devolution occurs in democracies where regions have historical memories of political independence and usually have a desire to preserve a distinct culture.

An excellent example is the United Kingdom. Five-sixths of the country's population and almost as much territory is English, with the remainder divided into Scot, Welsh, and Northern Irish regions and population. Until paramilitary action and political terrorism rendered Northern Ireland ungovernable by the early 1970s, the Irish had in place a regional legislative assembly called the Stormont. Both the Welsh and the Scots have strong nationalist movements represented in the British House of Commons. Each has an ancient memory of political independence.[18] Thus, considerable debate has developed over whether it is a good idea for each region to have its own legislature rather than being governed directly from the central government in London.[19] The amount of power vested in regional legislatures would equal the influence London would lose over local affairs. In many respects, this process is an inevitable one. The British government has widely ceded prerogatives to regional jurisdictions while retaining control over foreign affairs and other activities that require a nationally coherent policy. For it not to do so would only invite resentment and stronger efforts at outright separation.

Very often, either the political arrangement or political geography of a country does not allow for devolution strictly along the lines of geographical regions. Such arrangements are frequently based less on political formulas than on cultural divisions that follow religious, linguistic, and ethnic patterns. Sometimes all three come into play. For example, in Israel, both Arabic and Hebrew (as well as English) are considered official languages and are displayed everywhere from road signs to restaurant menus.

Moreover, Arabs and Jews usually belong to their own political parties. Arab Muslims administer their own school systems where the language of instruction is Arabic. Other countries, most of them with democratic political systems, have established an official tolerance and endorsement of a multilingual nationality. India counts fifteen languages as official, Switzerland three. Canada has long had two official languages, English and French, and an unwritten requirement over the last few decades that no national politician of any party can become prime minister without fluency in both.

devolution
The decentralization of the roles of a national government with a gradual and usually peaceful transfer of domestic authority to regional jurisdictions.

---

[18]The Scots are much more emphatic about devolution than the Welsh, whose support for devolution is only around 50 percent. See "Waking the Welsh Dragon," *The Economist,* January 18, 1997, 58.

[19]"Bricks from Straw," *The Economist,* July 22, 1995, 54.

Whether it is politically healthy to officially recognize and encourage these divisions is debatable. Some groups believe that one language and only one should characterize the nation. In south Florida, for example, English-speaking residents have occasionally expressed a resentment of the growing appearance of Spanish-only neighborhoods and shopping malls. It seems clear, though, that such divisions are permanent features of several democracies, and that the acceptance of cultural preferences may enhance internal peace. In fact, even the United States, which has long prided itself on the political integration of its many minorities, now has congressional districts where an English-speaking candidate is at a serious disadvantage. Besides Spanish-speaking voters, in a few districts in southern California, a candidate fluent in Korean or Chinese can have distinct advantages. President George W. Bush is able to converse rather well in Spanish, the first American president to do so. It is most unlikely that he will be the last.

Governments, especially but not exclusively democratic governments, are becoming more sensitive to the needs of historically ignored minorities. Indigenous peoples have frequently been victimized over the last five centuries, but governments are recognizing and rectifying this in the closing years of the twentieth century. In the northern regions of Norway, 80,000 Saami, descendants of people who arrived there 10,000 years ago, are no longer forced to learn Norwegian, and the central government encourages them to preserve their own culture. It is understandably difficult, though, to retain one's own culture amidst an overwhelmingly larger one.

4-5 The Industrial Democracies

Most of today's democracies are the products of processes that took generations to accomplish. And most current democracies are more democratic than they were generations ago. When the United States held its first national elections in 1788 for the presidency and House of Representatives, only about 100,000 voters out of four million inhabitants were eligible to participate.[20] Women were denied the franchise (the right to vote), as were all youths under the age of twenty-one. A tenth of the population were slaves, and in some states property and religious qualifications limited voting eligibility well into the nineteenth century.

Two centuries ago, the United Kingdom, like the United States, was one of a handful of countries that had any semblance of democratic governance. Its parliament can actually be traced back to the thirteenth century. Yet it did not seriously begin to extend the franchise until 1832 with the passage of the first of several Reform Bills, a process that went on well into the twentieth century. Until then, members of parliament were frequently elected from **rotten boroughs**; that is, from districts where only the candidate possessed enough property to vote, let alone stand for office. Some rotten boroughs had neither franchised nor disenfranchised people—the districts were underwater.

Industrialized democracies are sometimes described as societies that are reasonably comfortable places to live. Their citizenries generally enjoy a comfortable standard of living, high educational attainment, almost universal rates of literacy, relatively long life spans, and a degree of security in old age, attributes most of the rest of the world's population can only dream about. The *Human Development Index*, published by the United Nations, ranks about 130 countries on their quality of life. The top twenty or so countries are industrialized democracies (Norway ranks first, the United States sixth).[21] In nearly all of these countries, the bulk of the population enjoys a recognizable middle-class lifestyle that includes such amenities as car and home ownership, social security systems, national health care, public education

rotten boroughs
British electoral districts in which only one person owned enough land to be able to vote or stand for office. The candidate faced no opposition, simply voted for himself in parliamentary elections, and declared himself the winner.

---

[20]The membership of the U.S. Senate was not popularly elected until 1913, when the Seventeenth Amendment was ratified.

[21]*The Economist*, August 3–9, 2002, 82.

generally available from kindergarten through college, and affordable entertainment. The industrialized democracies only began to exhibit these features in the twentieth century, the result of steady progress and gradual spreading of the Industrial Revolution that began a few hundred years ago. The national wealth that the industrial and technological revolutions generated enabled quite a few people to become rich, but, more importantly, they gave an impetus to an expanding middle class that demanded and usually received more and more services and whose earnings, savings, and taxes could pay for those services.

Until the last third of the twentieth century, this phenomenon was restricted to Western Europe and North America. Industrialization and democracy seemed to be made for each other, though environmentalists would not necessarily agree. The devastation of World War II interrupted it, but by the mid-1950s, countries such as France and Germany were back to their prewar levels of economic production. By the early 1960s, the term **economic miracle** was being applied to Germany, but it might as easily have described the French and Italian recoveries as well. Just as impressive was the growth of the Japanese economy, which rapidly accelerated in the 1960s. Less than four decades after its defeat in 1945, Japan had the second biggest economy in the world.

All of these countries had something in common besides prosperous economies—they all had democratic political institutions. With the notable exception of Japan, industrialized democracies appeared confined to the West. This dramatically and noticeably changed by the 1980s as smaller East Asian countries such as South Korea, Singapore, and Taiwan established and sustained modern and productive economies.

economic miracle
The rapid economic recovery of a country militarily defeated and economically devastated. Germany and Japan, the defeated Axis powers in World War II, are generally regarded as case studies of countries that fully recovered both their economic importance and global standing in just a few short decades.

4-6 A Democratic Fragility: Immigration

Think about it: Over the last three to four generations (the last 100 years or so), the lives of hundreds of millions of people have been irrevocably transformed under the auspices of political democracy. When they were young, today's great-grandparents would have viewed the present world as the stuff of imagination or science fiction stories. The average life span has increased from about forty-five to nearly eighty, and it is no longer uncommon for some individuals to reach their hundredth birthdays. Indoor plumbing and electric service have provided a reliable and unprecedented amount of personal hygiene. Instant communication to nearly anywhere on the planet is available through telephone service, fax machines, and email.

It is no wonder that so many millions want to leave the lives they regard as dirty, boring, miserable, and without hope to find lives they regard as utopian and which most Americans and Europeans take for granted. More people than ever before are on the move. By 2000, an estimated 100 million people (nearly one out of every sixty human beings on the planet) from North Africa, Eastern Europe, the Middle East, Latin America, and South Asia were trying to immigrate to the more prosperous regions of Western Europe and North America. Immigration is frequently and, in some cases, mostly illegal. During the American Congressional 2006 elections, the immigration issue was an especially debated topic, especially in those states that have a common border with Mexico. Estimates vary but there is a consensus that there are between eleven and twelve million undocumented (or illegal) immigrants in the United States.

Most democracies during the 1990s and into the early 2000s became very skittish about allowing, let alone encouraging, immigration to their shores. In Western Europe, in particular, high unemployment rates nurtured a growing apprehension over the arrival of large numbers of African and Middle Eastern immigrants who, it was feared, would take jobs away from indigenous workers. Another fear was that some immigrants might turn out to be terrorists intent on murdering large numbers of people.[22] Nightmarish scenarios have been constructed to convince

---

[22]For a breakdown of the pros and cons of immigration see "The Longest Journey," *The Economist*, November 2, 2002.

governments to either help alleviate the terrible poverty in the Third World in order to lessen the desire to migrate to Western Europe or North America, or to seal the First World's borders shut against immigrants, or both. Some of the rhetoric borders on racism: The predominantly prosperous West and its one billion mostly white and comfortable inhabitants, alarmists warn, are in danger of being overwhelmed by an influx of millions (perhaps tens of millions) of the world's more than five billion nonwhites.[23]

The message seems clear. If Western populations desire to retain the integrity of their cultures and/or fear their dilution or simply have no desire to acquire greater population density because of a strain on resources, then an alternative must be pursued. If Western governments want immigrants to stay home, they will need to provide an incentive to do so. The West can supply this incentive in the form of substantial economic assistance, family planning, and health care. Otherwise, the world will continue to have obscenely unequal economies, and the West and a few Westernized countries will continue to get richer while much of the rest of the world grows poorer.

4-7 Emerging Democracies

Even authoritarian regimes able to create growing economies were becoming democratized by the 1980s. South Korea is a case in point. Like Japan, South Korea is an East Asian country and, like Japan, it was devastated by war. But South Korea, Taiwan, and Singapore, known as **East Asian dragons** (or **tigers**) (countries that have achieved a Western-style political system and economy), have shown that the road to democracy can differ from society to society. This was true in the West: While democracy progressed rather smoothly in the United States, France, and Britain during the 1920s and 1930s, it regressed in Germany, Italy, Spain, and Portugal during the same time and then made a comeback later.

East Asian dragons (or tigers)
The East Asian countries of South Korea, Taiwan, and Singapore whose economies and standards of living are approaching those of the West and Japan. Other countries such as Indonesia, Malaysia, and Thailand may soon be included in this group.

The same process seems to be going on in East Asia. Both South Korea and Taiwan are strong examples of authoritarian systems undergoing democratization, but in different ways:

> *South Korea:* The year 1987 was key. Demonstrations by students and a growing middle class ended the rule of the last of a series of militarily supported dictators and installed a popularly endorsed regime. Since then South Korea has, for the most part, held regular elections and has instituted other reforms that work to guarantee civil liberties.
>
> *Taiwan:* In 1986, the ruling party initiated democratic reforms in anticipation of rumblings among members of a growing middle class that wanted access to the political decision-making process. The reforms abolished martial law (in effect since 1949) and legalized opposition parties. After the generation that fled China in 1949 retired and the recognition of the People's Republic by the world community as the legitimate representative of the Chinese people, the Taiwanese understood that it was necessary to develop an acceptable (that is, democratic) polity.

As described in the Huntington analysis mentioned earlier, South Korea experienced a *transplacement,* "in which an authoritarian regime and a strong opposition first clash and then compromise when both realize that neither long-term repression nor revolution are feasible." Taiwan experienced a *transformation* that occurred "through management by liberalizers within the government."[24]

---

[23]For perhaps the gloomiest scenario of all, see Matthew Connelly and Paul Kennedy, "Must It Be the West Against the Rest?" *The Atlantic Monthly,* December 1994, 61–91.

[24]Steve Chan and Cal Clark, "The Price of Economic Success: South Korea and Taiwan Sacrifice Political Development," *Harvard International Review,* Winter 1992–1993: 24–26, 64.

The East Asian tigers have more in common with each other than with the Western democracies. There is no reason to expect South Korea, Taiwan, and Singapore to develop the same Western economic and political precedents at the same rate because of their tremendous cultural differences. World economic competition, while no longer between capitalists and communists, is now between at least two distinct forms of capitalism.

One form is familiar to most Westerners: *Individualistic capitalism* characterizes the American and British versions. It emphasizes intense, often ruthless aggressiveness to win short-term goals and immediate profits, a policy that bankrupted several dotcom companies in 2001 and 2002. Participants engage in competitive practices such as corporate raiding and extend minimal (if any) cooperation to either rivals, stockholders, or governmental agencies for the common good. The other form, *communitarian capitalism,* emphasizes the qualities frequently associated with the East Asian success stories: firm loyalty, long-term investment strategies, and policies that require teamwork, social responsibility, and a concern for sustaining growth by constantly updating and refining industrial techniques and workers' skills.[25]

Obviously, it is not impossible to locate both individualist and communitarian features in East Asian and Western societies, yet the distinctions are often crucial in understanding the economic and political processes in these societies. The East Asian democracies require and generally receive greater discipline and conformity from their citizenries than their Western counterparts. Such a requirement does not make them less democratic than those in the West: Social discipline and a lack of interest in individual expression sounds suspect in the West, but East Asians also enjoy lower crime rates and less violence than their Western counterparts.

Even assuming that democracy is the form of government many of the world's people prefer, it does not necessarily follow that American-style democracy will prevail in the end. Nor should it do so. Political culture, as indicated in the previous chapter, has a lot of impact in determining the kind of political regime that governs a society. It would be a mistake to assume that democracy evolves in just the same way in differing political cultures. It is likely that democracy means different things in different societies. Newer democracies will probably place less emphasis on the prerogatives of the individual than older (Western) systems.

4-8 Authoritarian and Democratic Blends

Why have some authoritarian regimes, such as South Korea, begun democratization processes, while others, such as Indonesia, are having a hard time getting started? Two reasons—economic development and the accompanying urbanization—have already been discussed. Apparently, both are necessary to democratization. A study of rapid economic growth in South Korea and Indonesia revealed that as the 1990s began, 70 percent of the South Korean population lived in towns and cities, while only 30 percent of Indonesians did, proportions that didn't change significantly a decade later.[26] With the bulk of the South Korean labor force concentrated in the cities, it was easier for workers to organize themselves and protest governmental excesses. Indonesia has a population four times that of South Korea spread out over a land area nearly twenty times as large. This makes it much more difficult to organize politically.

Moreover, Taiwan and South Korea are much more urbanized societies than Indonesia. An interesting theory suggests that democracies tend to develop faster in cities than in the countryside.[27] Cities, as centers of commerce and industry, are richer and are home to a larger middle class than rural areas. Ancient Athens,

[25]Lester C. Thurow, "Who Owns the Twenty-First Century?" *Sloan Management Review,* Spring 1992: 5–17.

[26]David Potter, "Democratization in Asia," in *Prospects for Democracy: North, South, East, West,* ed. David Held, 364–65 (Stanford, California: Stanford University Press, 1993).

[27]See "Cities," a survey published in *The Economist,* July 29, 1994.

FIGURE 4–1	Cornerstones of Modern Democracy

Renaissance	Protestant Reformation	Enlightenment	Industrial and Technological Revolutions
(1300s–1600s)	(1500s–1600s)	(1700s)	(1600s to present)
This period ushered in the rediscovery of ancient classical scientific learning that encouraged free inquiry, experimentation, and toleration of unorthodox ideas.	During the Reformation, the principle of separation of church and state developed, and links between citizenship and religious affiliation began to dissolve.	Contradictions between science and religious faith eventually encouraged an atmosphere of freedom of inquiry. This event helped produce advances in technology and democratization.	These revolutions introduced an increase in and redistribution of economic wealth to enable masses of people for the first time in history to become educated, travel widely, and dismantle theories of government.

(All dates are approximate.)

remember, was a city-state noted for commerce and, for the time, substantial wealth. Of course, plenty of countries are urbanizing without democratizing. This urbanization is going on so quickly that it may at least temporarily outpace any political development and, perhaps more ominously, any economic development as well.

Perhaps an even more compelling reason for some countries to democratize is that it is politically chic to do so. The industrial democracies command so much of the world's wealth, so much sophisticated technology, and such a preponderance of military strength that no single nondemocratic regime or combination of dictatorships can hope to challenge them. Moreover, several countries began to realize by the 1990s that to establish advantageous commercial relationships with these democracies, they would need to democratize themselves, or to at least reduce or eliminate their more brutal practices. The industrial democracy "club," in the immediate aftermath of the Soviet collapse, appreciated the fact that developing countries need economic assistance and could turn nowhere else for it.

Of course, whether all this will work out remains to be seen. Established democracies have their own problems. For a long time, Western democracies have been viewed as the product of cultural and technological revolutions as much as ideological and political ones. Figure 4–1 notes the events of Western historical epochs that serve as the cornerstones of modern democracy (and, by the way, tended to begin in cities).

To be sure, these processes began with and remain dominated by the West, and to an appreciable extent they were geographically restricted to the West. An important question remains: How successfully can democracy be transplanted to other countries and regions? Equally important, should transplantation occur at all? It may be better to let political processes work out naturally. One argument suggests that a country probably shouldn't be forced to become democratic before it's ready. A perhaps even more intriguing question is whether the more democracies exist, the more peaceful the world will become. Because democracies are inherently peaceful and consistently focus on economic prosperity, this theory goes, they are reluctant to fight wars with anyone, especially one another.[28]

This concept has not met with universal agreement. Some have argued, for example, that World War I (1914–1918) was fought between contenders who were fairly democratic, considering these were the early years of the twentieth century. Germany had a strong parliamentary system, as did its main antagonists, France

---

[28]"Democracies and War," *The Economist*, April 1, 1995, 17. One analysis found that "of the 416 wars between sovereign powers recorded between 1816 and 1980, only 12 were even arguably wars between democracies, and most of those had extenuating factors."

and Britain, and, in the last two years of the war, the United States. World War I notwithstanding, democracies have not recently been inclined toward international violence. They have tried to encourage other countries to become democratic in the belief that democracy is a good system and that the more democracies there are, the safer the world will be.

This is why the United States, for example, concerns itself with postcommunist Russia. The logic is appealing: Americans must assist Russia economically in order to make its democratic regime credible; as Russia democratizes, it will become more stable and the world will be more peaceful. But Russia is a non-Western country that missed most of the pivotal thinking of the Renaissance, Reformation, and Enlightenment. Its industrial revolution did not begin until industrialization had been well underway in the West for generations. Even at the time of the Soviet Union's collapse in 1991, more than 30 percent of the Russian labor force still worked in agriculture, many times the number in Western countries such as the United States, France, Germany, and the United Kingdom (where the proportions of agricultural workers range between 3 and 8 percent).

Free elections are the most evident characteristic of political democracy. Yet Russia's elections have not been particularly encouraging. Extremist parties on the left and right have support. Some observers remind the world of the ultimate fate of Germany's precarious and failed democracy between 1919 and 1933. A large proportion of the German electorate supported either extreme left or right political parties, until the moderate and democratic center shrank to the point where it no longer attracted enough support to maintain power. Too many Germans in 1933 were disillusioned with democracy to continue to sustain it.

Russia's democratic experiments remind political historians of Germany because of the attraction extremes have for large proportions of voters in both nations. Of course, precise historical parallels are impossible. But concern over the popularity of undemocratic parties and leaders in a democratization process is both understandable and legitimate.

4-9 Democracy's Future

There is little point in trying to predict democracy's future. For one thing, democracy is most likely still in its beginning stages as a political system. Yet, because democracies are also the leading economic powers in the world, other countries can reasonably be expected to pursue their example. However, this isn't a foregone conclusion. Only seven countries in the world have been consistently democratic for at least a full century. Five are English-speaking nations. And democracy is not an easy accomplishment. No democracy is a finished story, and although democracies closely resemble one another in their constitutional and political structures, no two democracies are quite the same.

Democracy's future is also uncertain because democratization sometimes proceeds haphazardly in places where it hasn't existed before. In much of Eastern Europe, Latin America, and nearly all of Africa and the Middle East, democracy is a precarious thing. Even optimists suggest that democracy inherently contains real dangers that could in the end destroy it. As pointed out earlier in this chapter, antidemocratic forces can do well in free elections and occasionally even win them.

Finally, one scholar has warned that care has to be taken not to revert to what he refers to as **tribal democracy**.[29] The earliest democracies were, understandably, tribal communities in which democracy functioned rather well, but only for those admitted to its processes as full and equal partners. For example, earlier in the chapter, the rather restrictive democracy of the classical city-state of Athens was mentioned. Modern political systems these days can actually function democratically if one overlooks the people who are refused admittance to their democratic

tribal democracy
A society that is democratic but extends democracy only to citizens who possess certain ethnic or religious characteristics.

[29]Raymond D. Gastil, "What Kind of Democracy?" *The Atlantic,* June 1990, 92–94, 96.

POLITICAL BIOGRAPHY

Pericles, History's First Democrat

Library of Congress, Prints and Photographs Division, LC-USZ62-107429

The earliest experiments in democracy began about 2,500 years ago. Democracy appeared in Athens under the auspices of the city-state's leader, Pericles (495–431 B.C.). It might be more accurate to give Pericles credit for democratizing Athens rather than for establishing a democracy. He governed by consistently winning office for three decades, a long tenure for a democratic politician; but this was an age that did not impose term limitations on its top political leaders.

Accomplishments attributed to Pericles include employing the unemployed in public works programs (a policy that helped build the Parthenon), paying citizens for jury duty and military service, and ensuring that every voter was also a legislator and could attend and deliberate in Assembly meetings.

Only a minority ever did, however, because most Athenian citizens were either too far away to conveniently travel to the meeting place or had no interest in participating. Even the judiciary was democratized in a sense: Hundreds of jurors could assemble to hear a case, and the outcome was based simply on majority vote. Apparently, few worried that juries could make mistakes.

Athens, of course, was an incomplete democracy. Pericles himself was referred to as *strategos autokrator*, or commander-in-chief of the army; in other words, he was an officeholder of unequalled power. This was an elected office, however; perhaps Pericles was simply a democratically chosen dictator. Ironically, one of his most controversial measures restricted Athenian citizenship. To acquire citizenship, one had to prove that both parents were Athenians. This rule was designed to prevent immigrants from becoming citizens for fear of diluting the original citizen fabric of Athens. This issue is a familiar one in most democratic societies today.

processes. Non-Shiite Muslims in Iran, for example, are severely discriminated against, while Shiite Muslims regularly vote in free elections.[30] The United States briefly regressed to a tribal democracy between 1942 and 1944, when the government interned citizens of Japanese descent, an obvious violation of the constitutional rights of 120,000 Americans. Their incarceration was not a happy memory either for them or for their fellow Americans who placed them in camps. The memory was revived after 9-11 when some Americans began to view citizens who are Muslim and/or of Middle Eastern descent as somehow less patriotic than other citizens or even in sympathy with terrorists. The dual notions that democracy has come a long way and still has a long way to go are equally reasonable assumptions.

Throughout their long histories, authoritarian regimes have varied considerably in terms of brutality and repressiveness. It seems reasonable for democracies, as they spring up in non-Western regions, to also vary in form and degree. Some may well remain tribal, restricting democracy to certain groups. After all, for most of their history, Western democracies themselves were restrictive and discouraged full citizen participation on the basis of race, ethnicity, gender, or religion. Just as these governments progressed, however, there seems little doubt that democracy will continue to evolve as a viable political system.

Chapter Summary

1. Despite the collapse of communism in Eastern Europe and the Soviet Union, the spread of democracy is far from guaranteed. Although it has expanded greatly over the last decade, many people around the world still view democracy with suspicion, distrust, or hostility.

2. Authoritarian forms of government preceded and still coexist with democratic forms. In several countries over the last decade, authoritarian regimes that have presided over substantial economic growth have gradually given way to democratization.

---

[30]Ibid.

3. Democratization is often resisted because of its association with modern morality, gender equality, and a secularized culture.

4. Samuel P. Huntington's concept of waves of democracy suggests that a third (and so far, successful) wave of democratic growth exists today. The first two waves were followed by reversals in which democracy receded, and there is no guarantee that a similar reversal won't slow the third wave.

5. Democracies are still rare in the Middle East and Africa. They are well established in Western Europe, are gaining footholds in Eastern Europe, have begun to tenuously appear in some of the former Soviet republics and East and South Asia, and are showing substantial promise in most of Latin America.

6. Firmly entrenched democracies do not require frequent changes in government. One political party may remain in control for several decades before giving up power peacefully.

7. Problems associated with severe demographic changes may influence a society's progress toward democracy. If the indigenous majority of the country is distrustful of a large ethnic minority, the majority may be tempted to deny the minority the full advantages of citizenship.

8. Several democracies or countries undergoing democratization seem destined to experiment with devolution. Many of these countries include regions that have long memories of political autonomy or outright independence. These regions often desire to reassert at least some degree of control over local affairs.

9. Many democracies, particularly those in close proximity to the Third World or developing countries, are encountering moral and political dilemmas as large numbers of desperate immigrants attempt to enter. Both legal and illegal immigration has become a major political issue in Western European and North American democracies.

10. Emerging democracies will democratize at their own rates and in their own ways. There is little reason to believe that future non-Western democracies will be carbon copies of the West.

Chapter 4 Quiz

1. Institutionalized government first appeared
   a. when democracy took hold.
   b. after the Congress of Vienna completed its work in 1815.
   c. about 10,000 ago.
   d. during the classical Greek period.

2. The Aryan Nation is a
   a. reference to Nazi Germany between 1933 and 1945.
   b. group in the United States that believes in racial purity.
   c. liberal religious organization.
   d. professional Canadian football team.

3. Restrictions on family size are rigorously enforced by the government in
   a. India.
   b. Mexico.
   c. China.
   d. Japan.

4. According to Samuel Huntington, democracy is currently experiencing its
   a. first wave.
   b. first reversal.
   c. third wave.
   d. second reversal.

5. The two countries in the Middle East with genuine claims to providing democratic political systems are
   a. Libya and Syria.
   b. Egypt and Saudi Arabia.
   c. Israel and Turkey.
   d. Jordan and Lebanon.

6. The three Baltic republics of Estonia, Latvia, and Lithuania all have significant ethnic minorities of
   a. Poles.
   b. Germans.
   c. Finns.
   d. Russians.

7. During the 1950s the term "economic miracle" was applied to describe the rapid post-war recovery of
   a. the United Kingdom.
   b. the United States.
   c. Germany.
   d. the Soviet Union.

8. Examples of East Asian tigers include all except which of the following?
   a. The Republic of (South) Korea
   b. Taiwan
   c. Indonesia
   d. Singapore

9. The Renaissance, Reformation, Enlightenment, and Industrial Revolution tended to facilitate
   a. monarchial rule.
   b. social breakdown.
   c. terror states.
   d. democracy.

10. The number of countries considered consistently democratic for at least a full century is around
    a. 7.
    b. 38.
    c. 43.
    d. 97.

PART 3

The Institutions of Government and the Political Process

The next four chapters emphasize the most basic features of modern political systems. Of course, some political systems are not modern. Many, for example, lack or prohibit a recognizable political party system (Chapter 8). On the other hand, the legislative, executive (including bureaucracies), and judicial functions, covered in Chapters 5, 6, and 7, respectively, are apparent in nearly all political systems. Even authoritarian systems (with some notable exceptions) evidence these three kinds of institutions, if only because they are useful to the regime. The chapters in this part concentrate on analyses of and examples from democratic regimes, discussing the important ways they resemble one another as well as how they differ.

Legislatures

KEY TERMS

impeachment
legislative councils
loyal opposition
minority government
parliamentary majority
parliamentary party

party discipline
party whips
referendum
religious constituency
Speaker of the House
vote of (no) confidence

Democratic systems usually have viable legislatures. No political democracy, in fact, functions without a representative assembly. Much of the progress of democratization in many countries is traceable to their national legislatures. The people elect a democratic legislature, and in the process they provide limited political prerogatives to their representatives for a stipulated term of office.

The notion of citizen-legislator is making a comeback, especially in the United States, where the idea of legislators with lifetime careers in politics is increasingly unpopular. Several members of the United States Congress have practically placed their hands on their hearts to insist they will serve no more than three terms, though several changed their minds anyway. Other democracies allow legislators to pursue lifelong political careers without any apparent adverse effects. Jacques Chirac, the current president of France, has been in national politics for forty years. The Israeli prime minister, Ehud Olmert, has been active politically for at least three decades. Both have held a variety of cabinet positions and have been in and out of government. Chirac is a former mayor of Paris while Olmert was mayor of Jerusalem.

referendum
A legal provision that allows the entire electorate in a region or a country to vote yes or no on an issue. The outcome becomes law without requiring legislative action.

In a crunch, it would be possible for people to make laws without a legislature. They could simply vote yea or nay in a national **referendum** on an issue. In fact, several democracies have constitutional procedures that allow the entire electorate to vote on such matters as taxation or whether to join an economic organization. One notable exception, the United States, has no provision for national referenda, though most states occasionally hold them.[1] For example, in the United States, Congress made the decision to join NAFTA (the North American Free Trade Association). Several European countries, in contrast, conducted a referendum on whether to join the European Economic Community. The referendum's outcome has the force of law.

Still, no country with the exception of Switzerland uses a national referendum on a regular basis.[2] France has used it only about a half dozen times since 1958, the year the Fifth Republic[3] was established. Many nations hold referenda on issues of critical importance or, as in France, when the executive wants to bypass the legislature. The referendum in effect makes the entire electorate a national legislature.

This chapter will emphasize democratic legislatures, but carefully and selectively. While all democracies have legislatures, they differ in their powers and in their relationships to the executive branch of the government.

---

[1]The United States Supreme Court in *City of Eastlake v. Forest City Enterprises, Inc.* (1976) maintained the right of the American people to legislate by referendum. See John T. Rourke, Richard P. Hiskes, and Cyrus Ernesto Zirakzadeh, *Direct Democracy and International Politics: Deciding Issues Through Referendums* (Boulder, Colorado: Lynne Rienner Publishers, Inc., 1992), 155.

[2]Switzerland by itself conducts about half of the nearly 1,000 referenda held annually throughout the world.

[3]Between 1789 and 1958, France experimented with a variety of regimes that included two empires, a restored monarchy, and four republics. Most of these ended because of military defeat, revolution, or both.

5-1 Legislative Beginnings

The legislature—normally an assemblage of chosen or elected representatives of the electorate—is probably the earliest and most durable political institution, one that maximizes access to the decision-making processes that impact entire societies. Legislatures can be traced back millennia: Classical Greece and Rome had vibrant legislatures. Rome even had a sort of two-chamber legislature. The Roman upper house was the Senate, a term that has obviously stuck, because Australia, Italy, France, Canada, and the United States still use it. The Roman Senate's membership, respectfully referred to as the "Fathers of Rome," was primarily representatives of Roman aristocracy. For the great majority of the citizenry who lacked aristocratic credentials, the Romans created popular assemblies, the equivalent of modern-day lower legislative houses. Bicameral legislatures are found elsewhere including Japan and South Korea, newer democracies that have also seen a need for upper and lower houses.

In the early centuries of the Roman Republic, the Senate consisted of energetic and public-minded members. It eventually deteriorated and became one of history's first "rubber-stamp" legislatures, agreeing to nearly everything the Roman emperor, often a product of the military and just as often an autocrat, wanted.

During the Greek city-state period and through the history of the Roman Republic, legislative assemblies functioned relatively well. They were responsible (as legislatures in parliamentary systems are now) for enacting laws as well as for furnishing the executive. In very small city-states, legislatures were composed of all adult male citizens, and these men made the decisions that immediately affected their own lives. If they voted to go to war, they became the soldiers; if they levied a tax, they paid it.

These assemblies were basically one-branch governments that selected, as in the case of Pericles, the civilian executive and military leadership, often for clearly defined terms of office. Some assemblies could grant life tenure for certain offices during difficult times. They could also grant emergency powers and create what might be called constitutional dictatorships, and they could function as juries in trials that involved the security of the state. Probably the body with the closest contemporary resemblance to these legislatures is the New England town meeting, where all residents are free to attend and to make decisions affecting their lives by majority vote.

Modern legislatures have deep roots. The British parliament, for example, has antecedents that are centuries old. Other European political systems are equally aged. Iceland boasts the oldest, longest-functioning national legislature in the world—theirs is nearly a millennium old, established when Scandinavian settlers arrived in the tenth century. All of this suggests that legislatures are time-tested political instruments for expressing the issues that are dominating public attention and dealing with them in an effective way. Legislative debates are basically clearinghouses that examine all sides of an issue before determining what will be done about it. The outcome of the debates and examinations is laws. For the most part, laws are both effective and obeyed. Some laws are quite frankly better than others and endure longer. Yet, in a flexible and democratic political system, laws can be revised or repealed as needed.

Not all legislatures, of course, are the same. Nor are all legislative bodies popularly elected. The strong social class divisions in Europe, for example, were long reflected in their national parliaments and, to an appreciable extent, still are. The institutions of upper and lower legislative houses developed because social class lines were very distinct. Membership in the upper houses, such as the House of Lords in Britain, required an aristocratic pedigree. Lower houses were filled with members of lesser social (but not necessarily lesser financial) standing. Hence, the British House of Commons was, as the name suggests, composed of members who were commoners, not members of the aristocracy.

Even the electorate itself reflects class lines. Neither members of the House of Lords nor members of the royal family can participate as either voters or candidates for seats in the Commons. To do so requires giving up one's title, at least for the duration of one's political career. The decline of upper houses and the rise in the power of lower houses corresponded to the widening process of democratization in several Western European countries in the early nineteenth century. By the early years of the twentieth century, most democracies were increasingly relying upon the popularly elected lower houses to make laws, and many had begun to restrict the legislative prerogatives of the upper house. A few countries, like Sweden, abolished their upper houses.

5-2 Legislatures in Parliamentary Systems

This chapter and the next show that, in many ways, parliamentary democracies remain one-branch governments. It is still the parliament (or, usually, the lower house of parliament) that supplies the top personnel of the executive department. The United States is actually one of a minority of democracies (France has been another since 1958) that chooses the executive independently of the legislature and that constitutionally provides for co-equal and separate government branches. Germany, Japan, and the United States are three of a small number of democracies that grant their upper houses substantial legislative powers. See Figure 5–1 for a direct comparison of the American and British systems of bicameral legislature.

Countries serious about representative government have concentrated tremendous powers in the legislative branch. Indeed, the legislature is often the only branch with any powers: The American system of co-equal branches is not a widely emulated arrangement. Even the United States began its political existence as a one-branch government; the Continental Congress was the only governmental body for a decade (1777–1787) until the Constitution was drafted and ratified (1787–1789), creating the familiar three-branch government.

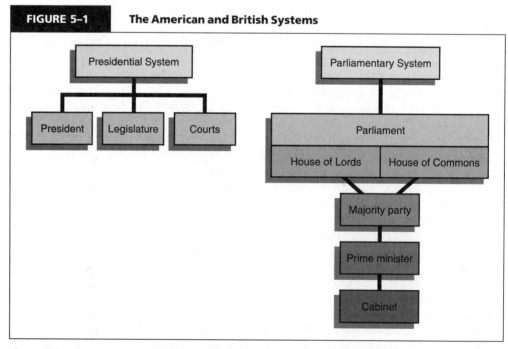

FIGURE 5–1   **The American and British Systems**

The presidential system in the United States is composed of three equal but separate branches: executive (president), legislative (Congress), and judicial (the courts).

A Note On	THE EUROPEAN PARLIAMENT

Legislatures can have regional importance that goes beyond national borders. The European Parliament is a legislative (some would say quasi-legislative) body that includes 567 members elected from twenty-five European countries. These countries belong to the European Union, a primarily economic organization. The Parliament's functions are still being clarified.

In a sense, the European Parliament is a legislature that doesn't legislate. It is unfair to simply refer to the European Community as a debating society. It does examine and evaluate the policies of the European Commission, a quasi-executive body. The most important aspect of the European Parliament is probably its potential. Its membership represents twenty-five countries and around 480 million Central and West Europeans. Countries in the eastern half of the continent gradually joined the European Union after the collapse of its communist regimes and elected representatives to the European Parliament. The Parliament may one day be regarded as one of the first critical steps toward political integration on a continental scale.

Some observers believe that in most parliamentary democracies, political power has been transferred from the legislative to the executive. This common observation may be exaggerated. After all, parliaments can bring down governments with a vote of no confidence. Moreover, democratic parliaments do not simply rubber-stamp anything the government proposes: Rank-and-file parliamentary members like to be asked for their opinions and insist on being informed by their party's leadership. It is almost a certainty that political power can more easily revert to the executive branch during periods of great urgency or when a country feels itself to be mortally threatened. Of course, the public and the executive may have conflicting points of view as to whether a mortal threat exists. For example, the September 11, 2001, terrorist events boosted both the popularity of the United States president and the public's confidence in his leadership. In view of such an endorsement, Congress was prepared for the most part to support and authorize a military response to terrorism. In the last months of 2002 and early in 2003, the threat of war with Iraq did not solidify support as readily. Instead, a national debate ensued as to whether such a conflict was either necessary or inevitable. That continued gradually dissolved after the official end of hostilities but was renewed during the insurgency that got underway by early 2004.

Legislatures can be unforgiving when neither occurs. When British Prime Minister Anthony Eden evaded giving a full account of a combined British and French invasion of the Suez Canal Zone in 1956, members of his own Conservative party were outraged. They might have been placated had not the United Nations forced both countries' military forces out a few weeks later through a rare cooperative effort involving the United States and the Soviet Union. Eden was forced to retire from the prime ministership by early 1957. President Lyndon B. Johnson (1963–1969) was besieged by members of Congress of both parties opposed to his escalation of the American involvement in Vietnam. In 2003 many Congressional Democrats opposed American military involvement in Iraq and challenged President Bush's policy in that military operation. This issue was an important one during the 2006 congressional elections.

In some instances, parliaments may have *too much* power or, perhaps more accurately, exercise too little responsibility. During the brief career of the French Fourth Republic (1946–1958), for example, the French National Assembly got rid of governments in rather quick succession. During this period, new governments were formed on the average of every seven months. When the constitution of the Fifth Republic was drafted, it shifted power from the legislative to the executive branch. The president of the Republic was to be selected in a separate popular election (purposely held at a different time from National Assembly elections). And French presidents justifiably claim to have a mandate from the people, because they must be elected by an absolute numerical majority.

There is no doubt that the focus of power in parliamentary systems has shifted from the legislature to the executive. The executive often proposes most legislation, though in Britain members of Parliament can introduce bills that reflect particular needs in their districts. Moreover, members of parliamentary systems usually have the opportunity to ask cabinet ministers questions. "Question time," a set, weekly period during which the prime minister must answer anything thrown at him by members of the opposition (this can be seen on C-SPAN on Sundays at 9 P.M. eastern time) is most beneficial to opposition members; they can get information from the executive branch, or, in many cases, embarrass the executive if he or she can't or won't provide information.

5-3　Legislatures in Nondemocratic Systems

Rubberstamp legislatures are in ample supply in dictatorships today. They exist only to provide the regime with a cloak of legitimacy and to enthusiastically voice approval of any and all government actions. Although the Soviet Union is gone, its legislature, the Supreme Soviet, will probably hold the record for consistent rubber stamping for a long time, with an unbroken unanimous endorsement of all legislation submitted to it for nearly seventy years. Much the same situation currently prevails in China's National People's Congress. The typical totalitarian legislature is huge, often composed of over 1,000 members who are carefully chosen for their loyalty to the regime and who can be counted on to support all executive decisions, regardless of whether the decisions are humane, in accordance with international law, or even consistent with their own country's constitution. Table 5–1 gives additional details on the legislative assemblies in selected nondemocratic political systems.

Understandably, there isn't much to say about the legislative process in countries that still employ rubber-stamp legislatures. Some countries have no legislatures at all. Most of these are traditionalist monarchies in the Middle East or elsewhere. Some do have **legislative councils** that act only in an advisory capacity and are dependent upon the monarch for continued service. In traditionalist monarchies such as the Kingdom of Saudi Arabia, the monarch usually relies on family members (the Saudi Arabian ruler typically has several hundred close family members in his retinue) for advice on policy matters.

legislative councils
Advisory bodies that monarchs in Persian Gulf states and other traditionalist regimes choose and maintain.

TABLE 5–1	Legislative Assemblies in Nondemocratic Political Systems*		
Country	**Legislature**	**Main Features**
Brunei	Legislative Council	29 members appointed by the Sultan
China	National People's Congress	All 2,976 seats controlled by Communist party
Iran	Islamic Consultative Assembly	290 members elected by several religious factions
Democratic People's Republic of (North) Korea	Supreme People's Assembly	All 687 seats controlled by Communist party

*Not all nondemocratic regimes have equally undemocratic legislatures. Iran does have relatively free elections, but it is very difficult for any candidate who does not subscribe to a fairly stringent religious agenda to win a seat.

5-3a Evolving Legislatures

The collapse of the communist regimes in Eastern Europe may have ushered in a new era for national legislatures. Although countries in Eastern Europe all had parliaments, during the Cold War they were ineffective. A parliament in a communist country exists primarily to endorse the policies of the executive branch, which in turn is dominated by the Communist party. In the 1990s, former communist countries elected legislators in competitive elections, but few candidates had any legislative experience. Those who did were former communist legislators who, understandably, were still inexperienced in the political art of compromise and negotiated legislation. One scholar made the following observation during the middle 1990s:

> New members in new parliaments are not well-equipped to face their new tasks. The members are inexperienced. Depending upon the duration of the dictatorship, few persons in society will themselves have any personal experience of democratic procedures. They will be asked to make new decisions on new problems without guidance or experience in the open expression of disagreements.[4]

The Eastern Europeans had to learn democracy from the ground up. They did reasonably well. Most have applied for membership in the European Union, an association that brings many economic benefits. In 2002, four Eastern European states and three former Soviet republics were admitted to NATO. In both cases, the requirements are stringent: Strong democratic institutions and an emphasis on free market economics must be present. The future success of political democracy in Eastern European countries may well depend upon the ability of new legislators to learn fast.

5-4 Upper Houses

Upper houses do matter, even though most of them lack substantial legislative powers. The House of Lords is not and does not pretend to be the equal of the House of Commons. Its lack of real power helps to explain why most members don't bother to go to the sessions. Others become bored with the proceedings and can go for decades without visiting the House of Lords: Inheriting a seat doesn't necessarily mean inheriting an interest in politics. If a member of the House of Lords does want a serious political career, he or she (there are now ladies in the House of Lords) can resign his or her peerage and stand for a seat in the House of Commons.

Memberships in many upper houses are won in rather undemocratic fashion (see Table 5–2). In a democracy, this fact alone generally makes the upper house less powerful than the lower house. Members are normally selected by regional or state governments, special electoral colleges, or the executive. The British monarch can often recruit members by simply appointing distinguished individuals (often leading politicians retiring from the House of Commons) life peers. The Senate in Italy is unusual in that most of its membership is popularly elected, but it still allows the creation of some lifetime appointments.[5]

Upper houses do matter in some political systems, and they attract very ambitious politicians. The United States Senate is an obvious example. The U.S. Senate is exceptional in that it is both a powerful and a popularly elected legislative chamber. Most upper houses, whether they have political significance or not, are filled with people who have either inherited their seats or have arrived at them without bothering with a popular election. For instance, a huge electoral college of over 80,000 members, most of them municipal councilors, choose the members of the

---

[4]David M. Olson, "The New Parliaments of New Democracies: The Experience of the Federal Assembly of the Czech and Slovak Federal Republic," in *The Emergence of East Central European Parliaments: The First Steps*, ed. Attila Agh, (Budapest: Hungarian Centre of Democracy Studies, 1994) 37.

[5]Former prime ministers, for example, may be elevated to one of seven appointed Senate seats. For an interesting insight into Italian politics, see Alexander Stille, "The Fall of Caesar," *The New Yorker*, September 11,1995, 68–83.

A Note On	UNICAMERAL LEGISLATURES

If upper houses do not have much real political significance in the legislative process, then why do they exist? Many countries have either eliminated upper houses or never had one in the first place. Because of their diversity, federal systems such as Canada and the United States usually find it convenient to establish upper houses to represent geographical units. Smaller and relatively homogeneous countries often get along nicely with a single legislative chamber. (Notable exceptions include countries such as Denmark and Norway, which, for historical reasons, have retained bicameral legislatures.)

Most unicameral legislatures, like most of the countries they are located in, are relatively small. Costa Rica, Israel, and Lebanon, for example, are countries with populations around or under six million. Their national legislatures have only 60, 120, and 99 members, respectively. Sweden, with a population of nearly nine million, is one of the larger countries with a unicameral legislature; its chamber has 349 members. South Korea is somewhat unusual with a population of around fifty million and a unicameral legislature (National Assembly) of 299 members. South Korea, though, is territorially small, about the size of Indiana. Legislation is not necessarily more efficient in countries with unicameral systems. As mentioned earlier, most countries assign limited roles to their upper chambers anyway. Moreover, a single chamber might very well be unable to handle the workload many legislatures increasingly confront. An exception to the general rule of small country/unicameral legislature is China. Even though China's population of 1.3 billion is spread out in the world's fourth largest state territory, the country's legislature is confined to one house.

TABLE 5–2	**Methods of Selection for Upper House Membership**

Country	Chamber	Form of Selection
France	Senate	Special electoral college of municipal councilors
Germany	Bundesrat	State governments
Italy	Senate	Mostly popular election; some appointees
Japan	House of Councilors	Multi-seat districts and proportional representation
United Kingdom	House of Lords	Mostly inherited or royal appointment
United States	Senate	Popular election

French Senate, and in Germany, the federal republic's sixteen state governments select the members of the powerful Federal Council (Bundesrat).

With some exceptions, upper houses tend to have substantial legislative powers in federal systems, such as Germany and the United States. In these systems, states or provinces completely or largely control a great many of their own affairs, including education, health care, public transportation, and taxation. Regional governments are less powerful or nonexistent in smaller and more homogeneous systems. In Germany, the Bundesrat consists of delegations of three to five members for each of the sixteen states (the exact number is based on the state's population). Each state government charges its delegation with advocating and protecting the state's particular interests.

The U.S. Senate and the German Bundesrat are arguably the most powerful upper houses in the industrialized democracies. Upper houses in most other democracies can at best delay legislation the lower house has passed. The power to delay legislation, however, should not be underestimated; it is often actually helpful to the legislative process. The well-educated and legal-minded members of the House of Lords on occasion make very useful revisions to legislation sent to them from the Commons.

TABLE 5–3	Selected Countries' Goverments	
Country	**Type of Legislature**	**Type of Governmental System**
United Kingdom	Bicameral	Parliamentary
Germany	Bicameral	Parliamentary
Japan	Bicameral	Parliamentary
India	Bicameral	Parliamentary
Canada	Bicameral	Parliamentary
Italy	Bicameral	Parliamentary
United States	Bicameral	Presidential
Brazil	Bicameral	Presidential
France	Bicameral	Presidential
Mexico	Bicameral	Presidential
Russia	Bicameral	Presidential
China	Unicameral	Totalitarian dictatorship
Israel	Unicameral	Parliamentary
Denmark	Unicameral	Parliamentary
South Korea	Unicameral	Parliamentary
Sweden	Unicameral	Parliamentary
Costa Rica	Unicameral	Presidential

Legislative assemblies have often been rather noisy and sometimes even violent in their debates. The majority party that controls the government in the British House of Commons and the minority party, politely known as the **loyal opposition**, are separated by a "sword's length," a tradition dating back to the time when members habitually wore swords and sometimes challenged one another to a duel. Shoving and brawling are still a regular feature in some of the newer democracies in East Asia. Taiwanese and South Korean citizens watch events in their respective National Assemblies for much the same reason Americans attend hockey games: A fistfight could break out at any moment.

Upper houses usually have smaller memberships than lower chambers. Most upper houses have precisely set memberships: two senators from each of the fifty states in the United States, for a total of 100; three, four, or five—depending on the state's size—from each of the sixteen states in the German federation, for a current total of sixty-nine. The relatively smaller size of the upper house allows its members to do business more efficiently—at least, most of the time. Many upper houses have delay tactics built into their parliamentary rules, although it is difficult to find one equivalent to the U.S. Senate's filibuster.

Most upper houses have limited powers because they are not popularly chosen; upper house members in nonelective systems cannot claim a popular mandate. In a democracy, this means that political power in most instances must reside in the lower house. This is especially true in parliamentary systems, where the lower house supplies the personnel for the executive. In presidential systems, the chief executive is chosen separately from the legislature.

Table 5–3 shows a list of selected countries with unicameral (one chamber) and bicameral (two chambers) legislatures worldwide.

5-5 Lower Houses

With a few important exceptions, most legislative business in a democratic political system is conducted in the lower house. In parliamentary systems, the same political party controls both the lower house and the executive. The opposition may actually

loyal opposition
In democratic regimes, the "loyal opposition" is usually the minority party in the legislature. The minority will challenge the government on various issues while awaiting the opportunity to become the majority in the next election.

TABLE 5–4	Some Distinctions between the U.S. House of Representatives and the British House of Commons	
Feature	United States	British
Term limitations	Three terms (6 years) in several states	none
Length of term	2 years	up to 5 years
Size of constituency	average of 560,000	under 100,000
Nominating process	mostly primaries*; possible run-off	interview by leadership of local party

*In some states, a party caucus or convention rather than a primary election is held to select candidates.

control the upper house, but, its power may be limited. For example, the Conservative party in Britain is in perpetual control of the House of Lords, but it influences legislation only in innocuous ways. In contrast, in a presidential system, where the executive and legislative are elected separately, opposing political parties may control each branch. During 1993–2001, for example, a Democrat occupied the American presidency; for most of that time a Republican majority controlled both houses of Congress.

From 1979 until 1997, the Conservative party held the majority in the British House of Commons and therefore chose the executive leadership. The British prime minister and the rest of the cabinet ministers hold seats in the Commons and are expected to attend its sessions. There is no division of powers in Britain as there is in the United States. This **parliamentary majority**, the party controlling both the House of Commons and the executive, is crucial to the passage of legislation. (Table 5–4 points out other distinctions between the lower houses in the United States and Great Britain.)

Parliamentary majorities are essential if a government is to be formed and to endure. In a parliamentary system, if a government proposes a piece of legislation and loses the vote on it, the government can collapse; the prime minister is ousted and a new majority may take over. To put it succinctly, no parliamentary government can survive without a guarantee of majority support for its policies. In the mid-1990s in the British House of Commons, the Conservative party controlled more seats than all other parties combined (even though it secured less than a majority of the popular vote, an issue to be examined in a later chapter). The Conservatives therefore controlled the government. However, in May 1997, the Labour party gained control for the first time since 1979 because the Conservatives became increasingly associated with Britain's economic decline. Moreover, the Conservatives themselves were politically disunited at that time and were fighting over ideology. Labour's leader, Tony Blair, became the new prime minister. Labour went on to win the next two parliamentary elections and in 2007 celebrated a full decade in control of the British government, its longest run of success in nearly a century.

Forming a legislative majority, however, often requires a coalition of two or more parties. The parliamentary democracy of Israel, for example, has produced government by coalitions since its establishment; no one party can seem to win a majority of votes. In such a situation, the executive must be carefully selected to represent all the parties in the coalition and all their political points of view.

The executive branch of government in a parliamentary system does seem to get most of its legislation passed. But it is also true that it carefully considers proposed legislation. After all, majority support is required, or the party may lose power; legislative proposals must be carefully crafted to secure the endorsement of rank-and-file members. Usually, **party whips** act as liaisons between the party

parliamentary majority
The majority party in a parliamentary system. The executive must receive consistent support from a numerical majority of legislators to continue in office and to secure the passage of its legislative program.

party whips
Legislators who work between the party leadership and the rank-and-file members; whips must ensure that on any parliamentary issue, all members will be present and voting, and they must try to persuade members to support the party's position.

BIOGRAPHY

Nancy Pelosi (b. 1940)

The 2006 congressional elections produced a Democratic party majority in the House of Representatives for the first time in 12 years. The then minority leader, Nancy Pelosi, became the nearly automatic candidate for Speaker of the House, a position being vacated by Dennis Hastert who had held the job since 1999. Representative Pelosi comes from an old political family (her father and brother served as mayors of Baltimore) and has served 20 years in the House, consistently winning re-election with 80 percent of the vote in California's eighth district in the San Francisco area.

It is important to know who she is (50 percent or the American people in a recent poll did not recognize her name in 2006). In 2001 she became the first woman in American history to become the House minority leader of a political party. In 2007 she became the first woman in history to become Speaker, next in line for the presidency after the vice president should a vacancy occur. Her differences with the Republican party are well known and her elevation to Speaker suggests that the congressional term during 2007-2009 should be an interesting one. Speaker Pelosi occupies a very strong position and is generally reputed to represent views that are in opposition to most of the Bush administration's domestic and foreign policies. The critical issue of Iraq will certainly be in play since a great many of Pelosi's supporters opposed the war and are currently calling for a quick or even immediate withdrawal of American forces. This matter will be a real test of the bi-partisan cooperation between Democrats and Republicans that both the president and the speaker are calling for. A great many Republicans, however, consider Pelosi as a spokesperson for the radical left of the Democratic party while their Democratic counterparts regards Bush as representative of the extreme right wing of the Republican party. American politics has usually been dominated by the ability of both parties to negotiate and compromise. Speaker Pelosi and President Bush both have a great deal to live up to.

leadership and rank-and-file members, helping to get proposed legislation in shape and then persuading party members to be present and voting when the legislation reaches the house floor. There seems to be a correlation between the size of a ruling party's majority and its leadership's respect for rank-and-file opinions. The more narrow the majority, the more influence rank-and-file members have on legislation.

5-5a Party Discipline

Party discipline, the efforts parties make to ensure that legislators support their parties' official position on legislation, is normally exerted during the legislative process. Party discipline is stronger in some systems than in others. American presidents, for example, expect little party discipline and even a fair amount of defiance from members of the same party in Congress. In parliamentary systems, however, parties require strong discipline not only to pass legislation, but to retain control of the government. Presidents can lose votes in Congress and even see Congress override a veto and still remain in office; prime ministers have no such advantage.

Party discipline has two complementary aspects. First, it is crucial to accomplishing legislative business. Both the government and the opposition need to know how many votes they can count on to either formulate or oppose legislation. Second, representatives need to be faithful to party policies if they want the party's support during the next campaign. In most democracies the majority of voters tend to cast their ballots more for the party than for the candidate.

Both the voters and the party leadership in a parliamentary system are horrified should a member of parliament defy the party line. A maverick parliamentarian has on occasion survived the displeasure of the party establishment, but consistent defiance is usually a sure-fire method of political suicide. The local party leadership will simply replace the delinquent parliamentarian with another candidate in time for the next election.

Breaks from party discipline in a parliamentary system can occur but are remarkably infrequent. After all, parliamentarians with similar ideological convictions naturally tend to vote together. Moreover, rank-and-file politicians tend to owe their careers to the party. It is very unusual for aspiring politicians to be elected to public office because of celebrity status or because they have enough money to

Party discipline
The efforts political parties make to get their own legislators to support the party line on various issues, to guarantee both party solidarity and party support for the individual members at election time.

A Note On   LEGISLATURE SIZE

Legislatures may become unwieldy if their membership grows excessively large. It's hard to determine an optimal size for a legislature that both allow it to represent the various interests in society and to complete its work efficiently. Consider, for example, some of the numbers: The British House of Commons includes 650 members, the French National Assembly 577, the American House of Representatives 435, the Japanese House of Representatives 480, and the Italian Chamber of Deputies 630. There is nothing magical about any number, and all of these numbers have changed from time to time. China's unicameral legislature, the National People's Congress, is the largest in the world with 2,985 members.

Legislatures that become much larger than 600 members do seem to have difficulty conducting business. During the last decades of the Soviet Union, each chamber of the Supreme Soviet had around 1,500 members. Some of the Supreme Soviet's committees were as big as entire legislative houses in several Western democracies. This huge membership made it almost impossible for various factions and coalitions to form, as they do in democratic legislatures. Large size was most likely intended to make sure that divisions never occurred or would not matter if they did. All votes taken were, by design, unanimous.

Predictably, upper houses are normally much smaller (the British House of Lords is a notable exception) and sometimes, though certainly not always, more efficient. The American, French, and Italian Senates have 100, 317, and 315, members, respectively. One of the most powerful upper houses in the world is the German Bundesrat (Federal Council) with just sixty-nine members. Only the United States Senate is popularly elected, and its powers are substantial. The U.S. Senate is perhaps the only upper house in a democracy that includes members who frequently challenge executive authority, perhaps partially because several senators may be eyeing the presidency themselves.[6]

Speaker of the House
The presiding leader of the lower legislative chamber. The Speaker has substantial powers when it comes to setting legislative agendas, recognizing members, and maintaining order. This term is used in the English-speaking democracies.

finance their own campaigns. They generally are elected (or defeated) on the basis of their party label. Political life rarely exists outside the party in a parliamentary system.

Even when party discipline is weak, as it is in the United States, there is usually no question as to who has the ultimate authority to decide which legislation to try to enact into law. Legislative roles differ from one system to another, however. The **Speaker of the House**, for example, has different powers in the U.S. Congress than the British parliament. While the American Speaker is expected to be partisan in advocating or opposing legislative programs, the British Speaker is expected to be completely nonpartisan, regardless of his previous political experience. The American Speaker always comes from the majority party, while the Commons Speaker, once installed in office, no longer belongs to any party and usually stays in office for a lengthy period of time regardless of which party controls a parliamentary majority.

The United States Congress may present at least a partial exception to most notions of party discipline or institutional control of party members. A member of Congress normally has an individual base of support that only modestly relies on the national party organization. Some U.S. legislators, especially from more populous states, are also nurturing presidential or vice-presidential ambitions. One or two of them have even been former vice presidents.[7]

---

[6]Most of these senators are not successful in their quest to become president. The last sitting senator to be elected president was John F. Kennedy in 1960, and no president since Richard M. Nixon (1969–1974) has served in the Senate. Still, these facts did not discourage at least four senators from seeking the Republican presidential nomination in 1996, including the eventual nominee. Robert Dole resigned his seat as the senior senator from Kansas in that year to run as the Republican candidate for president.

[7]The only example of a former American president returning to the Senate after leaving the presidency is Andrew Johnson. His tenure was brief, however. Johnson died several months after arriving at the Senate in 1875. Hubert Humphrey, vice president from 1965 to 1969, returned to the United States Senate in 1971 and remained there until his death in 1978. He had previously served in the Senate from 1949 to 1964. John Quincy Adams, America's sixth president (1825–1829), is the only former chief executive to pursue a career in the House of Representatives. His career in the House (1831–1848) was long and distinguished. Alexander Stephens, Confederate Vice President during 1861 and 1865, served three terms in the House of Representatives during the 1870s. In 2000 Hillary Clinton became the first former First Lady to seek and win election to the Senate. She was re-elected in 2006 and then prepared to seek the Democratic Party's presidential nomination in 2008.

All of this suggests that parliamentary systems are smooth-running affairs compared to systems that don't enforce strong party discipline. But this is not necessarily true. Challenges to the party leadership are far from unknown in parliaments—they simply come from the opposition party. In a typical parliament, cabinet ministers are also legislators and are therefore subject to scrutiny from the opposition. Opposing legislators seek every opportunity to ask embarrassing questions of a minister whose department is having trouble providing public services or who is suspected of corruption.

In fact, it is part of the loyal opposition's job to keep the majority on its toes. It often spends most of its time challenging government-sponsored legislation. Considering that the government controls a parliamentary majority and is nearly certain to win any vote, one might ask why the opposition bothers. The answer is simple. By stating in a public forum its ideological position on a piece of legislation, the loyal opposition reveals what it would do if it became the majority party after the next election. This enables it to offer an alternative to the electorate.

Infrequently, a **minority government** forms as the result of an indecisive parliamentary election. For example, the February 1974 national elections for the House of Commons yielded no party with an absolute majority of seats. The Labour party had a plurality of seats, however, and was able to join forces with the small Liberal party in an unofficial coalition. The arrangement was short-lived, as minority governments usually are, and another election was held eight months later that provided Labour with a small but workable majority.

Minority governments are understandably weak and usually of brief duration. The executive in such a situation tends to lose power to the legislature. The parliament, after all, has a majority of seats the government doesn't control. The government's best chance for survival is if the opposition is divided, as it often is in a legislature populated by several political parties. One other consideration may also provide a reprieve for a minority government: Legislators may not want to risk their seats again soon after an election and may cooperate with the government (at least to an extent) in an effort to avoid another electoral contest.

Occasionally, legislative proposals are neither partisan in origin nor require the imposition of party discipline when it comes to a vote. For instance, the question of whether to impose capital punishment on convicted murderers in Britain is a moral issue. In such matters, each individual parliamentary member is left to vote his or her conscience.

At first glance, a parliamentary system seems much more efficient than the presidential system in the United States and most other countries in the western hemisphere. This is because the lower house in a parliamentary government, thanks to party discipline, tends to approve nearly all legislation the government submits to it. Also, because there is no separation of powers in such a system, law, once approved, remains law unless the lower house repeals its own legislation. Such a repeal is unlikely to happen unless the legislation sponsor—usually the government—agrees. With the government in effective control of a parliamentary majority, an "elective dictatorship"[8] can prevail.

The best hope of blunting any lower house excesses in a parliamentary system rests with the unelected upper house. In Britain, for example, the House of Lords raised a hue and cry over the Police Bill the House of Commons passed, a bill that would allow law enforcement agencies to "break into anyone's home or office in secret, carry out searches and plant eavesdropping devices."[9] In this matter, the Lords practically condemned the bill as an affront to individual rights. The public concurred, and the Commons was moved to reconsider the legislation.[10]

minority government
Occurs in a parliamentary system when no party or coalition of parties can secure a numerical majority of legislative seats; a minority government functions only until a new election, which often occurs within several months.

---

[8]Anthony Lewis, "Champions of Liberty," *The New York Times*, January 31, 1997, sec. A.

[9]Ibid.

[10]Ibid.

5-6 The Legislature and Representative Government

The ideal of popular selection of legislators is generally regarded as admirable. Yet the selection process does not always permit the widest possible choices, even in democratic systems. From the time it gained its independence from France in 1943 to its collapse in the civil war that began in 1975 and 1976 and didn't end until about a decade and a half later, Lebanon functioned as the most democratic state in the Arab world. However, Lebanon's political system rested rather nervously on arrangements that reflected its sectarian character. Its numerous religious sects had to be politically accommodated to avoid violence.

Though ethnically and linguistically an Arab country, Lebanon's population is divided into a variety of Islamic and Christian communities. The 128 National Assembly seats are distributed proportionally among seventeen officially recognized **religious constituencies** (four Orthodox Christian, seven Uniate Christian, five Islamic, and one Jewish). The seventeen sects double as political parties at election time. Even the executive is determined by religious sect: The president must always be a Maronite Christian, the prime minister a Sunni Muslim. To complicate the situation even further, a Syrian army of 30,000 occupied a portion of Lebanon for two decades until 2005 and often dictated Lebanese domestic and foreign policy.

Prior to its civil war, the distribution of power in Lebanon was based on the population of each sect. That sounds fair until one learns that the last census was taken in 1932, when Christians were the majority. They aren't any longer; the Islamic sects are now the most likely majority, and they are understandably urging a redistribution of political power.

The arrangement in Lebanon was precarious and clumsy, but it was also a formula for civil peace that has endured for a third of a century. Lebanon's political system was not new. Some congressional districts in the United States have been bizarrely drawn as a result of the process called gerrymandering to purposely include African-American majorities with the assumption that such districts would elect African Americans to Congress. Decades ago, some district lines were drawn, at times rather bizarrely, to guarantee white majorities. Figure 5–2 illustrates the

religious constituency
A voting group politically defined largely by its predominant religious affiliation.

| FIGURE 5–2 | The Original Gerrymander—Massachusetts 1812 |

The practice of drawing district lines for partisan political advantage has a long history in American politics.

original gerrymandering, which occurred early in American history, to ensure one party's dominance.

By definition, democracies attempt to guarantee representation for the major segments of the population. Legislatures are therefore expected to reflect the electorate's major components and preferences. They rarely do so completely. In the United States, for example, only about a tenth of the 535 members of Congress are women. In contract, in Norway women occupy about half of the parliamentary seats. Norway also has a female prime minister. This makes Norway one of a handful of countries to achieve gender equality.

It follows that if some groups are underrepresented, others must be overrepresented. In the English-speaking democracies, elections are decided in a winner-take-all system: Whichever candidate receives a plurality of the votes wins the seat. Such an electoral process frequently means that a large minority or even a majority cast ballots for candidates who do not gain legislative seats. Some parliamentary systems are sensitive to this problem—they allow smaller parties that receive as little as 5 percent of the total vote (or less, in some countries) to earn seats. This more equitable arrangement, though, creates other problems that will be examined in a later chapter.

5-7 Powers and Limitations of the Legislature

No legislature is all powerful but some are more powerful than others, depending on time and place. Over the last several decades, some legislative authority has been gradually transferred to the executive in some systems. The amount of transfer varies by country and, to some extent, by the popularity and persuasive appeal of the executive. In the United States, a series of relatively weak one-term presidents, from 1961 on, made few inroads on lessening the prerogatives of Congress. In 1974, for example, Congress was instrumental in forcing Richard Nixon to resign the presidency and effectively appointing his successor, Gerald Ford. Legislatures in almost every democratic political system continue to serve as the recruiting ground for future members of the executive branch.

5-7a Legislative Selection of the Executive

Legislatures do more than pass laws. One of their important functions is to perform as an electoral college. The **parliamentary parties** in the British House of Commons, for example, choose their party leaders knowing that those leaders may become prime minister. When Margaret Thatcher resigned the prime ministership in 1990, the Conservative party selected John Major as her successor. When the majority party chooses its leader, it is actually choosing the next prime minister. The queen asks the majority party leader to form a government (a request that is never refused), and no one is surprised at the result.

In Germany, the chancellor is chosen directly by the Bundestag in a vote taken as a new session opens following a national election. The vote generally follows party lines. Thus, the leader of the party that controls a majority of Bundestag seats or has the support of allied parties becomes chancellor.

In the United States, the House of Representatives, in the rare circumstance that no candidate for president secures the required majority in the electoral college, can select the president. While this has happened in only two elections, 1800 and 1824, it has come close to happening on several other occasions. In the 1948, 1968, 1992, 1996, and 2000 elections, third-party candidates nearly prevented any candidate from securing an electoral-college majority, and in all cases they did prevent the victorious candidate from winning an absolute popular majority. In 2000 the Democratic candidate, Al Gore, received a half million more popular

parliamentary party
Those members of a political party who hold seats in the national legislature and are essentially the leadership of the party.

TABLE 5–5	Legislative Selection of the Head of Government
Federal Republic of Germany	Chancellor is chosen by a majority vote of the membership of the Bundestag.
France	No legislative influence; presidents are popularly elected, but the National Assembly confirms the president's choice of prime minister.
Japan	Prime Minister is chosen by a majority vote of the House of Representatives.
United Kingdom	Monarch asks leader of the majority party to form a government.
United States	If no presidential candidate secures an electoral-college majority, the House of Representatives will choose the president.

votes than the Republican candidate, George W. Bush. However, Bush won by securing just four more electoral-college votes than Gore, one of the tightest presidential elections in American history. (See Table 5–5 for a summary of how different legislatures select the head of government.)

Since the ratification of the Twenty-fifth Amendment in 1967, the U.S. Congress can also vote on a replacement, nominated by the president, if the vice-presidential office becomes vacant through resignation or death. When a vacancy occurred in 1973 because of Vice President Spiro Agnew's resignation, both houses confirmed Gerald Ford, President Richard Nixon's choice, as vice president. The next year, after Ford became president following Nixon's own resignation, Congress confirmed his choice of Nelson Rockefeller as vice president.

The government introduces most of the bills in a parliamentary system. In a presidential system, members of the legislature submit much legislation individually or collaboratively. The American president, however, is the "chief legislator" in one sense: Any of his supporters in Congress can introduce legislation the administration formulates. The president makes his policy desires known in an annual state of the union address as well as more informally in press conferences and in meetings with congressional leaders. The president rarely gets everything he wants, even if his party is the congressional majority. Members of the president's party tend to pay close attention to the preferences of their own constituencies, which may not be in concert with those of the administration.

Legislatures in both parliamentary and presidential systems do possess ultimate controls on the executive. In a parliamentary system, the government must at all times have the support of the legislative body. Should the government lose a **vote of confidence**, it usually has to leave office. The tenure of presidents is somewhat safer but is explored in greater detail in the following chapter. The American president, for example, serves a four-year term regardless of how many legislative battles he loses with Congress. The French president is assured of a five-year term even if his party loses control of the National Assembly.

Nevertheless, an unhappy legislature can usually remove a president in certain cases. **Impeachment** allows the legislature to make serious charges against a president and to remove him or her if found guilty of wrongdoing. In the United States, the House can accuse a president of "high crimes and misdemeanors," and the Senate tries the case. (The Senate actually receives the charges of impeachment from the House and then acts as a jury.) To be constitutional, there must be good reason to believe the president has broken the law. Only twice in American history has a president faced impeachment proceedings: Andrew Johnson was tried in 1867 and Bill Clinton in 1999. Both were acquitted. Another president, Richard M.

vote of (no) confidence
A device often used by the legislative opposition in a parliamentary system to embarrass or bring down the government. The government must win every vote of confidence; if it doesn't, it no longer controls the legislative majority, and a new government is formed.

impeachment
The process in place in presidential systems that allows legislatures to charge officeholders with wrongdoing and remove them from office if they are found guilty.

Nixon, resigned from the presidency in 1974 to avoid almost certain impeachment and likely conviction.

Impeachment suggests that Congress has a judicial role. The U.S. House of Representatives can bring impeachment charges not only against presidents but against federal judges. This has happened at least five times. Ironically, in the most recent impeachment case, the Senate convicted federal judge Alcee L. Hastings in 1989; Judge Hastings was removed from the judiciary but returned to public life after winning a seat in the House of Representatives from a congressional district in Florida in 1992. Hastings made history by being the first person impeached by the House to later be elected to it.

5-7b Recruitment of the Executive

In parliamentary systems, it is unheard of for the prime minister or a cabinet member to arrive in their positions without legislative experience. In stark contrast, in the United States serving in Congress before running for president may now be a disadvantage—of the five presidents who have served since 1977, only one, the senior George Bush (president during 1989–1993), had congressional experience, and Bush served only two terms in the House.

It is customary in parliamentary systems for cabinet ministers to rise through the ranks and establish seniority before securing a position in the executive branch. The typical cabinet minister often serves a couple of decades as an MP (Member of Parliament) before rising to the executive, usually as a junior minister. Legislative experience enhances the opportunities of the politically ambitious in a parliamentary system, while in the United States too much time in Washington makes one a suspected "insider."

But parliamentary politics has its own problems. Most members of Congress don't anticipate or even hope for cabinet posts; they prefer the comfort of a reliable constituency. Moreover, they are constitutionally prohibited from serving in both capacities simultaneously. However, failing to attain a cabinet position is a major disappointment for most parliamentary members. The British House of Commons is a case in point:

> Politics has become a profession, with a well-understood career structure. By this standard, most MPs are doomed to fail; at any one time, only around 14 percent of them are members of the government. The consequences are obvious. In the Commons bars and offices lurk many bored, soured souls. A few are dim-witted drones, but most are talented, frustrated, wasted people. The still-ambitious ones (often career politicians who have had no other job) are voting-fodder, humiliatingly dependent on the goodwill of the party bosses and whips.[11]

In parliamentary systems, the legislature also depends upon the executive to determine the next election date. Rank-and-file MPs can easily become nervous wrecks because they may not know the next election date much sooner than the public does. Everyone knows when, by law, an election must take place: In parliamentary systems, national elections are scheduled to occur from three to five years apart. A government in danger of losing the next election will let the clock run out. In 1964 and 1997, British Conservative governments, in trouble in the polls, waited until the last minute before the five-year limit ran out to set a date for elections. The prime minister can decide to dissolve parliament and call new elections before the scheduled term ends. In sum, a prime minister calls for an election when it appears the party has the best chance to win it.

At least MPs don't have to worry about term limits. Parliamentary systems have not seriously considered term limits and it is not a political issue for them. MPs can

---

[11]"Bagehot," *The Economist*, August 3, 1991, 58.

serve for indefinite periods as long as their party leadership—especially the leadership at the local district level—is happy with them and as long as they can win elections in their constituencies. These are not always easy tasks. New candidates for parliamentary seats may have to campaign in districts that have not elected anyone from their party to parliament in decades.

In presidential systems, terms of office for both the legislature and the executive are comparatively firm. In the United States, for example, members of the House of Representatives serve two-year terms. The House doesn't have to worry that the executive will dissolve it and call for new elections. By the early 1990s, though, many representatives were subject to term limits imposed by their state legislatures.

Sometimes individual House members impose term limits on themselves, "taking the pledge" not to serve more than a set number of terms, even without the prodding of their state legislatures. Politicians both in and out of Congress have suggested a constitutional amendment to place a limit on terms in both the House and the Senate. In American legislative politics, an excellent way to get elected to Congress is to promise to leave it quickly.

5-8 Legislative Tasks

National legislators have earned inconsistent evaluations from their constituencies. In the United States, for example, members of Congress are not considered much more trustworthy than used car dealers. Of course, too much cynicism can pose a danger to democracy. For every member of Congress who is accused in the media or actually brought to trial for some type of wrongdoing, many more steadfastly do their jobs and labor to benefit their home districts or states.

There is good reason to believe that the memberships of legislatures tend to represent both the moods and the demographics of their constituents. In almost every democracy, for instance, legislators must pay increasing attention to their elderly constituents. As the people over age 65 become the fastest growing demographic group (except for those over 85), their legislative representatives must respond to their concerns about health care, pensions, and living standards.

National legislators in democracies perform tasks critical to the political process:

1. They are in constant communication with their constituents and are therefore one of the few political organizations consistently aware of changing opinions on issues. Legislative members in all industrialized democracies have become accustomed to receiving volumes of mail, telegrams, phone calls, and fax and email messages on a regular basis. Their constituents consistently instruct them on what stands to take on the issues, how to vote, and, overall, how best to do their job.

2. Legislators in many countries have the responsibility of choosing the executive leaders. The German Bundestag, for example, elects the chancellor. (The vote, of course, is always in favor of the leader who controls a majority of seats in the Bundestag.) Both the Bundestag and Bundesrat choose the German president. Japan chooses its prime minister in a similar fashion, and in Israel, the parliament chooses the president. In the United States, Congress can choose a president if no candidate receives a majority of the electoral-college vote (though this has never happened in modern times).[12] With the ratification of the Twenty-fifth Amendment in 1967, Congress gained the additional constitutional responsibility to confirm a presidential nomination to fill a vice-presidential vacancy.

3. National legislatures govern themselves and can govern the executive. Prestige and authority go along with being a national legislator, and so does a great deal of responsibility. As noted earlier, the House of Commons forced Anthony Eden

---

[12]Congress has done this twice, in 1800 and 1824, and came close to it in 1948 and 1968 when third-party candidates threatened to secure enough electoral votes to deny a majority to either the Democratic or Republican candidate.

out of the prime ministership because he refused to be forthcoming about British involvement in a military attack on the Suez Canal Zone.

4. Finally and most obviously, legislatures draft, propose, debate, and pass legislation into law. In this sense, the executive and the legislature share the obligation of making laws. Individual members of parliament tend to have more to say if they belong to a narrow majority. The government that controls a majority of only a few seats must be concerned that a few defections, resignations, deaths, or independent-minded members could not only defeat government-sponsored legislation but could bring the government itself down. The following chapter shows that a democracy tends to induce an intimate and sometimes noisy relationship between the executive and legislative branches. This relationship can vary in significant ways between parliamentary and presidential systems.

Chapter Summary

1. Legislatures are an ancient political institution. They trace back to classical Greece 2,500 years ago when the first legislative assemblies began to meet in Athens.

2. Many modern legislatures have upper and lower houses that formed along the social class lines that characterized European societies hundreds of years ago. In most modern legislatures, the lower house has more real political power.

3. In a parliamentary legislative system, the lower house furnishes the executive from its own membership and at any time can withdraw support for the government.

4. Members of most upper houses are not chosen democratically and have little real power. However, they can help draft legislation and help revise legislation passed by the lower house.

5. Parliamentary systems differ from presidential systems such as the United States in that parliamentary systems have no division of powers between the executive and legislative branches of government.

6. Party discipline is a requirement in parliamentary systems. It ensures a productive legislative process and furthers the business of the government.

7. Representative assemblies only rarely represent all of the various social groups and are often disproportionate when it comes to representing gender, ethnic, and religious communities.

8. An important function of some national legislatures is to select the head of government. Some legislatures can, when circumstances dictate, remove the head of government from office.

Chapter 5 Quiz

1. A "rubber-stamp" legislature is common in
   a. totalitarian regimes.
   b. parliamentary democracies.
   c. ancient societies only.
   d. English-speaking political systems.

2. In Greece, city-states legislatures were generally composed of
   a. only the elderly citizens over age sixty-five.
   b. all adult male citizens.
   c. men and women over age twenty-one.
   d. top 10 percent of taxpayers.

3. The oldest functioning legislature is found in
   a. United States.
   b. China.
   c. France.
   d. Iceland.

4. Upper chambers with real political powers are found in
   a. France and Italy.
   b. France and Germany.
   c. Germany and the United States.
   d. the United Kingdom.

5. A unicameral national legislature is found in
   a. Japan.
   b. Mexico.
   c. Russia.
   d. Israel.

6. A minority government results when
   a. no party or coalition of parties controls a legislative majority.
   b. a legislative minority defies an election outcome.
   c. a small ethnic group controls the parliament.
   d. none of the above occurs.

7. Lebanon's National Assembly is based on representation from
   a. ethnic tribes.
   b. religious affiliations.
   c. mountainous and coastal areas only.
   d. urban and rural constituencies.

8. The German chancellor is officially chosen by
   a. absolute majority of the popular vote.
   b. a special electoral college.
   c. state government leaders.
   d. the Bundestag.

9. The only two American presidents who have faced impeachment proceedings are
   a. Richard Nixon and Bill Clinton.
   b. Andrew Johnson and Bill Clinton.
   c. Andrew Johnson and Richard Nixon.
   d. both Bush presidents.

10. Recent American presidents have had
    a. substantial experience as a national legislator.
    b. little or no experience as a national legislator.
    c. previous cabinet rank.
    d. diplomatic experience at the ambassadorial rank.

11. Which of the following statements does not apply to both the American president and the British prime minister?
    a. Both are installed by the legislative upper house.
    b. Both have term limits.
    c. Both have usually served in previous cabinet positions.
    d. all of the above.

The Executive: Presidential and Parliamentary Government

KEY TERMS

absolute monarchy
accidental president
bureaucracy
cabinet government
collective responsibility

constitutional monarchy
head of government
head of state
minority president

head of government
The top government officer who
exercises actual political power.

head of state
The ceremonial leader who *symbolizes*
national sovereignty and political
legitimacy.

The national leaders nearly everyone in a country can identify are the **head of government** and **head of state**. The former holds real power, while the latter may only perform ceremonial roles and activities. Americans have it easy in this respect: The two heads are combined into one office, the presidency. In the United States, however, the vice president (like a head of state) often doesn't have enough to do; recent occupants of the office have gratefully received meaningful assignments from the president. Vice presidents have also become presidents-in-training. George Bush (senior), Walter Mondale, and Al Gore were all vice presidents who ran for the presidency, though not always successfully.

In democracies, it is unusual for either head to be chosen by popular election. (France is a noteworthy exception to this rule and will be examined in more detail shortly.) Yet the head of government must be able to secure wide support for his or her policies to be effective. This normally happens through an election—if not a popular election, then election by a parliamentary majority.

A national executive personifies her or his country and is, fairly or not, held responsible for how well the country is doing. The executive makes decisions that influence millions of lives. The quality of these decisions and the chances they will be successfully implemented are determined by the level of cooperation the executive receives from the bureaucracy.

This chapter surveys the various dimensions of the executive office, including selection procedures and the extent and variety of executive powers. It emphasizes the role of the executive in democracies, but also touches on the diversity of executive offices and roles in nondemocratic systems. The U.S. political system is used as a comparative backdrop when appropriate. Most national executives have more power today than they have ever had; at the same time, they probably face more constraints. This chapter focuses on how effectively they use their powers to respond to their constraints and pursue their political agendas.

6-1 Presidential and Prime Ministerial Government

A political executive is, as the term implies, someone who executes government policy. In a democracy, the legislative and executive branches collaborate to both formulate and implement policy. In parliamentary systems, the executive component of the government can be realistically considered a kind of senior legislative committee composed primarily of the leadership from the party that controls a majority of seats within the legislature. In the nonparliamentary democracies, though, power is often less concentrated. An American president, for example, has less freedom of action than a British prime minister when it comes to making policy. A president usually has to negotiate policy, often in a bipartisan fashion, with legislators who as often as not are members of the opposition party.

6-1a The American Presidential System

Although he is the leader of the most powerful country in the world, the U.S. president is remarkably frail in several ways. Unlike a great many other democratic executives, the American president faces term limits and a frequently hostile legislative majority. Also, the public tends to become dissatisfied with their chief executive rather quickly. Since World War II, three Republicans, Dwight Eisenhower (1953–1961), Ronald Reagan (1981–1989), and George W. Bush (2001–2009) have been elected to and have served out two complete four-year terms.[1] Bill Clinton became the first Democrat to be elected to and complete two consecutive terms, despite an impeachment proceeding, since Franklin Roosevelt (1933–1945), and was only the third Democrat in the twentieth century to do so.

Even with these limitations, however, the American public still expects much from the office of the presidency. And successful occupants usually thoroughly enjoy the considerable prerogatives and powers the office provides. Teddy Roosevelt viewed his presidency (1901–1909) as a chance to use a "bully pulpit" and believed that presidents ought to be presidential: "My belief was that it was not [the president's] right but his duty to do anything that the needs of the nation demanded, unless such action was forbidden by the Constitution or the laws."[2]

Roosevelt was so enamored with the presidency that he even tried to make a comeback during the 1912 presidential election. He lost but certainly left an impact. Bill Clinton enjoyed the presidency so much that, during his last months in office, he slept as little as possible in order to savor the prerogatives as much as possible.

The American presidency has evolved into a carefully watched political phenomenon. While Americans seem to quickly grow to dislike presidents and often limit them to one four-year term, they still adulate and respect the office. They tend to distinguish between the office and the occupant with the utmost respect for the former and varying degrees of affection or dislike for the latter. It's no wonder: The American president is simultaneously head of state, chief executive of the world's only current superpower, diplomatic leader, commander-in-chief of the most powerful armed forces in the world, principal legislative leader (though the influence of this role diminishes when the president faces a congressional majority from the opposition party), and leader of his party.

United States presidents tend to represent the American political mainstream, which is usually slightly to the left or right of the ideological center. Would-be presidents who stray too far from the center or try to push the electorate too far to the left or right often come to unrewarding ends. Both the Democrat and Republican parties learned valuable lessons when each nominated presidential candidates from extremist wings. Republican candidate Barry Goldwater in 1964 and Democratic candidate George McGovern in 1972 ensured landslide victories for their opponents by offering programs with little popular appeal. Goldwater suggested the repeal of the Social Security Act of 1935, and McGovern proposed that the government provide a minimum guaranteed income for every American family. Both suggestions horrified and repelled huge segments of the electorate.

The American presidency has not only grown in stature and power. It is an office that requires its occupant to either sleep very little or be able to delegate tasks to cabinet secretaries, the White House office staff, and to such agencies as the Office of Management and Budget (OMB) and Council of Economic Advisors (CEA). There are simply more things for the executive branch to do than were foreseen by the founders of the republic more than two centuries ago. George Washington's first cabinet consisted of only four secretaries. Modern presidencies can have as many as twenty or more individuals with cabinet rank. The growth of the economy has made it feasible for the government to deliver more services and accept

---

[1]The first two almost didn't make it. Eisenhower suffered two heart attacks during his second term while Reagan was seriously wounded in an assassination attempt at the beginning of his first term. We assume that George W. Bush will finish his second term.

[2]Arthur B. Tourtellot, *Presidents on the Presidency* (Garden City, N.Y.: Doubleday, 1964), 55–56.

| FIGURE 6–1 | | Presidential–Vice-Presidential Relations | | |

F. D. Roosevelt	Kennedy	Carter	Reagan	G. W. Bush
1933–1945	1961–1963	1977–1981	1981–1989	2001–
Roosevelt named his vice president, Henry Wallace (1941–45), Chairman of the Board of Economic Warfare but the position was short-lived; he was removed after internal disagreements over policy.	Kennedy gave his vice president, Lyndon Johnson, office space in the White House, signifying a closer relationship, but in reality Johnson's role was minimal.	Relying on Walter Mondale's experience and delegating broader authority to him, Carter raised the value of the vice president as an advisor to the President.	Like Carter, Reagan chose for his vice president a Washington insider, George Bush. Bush brought experience in a variety of political arenas and received unprecedented status as a vice president, including a staff of seventy and a budget of $2 million.	The younger Bush has relied on his vice president, Dick Cheney, and delegated so much work to him that Cheney enjoys the most powerful Vice Presidency in history, causing some to dub him the "Co-President."

more responsibilities. The necessities of the times are another reason cabinets may grow. In 2002 the Department of Homeland Security was created in the aftermath of 9-11, for example, to confront and thwart the menace of terrorism.

Modern presidents, probably beginning with the Eisenhower administration (1953–1961), have provided vice presidents access to high-level meetings and substantive roles in policy formulation (see Figure 6–1). Vice-presidential involvement is important if only because several modern vice presidents have become presidents themselves, either because of a sudden vacancy created by assassination or resignation or by election in their own right. No one doubts that Vice President Dick Cheney is intimately involved in most domestic and foreign policy issues of the current Bush administration. His previous experience as a member of Congress and as Secretary of Defense during the first Bush administration (1989–1993) helps to explain his importance.

The modern American presidency is often beset with crises, and public opinion polls and voters evaluate how successfully the president responds to these. President Franklin Roosevelt (1933–1945), for example, rallied the full powers of the office and his own considerable persuasive abilities to lead the United States out of the Great Depression. He was also the American leader in World War II, a conflict that challenged the very survival of Western democracy. The loss of life associated with 9-11 could suggest that George W. Bush, who certainly did not intend to be a "war president," is confronted by a similar titanic struggle to preserve the American political democracy against an enemy bent on its destruction.

Despite these setbacks, the presidential office remains vibrant. For example, Congress may have declared war for the last time (in December 1941, against Germany, Italy, and Japan). The president can now dispatch American soldiers anywhere he can justify their presence. President Reagan ordered an invasion of Grenada, and the first President Bush ordered troops into Panama in 1989 and sent a half million troops to the Persian Gulf in 1990 and 1991 to deal with the menace Saddam Hussein posed to the industrial world. When President Clinton offered to send 20,000 American troops to Bosnia in 1996, the offer met with little criticism from Congress. Congress overwhelmingly supported George W. Bush's 2001 decision to send large numbers of American troops to Afghanistan to remove the Taliban regime and destroy the al-Qaeda network. Bush sent an American army to

FIGURE 6–2   **Military Actions by U.S. Presidents**

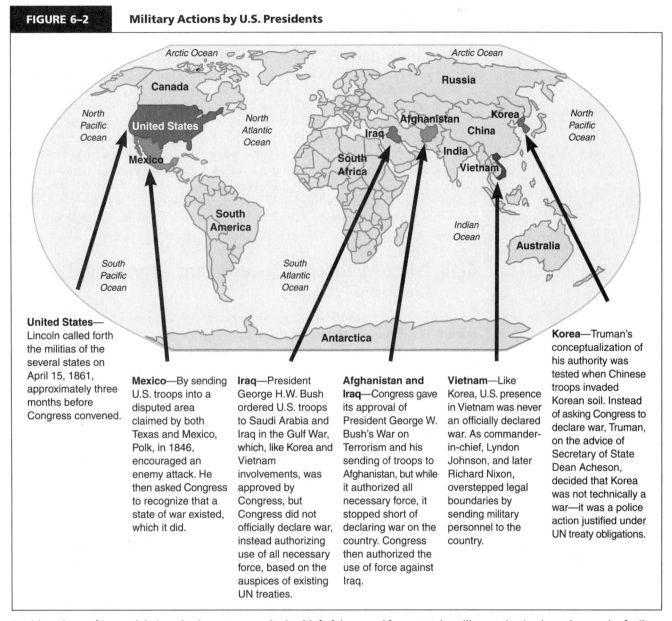

United States— Lincoln called forth the militias of the several states on April 15, 1861, approximately three months before Congress convened.

Mexico— By sending U.S. troops into a disputed area claimed by both Texas and Mexico, Polk, in 1846, encouraged an enemy attack. He then asked Congress to recognize that a state of war existed, which it did.

Iraq— President George H.W. Bush ordered U.S. troops to Saudi Arabia and Iraq in the Gulf War, which, like Korea and Vietnam involvements, was approved by Congress, but Congress did not officially declare war, instead authorizing use of all necessary force, based on the auspices of existing UN treaties.

Afghanistan and Iraq— Congress gave its approval of President George W. Bush's War on Terrorism and his sending of troops to Afghanistan, but while it authorized all necessary force, it stopped short of declaring war on the country. Congress then authorized the use of force against Iraq.

Vietnam— Like Korea, U.S. presence in Vietnam was never an officially declared war. As commander-in-chief, Lyndon Johnson, and later Richard Nixon, overstepped legal boundaries by sending military personnel to the country.

Korea— Truman's conceptualization of his authority was tested when Chinese troops invaded Korean soil. Instead of asking Congress to declare war, Truman, on the advice of Secretary of State Dean Acheson, decided that Korea was not technically a war—it was a police action justified under UN treaty obligations.

Presidents have often used their authority as commander-in-chief of the armed forces to take military action in places thousands of miles from the United States in order to secure and protect American personnel and property.

invade and occupy Iraq in 2003 without requesting a congressional declaration of war. Figure 6–2 shows a sampling of places and times the president has exerted his powers as commander-in-chief without a congressional declaration of war.

In one sense, American presidents who face no severe crises almost have a more difficult time. President Clinton, for example, saw his domestic policy agenda thwarted during his first term, especially after the Republican party achieved majorities in both houses of Congress in the 1994 elections. He turned to the foreign policy arena (which most of his critics and supporters maintained he had little interest in) to demonstrate presidential success. Israeli and Palestinian leaders signed two important accords at the White House in September 1993 and September 1995. An obviously pleased president sat between them, hoping to receive some credit as a peace broker.

When it was created, the presidency was a unique office—no other country in the 1790s had anything quite like it. The American presidency became a model for other political systems, particularly in the western hemisphere. Nearly all of the

Latin American countries have adopted a presidential form of government. Like the United States, quite a few have imposed term limits: by law, the Mexican president may serve only one six-year term, and Costa Rica has limited its presidents to a single four-year term since 1948. An important difference is that Latin American presidencies are strictly decided by popular election, without an electoral college.

The United States president is probably the most watched and studied political figure in the world. The electronic and print media observe his every move. His words have the potential to make millions of listeners happy or depressed. The outcome of his annual medical checkup is awaited with great anticipation; a presidential illness—even a mild one—can cause jitters in the stock and currency markets.[3]

National leaders in other countries are also carefully observed. Interestingly, though, they sometimes seem to have more extensive powers than their American counterpart. They also tend to last longer. Even democratically chosen executives can be quite distinct from one another when it comes to acquiring and exercising political power.

6-1b Prime Ministerial Government—The United Kingdom

An interesting characteristic of the American presidential system is that quite frequently American presidents seem to arrive at the White House without much national political experience. Popular generals such as Ulysses S. Grant and Dwight Eisenhower served in no public office before their elevation to the presidency. Colin Powell, a former Armed Forces Chief of Staff and hero of the Persian Gulf conflict, was considered a strong presidential possibility in 1996 despite (or perhaps because of) the fact he had never ventured into politics. He became Secretary of State in 2001. Warren Harding was governor of Ohio when he was elected president in 1920, but he was almost unknown outside his state. Harding may have received the Republican nomination for president, some believe, because he "looked presidential." Bill Clinton was an obscure governor of a small state. Billionaire Steve Forbes became a candidate for the 1996 and 2000 Republican presidential nomination with no prior political experience, but equipped with $25 million of his own money to spend on his campaign.

Prime ministers don't achieve office this way in most parliamentary systems. Candidates for the prime ministership are almost never war heroes[4] or billionaires (although millionaires aren't uncommon). The typical ascension for British heads of government is to work up through the ranks, starting in the House of Commons and working up to a top cabinet position: backbencher, junior minister, senior minister. (In contrast, no sitting member of Congress has become president since John Kennedy accomplished the feat in 1960.) Consider, for example, the qualifications a prospective prime minister's resume typically includes. He or she must

1. have long-time service in the lower (elective) house,
2. have previous Cabinet experience that includes such powerful ministries as foreign affairs, defense, or finance,
3. be leader of the majority party in parliament, and
4. be unrelated to the royal family.

In Britain, as in the United States, the party leader is usually from the party's center but is at least minimally acceptable to the various ideological wings within the party.

---

[3]The public is not always informed when the president has a health problem. For example, Grover Cleveland (1885–1889 and 1893–1897) had cancer during his second administration, though the public did not know it. See Robert H. Ferrell, *Ill-Advised: Presidential Health and Public Trust* (Columbia and London: University of Missouri Press, 1992). Woodrow Wilson suffered a stroke and Dwight Eisenhower a series of heart attacks, and the public was informed in these instances.

[4]Winston Churchill, prime minister during 1939–1945 and 1951–1955, was a veteran of the Boer War in South Africa (1899–1902) who even had a price on his head, placed there by the Dutch settlers who were at that time battling to keep British influence out of the country.

Although this section of the chapter is entitled "Prime Ministerial Government," it is as convenient and probably as accurate to apply the term **cabinet government** to a parliamentary system. In many respects, the cabinet is more critical than in the American system because of its membership. American presidents usually choose cabinet secretaries whose names are unfamiliar to the American public. Cabinet secretaries are often recruited from the ranks of career civil servants or from major corporations in the private sector. In some cases, they come out of an academic setting, as did Secretary of State Henry Kissinger (1973–1977).

In contrast, parliamentary systems such as the United Kingdom's produce cabinets filled with well-known and ambitious political personages, at least at the top levels. It is likely that one or more of them will eventually go on to become prime minister. The cabinet is viewed as preparatory training for the top job. However, it isn't unheard of for a former prime minister to occupy a cabinet position.

Another rather critical difference exists between American and British cabinets. When the prime minister makes his cabinet selections, he or she must be mindful of at least two interrelated considerations. First, the cabinet should reflect an ideological balance between the various wings of the political party. The prime minister himself is usually the product of a hard or soft ideological emphasis. If he comes from the more moderate elements within, say, the Conservative party, the prime minister will probably bring into the cabinet a representation of the right wing. Second, the prime minister must acquiesce to the political fact that all or most of the top cabinet positions will be filled by people who want his or her job. Usually, some are political allies or protégés willing to wait patiently for their turn until the prime minister retires. Others may not be so patient and are prepared to take full advantage of any opportunity to create a vacancy in the party leadership. Such individuals often represent various factions within the party who may believe the prime minister is taking the party in the wrong ideological direction.

The fact that senior-level cabinet appointments are more political than practical can, of course, detract from a minister's impact. He or she can easily serve in several ministries during a long career. Most ministers are therefore very dependent upon the civil servants attached to her or his office. Fortunately, the British civil service has an established reputation for objectivity and competence. A minister is expected to take full responsibility for his or her department's problems, even though ministers are shifted around a lot or occasionally dropped from the cabinet, usually for political reasons.

Most of the time, however, cabinet members offer at least a facade of political loyalty. Governments in the British and other parliamentary systems stand or fall together. This solidarity demonstrates **collective responsibility**. Before the government makes a decision, there can be (and usually is, if the decision is controversial) a great deal of debate at cabinet meetings. However, once a decision is finally made, the debate is over. Cabinet members are expected to present a united front to the public at large and, especially, in parliament. They unanimously defend the policy the government has formulated and decided to implement. A cabinet minister who for any reason simply cannot go along with the decision is expected to resign from the government while remaining a member of parliament.

Finally, the prime minister and cabinet ministers are members of the House of Commons. They must regularly respond to questions and charges from other members, who often word their challenges to create maximum embarrassment and discomfort for the government. Unlike their somewhat luckier American counterparts, who appear only infrequently in Congress and can often get away without appearing at all, senior British ministers are constantly on the firing line.

cabinet government
In a parliamentary system, the cabinet is composed of party leaders who stand or fall together, creating a cabinet government. Cabinet members must publicly agree and must maintain a parliamentary majority to retain power.

collective responsibility
Once a policy is formulated, all of the cabinet ministers in a parliamentary system assume responsibility for its defense and implementation.

6-1c Ceremonial Heads of State

The American president is both head of government and head of state. Parliamentary democracies separate the two offices. The British, for example, have enjoyed the institution of the monarchy for a millennium. The single interruption came in 1649, when Charles I was executed. It took only a dozen years, though, for remorseful subjects to restore his son to the throne. The people had grown weary of the puritanical government that ruled England in the interim.

The British monarchy survived over the next three and one-half centuries by gradually agreeing to give up political powers to popularly elected assemblies. Monarchies in other European countries that didn't accept their declining roles were ended, often in violence. For a monarchy to survive in a democratizing country, it needed to become relatively powerless. The less power a monarch possessed, the more public popularity he or she enjoyed.

The Japanese emperor is the technical head of state and remains thoroughly respected by his subjects, though he does not possess any significant power. Some Japanese continue to regard the emperor as divine though the imperial family has, since the end of World War II in 1945, disclaimed this honor.

Monarchies became symbols of national unity and enjoyed widespread respect and affection because they no longer participated in policy making. Unlike her prime ministers, Queen Elizabeth II of England consistently draws cheers and applause whenever she appears on public occasions. (This is not true of her children, however, whose occasional scandalous behavior has damaged the monarchy's prestige; her son and heir, Charles, has nowhere near the popularity his mother consistently enjoys.) In most democratic societies where they still exist, royal family members aren't even allowed to cast ballots in national elections—one of the only things they have in common with convicted felons. A goodly number of countries have dispensed with their monarchies. Italy and Greece did after World War II, and France broke with monarchy after 1870. Others, such as Spain, have abolished a monarchical institution, missed it, and restored it. In fact, exiled royal family members are usually available to be restored. No sooner had the communist regime of the Soviet Union dissolved than many Russians expressed a preference to re-establish the Russian monarchy. They wanted to return the Romanov family, which had ruled Russia from 1613 to 1917, when the last Russian tsar and his immediate family were shot, to the throne.

Many countries without monarchies have heads of state that are effective national symbols. Some systems, such as Israel, Italy, Germany, and Austria, have presidents. While the Austrian president is popularly elected, most aren't; instead, one or both parliamentary houses choose them. Without a popular mandate, there is little danger that a ceremonial president could actually become an influential political force.

A ceremonial president usually has a record of distinguished service, often having established a noteworthy career outside of politics. A ceremonial president can be a career politician, of course, but usually not one who has been successful enough to become a head of government. A prime minister, by contrast, has often made a good share of enemies on the way to the top and has been a partisan politician for decades. Former prime ministers normally retire to write their memoirs without expecting to serve in public office again.

What is the purpose of having a ceremonial head of state? They basically serve very few but still important functions:

1. As mentioned previously, a head of state is a symbol of national unification. He or she regularly appears at important events, lending a degree of dignity to them. The head of state also receives high-ranking personages visiting from other countries, including other heads of state, and travels abroad on goodwill visits to other countries.

2. After every election, the head of state asks the leader of the party (or coalition of parties) with a parliamentary majority to form a government. Most of the time, this is a pro-forma act because the head of state cannot act to contradict the results of a free election. On occasion, though, an election result

is extremely close and may even be in dispute. At such a time, the head of state can exercise, usually within carefully specified constitutional limits, an independent choice.

3. The head of state is the personification of political legitimacy. In most parliamentary systems, he or she appoints the head of government. In a clear-cut electoral outcome, as just mentioned, this appointment is fairly automatic. Yet, because Queen Elizabeth II, for example, represents 1,000 years of political traditions and institutions, she almost "anoints" a prime minister and confers legal authority on that person. In other words, she selects someone to safeguard British interests for the next four or five years.

4. The head of state provides stability in unstable or rapidly changing political situations. A long-reigning monarch (Queen Elizabeth II, for instance, came to the throne in 1952) will normally outlast several prime ministers, but even a presidential head of state can serve a term as long as six years. In a country such as Italy, where there have been more than fifty governments in the six decades since 1945, a long-serving and familiar head of state offers a reassuring presence that comforts a population that has an understandably difficult time keeping up with changes in government.

Some heads of state, especially the comparatively few who are popularly elected, have more authority than others. By and large, though, their powers are ultimately constrained by an electorate that makes its political preferences clear at the polls. Heads of state, therefore, only rarely challenge or disagree with the heads of government.

6-2 Selection of the Executive

In nondemocratic systems, national leaders are self-selected. A national leader in an authoritarian system will frequently seize power through a coup or a rigged election. Often a rigged election will follow a coup to ensure at least the appearance of legitimacy. Perhaps the easiest way to become and remain a national leader is through an inherited monarchy, another aspect of authoritarianism.

However, in this section of the chapter, the selection of the chief executive in three industrialized democracies is surveyed. Table 6–1 demonstrates that not all are chosen in a completely democratic manner. The table also shows that the distinct peculiarities of a political system and culture are instrumental in shaping the selection process.

6-2a France

The most democratic process for choosing an executive is through a direct popular election that requires an absolute majority of the electorate to officially endorse a particular candidate. In 1965, the French dispensed with an electoral college to

TABLE 6–1	**Direct and Indirect Ways of Selecting a Chief Executive**	
Direct Selection	**Indirect Selection**	
French president	American president	British prime minister
Electorate	Electoral college	Majority party
	Electorate	Electorate

POLITICAL BIOGRAPHY

Charles de Gaulle

© Wally McNamee/ CORBIS

The founder and first president of the Fifth Republic, Charles de Gaulle (1958–1969) reasoned that the French had spent a good deal of their history and blood trying to make up their minds between a republic and a monarchy. He also understood that the French had rarely been a united people. De Gaulle once asked how it was possible to govern a country that produced 200 different kinds of cheese!

The compromise was a seven-year presidency (later changed to five years) secured by an indisputably popular mandate. The president of the republic would be able to govern because the electorate had chosen him. He could also function as head of state because he would choose a prime minister and other cabinet officials to carry out the daily business of government and take the blame for anything that went wrong with the economy.

De Gaulle, who was primarily responsible for drafting a new constitution in 1958, also gave the president the authority to call for a national referendum. The French electorate may vote yes or no on any issue the president puts to them. The referendum is an excellent technique for bypassing the legislative branch and ensuring a direct link between the president and the people. De Gaulle had little respect for the National Assembly, which he considered divisive and inefficient.

Much of de Gaulle's political design seems to be working. When de Gaulle took power, France was on the brink of civil war. De Gaulle reasoned, apparently with justification, that the French people required strong but popularly chosen leadership with somewhat more authority than counterparts in most other democracies. The Fifth Republic has survived its founder by several decades and seems, unlike previous regimes, to have the confidence of the bulk of the French nation.

---

enable the president of the republic to come to office with a popular mandate. In effect, the French have a two-stage election for the presidency. The first ballot is the rough equivalent of a national primary as voters choose from any number of candidates. Only three or four are serious candidates, who come equipped with the support of major party organizations, substantial experience, and name recognition. Unless one of them wins an outright majority (which has not happened in the seven presidential elections since 1965), a second election or run-off ballot between the two top vote getters occurs two weeks later. One will secure an absolute majority and a mandate for a five-year term of office.

A plurality winner on the first ballot may not end up the majority winner on the second. For example, two conservative candidates may compete on the first ballot, with a socialist candidate opposing them, as happened in 1995. The socialist came in first. The strongest conservative candidate, Jacques Chirac, then overwhelmed his socialist rival, drawing support on the second ballot from those who voted for the losing conservative on the first.

Unlike the American and several Latin American presidencies, the French presidency does not have the constraint of term limits. The French believe their executive is entitled to serve as long as a popular mandate is retained. The insistence on a popular majority eliminates the possibility of a **minority president**, or a president who wins office without a majority or a plurality of popular votes. U.S. presidents can be minority presidents. Both Bill Clinton and George W. Bush failed to receive a majority of popular votes, but won their elections in 1992, 1996, and 2000 anyway.

Should a president leave office for any reason before the completion of his term, the French simply have another election for a full term. During the few weeks between the vacancy and the new election, the President of the Senate functions as interim president. There is no vice president who automatically fills out the remainder of the term. The French consider this another important democratic feature. Unlike the United States, France never has an **accidental president**, or a president

minority president
A phenomenon that characterizes American presidential politics: A candidate can win an election without acquiring either a majority or plurality of the popular vote.

accidental president
A phenomenon in American politics: the sudden and unexpected ascension of a vice president to the presidency.

who suddenly and unexpectedly steps up to fill a vacancy without direct election to the office.

A new president may begin his term with substantial popularity only to see it dissolve after one or two years. (Seven months after taking office in 1995, Jacques Chirac had a popularity rating of 11 percent, a record low for any French presidency.) He can also make a comeback, as Chirac did in the last stages of his first term, and secure re-election in the process. Chirac won a second term in 2002 with 80 percent of the vote on the second ballot, defeating the extremist right-wing candidate, Jean-Marie Le Pen. The French may be more patient with their chief executives than Americans, who are liable to get rid of their presidents after only one four-year term.

In a peculiar blend of presidential and parliamentary features, the French president appoints the prime minister and other members of the cabinet. Unlike a strictly parliamentary system, the French system forbids cabinet members to simultaneously hold legislative seats. They have no mandate of their own. If the economy sours, for example, a French president may simply allow the prime minister and/or other cabinet ministers to take the blame. It is not unusual for the president to go through two or more prime ministers in a single term of office.

It isn't surprising that many French prime ministers who remain in office for a respectable length of time and escape the onus of serious scandal desire to become president. Three of France's five Fifth Republic presidents were previous prime ministers. Chirac himself was a prime minister under two different presidents. The prime minister therefore has an especially important stake in the success of the government that holds the key to his or her own political future.

The president tries to remain politically aloof as the head of state and allow his prime minister to deal with the day-to-day workings of the government. This goal does not always meet with success, though. Within weeks of his ascension to the presidency in April 1995, Jacques Chirac announced that France would carry out a series of nuclear tests in its South Pacific possessions. The timing could not have been worse: The announcement came on the fiftieth anniversary of the atomic bombings of Hiroshima and Nagasaki. Neighboring countries around the possessions were outraged. In protest, the governments of Chile and New Zealand recalled their ambassadors from Paris, and Australia's prime minister called France's nuclear testing "an act of stupidity."[5] At least on the international level, the French president cannot escape responsibility for the policies of his or her government.

A French president must also assume responsibility for the direction of domestic policy. Chirac's "honeymoon period" was probably the shortest in French presidential history. Within a few months, he was being blamed for a 12 percent unemployment rate and for changing his mind too often on what to do about it.[6] He won again in 2002 only because of widespread disenchantment with his opponents. Consistent unpopularity persuaded him not to run for a third term in 2007.

6-2b The United States

Choosing an American president is an expensive and time-consuming matter. It is also a process watched avidly by most of the rest of the world. For the party out of power, the event begins as much as a year and a half before the national election. If an incumbent president is finishing a second term, even the party in power begins early to consider several candidates for the succession.

Glory may matter as much as money in American politics. Successful generals with no political experience such as Ulysses S. Grant (1869–1877) or Dwight David Eisenhower (1953–1961) can be so popular that their names and reputations can

[5]"Test and Shout," *The Economist*, September 9, 1995, 50.

[6]"France Strikes Against Chirac," *The Economist*, October 14, 1995, 57–59.

easily carry them to the nomination and to electoral victory. In fact, by the late 1970s, it was becoming increasingly fashionable to attempt to win political office by posing as someone with modest or no political experience. Presenting oneself as a "Washington outsider" and a "fresh face" was considered to be an excellent campaign strategy. This is why the former Chief of the Armed Services and hero of the first Persian Gulf conflict, Colin Powell, appeared to be a serious contender for the Republican nomination before he announced he would not be a candidate in 1996.

There is actually no sure route to the American presidency. Political leaders in other democracies customarily work their way up through the ranks into party leadership positions and high-level cabinet posts. In contrast, an American president need not have held any previous political office, or may have held an office in a small state—Governors Carter and Clinton, for example, were mostly unknown outside of their home states before they achieved success in the Democratic party primaries. No cabinet official has become president since 1928 when Herbert Hoover was elected. No sitting vice president between 1837 and 1988 won a presidential election.

If a candidate survives the primaries and goes on to win the national election, he or she may not even then be assured of a popular mandate. Voter turnout is miserably low in the United States and, because of the electoral college, a candidate can win the popular vote and still lose the election. Because this happened in 1888, 1916, and 2000, the potential is clearly there, especially if a strong third-party candidate runs.

It is only in the electoral college that a majority matters. Becoming president requires the support of a minimum of 270 electors out of a total of 538. Only on two occasions, in 1800 and 1824, has no presidential candidate achieved a majority in the electoral college. When a majority is lacking, the House of Representatives is constitutionally obligated to decide the outcome. A strong third-party movement may not be able to overcome Democrat and Republican dominance, but it has on several occasions threatened to throw the election to the House.

Some have suggested that the electoral college be abolished or reformed to reflect the proportions of the popular vote. The chances are slim that either will happen. Doing anything to the electoral college would require a constitutional amendment. Besides, there is a general satisfaction with the college, especially among the larger states, which have large electoral blocks. California, for example, has fifty-seven electoral votes, one-fifth of the total needed to win. If a presidential candidate can carry the eleven largest states, he or she will win the election even if an opponent wins the other thirty-nine. The electoral college also seems to provide a certain peace of mind—the electorate knows they can count on it to secure a final and usually indisputable election result.

Several presidents have actually been minority presidents, coming to the office with less than 50 percent of the popular vote. Bush won the 2000 election with only 47 percent of all ballots cast. He has a lot of company: Harry Truman in 1948, John Kennedy in 1960, Richard Nixon in 1968, and Bill Clinton in 1992 and 1996 all won close elections with under 50 percent of the popular vote. The 2004 election was the first since 1988 in which a candidate won an absolute majority of popular votes.

In some cases, it is possible to become president without any popular or electoral college votes. American presidents have a high mortality rate. Between 1841 and 1963, no fewer than seven presidents were either assassinated or died in office. An eighth, Richard Nixon, resigned in 1974. In all of these instances, the vice president assumed the office. Several other presidents, including Ronald Reagan in 1981, have survived assassination attempts.

Accidental presidents may have successful administrations. Then again, they may not: How well remembered are the accomplishments, for example, of President Millard Fillmore, Zachary Taylor's vice president, during 1850–1853? Vice presidents who suddenly become presidents have no mandate beyond the constitutional one. Fortunately, recent vice presidents have been much better prepared to assume the presidential office. This is because modern presidents, beginning with Eisenhower, have invited vice presidents to cabinet meetings and generally kept them well-informed. Some, like Walter Mondale during the Carter administration (1977–1981), have worked very closely with their presidents. A vice president is still selected by and must at all times be loyal to the president, but at least he or she is no longer an unknown or inexperienced novice.

6-2c The United Kingdom

The British prime minister, as is typical in parliamentary systems, is the leader of the majority party in the lower house. He or she must remain party leader in order to remain prime minister. The support of the House is forthcoming as long as the government's policies are generally acceptable, cabinet-level scandals are infrequent, and the party's parliamentary majority is maintained.

Whether prime minister or not, the party leader is dependent upon and requires the continual support of the party's parliamentary members. If a sudden vacancy occurs in the party leadership, there is no automatic successor. Both of Britain's major parties are restrictive when it comes to choosing their respective leaders.

There is no popular election except at the local level: A party leader, like the other 649 members of the House of Commons, is elected from a single-member constituency of about 100,000 people. He or she becomes party leader by securing the support of the party organization and, in particular, of the majority of party Members of Parliament (MPs). As in other democracies, the public opinion polls influence the status of the party leader and prime minister. Conservative Prime Minister John Major, for example, saw his leadership seriously threatened in July 1995 by John Redwood, an aspiring Conservative politician. Redwood understood that the polls indicated a general dissatisfaction with Major. (The dissatisfaction was confirmed in May 1997, when the Conservatives lost decisively to Labour.)

Redwood was correct in his assessment of public opinion, but Major rode out the 1995 storm primarily because he was still party leader and the party leader controls the party machinery. Most British Conservative party leaders tend to represent the ideological center of their party. That is where the bulk of any party's supporters are, and that is also where a good part of the British electorate is found. The Conservative party has a strong right wing, from which Redwood drew his support, but the party tends to stay with moderate policies and leadership. At the time, Major represented both. In 1940 Neville Chamberlain, who had become prime minister in 1937, had less skill. Because of his disastrous policy of appeasement toward totalitarian dictators, primarily the German regime of Adolf Hitler, Chamberlain was forced to leave the prime ministership by the party membership in the House of Commons.

Historically, leaders of the Labour party did not represent the ideological center of their party, as will be seen in Chapter 7. The Labour party lost four consecutive national elections between 1979 and 1992, in great part because of its proclivity to produce leadership too closely associated with its extreme left wing. Younger and more moderate leaders reversed this trend[7] in 1995, electing Tony Blair as party leader. He has since led Labour to two three consecutive wins in 1997, 2001, and 2005.

Of course, whether a party leader becomes prime minister (or remains as party leader) is determined by how well the party does at election time. A typical party leader will get two or three chances to gain a parliamentary majority and form a government. Some are rather successful at doing this: Margaret Thatcher became the longest-serving British prime minister and Conservative party leader in modern

---

[7]"Portillo's Complaint," *The Economist*, October 22, 1995, 63.

times by winning three consecutive national elections and remaining head of government for eleven years (1979–1990). She had become the Conservative leader four years earlier, in 1975. During the same sixteen-year period, Labour went through no fewer than five party leaders.

Becoming party leader requires a great deal of persistence and patience. These requirements were especially in evidence in the Conservative party during the past few decades. The Labour party in the 1990s began choosing younger and more dynamic leaders, electing Tony Blair as party leader while still in his late thirties. Successful party leaders in Britain, as in most of the industrialized democracies, usually emerge from moderate elements.

The ultimate selection of a prime minister also depends on the public perception of political personalities. British prime ministers tend to remain in power in great part because of their perceived or real strength of character. Like occasional American presidents, British prime ministers have sometimes been accused of being weak or ineffective. No such charge was ever leveled at Margaret Thatcher: She was affectionately known as the "iron lady." Presidents Jimmy Carter and the first George Bush were seen as being too soft to be effective. So was former Prime Minister John Major, Thatcher's successor, despite the fact that he successfully repulsed numerous intra-party efforts to get rid of him. Tony Blair is not known as weak. His support of the Bush administration's war on terrorism and war on Saddam Hussein got him into some trouble with elements in his own party during 2002 and 2003 who did not support the decision to go to war in Iraq.[8]

On the other hand, Winston Churchill, Britain's prime minister during World War II, was often characterized by both friends and critics as a bulldog in his relentless refusal to give in to an enemy he personally despised. Margaret Thatcher's nickname attests to her strong personal stubbornness and her forceful political style. When the British imprisoned Irish Republican Army agents in Belfast as common criminals and murderers in the 1980s, the prisoners threatened a hunger strike unless they were reclassified as political prisoners. Prime Minister Thatcher suggested they were free to starve themselves to death (a few did) and argued they at least had a choice they didn't allow their victims.

After a national election, the leader of the majority party or, in rare circumstances, the plurality party (the party with the most seats), in the House of Commons is expected to form a government by invitation of the Queen. The leader becomes Her Majesty's first or prime minister. In reality, of course, the government is already in place. The interview with the queen is a pro-forma or symbolic act. However, this symbolism does give a prospective prime minister's political legitimacy a boost. Queen Elizabeth II is, after all, the head of state. She confers the authority of the state to her government when she names a prime minister and requests that that individual form a cabinet.

6-2d Self-Selected Executives

Most of the world's government leaders are not popularly chosen through regular and honest elections. Nondemocratic regimes regularly display varying degrees of disregard for basic human rights. Some "honest" dictators sincerely desire to do what is best for their countries. Kemal Ataturk, for example, governed Turkey in a rather authoritarian manner during 1922–1935, but believed Turkey should be democratic. To prove his point he created two political parties to compete with one another in elections. Most dictators, however, are rather mindless of and insensitive to the suffering they cause their own citizens.

The Kim dynasty in North Korea has been previously mentioned. It is typical of perhaps five dozen countries governed by frequently despised and feared dictators.

---

[8]"Saddam's Feint," *The Economist*, September 21, 2002, 54.

In these countries, the political system exhibits several or all of the following characteristics:

1. The principal constituency is the military hierarchy. The dictator is often a military leader and sees the officer corps, many of whom he knows personally and who secured his power, as the means by which he can retain and expand power.

2. The dictatorship relies on secret police. Because a dictatorship cannot depend on voluntary citizen support, a secret police force, often run by a near relative of the dictator, reports and punishes any sign of dissent or opposition. For example, Bashir Al-Assad came to power in 2000 in Syria, when his father died, even though he was too young to be constitutionally eligible for the Syrian presidency. An obedient legislature quicky amended the Syrian constitution to lower the minimum age. He inherited support from the military and from the Syrian secret police and blunted all opposition to his ascension to the Syrian leadership. Dictators, it should be pointed out, occasionally hold sham elections in order to demonstrate how beloved and popular they are in their own countries. They don't seem to understand that they really aren't fooling anyone. In some dictatorships, several versions of the secret police actually spy on one another as well as on the general citizenry.

3. Power is vested in the dictator's close associates. Family members and/or retainers from a particular region or tribe are placed in positions of authority because the dictator does not have the luxury of choosing people on the basis of merit. This practice often leads to governmental incompetence, because totally unsuited people may be placed in high office. It also can encourage rampant corruption, because political leaders may feel they have a license to enrich themselves while they can, until the day the regime is overthrown.

4. The dictator is installed for life, or until overthrown. Unless the dictator is also a monarch, little or no provision is made for political succession. Thus, when a dictator is overthrown or dies after several decades in power, national turmoil may ensue. Dictatorships are rarely succeeded by democratic regimes. A country may wind up sincerely mourning the passing of a dictator when the alternative is chaos or civil war that will end only when another, perhaps even more brutal, dictatorship is established.

5. The dictatorship is especially oppressive to select groups. A dictatorship may be especially desirous of making life miserable for an ethnic or religious minority that has sought to establish political autonomy or to gain outright independence. This feature is a main characteristic of Nigeria, where the military regime is very fond of hanging dissidents based on both their opposition to government policy and on their tribal associations.

Monarchs come to power quietly and usually peacefully through inheritance. Unlike military dictators, monarchs rarely have to kill people to gain power. Currently, monarchies seem to be more powerful in the Middle East than in any other region. This is especially noticeable in the Persian Gulf, where several countries are traditionalist monarchies; the same royal house has been in power for several generations and is accustomed to having things its own way. Saudi Arabia is the best example of monarchial autocracy. During the 1920s the Saud family assumed control of most of the Arabian Peninsula and named the country after itself.

Several political democracies are described as **constitutional monarchies**. Britain's Queen Elizabeth, for example, and Japan's Emperor Akihito are constitutional monarchs. A constitutional monarchy is not a dictatorship because the monarch is usually stripped of real political power.

The rulers in **absolute monarchies** are certainly masters of their countries. Some of them, like the Saud family of Saudi Arabia, will not even hear of the possibility of a popularly elected legislature.

Some absolute monarchies may be evolving out of their absolutism. In Jordan, King Hussein (reigned during 1952–2000) permitted free elections. His son and

constitutional monarchy
A system in which a nondemocratic institution, the monarchy, is preserved by transferring any substantive decision-making power from the monarch to the parliament.

absolute monarchy
A system in which the chief executive holds all significant political powers and transfers power to his or her heirs.

successor, Abdullah II, has continued the practice, but still retains ultimate control over the country's armed forces. Unlike military dictators, monarchs are usually more relaxed about their positions. Even King Hussein, who was the target of innumerable assassination plots, is noted not only for his strong governing style but for his toleration of occasional dissent. Of course, outright opposition to the institution of the monarchy is not allowed.

6-3 Executive Powers

The powers of the head of government vary from system to system. Democracies have a great deal in common, but they are distinct from one another in significant ways. Consider, for example, what a French president can do in comparison to an American president:

- serve as many terms as elected (U.S. presidents are limited to two four-year terms)
- govern unilaterally, without the national legislature, during a state of emergency (which the president can unilaterally declare) for up to six months
- dissolve the lower house of the national legislature (but no more than once in a twelve-month period) and announce a national referendum, the result of which has the force of law

The British prime minister also has some helpful advantages an American president can only envy. Specifically, the prime minister can:

- ensure that a parliamentary majority equipped with party discipline will pass the prime minister's legislative proposals
- choose the time of the next national election, as long as the date is within five years from the most recent election
- normally rely on a majority of the party's MPs in the House of Commons to retain the prime ministership
- work without facing the restriction of term limits

6-4 Constitutional Restraints

Every democratic system places serious limitations on the powers of its government. Most have a constitution that guarantees the civil rights of the citizenry. Such guarantees often form the relationship between government and the governed and are explored further in the next chapter.

Restrictions on the powers of the executive are especially pronounced in most democratic processes. In many of the presidential systems in the Western hemisphere, the chief executive is limited to a precise number of terms, often just one term. In several of the Latin American democracies, dictators proclaiming themselves presidents for life are a disconcertingly recent memory. François "Papa Doc" Duvalier did this in Haiti and died in office. His son and successor, however, was thrown out of power a few years later and lives in exile in France. Some countries have constitutions that not only limit incumbents to one or two terms but prohibit immediate family members from seceding to power.

The United States is a recent convert to term limits. The Twenty-second Amendment, ratified in 1951, limits American presidents to a total of two four-year terms, or a total of ten years if a vice president takes over for a president and then is elected him- or herself. A comparative summary of term restrictions appears in Table 6–2.

Some presidential systems are more restrictive than others. The French president is probably the most powerful. He or she faces no term limits, is elected by an absolute popular majority, and has emergency powers that can be invoked when

TABLE 6–2	**Presidential Term Limits in Selected Countries**	
Country	**Length of Term**	**Renewable?**
Costa Rica	4 years	No
France	5 years	Yes
Mexico	6 years	No
United States	4 years	Once

the president thinks they are needed. Article 16 of the French Constitution states that

> When the institutions of the Republic, the independence of the nation, the integrity of its territory or the fulfillment of its international commitments are threatened in a grave and immediate manner and when the regular functioning of the constitutional governmental authorities is interrupted, the president of the Republic shall take measures commanded by these circumstances . . .

The president can determine when "a grave and immediate manner" exists, but the emergency powers themselves have limitations: The president is obligated to apply emergency measures with the cooperation of the prime minister and the presidents of the Senate and National Assembly.

Finally, government leaders, including presidents, are constitutionally required to obey the same laws as everyone else. They cannot bribe their way to power, rig elections, or arbitrarily repeal laws they don't like, although the latter becomes excusable and perhaps even justified in national emergencies. Lincoln, for example, suspended the writ of *habeus corpus*, which allows a citizen to challenge the government for imprisoning him or her without due process of law, during the Civil War from 1861 to 1865. This was clearly an impeachable offense, but a Congress dominated by Lincoln's party and determined to retain the Union's territorial integrity ignored it. Eighty years later, the U.S. government detained 120,000 Americans of Japanese descent, confiscating property from many, during World War II. No president could get away with such disregard for the law in peacetime.[9]

In most democratic systems, restraints on executive power are both constitutionally required and voluntarily self-imposed. In Britain, for example, there is basically nothing to thwart or delay a parliamentary act. National elections are required at least once every five years, but from 1935 to 1945, elections were not held because of the emergency of World War II. The prime minister simply refrained from asking the king to dissolve parliament. The leaders of the political parties, already bound together in national unity, agreed that elections would be held immediately after the end of the war in Europe. They were, and the regular democratic process was renewed.

When no restraints are imposed on government in general and on the executive in particular, government is usually ineffective or worse. Many authoritarian dictators are too busy maintaining power and building expensive (and often tasteless) monuments to themselves to be bothered about the needs of their people. While North Korea's economy was deteriorating and causing much human suffering, the country's leader, Kim Il Sung, constructed a statue of himself bigger than any building in the country. His son, Kim Jong Il, was responsible for having Japanese citizens kidnapped and forced to assist North Korean intelligence agents spy in Japan by acquainting them with Japanese culture.[10] Saddam Hussein, while

---

[9]Nearly half a century later the American government apologized to the survivors and offered compensation for their ordeal.

[10]"The Apologetic Kidnapper, " *The Economist*, September 21, 2002, 12.

decrying the economic sanctions the international community imposed on his country, was still able to scrape $1.5 billion together to build a total of eight luxury palaces for his family and himself. Authoritarian leaders think only reluctantly about the long-term interests of their countries, such as political succession, because they are much more concerned with their own survival and self-interest. In contrast, restraints on power help a government work effectively for the long-term good of its citizens.

6-5 Bureaucracy

It is difficult to imagine modern or modernizing societies attempting to deliver public services to an ever-demanding citizenry without a bureaucracy. Ideally, **bureaucracies** assist the executive in providing at least those basic services, such as police and fire protection, which make citizens' lives more secure and comfortable, as well as implementing policy for the executive branch. The rapid growth of technology has enabled the bureaucracy to deliver more services efficiently at an affordable cost. Because technology is often a double-edged sword, bureaucracy may also be perceived as increasingly intrusive in the private lives of individuals. Moreover, depending on the system, bureaucracies can be beneficial, but they can also be murderous. This section will briefly examine how bureaucracies work in various political systems.

6-5a The Executive and the Bureaucracy

Most civil servants (the more polite term for "bureaucrats") perform important activities. Assuring even minimal services to an industrial society of millions of people is a daunting task. It isn't as though bureaucrats haven't been at it for a long time. Sumerian kings, Chinese emperors, and Egyptian pharaohs relied on a professional civil service. Nearly five millennia ago these civil servants made sure taxes were collected, roads built, armies paid, and the pyramids constructed.

Until modern times, few bureaucracies thought much about training or developing skills. France has been a pioneer in this effort, developing the *grandes écoles,* special schools dedicated to preparing civil servants to serve the public interest. One French president, Valery Giscard d'Estaing (1974–1981), was a *grande école* graduate. French presidents almost invariably have several graduates in their cabinets.

Most countries, including the United States, have no equivalent to the *grandes écoles.* This is a pity, because the schools not only train civil servants, but can increase or decrease the number of students they admit. By limiting or enhancing the number of students, the French ensure that their bureaucracy does not become top-heavy. Many *grande école* graduates eventually seek better paying jobs in the private sector.

Occasionally, bureaucracies forget their reason for being. They fundamentally exist to help rather than hinder people. At the same time, citizens demanding services need to remember that their taxes pay for the services bureaucracies provide, and when they want more services, bureaucracies will grow and become more costly. If, for example, people want breathable air, a governmental agency is probably going to have to ensure that industry complies with antipollution standards. Of course, breathing healthy air will then cost all citizens more in taxes.

In a democracy, a bureaucracy is supposed to serve rather than control. (The latter is in ample supply in nondemocratic systems.) Even a bureaucracy with good intentions and substantial resources may not find it easy to provide public services. As urban areas have expanded and as national borders, particularly in Western Europe and increasingly in North America, have partially broken down as the result of economic integration, bureaucratic jurisdictions have become complicated and confused.

bureaucracy
The machinery of government that carries out the policies that the executive and legislative branches have formulated.

In both Germany and the United States, for example, it is common for an individual to work in one city (or state) and live in another. He may receive services where he works but pay taxes only where he lives.[11] In several European countries and in North America, city boundaries are even beginning to flow over national frontiers. Along the border between the United States and Mexico, towns on both sides regularly trade services and a great deal of the workforce in the southwestern United States comes from Mexico, much of it legal, some of it not. There is little doubt that in the near future, bureaucracies from a variety of national and local jurisdictions will have to cooperate to serve the needs of distinct populations that impact upon one another.

Clearly, bureaucracies must constantly reform and revise policy as demands change and grow and as resources become less dependable. Local and national bureaucracies may be unprepared for demographic shifts. In the United States, for example, the bureaucratic structure of the public school system has been unprepared to cope with dramatic increases in numbers and in ethnic diversity.[12] Citizenries in democracies tend to evaluate governments on the basis of their comfort level. Bureaucracies will therefore not go away, nor should one expect to see them significantly reduced.

Governments that have tried to drastically reduce the role of bureaucracies have not been especially successful. In a modern industrial society, it is probably futile to try to reduce the role of the bureaucracy in any substantial fashion. A population that is rapidly aging—a feature particularly apparent in countries such as France, Germany, and Japan—and that is increasingly dependent on medical care funded by the public sector and concerned about the relationship between monthly social security checks and the inflation rate is going to make increasing, not diminishing, demands.

Moreover, bureaucracies must sometimes deliver services to people who haven't paid for them. New York City officials, for example, get annoyed at the great number of people who derive their livelihoods in the city but live and pay their taxes in another jurisdiction. As metropolitan areas spill over and across national borders, as they have between the United States and Mexico, bureaucracies in each area may have to pool resources with their neighbors and combine certain services. In sum, bureaucracies are liable to grow rather than shrink in the years ahead because services are increasing. People like the services bureaucracies provide. They want their garbage picked up once or twice a week, their food supply to be guaranteed, their roads paved, and drinking water safe. What people don't like is paying for all of these services.

6-5b Bad and Ineffective Bureaucracies

A bad bureaucracy and a bureaucracy that is ineffective are not necessarily the same. Governments implement policy through various bureaucratic agencies. The political traditions of responsible government strongly suggest that policies be geared to protect and help people. Too often, though, a government can cause a great deal of harm to its own citizenry and sometimes to other nations. A government can formulate and a bureaucracy pursue policies that intentionally hurt or destroy entire communities.

Several governments, such as the Soviet Union under Stalin (1924–1953), China under Mao Tse-tung (1949–1976), and Germany under Hitler (1933–1945), have exhibited frightening and massive lethality. Tens of millions of people under the control of these regimes perished because of inhumane conditions that bureaucratic agencies planned, created, and maintained. A bureaucracy is supposed to do

---

[11]"Federal Jigsaw," *The Economist*, June 2, 1990, 51.

[12]"Next Population Bulge Shows Its Might," *The Wall Street Journal*, February 3, 1997, sec. B.

what a government tells it to. In some political regimes, the careers of bureaucrats are determined by how efficiently they carry out their assigned tasks.

Adolf Eichmann (1906–1962) provides an example of the negative nature a bureaucracy can take on. Eichmann was part of the Nazi regime in Germany. He was placed in charge of transporting Jews and other victims across Europe to concentration camps, where most of them died from exposure, disease, or hunger, or perished in gas chambers. After his capture in 1960 in Argentina by Israeli agents and during his subsequent trial, Eichmann insisted it was his job to pack people into cattle cars and ensure that they arrived at their destinations on schedule. What happened to them after their arrival was not his concern or responsibility. One observer at the trial suggested that Eichmann was such a mindless cog that he would have had his own father executed if ordered to do so.[13] Yet, in the sense of carrying out state-mandated policy, Eichmann was a "good" bureaucrat.

Unfortunately for their victims, neither the Nazi nor Soviet bureaucracies were inefficient. Obviously, efficiency can have its darker side. However, many national bureaucracies are inept to the point of tragedy. The ineptness is not always the bureaucrats' fault. At times, they simply may not have enough resources to accomplish much. For example, out of an eight-hour day, the typical Egyptian bureaucrat does actual work for only twenty-seven minutes on average.[14] The short workday cannot be attributed to sheer laziness. Egyptian bureaucrats, like most of their Third World counterparts lack the resources to fulfill their assigned duties. There are many more bureaucrats than financial and technological resources.

The Egyptian capital city, Cairo, has a population of perhaps sixteen million. No one is sure of the exact number. Nearly one of every four Egyptians lives in a city with a bureaucratic infrastructure geared to provide services for about a third of the current population. Each day, Cairo adds 1,000 new people to its population. There is no way the bureaucracy can even begin to provide the most basic public services.

The trend in Egypt and other Third World countries is clear: Most have more civil servants than they know what to do with. The government hires college graduates because the private sector cannot yet provide enough jobs for white collar workers. Egypt is a United States ally and the second largest recipient of American foreign assistance, about $2.5 billion annually. Much of this sum is used to support the salaries of educated civil servants who might otherwise conspire against the government.

There are limits to the services bureaucracies can provide and the powers they hold. In many cases, the limits are too weak to protect people from abuse; in others, the bureaucracy lacks the resources to do much. In either case, it is hard for the executive branch of a government to achieve its goals without a viable bureaucracy.

Chapter Summary

1. National political leaders are generally *heads of government*, the people whose parties win elections or who appoint themselves in dictatorships. Heads of state, in contrast, are not politically powerful, but provide a symbolic legitimacy for the government and unity for the nation.
2. The American presidency is the world's single most powerful political office because of the tremendous military and economic resources. However, it is an office subject to constitutional limitations and restraints other strong democratic executives do not have to face.
3. In parliamentary systems such as the United Kingdom, the prime minister is invariably an individual who has worked his or her way up the party hierarchy. American presidents can have a power base separate from the national party hierarchy.

---

[13]Hannah Arendt, *Eichmann in Jerusalem* (New York: Viking Press, 1963).

[14]Mary Anne Weaver, "The Novelist and the Sheikh," *The New Yorker,* January 30, 1995.

4. The cabinet in a parliamentary system stands or falls together. It is composed of the top leaders of the majority party or coalition members.

5. Ceremonial heads of state are useful symbols of national unity and political legitimacy in great part because they lack significant political power to do any harm.

6. Democratic executives are not always chosen in the most democratic process; they may be selected indirectly, as in the United States. In several Latin American countries and in France, the chief executive must be elected by an absolute popular majority.

7. Self-selected nonmonarchial executives often install themselves following a military coup, which may or may not have been violent.

8. Constitutional restraints on executive powers vary from democracy to democracy. They may also increase or decrease depending on whether a severe national crisis crops up.

9. A country's bureaucracy is supposed to implement executive policy. In nondemocratic systems, the policies enunciated by the dictator may be inhumane and even criminal.

Chapter 6 Quiz

1. The United States president who viewed the presidency as a "bully pulpit" was
   a. Teddy Roosevelt.
   b. Franklin Roosevelt.
   c. Ronald Reagan.
   d. Bill Clinton.

2. The presidential system is most widespread in
   a. Europe.
   b. Middle East.
   c. Latin America.
   d. East Asia.

3. A politician hoping to become British prime minister should probably have
   a. royal blood.
   b. membership in the House of Lords.
   c. long service in the lower house of parliament.
   d. a military background.

4. In the British parliamentary system, cabinet ministers are generally
   a. independently elected by the voters.
   b. members of the House of Commons.
   c. appointed by the Church of England.
   d. members of the House of Lords.

5. The French presidency
   a. is popularly elected.
   b. doesn't face term limitations.
   c. comes equipped with a vice presidency.
   d. a and b only.

6. Presidents receiving less than 50 percent of the popular vote in the United States have included
   a. George W. Bush.
   b. Bill Clinton.
   c. John Kennedy.
   d. all of the above

7. Britain is an example of a
   a. military dictatorship.
   b. theocracy.
   c. constitutional monarchy.
   d. republican form of government.

8. Unlike the American and French presidents, the British prime minister gets to
   a. trespass on certain civil liberties.
   b. determine the date of the next national election.
   c. choose a successor.
   d. achieve high office through a special electoral college.

9. "Papa Doc" Duvalier is an example of
   a. a popularly elected monarch.
   b. a dictator becoming "president for life."
   c. the Federalist Papers in practice.
   d. two-term presidencies in Latin America.

10. Adolf Eichmann is an example of a
    a. corrupt bureaucrat.
    b. democratic bureaucrat.
    c. good bureaucrat in terms of executing state policy.
    d. lazy bureaucrat.

CHAPTER 7

The Law and the Judiciary

laws
Rules that formalize and reinforce patterns of social behavior that the overwhelming majority of society's members consider acceptable and beneficial.

A body of laws or legal system is required for social and political coherence. Laws can come from a variety of sources or simply from a single source. They are usually based somewhat on the customs and traditions that characterize a particular society. Because customs and traditions vary from society to society, legal systems themselves are far from identical. Whatever their origins, **laws** are essentially rules that identify, formalize, and reinforce patterns of social and political behavior that the overwhelming majority of society's members consider acceptable as well as individually and collectively beneficial.

Laws serve complementary functions: They are intended to protect each person from the predatory actions of others and from outrageous acts the government may commit. Simply put by political thinkers from Aristotle to Thomas Aquinas to John Locke, without constant adherence to law, any government is liable to become arbitrary and tyrannical. Locke, for example, argued that

> whosoever in authority exceeds the power given him by the law, and makes use of the force he has under his command to compass that upon the subject which the law allows not, ceases in that to be a magistrate, and acting without authority may be opposed, as any other man who by force invades the right of another.[1]

This basically means that without law and its application, society is either chaotic or autocratic. In effect, Locke concludes that if a political authority violates or ignores the law, the authority itself is illegal. People have both the obligation and the right to rebel if that is what it takes to establish a political authority that behaves lawfully. Locke provided the argument against a disreputable government that the American revolutionaries adopted a century later. As this chapter will emphasize, laws must not only exist, they must possess integrity. Unless both ruler and ruled voluntarily and steadfastly accept and obey them, laws are meaningless. No citizen or government official, at least in a democracy, is above or is immune to the law.

The rule of law consists of "legal decisions based on predictable rules and precedents."[2] It is difficult to overestimate the importance of the rule of law. It has, for example, been conspicuously absent in Iraq both before and after the American presence that began in 2003. In countries such as North Korea, law is at all times dependent upon the whim of a brutal dictatorship. Few people feel the protection of the law when the law itself can easily be swept aside. Predictability is a critical issue in this context. Nearly everyone, regardless of lifestyle, possesses a desire to know what is going to happen next in life and in the lives of family and friends. This is not always possible, of course, but the prevalence and application of law provides a strong degree of comfort and, to a limited extent, predictability. They expect others to leave them alone if they prefer not to interact. Exceptions are often brutal and frightening. When, during the fall of 2002, a sniper shot and killed or injured several people going about their daily business in the Washington, D.C. area, great numbers of people became alarmed. An unknown number began to alter their lifestyles and started to avoid restaurants, convenience stores, and other public places.

---

[1]John Locke, *Second Treatise on Civil Government*, XVIII, 199 and 202.

[2]Robert L. Bartley, "About Freedom in the Free World," *The Wall Street Journal*, October 14, 2002, sec. A.

Some were considering simply staying at home.[3] All of this suggests both the importance and fragility of the law in people's lives. One or two murderers have the capacity to wreak havoc on hundreds of thousands by contributing in frightening ways to the breakdown of law.

This chapter will examine notions of law and the various formulations laws take as well as the relationship between law and justice. This examination will also consider where laws come from and how they relate to particular cultures. Finally, the chapter will review the place of the judiciary in the legal system.

7-1 Where Laws Come From and What They Are For

Laws come from human necessity. They are formulated to regulate the acceptable conduct of human activities. Laws are often based on well-established tradition and social norms that are formalized into a legal system.

7-1a The Reasons for Laws

Crime has always been present in human society, yet both the nature of some crimes and the motivations behind them change over time. Laws must therefore also be flexible and be prepared for change. This is a difficult challenge; because laws enforced over time acquire a degree of respect, society is often reluctant to change them.

Laws and legal codes appeared because human society requires at least a minimum of order and discipline. Plato's *Republic* was a vision of society without laws. In fact, Plato's view was that laws were unnecessary because nearly omniscient philosopher-kings could preside over justice. Yet even Plato gave up on this ideal and wrote a sequel to *The Republic* appropriately entitled *Laws*. Neither in Plato's time nor since then have philosopher-kings been commonly available.

Laws need to be revisited from time to time. A society must bring them up-to-date, if only because of rapid technological progress. Sometimes entire legal systems must be revamped. On other occasions, a legal system can survive longer than the political institutions that created it. When they formed the United States, the founders retained many legal traditions inherited from Britain. Though they fought the British for independence, they respected Britain's legal system—they simply believed the British government violated its own laws.

When the Soviet regime collapsed in 1991, the Soviet legal system largely survived, at least in the immediate aftermath. This legal system, though, was part of a discredited regime and economy. Much that had been illegal now became legal. Private businesses, for instance, now opened, new political parties formed, and publications critical of government policy sprang up without breaking the law.

The idea that a person's word is his or her bond has been a reality for much of human history. When human beings mostly lived in villages, societies were usually small populations made up of people who knew and, for the most part, trusted one another. In such a situation, lawyers were rarely needed. A modern society, though, may be composed of tens or hundreds of millions of people who have complicated business and political dealings with each other but never meet. Instead they deal with one another by email, fax, phone, or regular mail.

The regulation of human activities by laws rather than the personal whims of an all-powerful government is a notion that has taken root in numerous countries. Laws that are more or less equally applied to all citizens, including those who govern, do seem to create an environment that the great majority of people have confidence in and will therefore support. Of course, laws can also be warped in order to

---

[3] *The New York Times*, October 18, 2002.

instill fear in an entire population. The penalty, for example, for criticizing Saddam Hussein, his books, or any of his policies in Iraq before the collapse of his regime in 2003 could mean the partial amputation of one's tongue or compelled to watch other family members beaten to death.[4]

Generally speaking, crimes of violence are universally condemned. No government, even one that commits violence itself, can tolerate individual acts of violence. To do so, as Hobbes pointed out three and a half centuries ago, would create chaos and drastically reduce public confidence in government.

However, definitions of criminal acts are not always the same in every country because legal systems are never exactly the same. In the United States, for instance, there is no legal requirement to work. While it is necessary for most people to pursue careers spanning four decades or more, the wealthy few can cheerfully live off the income from their investments without fear of punitive action on the part of the government. In the Soviet Union, on the other hand, it was against the law not to work. This law made sense in a communist society: Those who don't work have no place in a workers' paradise. One was legally required to be productive on behalf of society and to be relentlessly self-sacrificing. Selfishness itself was not an option. **Antiparasite laws** thus ensured that every able-bodied member of Soviet society fulfilled his or her obligations to labor toward building communism. The antiparasite laws in effect outlawed the choice of not working or working in trades (such as felonious crimes like drug trafficking and prostitution) that were not considered economically productive by the regime.

It's also important to note that crimes are occasionally criminal acts used to camouflage even worse and potentially more violent crimes. For example, a cell of Hezbollah, a terrorist organization devoted to the destruction of Israel and the United States[*] and supported by the Iranian government, was based in Charlotte, North Carolina, in order to more easily acquire and then sell on the black market in Michigan millions of dollars worth of cigarettes.[5] Clearly, this was an illegal racketeering act. Much of the money collected then went to support the terrorist activities of Hezbollah in Lebanon.

7-1b Lawgivers and Laws

Countries and even entire civilizations have adopted legal systems that have long ancestries. Lawgivers appeared early in written political history. In some cases, there is only scant evidence that a lawgiver—an individual who alone or with a few aides—formulated laws that were intended to guide and monitor correct human behavior and punish misbehavior. It is far from accidental that some of the most memorable political personalities in history were individuals who took a substantial interest in or were authors of the legal system in the countries they governed. Hammurabi was referred to in an earlier chapter as the first leader in recorded history to codify laws. The biblical Moses is another example of an early leader who combined political and legal leadership. Moses was a lawgiver who transmitted a moral code that was applied to all members of society. The code was in this case of divine origin because Moses received its basis, the Ten Commandments, from a celestial source while spending forty days alone on Mount Sinai. To a large extent, though, the Mosaic law that evolved over several centuries was both a codification of existing customs and habits and a detailed arrangement for the conduct of daily life. Both the Hammurabi Code and the Mosaic law paid close attention to details of personal behavior. Neither separated the secular from the spiritual. Nearly a millennium later Confucius (551–478 B.C.) did much the same sort of thing in China.

antiparasite laws
Instituted by the Soviet government, these laws discouraged laziness by requiring all members of Soviet society to work.

[4]Nicholas D. Kristoff, "An Iraqi Man of Letters," *The New York Times*, October 8, 2002, sec. A.

[*]Hezbollah was responsible for the attack on American military barracks in Beirut in 1983 that left nearly 250 dead.

[5]Jeffrey Goldberg, "In the Party of God," *The New Yorker*, October 28, 2002, 83.

Confucius successfully encouraged a mixture of harmony, learning, and virtue as underpinnings of law. So pervasive was his influence that his legal scheme was adopted by the Chinese government for two and a half millennia until it was officially abandoned in 1912. However, Confucian legal philosophy is still apparent throughout much of Chinese culture even today.

The history of a society or even a civilization can be characterized by its legal traditions. Ancient Sparta, known for the harsh regimen it imposed on its citizen-soldiers, became a rigid and stern system only after a perhaps mythical law codifier, Lycurgus, admonished Spartans to distrust foreigners, ignore the arts, and devote themselves solely to military training and civic duty. Thus, the term *Spartan* came to mean someone who lives simply and submits to harsh physical discipline. Another Greek law codifier was Draco—an Athenian—who for good reason inspired the term *draconian legislation.* Draco's code emphasized not the law itself, but what would today be regarded as drastic punishment for breaking the law. The death penalty was applied for several dozen crimes, such as stealing food, that are currently regarded as misdemeanors for which the penalty might be a simple fine or thirty days in jail. To put the punishment in context, however, those who lived in ancient times led a precarious existence in which stealing food could result in death. Punishments are still inhumane in some places. Hama, Syria, an entire town of 20,000—men, women, and children—was wiped off the map by military forces because of a rebellion in the town against the regime.

Lawgivers and law codifiers have left a strong imprint on legal systems. They have also caused considerable debate. Many people assume that laws, especially those with a moral content, are absolutely binding on every generation. The ancient legal codes are, to varying extents, still in force. They are applied in the origins of laws and punishments against the more heinous crimes of murder and rape. Most of the ancient lawgivers and codifiers, including those previously named, claimed to be legislating with a divine purpose. As the world has (unevenly) moved into more modern times, though, the authority to make laws has become increasingly secular and more flexible.

In modern societies, it is especially difficult to escape debate on issues that some regard as sacrosanct and others see as reactionary or nonsensical. Natural law and divine law are two concepts that tend to supplement one another. Both assume that a law divinely revealed or reasonably thought out is absolute everywhere, throughout time. An opposing school of thought, known as **positive law**, suggests that absolutism simply doesn't work: Change is constantly occurring, and laws cannot remain immutable. Moreover, while different societies undergo change at different paces, they nevertheless remain distinct from one another. Laws that protect one form of behavior in one society may not be found in another society where that particular behavior is patently illegal. Adultery by a married woman in the United States may result in a divorce, but in Saudi Arabia could result in the public beheading of the culprit. Law is a complicated matter and normally subject to the cultural norms of the society in question.

positive law
The philosophy that law is what a particular society decides it is for itself alone, not an absolute.

It should be noted that lawgivers and law codifiers are those who are attempting to craft a system of legal behavior that genuinely benefits the greater community. Dictators, in contrast, view law as an inconvenience to be ignored at best or violated on personal whim at worst. Iraq's former president, Saddam Hussein, for example, won a presidential election in 2002 without an opponent and with almost exactly 100 percent of the popular vote. In celebration he ordered the release of thousands of prison inmates, some of whom actually deserved to be in prison for capital crimes. Others were simply those viewed by Hussein's regime as political enemies.[6] Murderers and rapists were let loose on Iraqi society. The government's secret police were expected to arrest them again after the regime's compassion was demonstrated.[7]

---

[6]"Saddam Ceausecu?" *The Wall Street Journal,* October 22, 2002, sec. A.

[7]Ibid.

A number of these individuals joined the resistance against the American-led coalition later in 2003.

7-1c Law and Morality

Legal systems almost always include some moral values that a society has cherished for generations, sometimes for centuries. Murder was most likely considered immoral long before it became illegal. As one scholar has asserted,

> It is of course clear (and one of the oldest insights of political theory) that society could not exist without a morality which mirrored and supplemented the law's proscription of conduct injurious to others.[8]

At the same time, however, the state's physical enforcement of a particular morality is usually self-defeating. While most people would agree that society is probably better off adhering to standards of moral conduct, most would also be more likely to adhere to moral standards arrived at through reasoned argument and persuasion.[9]

Laws formalize customs and traditions that have existed for generations. A law works well when:

1. Everyone without exception is obligated to obey it. Laws lose credibility if they don't apply equally to everyone.
2. Compliance is voluntary and nearly universal. A bad or silly law is quickly found out when large segments of the population oppose or simply ignore it. When the United States attempted, through the Constitution's Eighteenth Amendment, to prohibit the sale and consumption of alcoholic beverages in the 1920s, the experiment failed and the constitutional amendment was repealed (by the Twenty-first Amendment) because so many people refused to obey a law they regarded as either unnecessary or absurd.
3. It is enforceable. While most people will obey a reasonable law, a few won't. The state must be prepared to ensure compliance by pursuing the alternatives of incarceration and/or financial penalties.

Morality has always underpinned the law. As one scholar succinctly expressed it, in both civil and criminal cases, the law's "function is simply to enforce a moral principle and nothing else."[10] This seems an easy principle to follow until one remembers that morality is supposed to be absolute—that is, never changing— while the law must be flexible. And even morality is not always absolute. Slavery was considered by its defenders as a very moral way of dealing with those who they believed were racially inferior. Such a condescending view is considered repugnant by today's standards, but was a convincing argument for those in the early nineteenth-century American South who owned slaves.2003.

7-1d Laws and Obedience

Most people generally obey the law because it is almost always in their self-interest to do so. People believe that the law requiring them to stop their cars at red lights, for example, is an excellent idea, and they consistently obey it. In fact, it is difficult to think of one good reason not to do so.

Laws are relatively painless to obey when they make sense. Most laws do make sense most of the time, but it is sometimes questionable whether the punishment

---

[8]H. L. A. Hart, *Law, Liberty, and Morality* (Stanford, California: Stanford University Press, 1963), 16.

[9]Ibid., 45.

[10]Patrick Devlin, "Morals and the Criminal Law," in *On Liberty,* John Stuart Mill, ed. David Spitz, (New York and London: W. W. Norton, 1975) 179.

for breaking a law is sensible. For example, several Western democracies have engaged in a serious debate about drug laws. Is it reasonable to imprison people who commit nonviolent criminal acts such as smoking marijuana? Should a person who uses marijuana to alleviate the discomfort associated with multiple sclerosis be considered guilty of possession of an illegal drug? According to Florida law, such a person is destined to go to prison—and in fact, one has.[11] In another case, a law-abiding dentist who had unwittingly lent money to someone running marijuana was convicted for conspiracy to distribute illegal drugs.[12] Laws that aren't sensible can be expensive; it costs over $30,000 annually to imprison one person in the United States.

Still, people are required to obey laws even when they disagree with them. This principle may sound peculiar, but people adhere to it in many cultures and nations, particularly in the democracies. Most laws that result from democratic processes and institutions enjoy nearly universal compliance because of the procedures by which they are adopted and implemented. Moreover, people in democracies know they can resort to the same processes and institutions to change laws they disagree with.

In an increasingly global society, it may be a good idea to have laws that make sense to anyone. With occasional exceptions, Americans find it easy to obey laws in other democracies, for example. Although they encounter some unaccustomed inconveniences in nondemocratic systems, such as restrictions on personal travel, the inconveniences are modest compared to those the permanent residents of these countries usually endure, if only because Americans are in these areas for short durations.

Nearly all legal systems contain numerous common features. This is hardly surprising, because all members of these societies are human. The fact that people all experience similar needs and apprehensions suggests that a universal legal system might apply to everyone.

Throughout the Western democracies, an independent judiciary has been instrumental in protecting individual rights. Many democracies, particularly the English-speaking ones, build on the judicial outcomes of cases. Courts do not explicitly make law—that task belongs to the legislatures—but they do interpret laws. The result is **case law**. The courts often make meaningful changes in existing laws by interpreting the law in new ways.

case law
Law based on judicial interpretations of existing laws and statutes. Court decisions become law themselves.

As an example, the United States Supreme Court legalized abortion in January 1973 in *Roe v. Wade*. This one decision forced several states to revise their abortion laws because any Supreme Court decision becomes the law of the land. The Court would have to reverse its decision or Congress would have to pass a constitutional amendment (which two-thirds of the states would then have to ratify) for the United States to again outlaw abortion. On the thirtieth anniversary of the decision in 2003 and beyond, the issue was still being noisily debated. Those who are anti-abortion have not given up trying to reverse the decision. While law may have a moral basis, as discussed earlier, there can still be an argument as to how morality itself is defined. Abortion is such a serious controversy simply because the country is split over whether abortion is tantamount to murder or whether a woman has sovereignty over her own body.

Why did the Court issue its 1973 opinion legalizing abortion? No previous Court had done so mainly because neither its members nor the public was ready to accept such an outcome. The Court was aware of changing public sentiment and a growing women's movement, and the law was changed to reflect those trends. This is not to say that abortion became any less controversial after *Roe v. Wade*; in fact, it was quite the contrary. Nevertheless, this example shows how case law

---

[11]Anthony Lewis, "First, Do Less Harm," *The New York Times*, March 1, 1996, sec. A.

[12]Ibid.

reflects changing social and technological circumstances—abortion became more acceptable as a growing number of women argued that their bodies were their own domain and no one else's, and as the medical profession became better able to develop safe procedures.

7-2 Case Law and Code Law

In modern societies, the law for several generations has appeared to lag behind social and technological developments. For example, in 1900, the average life span in the United States was forty-eight for men and fifty-one for women. A century later these numbers had increased to seventy-eight and eighty, respectively. Countries in Western Europe, Japan, and a few other Westernized societies had similar statistics. Since the 1970s Congress has enacted new laws blunting discrimination on the basis of gender, age, or sexual orientation and has been developing new programs for health care, social security, and welfare. Legal systems and judicial interpretations of the law change because society is not static. Case law has demonstrated its usefulness as judges face new social, economic, and technological conditions and render decisions accordingly.

While the English-speaking democracies have relied heavily on case law, most other democracies, especially on the European continent, rely on **code law**. For Americans unfamiliar with code law, its most remarkable and perhaps most frightening aspect is the absence of an automatic presumption of innocence in a criminal case. Still, an accused individual is far from unprotected. A code of laws gives as much opportunity to someone charged with a crime to demonstrate innocence as it gives a prosecutor to demonstrate guilt. A trial judge in a code law system can and usually does take a more participatory role than his or her counterpart in a case law system. For example, the judge does not hesitate to question witnesses.

In the English-speaking democracies, it is difficult to imagine a trial without a jury. Justice appears to be better served when a panel of jurors evaluates a defendant's plea of innocence—jurors who have been carefully screened by both the defense and prosecution to ensure fairness. Nevertheless, jurors come from all walks of life, and few are extremely familiar with the law. For obvious reasons, such jurors may or may not follow the letter of the law in rendering a decision.

Countries that have long relied on judges or tribunals are slowly adopting the jury system in selected categories of cases. Spain, for example, has turned to jury trials for fraud cases. However, some cases are so complex that jurors are understandably unable to reach a verdict. The details of a 1994 murder trial in the United Kingdom were so intricate that several jurors used a *Ouija* board in an attempt to consult one of the murder victims![13] Their eventual guilty verdict was later reversed for that reason.

Case law is an evolving set of legal principles whose origins trace back to English **common law**. Common law is also based on judicial decisions, some of which go back to the Middle Ages. By the seventeenth century, the English began collecting and systematizing these decisions into a body of law. **Statutory law**, law enacted by a parliament or other legislative body, came later; it supplements and supersedes case law. Figure 7–1 shows the differences and places where each type of law is used.

Modern code law goes back two centuries to the **Napoleonic Code**, named after Napoleon, founder of the first French Empire (1804–1814). The Napoleonic Code evolved in early nineteenth-century France and was adopted (sometimes in revised form) by Belgium, Italy, the Netherlands, Portugal, and Spain. A century later, the German Civil Code became the model of codification for Germany Scandanavian's neighbors.

code law
Law based on written codes that give judges little leeway in interpreting established laws.

common law
Law based on judicial decisions that trace back to the Middle Ages in Britain. Common law is the antecedent of case law.

statutory law
Law based on parliamentary or congressional legislation.

Napoleonic Code
The first legal code to be established in a country with a civil law legal system.

---

[13]"A Mystery," *The Economist,* January 27, 1996, 51.

FIGURE 7–1   **Code Law versus Case Law**

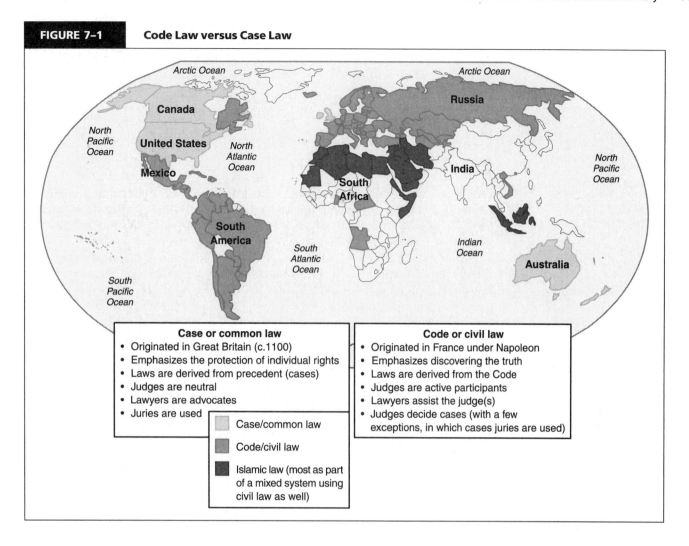

Case or common law
- Originated in Great Britain (c.1100)
- Emphasizes the protection of individual rights
- Laws are derived from precedent (cases)
- Judges are neutral
- Lawyers are advocates
- Juries are used

Code or civil law
- Originated in France under Napoleon
- Emphasizes discovering the truth
- Laws are derived from the Code
- Judges are active participants
- Lawyers assist the judge(s)
- Judges decide cases (with a few exceptions, in which cases juries are used)

- Case/common law
- Code/civil law
- Islamic law (most as part of a mixed system using civil law as well)

As the French armies conquered and occupied much of Western Europe during the early 1800s, the French government under Napoleon found the various legal systems archaic. Moreover, because Napoleon intended his empire to endure long after his demise, it was reasonable to conclude that laws would need to be standardized. Ironically, the Napoleonic Code has long survived the empire and may be the most useful part of its legacy. The Code was instrumental in modernizing European law, first in France and eventually in much of Western Europe. Unlike Britain, France had not developed a tradition of common law. The Code enabled the French to standardize their laws, many of which go all the way back to Roman times.

More than two millennia ago, the Romans developed a very practical legal system after they had conquered the Mediterranean world. As long as local legal systems did not interfere with or pose a challenge to the Roman state's authority, the Romans left the local systems alone. At the same time, though, Rome appreciated *ius naturale*, or **natural law**. Natural law is law that is universal and absolute: It applies to and prevails over all peoples throughout time.

In nearly all societies, for example, murder is considered the most heinous crime. Other "wrongs" such as thievery, fraud, and rape are severely punishable offenses wherever they occur. These "intrinsically" wrong activities can never be right, regardless of circumstances. People know they are wrong because no reasonable mind would doubt their wrongness.

Put another way: Some activities are genuinely evil, and they cannot under any circumstances be used for good. To emphasize this last point, one sixteenth-century

natural law
Law that is universal and absolute: It applies to and prevails over all peoples throughout time.

natural law theorist, Hugo Grotius, invoked divine authority as final proof just in case reason doesn't totally convince. Grotius argued that evil is evil and good is good. It is impossible for either to become the other; not even God can make evil into good. As Grotius put it,

> Just as even God, then, cannot cause that two times two should not make four, so he cannot cause that which is intrinsically evil to be not evil.[14]

7-3 Religious Law

Presumably as rational beings, people discern natural law through their ability to reason. For many, however, reason is not an entirely reliable basis. For some, reason can even lead to wrong conclusions, and not everyone entirely trusts reason. On what other basis do people decide right and wrong in order to create laws?

Hundreds of millions of people rely on and adhere to religious law because they believe it is indisputable. Religious law is, they argue, divinely revealed; it cannot be challenged or appealed. Secular law must therefore be subservient to and consistent with religious morality. Because a criminal act constitutes sin, penalties for sin are prescribed in holy writ and the secular authorities implement punishment accordingly. In such a system, usually referred to as a **theocracy**, religious considerations dominate the legal and judicial process.

Generally, religious law neither acknowledges nor condones the Western concept of separation of church and state. If, for example, a citizen in a theocracy refuses to respect the Sabbath, the state executes a punishment for sin, whether it be a flogging or a fine. Western society is certainly not without experience in this type of government. The authorities in the earliest American colonies insisted on punctual church attendance. Even today, "blue laws" in many American communities require drinking establishments and places of entertainment to close on Sundays.

The judges in theocracies receive training entirely in religious law. They are less free, therefore, to evaluate a case on the basis of their own interpretations. In many instances, they have no discretion at all. Divine law as revealed in holy writ is often interpreted literally.

In many political systems, religious law and secular law often conflict. In theocracies, this conflict is minimized because religious law automatically takes precedence over any other legal system. In secular societies, especially those that include substantial religious diversity, certain religious practices that seem perfectly reasonable to the practitioners may violate secular law.

By the early 1990s, France's Muslims represented the largest Islamic community in Western Europe and the second largest denomination in France. Muslim men may marry more than one wife at a time (though this isn't a religious requirement).[15] While this custom is acceptable within Islamic tradition, it violates French law. This presents an unresolved controversy in France and may introduce one into other Western countries where Muslim communities have formed. Different societies, though, encounter different problems. In the United Kingdom, the state must support religious schools—at least Christian and Jewish schools—as well as the regular school system; this practice is considered unconstitutional in the United States. However, the growing Islamic population in Britain is now seeking to gain state support for their school system. Some of the public fears that Muslims would not teach the usual academic subjects but instead would emphasize religious indoctrination, and they are questioning whether the government should support

theocracy
A political system where religious considerations dominate the legal and judicial process.

---

[14]Grotius, "*De jure belli ac pacis*," quoted in *A History of Political Theory*, 4th ed., eds. George H. Sabine and Thomas L. Thorson (Hinsdale, Illinois: Dryden Press, 1973) 394.

[15]According to the Koran, Muslim men are allowed to take up to four wives as long as they can fully support them.

these schools. Of course, some Christian and Jewish educational facilities probably emphasize religious doctrine over traditional academics as well.

An even more ominous situation has prevailed in the West Bank of the Jordan where Israeli military forces have occupied a hostile population of Palestinian Arabs. Nearly 250,000 Israeli settlers live among over two million Palestinians. Different codes of law pertain depending upon the community. Israeli law that offers the usual guarantees of a democratic state applies to the Israeli Jews who live in the West Bank, but military law applies (unevenly) to most of the Arab population. To complicate the situation further, Israeli law also applies to the one in five Israeli citizens who are Arab. There are obvious advantages to being governed by Israeli civil law rather than by Israeli military rule. It has become a debatable issue whether a full democracy can maintain this sort of divided legal regime.[16]

In the end there is no feasible way in which secular and religious law can be separated, even if secular and religious institutions are constitutionally kept separate. Some Islamic countries, among others, don't try. Most Christian countries have at least some history where religious doctrine spilled over into secular lawmaking. In many it still does. The United States is a very secular society, but December 25, a Christian holy day for the better part of twenty centuries, is a national holiday. Where the overwhelming portion of a citizenry is of one religious persuasion there is little doubt that those values will influence secular habits. This is why liquor stores are closed on Sunday in most American states. Minority religions, at least in the democracies, are usually accepting of this fact as long as their own religious prerogatives are not interfered with.

7-4 Law in Nondemocratic States

Citizens in Western democratic societies are accustomed to seeking the protection of law, and they assume that the state will apply the law fairly and equally. They also expect the law to prevent the state itself from making unwarranted intrusions into their lives and property. Most democratic constitutions include substantial lists of individual protections such as the Bill of Rights (in the American Constitution) or the Rights of Man (in the French).

Other systems have protections, but they are not as formalized. Britain, for example, pioneered such concepts as *habeas corpus* as well as the right of trial by jury, but it has yet to draft a permanent written constitution.[17] Israel, like Britain, also lacks a written constitution. Unlike the Anglo-American systems of justice, however, Israel has refrained from instituting trial by jury, preferring to rely instead on panels of judges.

It is difficult to understate the status of individual rights in nondemocratic states. Put bluntly, the security and welfare of the state takes precedence at all times over individual concerns. Often a regime's leader does not distinguish between personal desires and law. A dictator only infrequently believes that the rule of law is preferable to personal whim and is usually aghast at the notion that laws should apply to the ruler as well.

This is not to say that nondemocratic systems have no legal systems at all. On some levels, there are bodies of laws that actually work. Rigidly totalitarian systems such as Nazi Germany or the Soviet Union retained the usual laws against thievery, for example: These laws would at least be recognizable to citizens in Western democracies (though the penalties for such a crime would almost certainly be harsher than in the West). However, dictatorial regimes are much more concerned with what they regard as **political crimes**. These normally include any demonstration of opposition to the regime's policies or irksome clamoring for the regime to change its ways and guarantee human rights. Such regimes characteristically formulate and enforce laws

political crimes
Acts that demonstrate opposition to a regime's policies or that clamor for change.

---

[16]"When Good Men Turn Racist," *The Economist*, October 19, 2002, 42–43.

[17]Alexander MacLeod, "Britain's Constitutional Question," *The Christian Science Monitor*, March 3, 1992, 12.

FIGURE 7–2	Political "Crimes"

If you've ever...		You've broken the law in...	
	Demonstrated (marched in a parade, participated in a sit-in) against the government or a governmental policy		Cuba
	Written an essay or article criticizing the government or a governmental policy		Iran
	Published a newspaper, brochure, or pamphlet taking a position against the government's position		Pakistan
	Been a conscientious objector without a solid religious reason		Switzerland
	Organized a meeting of a political party outside of the capital city		Uganda
	Gotten on the Internet		DPRK (North Korea)

that violate both human decency and common sense. Figure 7–2 shows some places where common activities Americans take for granted are illegal.

Because of a nearly universal respect for the principle of state sovereignty—the jurisdiction a regime retains over the internal workings of the country it governs—governments can literally get away with murder if they are willing to ignore world public opinion, the condemnation of human rights organizations, and, at worst, economic sanctions. Most are willing to ignore these external voices, but some do revise or abolish laws the world considers injurious to human welfare. South Africa, for instance, began in the late 1980s to repeal the decades-old apartheid laws that ensured race separation and preserved the economic and political privileges of the white minority. These laws were repugnant to most of the world community. A combination of global displeasure and economic sanctions seemed to at least accelerate the reforms that led to the establishment of more democratic institutions.

An important distinction between democratic and nondemocratic legal systems has to do with ideology. Racial purification laws in Nazi Germany and economic demands in the Soviet Union are cases in point. During the Nazi regime, Germans were legally forbidden to marry non-Aryans or employ non-Aryan physicians and lawyers (Aryans were whites of Nordic heritage). Some laws were humiliating and lethal: German Jews were legally forbidden to have private vegetable gardens or use public swimming pools or, in the final stages of their persecution, allowed the right to live at all. The Nazi ideology held Aryans to be a "superior race," and the laws reflected this thinking.

In the Soviet Union, antiparasite laws asserted that every adult member of a socialist society had a responsibility to work. Because everyone was legally required to work in the Soviet Union, the country technically experienced no unemployment problems. The Soviet and other communist systems stressed **economic rights** in their constitutions—the right of every worker to a pension and free medical treatment. Such a focus stands in stark contrast to the legal and political rights normally guaranteed in Western democratic constitutions. In the United States, for

economic rights
The right to a pension and guaranteed medical treatment, earned by each ablebodied individual who fulfills the duty to work in a socialist or communist system.

example, a citizen has a constitutionally protected right to vote, but not a right or, for that matter, an obligation, to hold a job.

Totalitarian legal systems often attempt to enforce a particular form of human behavior. Article 10 of the 1977 Soviet Constitution, for example, explicitly denied the right of an individual to be selfish. While such a requirement may strike a Westerner as bizarre, in the Soviet Union, the legal and judicial systems cooperated with the political and ideological institutions to define acceptable human conduct. In a commonwealth of workers, all laboring for the welfare of the whole, no one had the right to be self-serving.

It may not come as a surprise to learn that the judiciary in a dictatorial system views its mission as protecting state and society *against* the individual. Defense lawyers are state employees. In fact, in the Chinese communist system (as in the former Soviet system), it is not unusual for a defense lawyer to occasionally denounce the defendant, particularly if the defendant is accused of heinous "crimes against the state." During the purge trials under Stalin in the Soviet Union during the 1930s, even the defendant might denounce him- or herself (usually as a result of torture or threat) and beg the court for punishment (usually by execution). The court rarely turned down such a plea. Defendants who cooperated in enthusiastically condemning themselves were assured that their families would be spared.

Many laws in a totalitarian society are never revised or updated because the ideology they are based on is itself inflexible. This system works quite well on the state's behalf but is often to the individual's detriment. That, after all, is the intention of the legal system in a communist regime: The collective takes both legal and political precedent over the individual members of the society.

The Chinese political system offers a more current case in point. China is still a totalitarian state with a Communist party dictatorship firmly in control of the government and the (increasingly free-market) economy.[18] To continue its rapid economic development, China must keep technologically up to date. Yet the more technology the Chinese adopt, the more legal dilemmas crop up for the state. The regime understands the critical need for information but wants to control its availability. By early 1996, for example, the government published new laws regarding the regulation of the Internet in China.[19] These laws require that a government channel be used for making international connections, overall supervision by the Ministry of Electronics, and the banning of any production, retrieval, or duplication of information considered harmful to state security.[20] The Internet is perhaps the greatest challenge to totalitarian government.

It may actually be in the interest of the Chinese government to remove restrictions to the Internet because even a totalitarian society can thrive on information. For example, a poll indicated that one-fourth of China's population, some 300 million people, have never heard of AIDS.[21]

There is little evidence thus far that China's rapidly expanding economy is helping to democratize its political system. Nor does the legal system seem to be awakening to human rights. China still executes more people annually than the rest of the world's countries combined.[22] Some evidence shows that the situation is actually getting worse: In 1980, twenty-one crimes were punishable by the death penalty; by 1995, this number had risen to eighty.[23] By the early 2000s, it had become common knowledge that the Chinese authorities were routinely "harvesting" body organs

---

[18]China's economic growth was strong throughout the 1990s and into the new century. In 2002, the economy was growing at a remarkable rate of around 8 percent. See Peter Wonacutt, "China's Output Grew 8.1% in Period," *The Wall Street Journal*, October 17, 2002, sec. A.

[19]Seth Faison, "Chinese Cruise Internet, Wary of Watchdogs," *The New York Times*, February 5, 1996, sec. A.

[20]Ibid. See also Elisabeth Rosenthal, "In China's Legal Evolution, the Lawyers Are Handcuffed," *The New York Times*, January 6, 2000.

[21]Rob Gifford, "China Gives AIDS High Profile," *Morning Edition*, NPR, December 1, 2003. Three hundred million Chinese is less than one-fourth of the total population but is the equivalent of the entire U.S. population.

[22]"Death Sentences and Executions in 2002," Amnesty International, http://web.amnesty.org/library/index/ENGACT510012003 (accessed December 18, 2003).

[23]"China's Arbitrary State," *The Economist*, March 23, 1996, 31–32. In 1996, at least two thieves were shot for stealing cows.

from executed criminals to sell on the open market. In 2003, Amnesty International noted that even people suffering from Severe Acute Respiratory Syndrome (SARS) who break quarantine could be subject to the death penalty in China.[24]

Governments that are unrepentant about safeguarding basic individual rights are often difficult for Westerners to deal with. During the 1970s and 1980s, when the international community began imposing economic boycotts on South Africa, the United States had to decide how to deal with the most prosperous country on the African continent—a country that was also severely violating human rights. The boycotts apparently did have an impact because the apartheid regime was gradually, and for the most part, peacefully, dismantled during the 1990s.

A similar dilemma involves the Southeast Asian country of Myanmar (formerly Burma). Some large American companies, such as Levi Strauss, withdrew from Myanmar in the early 1990s because of the government's miserable human rights record. Opponents to the military regime are frequently arrested or simply disappear. PepsiCo, on the other hand, did not withdraw until 1997, after increasing pressure from boycotts.[25] At the same time, the United States imposed economic sanctions on Myanmar, a country with a rapidly growing economy.[26]

Legal and moral arguments trip over each other in such a situation: Levi Strauss has argued that Myanmar's human rights record must improve before it will consider returning. PepsiCo, on the other hand, originally argued that Myanmar would inevitably democratize as its economy grows, and PepsiCo would help it economically. They also maintained that, in any case, it wasn't up to American corporations to interfere with or dictate foreign policy.[27] Meanwhile, the government in Myanmar continues to promise significant reforms.[28] Obviously, there is no easy answer. But it is apparent that issues such as human rights under different systems of law will continue to affect the global economy as well as the relationships between democracies and nondemocratic regimes.

7-5 Judiciaries

In democratic societies citizens who feel they have been wronged by an event or victimized by others normally apply to the judicial system for recourse. The American legal system has become famous for awarding huge sums of money to those individuals who can convince a court that they have been terribly exploited or injured. A woman successfully sued McDonald's for serving her excessively hot coffee that she then spilled on herself, suffering burns.

Judicial systems are not unlike their executive and legislative counterparts in terms of organization; the higher an agency is in the hierarchy, the greater the prerogatives of the agency. The American federal court system, for example, is arranged as outlined in Table 7–1. In addition to the national court system, of course, there are also regional or state and local systems. Even nondemocratic systems seem to generally follow the pattern of higher and lower courts.

The powers and prerogatives of judicial bodies vary from country to country; even as democracies differ substantially. The American federal judiciary, for example, long ago established the principle of **judicial review**, or a court's ability to declare an act of the executive or the legislature unconstitutional. Other democratic systems have constitutionally mandated judicial review but limited its

judicial review
The court's ability to declare an act of the executive or the legislature unconstitutional, whether on the state or national level.

---

[24]"People's Republic of China: Continuing Abuses under a New Leadership—Summary of Human Rights Concerns," Amnesty International, http://web.amnesty.org/library/Index/ENGASA170352003 (accessed December 18, 2003).

[25]"PepsiCo to Sever All Ties with Myanmar," *Los Angeles Times,* January 28, 1997.

[26]U.S. Department of the Treasury Office of Foreign Assets Control, *What You Need to Know about U.S. Sanctions against Burma* (Myanmar), Washington, D.C.: July 29, 2003, http://www.ustreas.gov/offices/eotffc/ofac/sanctions/t11burma.pdf (accessed December 18, 2003).

[27]Ibid.

[28]Marwaan Macan-Markar, "Myanmar Promises Reform ... Yet Again," *AsiaTimes Online,* December 18, 2003, http://www.atimes.com/atimes/Southeast_Asia/EL18Ae01.html (accessed December 18, 2003).

| TABLE 7–1 | The Federal Court System of the United States |

Court	Original Jurisdiction	Appellate (appealing the original decision) Jurisdiction	Caseload (number of cases per year)
Supreme Court **1 Court** **9 Justices**	1. Lawsuits between two or more states 2. Lawsuits between the United States and a state 3. Cases involving foreign ambassadors and other diplomats 4. Lawsuits between a state and a citizen of a different state (if begun by the state)	1. Lower federal courts 2. Highest state court	1. Approximately 130 signed opinions 2. Approximately 4,500 petitions and appeals 3. Fewer than ten cases of original jurisdiction
Appeals Court **12 Courts** **135 Judges**		1. Federal district courts 2. U.S. regulatory commissions 3. Certain other federal courts	1. Approximately 41,000 cases
District Court **94 Courts** **515 Judges**	1. Federal crimes 2. Civil suits under federal law 3. Civil suits between citizens of different states when the amount exceeds $50,000 4. Admiralty and maritime cases 5. Bankruptcy cases 6. Review of actions of certain federal administrative agencies 7. Other matters assigned by Congress	(No appellate jurisdiction)	1. Approximately 49,000 criminal cases 2. Approximately 218,000 civil cases

Source: Annual Report of the Director of the Administrative Office of the United States Courts (Washington, D.C.: Government Printing Office, 1990); Harold W. Stanley and Richard G. Niemi, *Vital Statistics on American Politics*, 2d ed. (Washington, D.C.: Congressional Quarterly Press, 1990); Bureau of the Census, *Statistical Abstract of the United States*, 1990 (Washington, D.C.: U.S. Government Printing Office, 1990).

application. France's Constitutional Council has been able to decide on the constitutionality of a legislative bill only since 1974. The German Federal Republic's Constitutional Court is specifically charged with protecting individual rights. Interestingly, the Constitutional Court can ban an extremist political party if it concludes that the party's program is potentially injurious to these rights.

The United States places a strong emphasis on separation of the judiciary from the other two branches of the federal government, as well as from the vagaries of public opinion. In a democracy, a judiciary must function beyond the influence or control of other political institutions to maintain impartiality. However, the judiciary in most democracies is not a co-equal branch of government. In Britain, for example, no high court can declare a law that parliament has passed unconstitutional. In most parliamentary systems, the parliament's decisions supersede court decisions. Only parliament can reverse, revise, or abolish the laws it enacts.

Other systems have judiciaries that can exert powerful influence but that also reflect the peculiar political cultures of their countries. In Costa Rica, one of the oldest and most stable democracies in Latin America, a special judicial body called the Supreme Electoral Tribunal oversees and monitors elections to watch for any voting irregularities. The Tribunal can order the results of an election void if it finds evidence of fraud. Many countries, including the United States, do not have an equivalent body, although the normal judicial processes seem to adequately cope with election fraud. Costa Rica, however, does not take the protection of the normal processes for granted.

Judiciaries in most societies are limited in scope. This is true for many of the same reasons that even authoritarian governments are limited in power. The rule of law remains tentative in much of the world, where communication and transportation systems are either primitive or nonexistent. In such places, traditional customs and cultural values underlie much of the legal system, and the people themselves enforce these traditions in an almost religious fashion. In 1994 Saddam's two sons-in-law fled Iraq to Jordan with valuable information about military installations. Their wives grew homesick and persuaded their husbands to return the next year after Saddam publicly forgave them. They, their father, and another brother were quickly murdered by a mob instigated by Saddam's son, Qusay. The mob needed little encouragement because its members viewed the victims as an embarrassment to the entire clan. There is little doubt that there were cousins in the mob who eagerly participated in the murders.

Clan dignity and honor superseded any protections the law or government might offer. It is unlikely that any judicial body in Iraq would have either the desire or the courage to prosecute anyone in this episode. In the Iraqi view, justice was simply meted out to those who had disgraced their clan. In this sense, justice was more important than legality.

Judiciaries have modest authority in parts of the world that either lack or question governmental authority. They are usually mouthpieces for a regime that equates dissent with treason. An independent judiciary in a country ruled by a dictatorship would be a contradiction in terms.

The relentless advance of technology in modern and modernizing society has created huge gaps in the application of the law. In effect, judicial bodies are often being asked to make determinations where the law may be unclear or may not yet exist. Of course, in many societies formal judicial bodies may not even exist. Justice may simply be left to local village elders or even to public opinion when it comes to crimes that are an affront to the religious or social sensitivities of the population.

Judiciaries in modern societies, in contrast, are practically under siege to increasingly decide what is legitimate privacy and how much of it can or should be protected. In the United States this issue has reached great poignancy since 9-11. How much privacy is the individual entitled to in an era when national security is being threatened? The American judicial system is in the process of reaching a decision on this matter. Are American citizens of Middle Eastern extraction entitled to less privacy than the rest of us? Such questions will be debated for a long time.

The European democracies are somewhat more conscientious about this issue than the United States. In October 1995 most Western European countries jointly established "a comprehensive set of data protection guidelines." Privacy in Europe is protected somewhat more than in the United States where there has been no federal legislation on this issue since 1974. In the quarter century since then much has happened. With the advent of greater access to computer technology it is rather easy to compile dossiers on every American who uses a credit card or a phone. Databases contain an ever-growing bank of information on people's buying habits, hobbies, the size of their bank accounts and stock portfolios, what they read, and the movies they watch. The databases are found in both government agencies and marketing organizations in the private sector.

In contrast to the United Kingdom, though, the United States is far ahead in its protection of individual rights. Britain does have a Bill of Rights that tends to emphasize parliamentary prerogatives and it doesn't have a constitution, even though four-fifths of the population believes that drafting one is a good idea. In effect, parliament has become the ultimate judicial arbiter because it alone has the authority to revise or repeal any measures it passes into law.

Of course, laws and judicial decisions are normally impacted by the times in which they are formulated, revised, or repealed. During the early years of the twenty-first century, as global terrorism became an increasing danger and nightmare scenarios of destruction became increasingly realistic, discussions about limiting the constitutional rights of various individuals were being taken seriously in several democracies, including the United States. This is not to say that democracies cannot survive temporary lapses during severe and desperate times. After all, Abraham Lincoln suspended *habeus corpus*—the legal justification for arresting someone—during the Civil War, something no president before or since Lincoln has done. *Habeus corpus* was immediately restored once hostilities were ended.

The judiciary in most democratic countries simply does not enjoy the relationship with the legislative and executive branches the federal courts in the United States have been designed to enjoy. In particular, the judiciary usually lacks judicial review and the power to overturn executive and legislative decisions. However, the French have a limited form of judicial review in their Constitutional Council. Since 1974, the Council has had the authority, which it infrequently uses, to decide on the constitutionality of a legislative bill. Council members, unlike their U.S. Supreme Court counterparts, do not receive life tenure. The presidents of the Republic, National Assembly, and Senate each choose three justices for nine-year nonrenewable terms of office. Thus, it is likely that the justices will represent a variety of viewpoints because the three presidents can come from different political backgrounds.

The German courts also have a form of judicial review. Because of the American occupation of Germany in the years immediately following World War II (1945–1949), a strong American constitutional influence exists. Moreover, both Germany and the United States, unlike the British and French systems, are federal republics with histories of disputes between state and federal governments. Accordingly, the Germans also have a close approximation of judicial review that tends to emphasize protection of individual rights. In Germany, the executive is completely removed from the selection of justices. Each of the two legislative houses chooses eight justices. The sixteen justices divide their labor: Half deal with conflicts between the federal and state governments, while the other half concentrate on individual civil liberties.[29]

The legal process is rarely simple or uncontroversial. The seemingly relentless march of technology has forced all branches of government to deal with legal questions that simply did not arise earlier. The inalienable right to life is in many societies the primary natural right of every citizen. In Western societies, citizens are now grappling with the question of whether every person also has a right to die at a time and place of his or her choosing. Is it legal for a physician, trained to support and sustain life, to ignore state prohibitions against "assisted suicide"? The American courts have not yet made a final ruling on whether assisted suicide is illegal,[30] and in all likelihood won't before the Supreme Court takes on the issue.

Independent judiciaries understandably dread court cases that involve strong doses of morality. Life-and-death issues such as abortion, capital punishment, and euthanasia are rarely resolved in the public mind, even after a court decision is made. These issues are constantly revisited because any judicial decision on such a matter usually dissatisfies a large proportion of the citizenry. It may be that when all is said and done, people expect too much of the judicial system precisely because they have placed so much authority for determining right and wrong in its hands.

Moreover, the world has entered a period of judicial process guided by international law that is already generations old. Global law is not a new concept. Both the United Nations and other international agencies coordinate and regulate health standards, monetary exchange, information technology, and world commerce. In a rapidly shrinking world, cultures are being exposed to one another in countless and relentless ways. There is little doubt that the judiciary will have to continue to formulate previously unneeded legal remedies as interaction among peoples becomes unavoidable.

---

[29]For a succinct summary discussion of the German Constitutional Court, see David P. Conradt, *The German Polity*, 3rd ed. (New York and London: Longman, 1986), 204–206.

[30]"Dr. Death Walks," *The Economist*, March 16, 1996, 34–35.

Chapter Summary

1. Nearly every society has instituted some sort of legal system that most of its citizens voluntarily obey. Laws are useful devices that help people understand what constitutes socially acceptable behavior.
2. Ancient legal systems often came from mystical lawgivers who usually claimed that their laws were divinely inspired or sanctioned.
3. Many laws in both ancient and modern societies have their basis in natural law, universal moral values that prohibit such actions as murder.
4. Laws also may arise from custom and tradition. A society usually accepts such laws easily.
5. In the end, even in nondemocratic societies, people obey the laws only if they are willing to do so. Laws that make no sense or seem out of step with the times are either ignored or challenged.
6. Case law has evolved primarily in the English-speaking democracies; its origins trace back at least a millennium. Code law usually prevails in the continental European countries.
7. Countries that apply religious law are rarely democratic. Regimes employing religious law in effect do not distinguish between church and state. Instead, they invoke the precepts of a particular faith to govern the society and to attempt to control elements of daily human behavior.
8. Other kinds of nondemocratic systems apply laws in a discriminatory fashion; these laws are often based on the personal whim of a dictator, or emphasize the ideology the regime has adopted.
9. Judiciaries are not always independent from or uninfluenced by the government, especially in dictatorial regimes. In democratic systems, judiciaries usually have the opportunity to make independent decisions and to affect the political process itself.
10. With the relentless advance of technology, judiciaries may be asked to resolve questions beyond the expertise of the judges.

Chapter 7 Quiz

1. In Plato's *Republic,* laws
   a. were modeled on holy scripture.
   b. were remarkably similar to those in ancient Japan.
   c. didn't exist.
   d. were borrowed from Egypt.

2. The ancient personality, Draco, was a
   a. lawgiver.
   b. totalitarian dictator.
   c. military leader.
   d. philosopher-king.

3. Antiparasite laws were applied in
   a. the Soviet Union.
   b. Saddam Hussein's Iraq.
   c. Germany during World War II.
   d. the United States during the Depression.

4. Draconian legislation is a term that refers to
   a. legal reforms in Europe during the twentieth century.
   b. severe laws applied during the American Civil War.
   c. the Hammurabi Code.
   d. the ancient legal code of the Greek city-state, Athens.

5. Common law is
   a. practiced in England.
   b. the basis of the Napoleonic Code.
   c. found throughout continental Europe.
   d. the basis of Sharia.

6. Statutory law
   a. is enacted by a legislative body.
   b. decreed by appointed judges.
   c. borrowed from religious laws.
   d. is created by constitutional amendment.

7. The largest Islamic community in Western Europe is located in
   a. Germany.
   b. the United Kingdom.
   c. Spain.
   d. France.

8. The concept of political crimes is generally found in
   a. democratic societies.
   b. authoritarian systems.
   c. only in the United States.
   d. the electronic media of the West.

9. The principle and practice of judicial review is most widely applied in
   a. Costa Rica.
   b. France.
   c. the United States.
   d. China.

10. *Habeus corpus* is
    a. the legal justification for arresting someone.
    b. the cornerstone of legality in authoritarian systems.
    c. the justification for global terrorism.
    d. often suspended in the United States during the Depression.

CHAPTER 8

Political Parties and Electoral Systems

8-1 The Purpose of Political Parties

Political parties are present in all democratic and most nondemocratic systems. In democracies, a political party is interested in two main activities: winning elections (and increasing the number of its members holding public office), and exercising political power to advocate or oppose different pieces of economic and social legislation. Most parties tend to be pragmatic rather than ideological: They prefer to win elections rather than consistently go down to defeat while preserving a purist ideology that irritates most voters. Finally, parties in democracies regularly participate in constitutionally guaranteed elections where the electoral outcomes are respected by both the winners and the losers.

A party in a nondemocratic system is a very different thing. It is often the creation and/or the tool of a dictator who uses the party to retain and expand her or his power. Such a party is uninterested in holding, let alone participating in, regular and free elections. Because such parties usually ban political opposition, there isn't much point to elections anyway. A single-party system occasionally does find elections useful. Its candidates can't lose, and even an election that is obviously rigged provides a small degree of legitimacy for the regime. The opposition is either nonexistent or clearly understands its function is to consistently lose elections.

In yet another arrangement, a nonparty system, all parties are banned because they are viewed as a potential threat to the regime, such as in Saudi Arabia. Moreover, Saudi Arabia is governed by Sharia law and the regime feels that any other possibility that might be proposed by an independent political movement would be harmful to what divine authority prefers. Absolute monarchies such as Saudi Arabia and Brunei have never allowed parties to function in any modern sense. These regimes equate political parties—not entirely incorrectly—with political opposition and factionalism, which they in turn equate with treason.

This chapter will concentrate mostly on political systems that include parties. One-party systems, of course, are not competitive, although intraparty competition may flare up between factions that represent a spectrum of ideological viewpoints or interpretations. Personalities are also important factors in one-party systems; competition between claimants to party leadership can become strident. Often, a phenomenon known as the cult of personality can occur, in which devotion to one leader becomes all encompassing and slavish to the point of worship. When a founding leader, such as V.I. Lenin in the Soviet Union or Mao Tse-Tung in China dies (in 1924 and 1976, respectively), complex succession issues can arise as loyal followers struggle to adjust to the change in leadership while potential successors fight to inherit the mantle of leadership.

In a single-party system, the party serves a quite different purpose than its counterparts in multiparty political systems, where several parties submit their programs to an electorate on a regular basis. The party is less concerned with elections than it is with retaining and expanding the party elite's control. The former Soviet Union, for example, was often referred to as a party-state because the party created and then used the state to carry out the party's ideological programs and to preserve the party elite's privileges.

Finally, intensely nationalist and theocratic political parties are currently functioning in several developing countries that are in the process of becoming political democracies. Two examples are the Islamic Welfare Party in Turkey and the Bharatiya Janata Party (BJP) (Hindu party) in India. Both parties have done very well in free elections, are in power in several states and regions, and have achieved national electoral success. Both advocate a rigorously religious lifestyle for the citizenry, insisting on strict adherence to religious holidays, dietary laws, and standards of feminine modesty, and support morality with the full strength of the state.

8-2 Political Parties

Most political systems come equipped with parties. Democracies normally have two or more parties competing in regular elections while authoritarian systems normally have outlawed all parties except the one that is official and state supported. A few countries such as Saudi Arabia have banned all political parties and consider them a nuisance.

8-2a Party Recruitment: Leaders and Followers

It is difficult to imagine a functioning democracy without a competitive political party system. Yet parties arose in the more mature democracies as an afterthought, and people often distrusted them, believing them to be sources of social division. In several cases, parties were instead the *result* of social division. In 2000, for example, Ralph Nader, a longtime and well-known consumer advocate, ran for president on the Green Party ticket and received 3 percent of the popular vote.[1] The environmentalist movement that supported Nader was not really hopeful of winning, but did assume that its take on ecological issues was gaining a national constituency. In retrospect, political parties seem to be a natural development in almost any democracy: Like-minded people tend to associate with one another in a political organization to pursue agreed-upon political goals.

Political parties certainly seemed to develop as an outgrowth of the democratic process. As the franchise (right to vote) was extended in the democracies during the nineteenth and twentieth centuries, parties evolved as vehicles for winning elections. The Democratic party in the United States and the Conservative party in the United Kingdom were among the first to understand this process. In the early decades of the nineteenth century, as the franchise was extended in both countries, these parties won elections because they made broad appeals to different sections of an expanding electorate. Parties were unnecessary before voters and elections existed; officeholders who were appointed to or inherited their positions had little need to form political organizations, preferring instead to develop and rely on personal followings.

With the advance of democracy in North America and Western Europe, political leaders realized they needed to establish permanent and fully active organizations to win elections and remain in office. In fact, this lesson has not been lost on leaders in nondemocratic systems. In single-party states such as Syria, party organization is important not for campaigning but for mobilizing masses of people to appear "spontaneously" at strategic times to support and celebrate the political leadership. The sight of hundreds of thousands or millions of people surging down a capital city's main avenues chanting their leader's name can be impressive to an outsider and, even more importantly, to the participants themselves.

---

[1]Nader ran again in 2004 and got even fewer votes.

In authoritarian systems, parties also can provide the means for getting ahead politically. A substantial proportion of the adult population normally join the only legally sanctioned party because of the benefits membership can bring: better housing and food, educational facilities, health care and, for those at the upper rungs, a car and perhaps travel abroad. Party members are genuinely loyal to and work hard on behalf of the regime because they have an important stake in its survival. The Ba'ath party in Syria and the Communist party in China and North Korea offer individuals the opportunity to advance themselves economically and socially in return for unstinting loyalty to and identification with the party. Party affiliation normally results only after an applicant is carefully screened and evaluated for the staying power of her or his loyalty.

The politically ambitious in democratic societies quickly learn that they will get nowhere without the support and label of a political party. It is rare for anyone in the United States or the United Kingdom, for example, to be elected to office without a party endorsement. One of the rare exceptions is Strom Thurmond of South Carolina, who was elected to the United States Senate on a write-in vote as an independent in 1954. Thurmond, who finally retired in 2003 at the age of 100 from the Senate, was able to accomplish this rare feat because he was already well known and respected in the state as a former governor who catered to his constituents. He was also a veteran of World War II and had landed in France on D-Day. Thurmond then ran as a Democrat until he changed to the Republican party in the early 1960s. No one else in modern times has been able to equal Senator Thurmond's feat. Even nationally known or popular figures such as Sonny Bono, a comedian-singer who was elected to Congress in 1994, require a party label to have any realistic hope of success.

Of course, some party systems are less strict than others when it comes to recruiting leadership. In the parliamentary systems of East Asia and Western Europe, an aspiring officeholder is expected to work her or his way through the ranks. In Britain, for example, a young man or woman who aspires to eventually become a cabinet minister usually starts out in one of the 650 single-member districts as one of several potential party candidates. Once selected by the party, the young politician is expected to tow the party line even if this guarantees electoral defeat. Defeat in this sort of situation may actually benefit a candidate; local party selection committees see the candidate as dependable. The reward for such party loyalty frequently is an opportunity to stand for a seat in a "safe" district the party has traditionally done well in.

Primary elections in parliamentary systems are rare. The local district party organization—not the voters—interviews applicants and then chooses the party candidate. Once a parliamentary seat is secured, its holder is still obligated to submit to party authority: The holder is told to vote the party line and refrain from speaking during parliamentary sessions unless the leadership specifically requests the holder's comments. A young party member may then gain opportunities to move from the back to the front benches if the seat is held in re-election campaigns and as vacancies in junior ministries become available. A noncooperative individual or political maverick has little chance to rise in the party hierarchy in a parliamentary system. Few people get to parliament without passing the party leaders' careful screening.

Sometimes, the process is put on the fast track in times of desperation. When Britain's Labour party chose Tony Blair as party leader, he was still in his late thirties. The party was desperate to revive its electoral fortunes; between 1979 and 1992, Labour had lost four consecutive elections. This was enough to induce both the party leadership and rank-and-file members to move the younger generation up on the fast track. When Blair became prime minister in 1997, he also became the youngest British head of government in the twentieth century.

The United States is an unusual political system because it is possible to achieve the highest political offices without moving through the party ranks. Only

FIGURE 8–1   **Working the Way Up the Ranks**

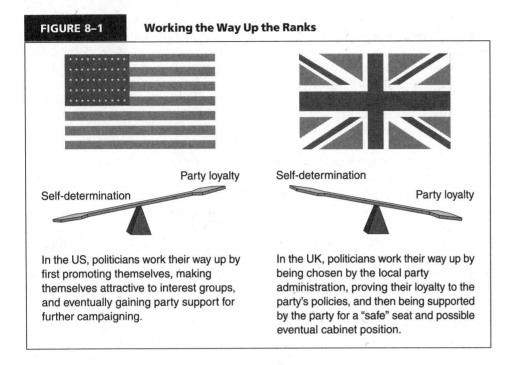

In the US, politicians work their way up by first promoting themselves, making themselves attractive to interest groups, and eventually gaining party support for further campaigning.

In the UK, politicians work their way up by being chosen by the local party administration, proving their loyalty to the party's policies, and then being supported by the party for a "safe" seat and possible eventual cabinet position.

infrequently does one move directly, say, from the Congress to the presidency. In fact, this hasn't happened since the 1960 election placed Senator John Kennedy in the White House. The executive experience gained by state governors has worked well on behalf of several presidential aspirants (Ronald Reagan, Bill Clinton, and George W. Bush being recent examples). This, of course, is not a hard and fast rule: Several possible presidential contenders in both parties who are members of the Senate are expected to offer their candidacies in 2008, though no one from the House of Representatives is likely to do so. Figure 8–1 compares the methods of ascending the political ladder in the United States and the United Kingdom.

Dwight Eisenhower, a national military hero, became president without holding any prior political office or even belonging to any political party. Yet Eisenhower is an exception. Despite the lip service given to the notion of "citizen-politicians," the experienced politician equipped with a long record of service to the state, country, and party usually becomes a candidate for president. The two major party candidates for president in 1996, for example, had both political longevity and party service. The Republican candidate, Bob Dole, rose through the ranks of his party during his long tenure in Congress (1961–1996). The Democratic candidate, Bill Clinton, had served six terms as governor of Arkansas before moving into the White House in 1993. His successor, George W. Bush (2001–), had been elected governor of Texas in 1994 and 1998 and, of course, bore a well-known Republican party name because his father had been vice president and president.

One-party systems are far different. No matter how well known or popular a military or sports hero may be, there is no corresponding political standing unless the individual is a member of the party organization. In one-party systems, membership in the only legal party makes one a member of the political elite. Party members receive perks ordinary citizens usually lack, such as better housing and medical care. The higher the party rank, the more services a member can expect. The former communist systems of Eastern Europe and the current ones in China and Cuba offer excellent examples of this.

To attain political greatness in a communist system, one must begin early, usually by joining the communist youth league. In the former Soviet Union, a child could start the process by joining the preadolescent Young Octoberists. The party carefully screened promising youths who applied for party membership to ensure they would be loyal to the leadership and ideology. Admittance to full party membership in the typical communist system included a probationary period of one to two years.

Absolute loyalty to party doctrine and the pronouncements of the leaders was required. Once accepted, the Communist party member remained a member for life unless he or she became the victim of a purge. During the dictatorship of Joseph Stalin (1923–1953), an atmosphere of paranoia pervaded both the Soviet state and the Communist party. Millions of party members were expelled, thousands were put on trial for counterrevolutionary activities, and most of them were executed or sent off, sometimes with their families, to Siberian labor camps—which usually amounted to a death sentence.

From the beginnings of the Communist regime in the 1920s to its end in 1991, the 6 to 8 percent of the adult population that belonged to the Soviet Communist party became a privileged class in a theoretically classless society. Recruiters began to focus on the children of party members in good standing. So long as party members retained political loyalty to the party leadership, they were assured of rewards for themselves and their families. For all practical purposes, this process created a Soviet aristocracy that enjoyed many lifestyle benefits. Party members could even secure products from the West that were officially banned for the general population, including reading materials and travel opportunities.

The Soviet Communist party became the most corrupt political institution in the country. It also was apparently the most incompetent. As the Soviet economy deteriorated and verged on collapse, the party hierarchy, or *apparatchiks*, were obsessed with retaining their privileges. In the last years of the Soviet state's existence, the leadership was hopelessly out of touch with the needs of the citizenry, tied to an outmoded and dated ideology, and helpless or unwilling to implement desperately needed reforms. The Soviet leadership also preferred to sustain the country's superpower status and nuclear parity with the United States. The Soviet nuclear arsenal was about as large as the American one and the leadership was determined to keep it that way and to project Soviet influence on a global scale. However, the Soviet economy could not sustain both a high military buildup and a robust civilian standard of living. A much higher proportion of the Soviet economy than the American one went into military preparedness. In the end, it was too much for the system to keep up.

Although the Soviet example may be extreme, there is little doubt that one-party systems are, at best, inefficiently responsive to the country's citizenry. Recruitment of both leaders and rank-and-file members tends to become incestuous. Eventually, the more qualified people in society are excluded from recruitment and governance. The party gradually loses its effectiveness and loses the confidence and respect of the governed.

Mao Tse-Tung established the Chinese Communist party during the 1920s and led it for the next half century. Mao saw no reason to have competitive elections or to tolerate real or potential opposition. It is estimated that Mao holds the record of civilian deaths of one's own fellow citizens. In about fifty years, a total of 70 million Chinese starved through incredibly inept economic planning or were simply executed or worked to death.

8-2b Political Parties and Interest Groups

Interest groups are fixtures in every political system and are very visible in democratic politics. In fact, it is as difficult to imagine a democracy without active interest groups as it is to imagine a democracy with no political parties. An interest group is an organization of individuals who seek to influence the outcome of government policies on issues of special concern to them. Pro-life and pro-choice organizations, for example, are especially interested in legislation that determines abortion policy. To have its way, an interest group may raise money on behalf of a candidate sympathetic to its point of view and mobilize volunteers to work on behalf of that candidate in a political campaign.

Depending upon their resources and expertise, an interest group can provide a great deal of help to a candidate who has a shortage of both. Better-endowed organizations such as the American Medical Association and the National Rifle Association can generate letter-writing campaigns to people already in office as well as raise much-needed and often substantial sums of money for a candidate's campaign. The arrival of large numbers of faxes, telegrams, letters, and electronic messages can be very persuasive to an officeholder soon to seek re-election or a candidate hoping to win political office.

Interest groups frequently exercise influence beyond their numbers on both parties and government, but their influence is usually consistent with their resources. Some kinds of interest groups may represent an overwhelming number of members of an organization; this is especially true of **professional interest groups**, which exert influence on behalf of members of certain professions. Most practicing attorneys in the United States, for example, belong to the American Bar Association (ABA). The ABA regularly assumes it speaks for all lawyers by protecting what it views as the interests of the profession.

Interest groups are also called (usually by their critics) lobbying or pressure groups. Whichever term is applied, their function is the same: to advance the cause of a group's political agenda, which is usually centered around a position on a particular issue or a small set of similar issues. Interest groups tend to be single-minded. Interest groups are frequently at odds with and in competition with one another. The competition seems to be especially severe in the case of **single-issue interest groups**, or groups that seek to shape policy on one particular issue. Some consider their cause of such overriding importance that their support for or opposition to a party or a candidate depends solely upon the position the candidate has taken on the relevant issue.

Legislation considered favorable to one interest group can be viewed as detrimental to another. Animal rights' activists, for example, have encountered unexpected opposition from AIDS activists.[2] The animal rights' groups don't want animals used for medical and scientific experimentation that is often painful and lethal to the animals. AIDS activists argue that while it is unfortunate that medical research may result in pain and death to animals, the experiments are conducted to relieve human suffering and save human lives. The lives of human beings, they argue, are more important than those of animals, and experimentation is needed if AIDS is to be cured or a preventative inoculation is to be developed.

Few causes are, after all, devoid of controversy. Even consumer and health groups whose efforts have tremendous popular support occasionally encounter organizations such as the American Civil Liberties Union, whose lawyers worry whether a ban on television commercials for tobacco products may be an abridgement of the First Amendment's freedom of speech clause. In 2003, Alabama Supreme Court Chief Justice Roy Moore placed a monument of the Ten Commandments in the rotunda of the Alabama Supreme Court building. He was severely criticized by both liberals and conservatives and sued by the American Civil Liberties Union for bridging the gap between church and state (making a religious statement in a government building). The display of the Ten Commandments may not be offensive to practicing Christians and Jews, but could easily be offensive to America's other growing religious minorities such as Islam.

Interest groups in democracies often link their prospects for success with a political party that suits their ideological needs. The British Labour party, for example, in part grew out of the trade union movement it has been closely associated with throughout its history. Unions are the most vocal and the largest support base for many democratic socialist parties throughout Western Europe, while business,

professional interest group
An organization that strives to lobby for and reflect the values and preferences of career professionals such as lawyers or physicians.

single-issue interest group
An organization that seeks to influence policy according to a usually uncompromising point of view on a particular issue, such as abortion or capital punishment.

---

[2]"Weekend Edition," NPR, June 23, 1996.

commercial, and professional organizations tend to align with parties to the moderate right of center. Britain's Conservative party, Germany's and Italy's Christian Democratic parties, and the United States' Republican party are all noteworthy examples of parties that are allied with interest groups representing these types of organizations.

Larger parties understandably enjoy and depend upon the support of numerous interest groups. Occasionally, though, a large national party may become too closely associated with a particular interest group for its own good. One of the misfortunes to befall the British Labour party during the 1980s was the public perception that the large trade union bosses almost completely controlled Labour's organization and parliamentary members. Regardless of whether the perception was the reality, it was strong enough to convince substantial numbers of voters that Labour was not a national political party as much as a vehicle functioning expressly to serve the demands of trade unions. Labour lost five national elections in a row between 1979 and 1992.

There is little doubt that interest groups are both important and powerful (though their power should not be overestimated). Many have the ability to raise the huge amounts of money candidates and parties require to run their campaigns and maintain their organizations between campaigns. American politics is especially susceptible to interest group influence because many candidates for Congress are on their own financially and can expect little or no direct support from the party organization. If they aren't independently wealthy, congressional candidates need and depend upon contributions from interest groups. Consider the expense of running a campaign for the U.S. House of Representatives or the Senate in 2006: The average expenditures of $1.3 million for a House seat and $9 million for a Senate seat can be very compelling reasons to a candidate for accepting an interest group donation.

This is in substantial contrast to the European democracies, where party discipline is so strong that interest groups are hard put to exert influence on individual members of parliament. No member of a typical European parliament, for example, can afford to offend his or her party leadership; to do so risks political disaster. Deciding between party loyalty and interest group pressure doesn't require a great deal of thought. One analyst quoted an anonymous source as observing that "Whatever an interest group might threaten to do to a deputy who doesn't vote as it wants is nothing compared with what the party will do if the deputy doesn't vote as it wants."[3]

It's safe to say that while nearly every political society has interest groups, sometimes thousands of them,[4] these groups have more freedom to operate and are a lot more active and independent in the democracies. They also exist and compete, however, in nondemocratic societies, and they often have goals similar to those of their democratic counterparts. Ultimately, any interest group serves its own interests. During the Soviet Union's final years, its most powerful interest group, the *nomenklatura* (the top 250,000 or so Communist party bureaucrats and their families) fought desperately to preserve its own prerogatives, including access to luxurious housing, cars, quality food, and medical care unavailable or unaffordable to the rest of Soviet society. Certainly this was not an interest group in the sense most Westerners understand. However, in the Soviet system it was an interest group within the Communist party structure that rewarded loyalty and granted favors in return.

In the average authoritarian system, the most powerful interest group may be the military and/or a landed aristocracy, as many Latin American countries have demonstrated for most of the twentieth century. Even a single family with numerous retainers may be an extremely influential group. A few hundred princes of the

---

[3]Michael Gallagher, Michael Laver, and Peter Mair, *Representative Government in Western Europe* (New York: McGraw-Hill, 1992), 134.

[4]By the early 2000s, the United States had an official count of approximately 4,500 Political Action Committees (PACs). Each one represents an interest group with a political concern.

TABLE 8–1	Party Dominance in Some Major Democracies	

Country	Political Party	Period of Time
Germany	Christian Democratic	1949–1969 and 1982–present
Israel	Labor	1949–1977
Japan	Liberal Democratic	1947–1993
United Kingdom	Conservative	1951–1964 and 1979–1997
United States	Democratic	1933–1993*

*This sixty-year period reflects a Democratic-dominated Congress interrupted infrequently and briefly by a Republican majority in one or both houses. It is noteworthy to also add that Republicans dominated Congress during 1995–2007 and controlled the presidency between 1945 and 2009—thirty-six years to the "Democrats'" twenty-eight years.

House of Saud control Saudi Arabia. In Syria, power is monopolized by the military. Hafez Al-Assad, a product of the Syrian Air Force and the Ba'ath party, ruled from 1970–2000. Before his death, he handpicked as his successor his son, Bashar. According to Syria's constitution, Bashar was then actually too young to become president, though the Syrian legislature quickly changed the constitution to accommodate Bashar's youth.

8-2c Types of Party Systems in Democracies

Democratic party systems tend to fall into two general categories: strong two-party systems and multiparty systems. Many of the English-speaking democracies favor two parties. However, a significant and permanent third party exists in the United Kingdom, and occasional third parties and, in some cases, fourth and fifth parties, arise from time to time in Canada, Australia, and, rarely, the United States. The Western European countries usually have institutionalized multiparty systems. Newer democracies such as India and Japan also enjoy the benefits and disadvantages of multiparty systems.

In the United States, the Democratic and Republican parties over time created a duopoly that emphatically discourages the rise of third parties. Third-party movements or individual candidacies have sprung up at the national level with varying degrees of success. Substantial third-party efforts were mounted in the modern presidential races of 1948, 1968, 1980, 1992, 1996, and 2000. At the local level, though, third-party movements have been regularly squeezed out of the electoral process for lack of funding and an ability to secure even a modest core of popular support. The Libertarian party in Alaska is an exception and has been able to elect a few candidates to the state legislature. The Republican party, founded in 1854, is the only successful third-party movement in American history. Within a few years of its founding, the Republican party overtook and replaced the fading Whig party.[5]

The two-party system suggests in theory that two major political organizations control the policy process. Keep in mind, though, that a two-party system frequently means one or the other party is politically dominant for decades or even generations at a time. Table 8–1 summarizes some major examples of party dominance in different democratic systems. Whether a long epoch of one-party dominance is healthy or desirable for political democracy is debatable. But regardless of one's position on this issue, such dominance is the result of regularly held free elections.

---

[5]The Whig party seemed doomed, anyway. During its entire history, the Whigs were able to elect only two presidents, both of whom died in office—one, William Henry Harrison, just thirty days after his inauguration.

The two-party system usually creates a clear winner—though not always. Some fundamentally two-party systems include permanent third parties that occasionally win enough parliamentary seats to prevent either major party from securing a majority. Two important examples include the Liberal party in the United Kingdom and the Free Democratic party in Germany. Both parties suffer from severe electoral disadvantages, yet both cause the major parties to look over their shoulders. None of the major parties in either the United Kingdom or Germany has won a majority of the popular vote since the 1950s.

In a parliamentary democracy, a political party participates in a national election in hopes of securing control of both the legislative and executive branches in one effort, or at least of winning enough parliamentary seats to help form a coalition government with one of the other parties. The majority party leader or the leader of a block of parties with a parliamentary majority takes control of the government and becomes prime minister. A vote for the party of choice is in effect a vote for a head of government.

The United States presents a major exception to this rule. Because it is a presidential rather than a parliamentary system, the American system is often characterized by a divided government or, less politely, political gridlock. Republican President George Bush, for example, faced a Democratic congressional majority during his term (1989–1993), while his successor, Democratic President Bill Clinton, was confronted with a Republican congressional majority halfway through his first term (1993–1997). A longer episode of political gridlock occurred from 1969 to 1993, when the Republicans controlled the presidency (except during the Carter years, 1977–1981) but never controlled both houses of Congress.

8-2d Multiparty Systems

Multiparty systems are more common than two-party systems in democracies. Many of the smaller parties in a multiparty system tend to resemble single-issue interest groups, forming around one issue and attempting to make policy on it. During the 1950s, the West German Federal Republic system included the Refugees Party. The Refugees succeeded in securing parliamentary seats but eventually dissolved because their concern—getting ample government assistance for East German refugees—was satisfied as the refugees integrated into the growing West German economy. During the same period, the Poujadist party in France achieved temporary success simply by calling for an abolition of most taxes. It was, in effect, an anti-tax party.

regional or separatist political party
A political movement with an appeal in a precise geographical part of the country or to a particular segment of the national population.

Other small parties have substantial staying power. **Regional or separatist political parties** have appeared in several Western European democracies. In Italy, for instance, the Lombard League seeks to detach the northern half of the country from the remainder or—what amounts to the same thing—throw the southern portion out of the Italian state. The Lombard League is convinced that the south is a drag on an otherwise prosperous economy. In Britain, the Plaid Cymru, or Welsh Nationalist party, and the Scot Nationalist party (generally and affectionately referred to in Britain as the Welshnats and Scotnats) draw a respectable segment of the vote, usually between 20 and 30 percent in their respective regions. Both desire separation from, or at least greater autonomy in, an English-dominated United Kingdom. These parties contribute to the weakness of the two-party system and even hint at the rise of a multiparty system, at least in their respective regions, because both the Welshnats and Scotnats regularly win parliamentary seats.

religious party
A political organization with a religious agenda that calls for laws and lifestyles to be consistent with a scriptural doctrine.

In some multiparty systems, such as India and Israel, **religious parties** have consistently done well at the polls. In the 2004 elections in India the Bharatiya Janata Party (BJP), a Hindu nationalist party, won the second largest amount of seats in the parliament. In 2006 in Israeli national elections three religious parties won a combined total of nearly a fourth of the parliamentary seats. While the religious parties in both countries received less than 25 percent of the popular vote, this is a very significant proportion in a multiparty system and normally cinches their inclusion in a coalition government.

Extremist parties, parties with radical viewpoints on the left or the right, can also do well in multiparty systems and can even threaten the larger parties' dominance. Since the 1980s, the National Front in France has regularly drawn support from 15 to 20 percent of the electorate in national elections. The Front has done even better on the local level and controls the municipal governments in several large cities. In the 2002 presidential elections the National Front's leader, Jean-Marie le Pen, received nearly a fifth of the votes cast, enough to make him the second leading candidate after the winner. Le Pen was able to beat out the Socialist candidate, normally the primary opponent to the Conservative candidate. The National Front's political program is basically anti-immigrant and anti-Semitic. In India the second largest party with representation in the country's parliament is the Bharatiya Janata Party (BJP) that began its career as a relatively extremist party calling for the removal of non-Hindus from India. It has since modified its stance, but continues to identify India with Hinduism.

Communist parties have traditionally represented the extreme left in most parliamentary systems. In some parliamentary systems of Western Europe, they have attracted rather sizable followings, and in France, they are the junior partners in a coalition government with the Socialists. During the 1980s the Italian Communist party was the most successful, often winning as much as 30 percent of the popular vote in national elections. Italian Communists did even better in local elections and have won mayorships and municipal council majorities in several Italian cities. For a time, the Italian party was the largest communist party in Europe and the second largest party in Italy. The end of the Cold War significantly reduced the electoral hopes of communists and all but wiped the party out in some countries. It has occasionally resurfaced under another name, such as the Party of Democratic Socialism in Germany, though professing a less doctrinaire political program.

Mainstream parties are usually the biggest and most successful players in a multiparty system. A mainstream party normally receives a fourth to a third of the total vote. It is rare but not unheard of for such a party to win a majority; the Liberal Democratic party in Japan did so for decades. Most of the time, though, a multiparty system has a strong party slightly to the left of center and one to the right. The leftist party is usually called the Socialist, Social Democratic, or Labor party, while the rightist one is the Conservative or Christian Democratic party. Whatever they are called, these parties tend to be centrist and moderate though they also come equipped with hard-line wings on either the left or the right—or, on occasion, both.

These are the parties that are the principal opponents in national elections and the ones that lead in the formation of coalition governments. Typically, the party with the greatest electoral support is one of the larger parties and attempts to form a government by combining forces with one or several of the smaller parties. This is not always an easy feat. Smaller parties invited to join the government are expected to be ideologically compatible, willing to accept ministerial posts in proportion to their parliamentary numbers, and committed to remaining in the government for the term of office. As one might guess, it doesn't always work out quite that way.

With some justification, multiparty systems can claim to be more democratic than two-party systems. In a multiparty system, every constituency of any significant size in an electorate can usually find a political party to express its point of view. Consider, for example, the names of some of the parties found in multiparty systems: the Women's Rights party, the Agrarian or Farmers' party, the Veterans' party, the Green or Environmentalist party, and the Refugees party. Some of these parties sound rather exotic to American voters unless they realize that there have been American parties called the Vegetarians and the Prohibitionists. Of course, interest groups operating in two-party systems are perfectly capable of articulating

extremist (political) party
A political organization on the radical left or right that espouses an ideological viewpoint that usually (but not always) lacks popular support at election time.

mainstream (political) party
A political organization that strives to win elections by appealing to moderate, centrist voters and, when necessary, playing down its ideological bases by emphasizing pragmatism and flexibility.

their point of view within one or both of the parties; in this sense, one could argue that interest groups make two-party systems more democratic.

One group of parties in multiparty systems is in reality composed of interest groups, because such parties are normally concerned only with a particular issue they consider to be of paramount importance. The Green party that has earned uneven electoral success since the 1980s in Germany is an example. Greens often pursue with relentless dedication a narrow platform of environmentalism that their followers regard as all-consuming. Most of these parties understandably appeal to a hard-core constituency that only infrequently expands into a broader base, but such parties frequently possess the electoral ability to win parliamentary seats and can tip the balance of power when a larger party is attempting to form a coalition government.

A second group of parties in multiparty systems tend to be characterized by strong ideological statements and long histories. The socialist parties active in Western European politics since the beginning of the twentieth century provide the best example. Their platforms tend to be strongly ideological. Many of them, however, have mellowed over the last few decades—perhaps because mellowing has become a requirement for political survival. Many Western European socialist parties have met with little electoral success during recent decades. They have had to seriously modify their programs and support a strong free market to appeal to a growing middle-class electorate. Once they make this move toward the center, socialists then find themselves less socialist and more electorally successful. By the early 2000s, several members of the European Union had left-of-center governments. These included the Labour party in the United Kingdom and the Democratic Socialist party in Germany. The latter had back-to-back electoral victories in 1998 and 2002 while the Labour party achieved similar success in 1997 and 2001. Neither party had been able to enjoy such an accomplishment for two generations previously.

A peculiarity in some multiparty systems involves one party that emerges with enough strength to dominate the government without the need for coalition partners. This is unusual, but it has occurred in a number of countries. For decades, the Liberal Democratic Party in Japan and the Congress party in India won elections so resoundingly that the several opposition parties combined did not hold as many parliamentary seats.

Some multiparty systems start out with a multitude of parties and become streamlined over time. When Germany's sovereignty was restored after World War II in 1949, a dozen or so parties competed in the first parliamentary elections. Most of them won seats. By the late 1950s, the number of parties capable of winning seats had been reduced to three, and Germany appeared headed for a two-party system. In recent years, however, the number of viable parties has increased to five, in part because of the new political constellation produced by East Germany's unification with the Federal Republic in 1990. It now appears that Germany is reverting to a multiparty system.

The results of the 2006 elections to the German lower house, the Bundestag, are instructive (Table 8–2). Members can earn seats in either local or national elections. Only two parties, the Christian Democrats and the Social Democrats, have the ability to win races in districts that elect just one member from all candidates. The other parties all rely on winning at least 5 percent of the national popular vote, and thus earning that portion of seats. Occasionally, a small party may be strong enough regionally to win seats directly in a few districts where it may have a regional stronghold. The only party to do this in recent elections is the Left party (communist and allied groups), which received only 4 percent nationally in 2002 but won in two districts, all of them in the old Communist party stronghold of Eastern Germany. By 2006 this party had transformed into the Left and broadened its base in both eastern and western Germany.

Extremist parties are usually ignored when it comes to forming a coalition government because their agendas are unacceptable to other potential coalition

TABLE 8–2	2006 Bundestag Election Results	
Political Party	**Percent of Popular Vote**	**Number of Seats**
Christian Democrats*	35.2	225
Free Democrats	9.8	61
Social Democrats	34.3	222
Greens	9.1	51
Left**	8.7	54

*Combines the national Christian Democratic Union and the Bavarian Christian Socialist Union.

**Inclusive of the Communist and allied parties.

partners. Of course, some parties generally considered extreme can do so well in elections that it is politically impossible to shut them out. Parliamentary results in the world's largest democracy, India, provide a case in point. The Bharatiya Janata Party (BJP) stands for strong Hindu nationalism and is widely regarded as uninterested in the interests of non-Hindus (about 15 percent of the population, or close to 150 million people), most of whom are Muslims. One of its political goals was to advocate the destruction of an Islamic mosque built on the site of an ancient Hindu temple, enabling the construction of a new Hindu temple.

Of course, not all religiously oriented parties are extremist, nor are all extremists successful at the polls. In some countries, such as Israel, a hard core of religious enthusiasts can usually guarantee a steady turnout at the polls. In the most recent elections (2004), religious parties achieved their traditional goal of ensuring that the largest party would be able to secure a majority of seats. One would have to outbid (or perhaps outbribe) the other to win the support of the religious party leadership in order to form a government.

In more secular systems, such as Germany's, both major parties may be denied outright majorities in one parliamentary election after another because of a third party such as the Free Democrats in Germany. Since 1949, the Free Democrats have been the junior partner in every German government, except the one ruling from 1966 to 1969, even though they consistently receive less than 10 percent of the popular vote.

A few general conclusions can be drawn regarding smaller but viable political parties:

1. They can be confident they will be decisive in determining which of the larger parties forms the government;
2. They can tip the balance of power and earn inclusion in any new government, usually with a disproportionately large number of cabinet ministries; and
3. They can exert power over their larger coalition partner(s) by threatening to leave the government, thereby reducing or eliminating the government's parliamentary majority, unless their policy preferences are at least partially placated.

8-2e Two-Party Systems

A two-party system is not always as simple as it sounds. Two-party systems are rarely pristine. Third parties frequently appear and can seriously challenge one or both major parties and, on infrequent occasions, even replace a major party. The American two-party system has been remarkably durable: The modern Democratic party goes back at least to the early 1830s or, in the opinion of some, earlier still to the Jefferson presidency (1801–1809), while the Republican party was founded in 1854.

The British two-party system is about as old. But in both the American and British systems, third parties have risen and faded at different times. The Liberal Democrats in Britain, however, have been a third party for nearly a century and have demonstrated remarkable staying power.

The two major parties in a two-party system are also prone to be divided houses. The Republican party in 1992 and 1996 faced a challenge from its hard right or more populist wing, led by Pat Buchanan. This wing was adamant in its refusal to compromise on abortion, arguing that the procedure is wrong under any circumstances. It took equally extreme views on immigration (favoring severe limitations); exhibited deep suspicion of the American role in the global economy, preferring a strong program of economic protectionism; and disliked the 1990s emphasis on foreign policy, preferring nationalism to internationalism. In those same years Ross Perot's independent candidacy probably drew votes away from the Republican party's presidential ticket and helped to elect and re-elect Bill Clinton in 1992 and 1996. Mainstream Democrats had their own problems with an uncompromising left wing that vocally supported affirmative action, homosexual rights, and multiculturalism. In 2000 Ralph Nader almost certainly drew votes away from the Democratic presidential candidate and may have helped ensure a Republican presidential victory. His second run for the presidency in 2004 was so weak that his candidacy probably hurt no one and did not impact on the election's outcome.

Major parties in the two-party systems occasionally find themselves in serious trouble. Political obituaries have been written for most major parties from time to time. Yet the major parties tend to survive and have demonstrated remarkable resilience. Over the last century, either the Democrats or the Republicans were expected to collapse on several occasions. Their supposedly imminent demises are briefly summarized in Table 8–3.

In all of these cases, the major party recovered and eventually went on to prosper. Democrats and Republicans have also withstood challenges in presidential races that threatened to deny either of the major candidates an outright victory in the electoral college and to throw the race into the House of Representatives. Over the last half-century, this threat loomed seriously in the elections of 1948, 1968,

TABLE 8–3	A History of Near-Party Collapse in the United States
Times of Democrat "Collapse"	**Reason**
1890s	Rise and serious challenges of Populist Party
1972	Disastrous presidential election result after party's left wing provided candidate and platform
Times of Republican "Collapse"	**Reason**
1929 and 1930s	Stock market plunge and Great Depression blamed by many on Republican presidency of Herbert Hoover
1964	Disastrous presidential election result after party's right wing provided candidate and platform

1980, and 1992. In all four races, the winning Democrat or Republican was denied an absolute popular majority.

Much the same could be (and in fact, was) said regarding the British Labour party during the 1980s and 1990s. The Labour party during this period was barely able to secure a third of the electorate's votes in national elections. A major party in a two-party system is surely in trouble if it is consistently unable to win at least 40 percent of the vote. Nor have the Conservatives escaped expectations of political death. In 1996, numerous prognosticators predicted disaster for the Conservatives in the next parliamentary elections; in 1997, their predictions were at least partially proved true when Labour handily won the elections and formed a new government.

The Democratic party in 1972 and the Republican party in 1964 were humiliated in the presidential elections, as each received barely 40 percent of the popular vote. In both of these cases, the party faced electoral disaster because it had veered much too far from the political mainstream for its own good. The Republican candidate in 1964, Barry Goldwater, frightened voters with what seemed at the time an extremist right-wing platform, while the Democratic candidate in 1972, George McGovern, did the same with a platform produced and dominated by the left wing of the party.

In Britain, Labour annoyed middle-class voters in the 1970s and 1980s by its apparent subservience to the trade union movement. The more moderate Labourites understood that the perception to some extent agreed with reality. It is impossible for a political party to win national elections in a democracy by restricting its appeal to a segment of the electorate. In this case, the segment was the working class, which was gradually diminishing in numbers as more and more Britons became better educated and moved into the middle class. By the middle 1990s, Labour had succeeded in positioning itself as a centrist party no longer in the hands of union leaders or tied to a socialist ideology with minimal popular appeal. Shortly thereafter, it succeeded in taking over the government.

There are few two-party systems in the purest sense. The American system probably comes the closest, because in a typical year the two major parties can expect to win the votes of 95 to 98 percent of the electorate. Plenty of atypical election years crop up though. Most two-party systems can be considered modified multiparty systems in which the larger parties tend to draw various ideological points of view into their ranks. The Republican party, for example, contains both pro-life and pro-choice supporters, both crucial to electoral victory. In contrast, multiparty systems may include two, three, or, infrequently, four large parties, none of which has much of a chance of winning a parliamentary majority, in addition to numerous smaller ones.

8-2f Are There One-and-a-Half-Party Systems?

In established democracies, there is an assumption that the major parties alternate in power. Generally speaking they do, but not as frequently as one might expect. In the United States, for example, the Republican party dominated the presidency from 1861 to 1933 with occasional exceptions (1885–1889, 1893–1897, and 1913–1921), while the Democrats remained the majority party in Congress for sixty years (1933–1993). The British Conservative party controlled the government for eighteen uninterrupted years (1979–1997). Germany's Christian Democratic party (with help from the Free Democrats) controlled the government during 1982–1998.

One party may dominate without a serious rival for decades or even generations. The Labor party in Israel controlled the country's coalition governments for twenty-eight consecutive years, from 1949 to 1977, without a break. The Liberal Democrats in Japan held power for more than four decades after the country regained sovereignty in 1947.

One-party dominant systems normally exist in countries that are not full-fledged democracies, most of them in the developing world. Such a party tends to evidence the following characteristics:

1. The political leaders are also the founders of the state; the first generation of leadership is often venerated for leading the country to independence from a colonial status.
2. The party is so closely associated with state institutions that it is difficult to imagine the party and state distinct from one another.
3. Party workers and supporters fill most political offices and effectively discourage opposition parties in seeking to win national and most local elections.
4. After about two generations in power, the founding party becomes increasingly sensitive to opposition, which by this time is usually attracting popular support or public discontent as the corruption and conspicuous arrogance of the ruling party grows.

There is always a danger that these traits will appear if a party stays in power too long, even if it submits to regular free elections. A founding party often earns or renews the electorate's support only after being in power for a twenty or thirty-year period and then decisively losing a national election. If it accepts defeat gracefully—as did Labor in Israel, the Liberal Democrats in Japan, and the Congress party in India—it eventually makes a comeback.

The *Partido Revolucionario Institutional* party (PRI) in Mexico has yet to do either. The PRI has governed Mexico since the late 1920s. It never lost a national election (although critics contend that the PRI won the 1988 and 1994 presidential elections with fraudulent ballots) until 2000. It lost several state elections to parties on its left and its right. Many observers believed that once the PRI finally lost a presidential election and left power peacefully, Mexico will advance to a more mature and more stable democracy. This happened in 2000 when the leader of the conservative opposition party, Vincente Fox, won. Fox's administration, which came to an end in 2006, was an overall disappointment. He was unable to reduce poverty and relations with the United States, Mexico's biggest economic partner, became increasingly strained as large numbers of Mexicans attempted to enter the United States in search of jobs and better economic conditions and as Americans became less tolerant of essentially porous borders with Mexico.

In such party systems, which include a legal but underdeveloped opposition, people may experience a high degree of frustration with the political process. However, they may also evidence a great deal of patience. In the examples just discussed, opposition parties patiently waited for decades (and some are still waiting) to achieve power, repeatedly contesting elections and accepting defeat peacefully. The ability of such parties to remain peacefully but actively in the political wilderness for a lengthy period of time gives a great deal of credence to the claim that democratic institutions are working.

8-2g One-Party Systems

party-state
A one-party system where the party dominates all state and social institutions. The state is simply an agency of the party to implement party programs and agendas.

A one-party system is another matter entirely. Such a system is often referred to as a **party-state**, because it is often the party that determines the nature of the government and of the political institutions. The former Soviet Union was an excellent example of a party-state. In a one-party system, the party dominates all state institutions. The state is simply an agency of the party and is in place only to implement party programs and agendas. Opposition political organizations are banned and, ideologically speaking, for good reason: In a communist system, the ruling party is the only legal party because it is the only party that represents and advocates on behalf of the working class, and working class members are the only people who matter because workers are a society's only productive members.

Under such a system, other political parties, by definition, are both unnecessary and wrong. Communist systems, like one-party systems everywhere, have a very pronounced tendency toward self-righteousness. During the last decades of the Soviet regime, it was not only wrong but indicative of clinical insanity to oppose the party and be unhappy with all the party was doing to improve society. Opponents were sometimes institutionalized in mental asylums until "restored to sanity," usually with electric shock treatments. Because such people supposedly detract from and may be injurious to the cause of the working classes, they cannot be allowed to function freely in a proletarian paradise.

All of this may sound as if the average person in a one-party state would have little to do with politics. One would think the absence of competitive elections would result in a disinterested citizenry. Yet the last thing any self-respecting totalitarian regime wants is political apathy among its people. In fact, the citizen has no legal right to be apathetic. A good citizen accepts without reservation the party's ideological goals. The citizen must also do this enthusiastically and be prepared to assist the party to fulfill these goals.

Drumming up enthusiasm is not easy in a one-party state, but most one-party systems attempt to do so. The German Nazis, Italian Fascists, and Soviet Communists all put substantial resources into youth organizations, for example, intending to produce a new generation of selfless, disciplined, and obedient citizens whose first loyalty would be to the regime and the party that was inseparable from it. The Ba'ath (Renaissance) party in Iraq under Saddam Hussein's regime (1968–2003) and in Syria since the 1950s was modeled on the Nazi structure and, like the Nazis, is completely ruthless toward any opposition. Professional organizations, labor unions, the media, and even the military were laced with party agents who ensured that every organization's members were thorough in their devotion to the goals of the party.

Enough of the adult population—say, 6 to 8 percent depending upon the country—belonged to the party in these systems to guarantee that the party's continuance and effective control would not diminish over time. In these one-party systems, party members became the most powerful interest group. Those who gained membership were envied by their fellow citizens, for the honor of membership meant joining society's political elite. It also meant great privileges.

Privileges aside, membership meant a lot of hard work. Party workers were expected to mobilize the masses to turn out for an election or referendum (to endorse the party's choices) or for a national holiday's parades (to illustrate the near-hysterical happiness that accompanies the good fortune of living in a perfect society). More ominously, party members were also expected to keep their eyes open for any hint of discontent or hostility towards the regime.

There may be a fatal flaw in one-party systems that dooms them to self-destruction. Without competition, meaningful elections, or any reason to know about—let alone respond to—public opinion, the state often eventually succumbs to institutionalized corruption, when the party becomes incapable of telling the difference between protecting its own interests and those of the country. In the end, the loss of public confidence in the party becomes so great that repair is impossible. Because the party and the state are politically inseparable, they can both collapse at the same moment. This is certainly what happened in the Soviet Union in 1991.

8-3 Elections and Electoral Systems

There are still some countries in the world that do not hold any elections, free or otherwise. All democratic and a good number of nondemocratic countries hold elections, but for different reasons. In democracies, elections are usually constitutionally mandated, and the political culture has induced the citizenry to expect and even look forward to participating in them at regular intervals.

8-3a The Point of Holding Elections

Elections in democracies provide the most important and widespread manifestation of popular political participation. They are the essence of what makes a political system democratic: The electorate decides who will govern and what policies will be enacted. While elections are commonplace in democracies, electoral systems differ somewhat from country to country. Voter registration requirements such as age and residency may differ slightly, for example. Overall, though, universal suffrage has been achieved in every full-blown democracy. In some democracies—the United States is an exception—even convicted felons can vote.

Voter turnout of the eligible electorate can be very high. Some countries come close to getting 90 percent of their people to the polls but a few, the United States being the most blatant example, do well to see 50 percent cast ballots (see Table 8–4). Americans are notorious for exercising their democratic right not to vote.

The dismal voter turnouts in the United States are a source of frustration for political scientists. They have suggested several reasons why American turnouts are so low compared to voter turnouts in other democracies:

1. American elections are always held on Tuesdays, although nobody seems to know why. Tuesday is a workday and a school day; this makes it difficult for voters to vote. European elections are usually held on Sundays, a nonworking day for most voters.

2. American elections are seemingly endless. There are off-presidential year elections and even local elections between national election schedules. Primaries precede the general election campaign, consuming media attention for months at a time and leaving many voters bored and exhausted. Americans have more elections than most democracies and longer campaign seasons than any. The 2004 national election campaign began in the snows of Iowa and New Hampshire in February and went on until Election Day in November, mercifully ending media coverage. National election campaigns nearly everywhere else are much shorter in duration, perhaps six weeks at the most. They may occur at five-, six-, or even seven-year intervals, as opposed to yearly elections in the United States. American voters seem to experience electoral fatigue because elections are frequent and campaigns seemingly endless.

3. The European systems tend to have more partisan voters. Up to 40 percent of American voters classify themselves as Independents. Neither Republicans nor

TABLE 8–4	Electoral Turnout in Recent Elections in Selected Countries

Country	Percent Turnout
Australia	94
Belgium	85
United Kingdom	78
Germany	77
Israel	77
Norway	76
Japan	73
Canada	69
France	69
United States	53
Switzerland	46

Source: Adapted from Russell J. Dalton, *Citizens Politics,* 2d ed. (Chatham, New Jersey: Chatham House Publishers, 1996), p. 45.

Democrats can win an election without substantial support from voters who consider themselves unaffiliated with any political party.

As Table 8–4 illustrates, voting Americans may be an endangered species. Only the Swiss have a lower voter turnout among the established democracies. Perhaps this isn't entirely negative, though. Not voting is one's choice in a democracy, and millions who make this choice have intelligent reasons. Many of the fifty million Americans who could vote and don't are making a conscious decision because of their displeasure with the available choices. There is a certain number of nonvoters who neglect to participate probably because their political apathy may mask an enthusiastic endorsement of the political and economic system. This explanation implies that the success story of the United States discourages people from voting, an ironic commentary on the American polity.

Moreover, Americans understandably become worn out from the relentless frequency of elections. Most of those who do vote visit the polling places more often than their counterparts in other nations:

> No country can approach the United States in the frequency and variety of elections, and thus in the amount of electing. No other country elects its lower house as often as every two years, or its president as frequently as every four years. No other country popularly elects its state governors and town mayors, or has as wide a variety of nonrepresentative offices (judges, sheriffs, attorneys general, city treasurers, and so on) subject to election. Only one other country (Switzerland) can compete in the number and variety of local referendums, and only two (Belgium and Turkey) hold party "primaries" in most parts of the country.[6]

No matter how many elections there are or how often elections are held, it is critical that the campaign and election themselves are conducted fairly, that voting activity is free of intimidation, and that both winners and losers accept the election outcome peacefully. These conditions are very important in any effort to promote the efficacy of a democracy. Any election in a democracy is an indication that the system is working and that, regardless of whether people are satisfied with prevailing economic and social conditions, they still have confidence in the overall political process.

None of this means, however, that even fair and punctual elections always yield the best possible results. The Nazi party was the largest recipient of the popular vote in the 1932 German elections, nearly 40 percent. As a result, the Nazis took power in early 1933 and almost immediately began to suspend democratic processes; the Germans had to wait seventeen years and lose World War II before voting in their next free elections.

Still, people are better off with than without elections. Some parties and politicians will always want to win elections only to end them. But freely and fairly conducted elections provide the following advantages:

1. An entire electoral population gets an opportunity at regular intervals (normally between two and five years) to evaluate and choose new or veteran political leadership.
2. The policy debates that surround elections enable electors to decide, with (it is hoped) objective information, which economic and political policies they want the government to adopt.
3. Popular support is mobilized on behalf of a position or candidate. For all of its clumsiness, a political rally (even one with planned "spontaneity") suggests a degree of popular endorsement.
4. Finally, elections renew the contract between the government and the governed and illustrate the people's commitment to the political system.

---

[6]Ivor Crewe, "Electoral Participation," *Democracy at the Polls*, ed. David Butler et al. (Washington, D.C.: American Enterprise Institute, 1981), 262.

Nondemocratic systems also find reasons to have elections. Communist states hold elections on a fairly regular basis. True, communist candidates for political office run unopposed, and one-candidate elections do not excite the electorate. Voters are still expected to cast ballots, though, and they are encouraged to exercise the limited choice available to them: They could vote for the candidate or vote against the candidate by striking his or her name out. This latter option did occur—it happened often enough to be the cause of some embarrassment to the party in the Soviet Union.

8-3b Types of Electoral Systems

single-member (SM) district
A region in which the constituency elects one representative, usually the individual who receives a plurality of the votes cast.

plurality
Simply the largest number of votes cast, which need not be a majority, for a candidate in an election.

proportional representation (PR)
An electoral system that allots legislative seats to political parties on the basis of each party's percentage of the total popular vote.

multimember districts
A region in which the constituency elects two or more representatives who may or may not be from the same political party.

Two general electoral systems are widely used: **single-member (SM) district** systems are found mostly but not exclusively in the English-speaking countries. As the term suggests, in SM systems, the country is divided into electoral districts roughly similar in population, and each one furnishes one member to the legislature. This is a winner-take-all system. Normally, a candidate is required to capture a **plurality** of the vote—the largest number of votes cast, even if less than 50 percent—to secure the seat.

The other and more popular electoral system is **proportional representation (PR)**. In a parliamentary election, a political party receives representation in the national legislature *in proportion* to the percentage of popular votes the party receives in an election. Ten percent of the popular vote normally provides a party with ten percent of the parliamentary seats.

Variations and combinations of both of these systems exist. Until 1996, for example, Japanese elections were conducted in **multimember districts** that elected three, four, or five candidates to parliamentary seats. Both Germany and Japan now use both SM and PR.

SM works well in the United States, where it is common for either a Democrat or a Republican to receive an absolute majority of votes in a district. Absolute majorities are far from common in the United Kingdom, however, where there are often at least three serious candidates contesting a seat. The Liberals, the long-time third party of British politics, can win as many as a fourth or even a third of the votes in many single-member districts and have won a fifth or more of the total vote in national elections. Even such a respectable proportion does the Liberals little good; they are usually edged out by one or the other major parties and have to make do with winning only thirty or forty seats of 646 in the House of Commons. A glance at Table 8–5 demonstrates why Liberals would prefer a revision of the current electoral system to proportional representation. The same glance explains why the Labourites might prefer the current system, at least for the time being.

The SM system does not necessarily sentence a third political party to permanent minority status. The Liberals could certainly make better use of their electoral base of 20 percent if their supporters were concentrated in one region of the country. A regional proportion of 30 to 40 percent would make the Liberals a

TABLE 8–5	**Popular Vote and Seat Distribution in the British House of Commons**			
Political Party	**Percent Popular Vote**	**Percent of Seats**	**Actual Number of Seats Won**	**Number of Seats If PR Were Used**
Conservative	32.3	30.0	196	209
Labour	35.2	54.8	354	227
Liberal Democrat	22.0	9.6	62	142
Others	10.5	4.8	31	68

Source: Data from the 2005 parliamentary elections, *CIA Factbook, 2006.*

serious contender for parity with the Conservatives and Labourites. Of course, there is no humane or sensible way to group all Liberal voters in one region.

The SM system tends to produce a government controlled by a single political party. This is not to say that PR systems can't produce stable governments with several parties sharing control; successful coalition governments form all the time. In fact, coalition governments may be more successful than single-party governments, if only because they often have a broader base of popular support.

Electoral Systems

Characteristics of SM Systems

1. Single-member systems promote efficient and decisive electoral outcomes, usually placing a single majority party in control of the government.
2. SM systems encourage two large parties to be pragmatic and moderate in their policies by co-opting issues of concern to smaller parties.

Characteristics of PR Systems

1. Proportional representation systems allow for numerous minority constituencies to elect representatives to parliament.
2. PR systems encourage a coalition government that represents a variety of opinions and ideologies.

The Israeli Electoral System

For electoral simplicity, it is difficult to beat the Israeli system for the following reasons:

1. The entire country is treated as a single constituency.
2. A voter casts one ballot on behalf of the party list of her or his choice.
3. The list can include up to 120 names for 120 parliamentary seats.
4. A party receives a total number of seats in proportion to the number of votes it receives in the national election.

On the other hand, some PR systems can get out of control. The 2001 Italian election is a case in point: The 628 seats of the Chamber of Deputies ended up divided among no fewer than twenty-six parties and parliamentary groups.[7] The largest of these parties, the Progressives, carried only a fourth of these seats. The two largest parties together accounted for only about 43 percent of the total vote. Forming a coalition government in these conditions is a political nightmare. It is also a partial explanation as to why Italy has had fifty governments over the last sixty years.

The most obvious compromise in any debate over the relative merits of SM and PR is to offer an electoral system that uses both. Germany, for example, has done so since 1949. Each German voter casts two ballots, one for a general party list and one for a favorite candidate in the voter's district. In the German lower house, the Bundestag, half of the 656 seats are determined by each type of vote.

The two larger parties, the Christian Democrats and the Social Democrats, usually win all of the SM seats between them. A smaller party that can manage a constitutionally required **threshold** of 5 percent receives seats in the general election proportional to the total vote. With one notable exception (1966–1969), every German government since the late 1950s has been a coalition between one of the largest parties and the Free Democrats. The objective of applying both SM and PR

threshold
A requirement that a political party receive a minimal percentage of the popular votes cast in order to receive parliamentary seats. In Germany, the threshold is 5 percent; in other countries, such as Israel, the percentage can be lower.

---

[7]"Mess Continues," *The Economist*, January 20, 1996, 49.

systems is to ensure representation in the Bundestag for any party that receives a respectable showing on election day, while avoiding any serious possibility that the government would be immobilized by and fragmented between too many parties.

8-3c Referendums

The public is active in determining policy through such devices as referendums. In a referendum, the public (or, more realistically, interest groups concerned with a particular issue) petitions to allow the electorate to decide on a legislative action with the ballot box.

In a real sense, every election is a referendum because voters determine whether to retain one government's policies or replace them with alternatives. Most democracies also have a provision for a formal referendum to implement or reject a proposed policy on the basis of popular will. (French presidents have used their ability to call for national referendums on six occasions since 1958, usually when they simply wanted to circumvent or ignore the national legislature.) In a referendum, the voters might decide, for example, whether their taxes should be raised or lowered. If a simple majority passes a referendum, it generally has the force of law, and the legislature cannot override it.

American presidents do not possess the power to authorize referendums, nor are they likely to acquire it. Congress is certainly not about to lessen its authority by allowing a president to bypass its prerogatives and appeal directly to the electorate. However, referendums are legal and are frequently held on the state and local levels in the United States. In fact, about half of the 900 or so referendums held each year in the world occur in the United States. American voters are increasingly asked to vote on referendums that involve social and moral issues, such as homosexual marriage, at the state and local levels. Problems are sometimes inherent in this sort of a referendum when constitutional issues are involved. Even a referendum passed by an enthusiastic majority will not ultimately become law if any part of it violates a constitutional provision.

electronic democracy
An electoral system in which each participant or voter can register direct approval or disapproval on issues through a computer or other electronic device.

In a modern society with tens or hundreds of millions of people, a referendum may be as close as it is possible to come to direct democracy. Moreover, in the age of rapidly advancing computer technology, an **electronic democracy** may actually be feasible. This possibility was first advocated during Ross Perot's 1992 presidential run, when televised national "town meetings" became part of the campaign. Universal voting on national issues could be handled through electronic voting, with the entire electorate participating through devices such as email and fax machines.

As a rule, political parties don't have much affection for referendums because they tend to lose control of the legislative process if the electorate can directly resolve an issue. Electronic democracy could make public officials more responsive to and perhaps more knowledgeable about the public will. They could test their proposals for public approval or disapproval before making them law. On the other hand, public officials could also become confused because the public often changes its mind. In any case, it is unlikely that political parties will become obsolete in the face of electronic democracy. Candidates will still need party organizations to raise money, recruit supporters, and mobilize voter turnout

Chapter Summary

1. Political parties exist in both democratic and nondemocratic political systems. In the democracies they seek to win elections, whereas in nondemocratic systems they are more interested in extending the power and control of the party leadership.
2. In democracies, a political party is usually critical to the success of an aspiring politician because one is expected to work his or her way up through the ranks. The United States is an exception; here, a popular nonpolitician can occasionally win political office.

3. Interest groups have a pervasive influence over political parties; in some cases, they even become political parties. At the same time, a political party must be careful not to become associated too closely in the public mind with a particularly influential interest group.

4. Party systems are generally classified as either two- or multiparty. Multiparty systems may be just as stable as two-party systems, even when a coalition government forms. One-party systems are usually dictatorships. Nonparty systems also exist in authoritarian regimes.

5. Extremist parties often do well in free elections. Their electoral prosperity usually rises when bad economic times or other causes of social unrest crop up. Within their own regions, separatist parties can often effectively compete with larger parties.

6. Electoral systems are usually based on either single-member districts or on proportional representation. In some instances, combinations of the two are available.

7. A referendum enables an electorate to either petition a legislature on an issue or, in some cases, to override the legislature altogether.

Chapter 8 Quiz

1. The Ba'ath party in Syria is an example of a(n)
   a. majority party in a multi-party system.
   b. authoritarian party.
   c. movement taking power after a free and competitive election.
   d. theocratic movement in the Middle East.

2. Strom Thurmond is a rare example of a United States senator who
   a. was still in office at the age of 100.
   b. won an election as an independent.
   c. switched political parties in the midst of a successful career.
   d. all of the above.

3. Presidents Ronald Reagan, Bill Clinton, and George W. Bush are all examples of
   a. senators who became president.
   b. governors who became president.
   c. military leaders who became president.
   d. cabinet officers who became president.

4. Animal rights advocacy is an example of a
   a. political party.
   b. professional interest group.
   c. single-issue interest group.
   d. mass movement opposed to goals of the American Civil Liberties Union.

5. *Nomenklatura* is a reference to the former Soviet Union's
   a. top scientific community.
   b. military elite.
   c. secret billionaires.
   d. top-tier Communist party bureaucrats and their families.

6. The most successful third-party movement in the United States is the
   a. Greens.
   b. Democrats.
   c. Republicans.
   d. Libertarians.

7. The Lombard League in Italy is an example of a
   a. theocratic party.
   b. mainstream party.
   c. refugee party.
   d. regional or separatist party.

8. The Bharatya Janata Party in India is an example of
   a. a nationalist party.
   b. a single-issue interest group.
   c. an Islamic party.
   d. an Asian communist party.

9. In the American presidential elections of 1948, 1968, 1980, and 1992
   a. neither the Democratic or Republican candidate won with a popular majority vote.
   b. the House of Representatives had to decide the outcome.
   c. there were significant third-party challenges.
   d. the Socialist party made important gains.

10. Consistently low voter turnouts are found in
    a. Australia.
    b. Belgium.
    c. Canada.
    d. the United States.

11. English-speaking democracies tend to favor electoral systems that have
    a. proportional representation.
    b. multi-member districts.
    c. single-member districts.
    d. at-large constituencies.

PART 4

Ingredients of International Politics

The fast-changing world necessitates these three chapters (9, 10, and 11) on political economy, political geography, and political violence. The 1990s was a decade that saw unprecedented economic growth across the planet, particularly in East Asia. Between 1972 and 1997 China's economy quadrupled and has continued to grow at an annual rate of between 8 and 12 percent in the early years of the twenty-first century. By 2006 China had become the fourth largest economy in the world. Even the dotcom bubble burst that occurred in 2001 had stalled but not blunted economic growth. However, the last couple of decades also saw economic disparities accelerate. Economic growth or the lack of it impacts on both a country's hopes for political democracy and the sustaining or establishing of political stability. The recession and stock market decline during 2000–2002 impacted much of the world as large corporations went bankrupt and more workers became unemployed, but by 2005–2006 most ecnomies had more than recovered. What ensures a country's stability, longevity, and perhaps even its survival? Its physical location, the quality and quantity of its population, and the behavior of its closest political neighbors are all important determinants. States have been known to disappear. Some have disappeared and reappeared. Finally, political violence, despite and in some cases because of the advance of democracy, characterized a good part of the twentieth century from world wars to terrorism. It is often political violence that makes states appear or disappear.

CHAPTER 9

The Global Political Economy

Those who are fortunate enough to live in relatively prosperous societies are generally aware that they are usually the beneficiaries of an evolving global economy. They are the consumers of products that are made across the planet. By the early years of the twenty-first century, despite the shadow of terrorism and the potential of war in the Middle East or on the Korean peninsula, most countries understood the importance of participating in and benefiting from a global economy. Those that didn't tended to focus on their military prowess. North Korea is a menace to its own people as well as others because it spends 31 percent of its gross domestic product on its military,[1] a horrific proportion in any society, but especially egregious in a country where large numbers of people live on the verge of starvation.

One important reason the Cold War wound down during the late 1980s was the increasingly undeniable realization that the industrialized and technologically proficient countries were leaving the Soviet Union and other communist societies behind. Given its antiquated and bureaucratically impaired economy, there was not much that the Soviet system (or its imitators) could do to remedy this. No longer was the world divided simply by the ideological contrast between communism and democracy; a growing economic rift divided it as well.

In the immediate aftermath of World War II, most of the industrialized powers needed to rebuild their shattered economies. The war's destruction in Europe and Asia was devastating to many countries. But the American economy, unlike many of the others, had actually expanded. The United States was the only major participant that had not been repeatedly bombed or militarily occupied or both. As the war ended, the American economy made up nearly half of the global economy, an unnatural and even undesirable situation that couldn't be sustained. It wasn't, of course, and while the United States still had the world's largest economy fifty years later, its proportion had diminished to a still impressive quarter of the total. The planet had changed in other dramatic ways that seemed irreversible: The population had more than doubled from 2.6 billion to 6.5 billion by 2006, and both overall global wealth and regional poverty had grown substantially.*

This chapter will explore the global economy, examining how governments and economies interact and produce both benefits and negative effects. It will consider the growing impact of the global economy on the lives of countries and individuals. Moreover, it will discuss how the world is splintering into more and more countries even as, paradoxically, entire regions of the world integrate economically.

Never before has the world seen such a prosperous lifestyle as that of citizens in the industrialized nations at the close of the twentieth century. One indication is the automobile. Researchers have noted that while the world's population more than doubled during the half century from 1945 to 1995, the total number of automobiles increased 1,000 percent, from fifty million to 500 million.[2] To this total one could add another quarter billion trucks and motorbikes.[3] The globalization

---

[1]Barry R. McCaffey, "North Korea's Global Threat," *Wall Street Journal*, sec. A, December 12, 2002.

*The world's population is increasing by about 90 million people annually, but is expected to level off to under 10 billion by or before the middle of the twenty-first century.

[2]"Living with the Car," *The Economist*, June 22, 1996, 3.

[3]"The Poor and the Rich," *The Economist*, May 25, 1996, 25.

of the internal combustible engine—and its accessibility to hundreds of millions of people—suggests unprecedented and increasingly widespread wealth.

Yet unprecedented poverty also remains. At least a billion people on this planet live in an extremely impoverished state, and they have little or no prospect of ever escaping this condition. A total of 1 billion people currently living have never received or made a phone call. Their misery is a mystery to many economists who wonder why countries with substantial natural resources remain poor.[4] On the bright side, many societies that seemed hopelessly poor thirty or forty years ago are vibrant today: South Korea was an economic backwater in the 1950s, but by 2006 it had the tenth largest economy in the world, and by 2020 it is expected to rise to seventh (which would put it ahead of Russia, Italy, and the United Kingdom). Because politics and economics are frequently intertwined, both this connection and its implications will be explored in this chapter. The relationship between politics and economics is critical for political stability; it seems that democracies cannot thrive in poor societies, while brutal dictatorships seem to manage quite well with an impoverished populace. However, this observation can sometimes be simplistic: The largest economy in the world by 2020 could well be China's, a country that is not currently making a great deal of progress toward democratic political processes. Thus, the tantalizing question of whether economic growth softens some nondemocratic regimes also needs to be explored.

9-1 Some Basic Principles

The last quarter century has seen dramatic changes in the world's economy. Many people are indeed getting richer, at least on paper. In 1974, for example, the capitalization of all the world's stock markets was about $900 billion. By 1994, this figure had grown to $15 trillion in constant dollars.[5] A decade later this number had almost doubled. The stock market reversals of 2000–2002 slowed but did not stop this growth and by 2005 nearly all of the decline had been recouped. The world has never before seen such a rapid or widespread growth in wealth. Most of this remarkable increase came in Western economies and indicated the growing gap between the West and the communist sphere, as well as between the West and the developing countries. But recently, the most impressive advances have been in East Asian countries, where

> the incomes of many of their citizens have doubled in a decade: their people also eat better, drink cleaner water and live longer, and more of their children survive early illnesses, get a better education and can find a job at the end of it.[6]

That is certainly good news. The bad news is that many other people are not getting any richer and may be getting poorer. According to the United Nations Development Programme (UNDP), people in seventy countries have lower average incomes than they did in 1980, and those in an alarming forty-three are even poorer than they were in 1970.[7] If one takes the long (and optimistic) view, the quality of life for most national populations has improved. Even in Africa, where poverty is endemic in some countries, living standards have improved by 21 percent overall since 1980. But while averages are up, those who lost ground are even poorer than they were a quarter century ago. Many African countries are plagued by war and government corruption and, frequently, both. Sudan, territorially the largest country in sub-Saharan Africa, has been embroiled in a civil war since at least 2003 that, in its western regions, principally Darfur, features slaughter literally on a genocidal scale.

---

[4]Ibid.

[5]"Cities", *The Economist*, July 29, 1995, 4.

[6]"A Global Poverty Trap," *The Economist*, July 20, 1996, 34.

[7]Ibid.

As studies of most of Africa suggest, progress can be painfully slow. An annual economic growth rate of 2 to 3 percent is not inconsiderable over the long term, but populations may wait decades before they experience a noticeable improvement in the quality of life. Moreover, there is no guarantee that such progress is either inevitable or sustainable.

Some economies can actually regress, often rather quickly. This happens most vividly when the political system itself collapses. The Eastern European countries and former Soviet republics (FSRs) had stagnated for years before their communist regimes imploded. Reformers wanted to establish free market economies in a hurry, so they implemented **shock therapy**—dismantling the collectivized, state-controlled system and replacing it with a free market. The reforms produced mixed results as national economies disintegrated and were characterized by frighteningly rapid declines in gross domestic products (GDPs). Millions of people in the FSRs had become accustomed to a social system that provided for their basic needs, though the provisions were often primitive. These citizens suddenly confronted the disappearance of subsidized (if often inadequate) foodstuffs, rampant inflation (officially nonexistent in the Soviet Union), and the dismantling of an extensive state welfare system (especially disconcerting to older people dependent on government pensions). FSRs such as Estonia, Latvia, and Lithuania had improved their economies in the decade following their renewed independence to such an extent that they were being admitted by 2002 to the European Union, a sure sign of progress.[8]

Zimbabwe, a sub-Saharan African country that once enjoyed a relatively high standard of living, is under the control of Robert Mugabe, the leader of an autocratic regime that is both corrupt and inept. The country had a negative 7 percent economic growth rate in 2005 with a nearly 150 percent inflation rate. Mugabe has rigged elections, forced productive farmers off their land to make way for supporters to gain property even though they know nothing about farming, deposited huge amounts of money in foreign banks, and interfered in the politics of neighboring states. Zimbabwe has become a country that is a poster child for disastrous governance.

During the Cold War, it was convenient, if not completely accurate, to divide the world's countries into the following three groups:

First World—The democratic and economically advanced countries of Western Europe, North America, Japan, and a few Westernized societies such as Australia and Israel. The bulk of the population in these regions enjoyed the highest living standards and quality of life in the world. Welfare programs at least partially alleviated the substantial pockets of poverty that existed.

Second World—The communist countries of the Soviet Union and Eastern Europe, where the economy was industrializing but not advancing appreciably and lagging behind the First World. Compared to the First World, the standard of living in these countries was abysmal. Communist systems achieved the distinction of equalizing poverty, making it easily available to the entire society with the exception of the party hierarchy. The average citizen had to wait years before getting a telephone and had little hope of owning a personal car (though public transportation was usually more than adequate).

Third World—Most of the rest of the world in the "underdeveloped" regions of Asia, Middle East, Africa, and Latin America. The economy in many of these countries was characterized by extremes of wealth and poverty with a decidedly underdeveloped middle class. Several countries were considered Third World only in a nominal or geographical sense. The populations of the East Asian "tigers" (or "dragons") enjoyed rising living standards that were increasingly similar to First World countries, and Chile, though part of Latin America, was

shock therapy
The sudden and rapid dismantling of a collectivized economy and maximized state control, replaced with a free market and minimal government supervision.

---

[8]These three Baltic republics (Estonia, Latvia, and Lithuania) were sovereign states between 1920 and 1940, when they were absorbed into the Soviet Union.

quickly developing a modern economy equipped with an expanding middle class. China was sometimes placed in the Second World and sometimes in the Third World category. China is rapidly becoming a First World country.

Well before the Cold War ended, this three-world model ceased to make sense. The terms are still used, however, because improved substitutes haven't been found. The term *Third World* is perhaps the most misleading because this group contains so much diversity and represents many times the population of the first two combined. The "Third World" is a vast place with three-fourths of the human race. The differences between rates of economic development and political democratization in these countries are so gaping that it makes little sense to classify them together. As one observer has explained,

> Today, two new forces are finishing off the tattered Third World idea. The first is the West's victory in the Cold War. There are no longer two competing "worlds" with which to contrast a "third." Leaders can't play one superpower off the other, or advertise their misguided policies as alternative to "equally inappropriate" communism and capitalism. The second is rapid growth in many once poor countries.[9]

Besides, many so-called Third World countries have long demonstrated a strong resemblance to First World countries, achieving and sustaining remarkable levels of economic growth. Several are also in the process of democratizing.

Third World societies are, of course, distinct from one another in history, culture, and economic development. Moreover, even within a developing country, some regions are almost certainly more advanced than others. In the state of Bihar in India, poverty is endemic for the usual reasons: illiteracy, malnutrition, overpopulation, and miserable sanitary conditions. Perhaps most telling of all, over 90 percent of adult women in Bihar are illiterate (and in some parts of the state, the percentage rises to 98). At the same time, India's middle class is growing, and its democracy has worked well since the country achieved independence in 1947.

A more comprehensive way of looking at the global economy can be described as follows:

1. Well-established, high living standards among the great majority of the population are currently limited to Western Europe, North America, Australia, New Zealand, Israel, Japan, and the "**little tigers**" of East Asia—South Korea, Singapore, and Taiwan. These regions account for only a seventh of the world's population of 6.5 billion but together create two-thirds of the global economy.

2. The former "Second World" of Russia, other former Soviet republics (FSRs), and most Eastern European countries are in a state of transition. A few of these countries—the Baltic states, Czech Republic, Hungary, and Poland—seem to be successfully developing both democratic institutions and working market economies. Geographically, ideologically, and even religiously, these countries have been close to and are hopeful of rejoining the West. The majority of the FSRs are still tentatively exploring the possibilities of a noncommunist world. All told, this region contains about 400 million people, about half the number in the first group.

3. A third group of slowly developing countries is defined by no single geographical region but consists of at least 100 countries scattered throughout the developing world. The Asian "**tiger cubs**" of Malaysia, Indonesia, and Thailand could fall into this category. So could Chile and perhaps Argentina and Mexico. India raises the biggest question; it is so huge and diverse that it could almost be treated as several countries. Some parts of India are doing well, others dismally. Overall, this group probably contains another 400 million people, which increases to 1.4 billion if India is added in. (China and India are such large countries that it isn't unreasonable to place each in a category by itself.) China, while

"little tigers"
Smaller countries located in East Asia with strong and growing modern economies, specifically South Korea, Singapore, and Taiwan.

"tiger cubs"
Relatively large countries in East Asia and Latin America attempting to modernize their economies. Chile is a successful example of this characterization.

---

[9]Charles Lane, "Let's Abolish the Third World," *Newsweek*, April 27, 1992.

a rising economic power, has very uneven distribution. The eastern third of the country that is on or is in close proximity to the Pacific coast had in 2006 a per capita income of $4,000; the remaining two-thirds of the country is rural and undeveloped with a per capita income of only $1,000.

4. Countries with valuable natural resources that enjoy global demand, such as the Persian Gulf states, could make up a fourth category. Their economies are rich, and their populations may be coddled in the sense that their overall needs are provided by the regime's largess. This policy does not, however, encourage real economic development. In many other instances, corrupt and/or incompetent governments and megalomaniac dictators keep the population relatively poor. It is difficult to be sure, but perhaps half a billion people live in these countries.

5. Nearly a fourth of humanity lives in the least desirable places, where the life span is barely half of the life span people in the first category enjoy. Most Africans, a large proportion of South Asians, Latin Americans, and Chinese live in conditions that can only be described as abject poverty. In some cases, the country has too small an infrastructure in place to build on. Several countries, such as Somalia, Rwanda, and Burundi, have no infrastructure at all; they do not exist in any modern sense except on maps. Their governments are either nonexistent or unable to control much more than the capital city. Most of the population is endemically poor because of relentless civil strife, political corruption, and even wholesale massacre, or because of natural disasters such as desertification.

These categories demonstrate the great unevenness of economic development. Surprise upturns and downturns further complicate the picture. In the 1950s, the Philippines was the most prosperous country in East Asia. Today, it is one of the poorest. A national poll taken in 2005 revealed that 40 percent of Filipinos would leave the country if they were able to do so. In 1980, Nigeria, the largest country in Africa, had a larger economy than South Korea, Thailand, or Malaysia. By 1990, all three had larger economies than Nigeria, even though Nigeria has substantial reserves of oil.[10]

Economies can and sometimes do regress. What goes wrong? Several potential problems are always on the horizon. A country can degenerate into civil war, and the war can drag on for years, decades, or even generations. A country may be ruled by a dictatorship more concerned with enriching itself than encouraging economic progress. The Philippines was moving along well until two decades of the Marcos regime (1965–1986) shattered the economy. The Marcos family and its retainers systematically robbed the national treasury. To this day most of the looted monies have not been located.

Another problem arises when a country relies too heavily on a particular product such as oil and leaves itself at the mercy of fickle world markets, as Nigeria has done. Ironically, possessing a natural resource that the rest of the world constantly demands can hurt a country's chances to develop. It is almost better to have too few resources; then the country places greater reliance on the most valuable resource of all—the population. Countries such as Singapore, Japan, South Korea, and Israel have all been mentioned as economic success stories: None of them have attained economic modernity because of any resource other than an educated, skilled, and diligent work force.

It seems clear that an increasing number of non-Western countries are doing well for themselves economically and are fashioning their own democratic styles. Many of these newly industrialized countries (**NICs**) are located in East Asia, but it would be wrong to assume that they are all the same. South Korea, Taiwan, and Singapore compete as much with one another as they do with the American and European economies, and they all worry about the predominance of the huge Japanese economic system and the potentially even larger Chinese economy. Japan currently possesses the second largest economy in the world, while China could have the

NICs
The acronym for *newly industrialized countries*, most of which are located in East Asia and Latin America.

[10]Keith B. Richburg, "Why Is Africa Eating Asia's Dust?" *The Washington Post National Weekly Edition*, July 20–26, 1992, 11.

world's largest economy in half a century if current trends—trade and commerce, technological education, and manufacturing—continue and the emphasis on the free market is not curtailed by Communist-party bureaucrats.[11]

The world economy is not yet global, but it is certainly globalizing. Perhaps if one insists on categorizing countries, it might be logical to group them into three worlds after all: The North American and West European world, where established democracies and advanced economies are taken for granted; the up-and-coming NICs in Asia and elsewhere, where advancing economies are helping to provoke demands for democratic reforms with as yet uncertain success; and the remainder of the world's countries, many of which are now attempting with varying degrees of success to find the formula for sustainable economic development.

9-2 Democracy and Capitalism

Capitalism has become "the mode of production of a globalized economy,"[12] but capitalism alone doesn't guarantee democracy. While the world now has unprecedented global wealth, this wealth is concentrated in a minority of the world's countries. The fact that nearly all rich countries are democratic is meager consolation to poor places that are neither. In 1995, the seven largest economies, usually referred to as the **G7**, were all Western with the single exception of Japan. Together these seven countries account for nearly half of the world economy—46 percent—though they contain only a tenth of the world's population. Moreover, while the rich in this context may not be getting richer, they aren't becoming less rich, either. The G7's proportion of the world's economy has remained fairly constant since 1960.[13] See Table 9–1 for a comparative list of selected countries according to their overall Gross Domestic Product (GDP) and per capita GDP.

G7
The top seven economies of the world—the United States, Japan, Germany, France, Italy, United Kingdom, and Canada. These countries may be joined in the near future by rapidly advancing economies such as China's. The G7 is sometimes expanded to G8 as a courtesy to Russia.

It is true that both democracy and free markets seem to be catching on in non-Western regions. It also seems at least partially true that some cultures remain resistant to either or both. Governments that desire to maximize control of their citizenries and enrich only a small elite lack any reason to encourage a free market and the social openness a free market promotes. India is the world's largest democracy, but its economic development has been stalled by ancient traditions that discourage Hindus from adopting free-market approaches to the economy. Not all Indians have followed these traditions, but hundreds of millions have. India's political elite have been wary of emulating the economic habits of those who colonized the country for centuries.

India, according to some experts, must turn its back on its own form of **autarky**, a largely discredited model of economic nationalism that emphasizes producing as much as possible within a country's own borders and avoiding foreign markets and international commerce. A government may favor autarky when it fears outside influence. In China, foreign trade was discouraged during 1949–1976 when the government insisted that the country could fend for itself without outside interference. It couldn't, of course, and hundreds of millions of Chinese endured deplorable economic conditions. During the Cultural Revolution (1966 to about 1971) the regime even encouraged "backyard furnaces"—devices to produce steel literally in the backyards of peasant homes (the peasants were expected to energetically produce steel after ten hours of farming). While economic success stories such as Singapore, Taiwan, and South Korea depend on foreign trade, India is more self-reliant.[14] It is also lagging behind in the remarkable economic growth these countries have experienced for more than a generation.

autarky
An economic system in which a society strives to achieve economic self-sufficiency within its own borders and become independent of foreign markets and international commerce.

---

[11]For some interesting insights into China's evolving economic culture, see Kathy Chen, "China's 'Oprah' is Part Gossip, Part Glamour," *The Wall Street Journal*, May 12, 2006, A15 and A17.

[12]Kathryn A. Manzo, *Creating Boundaries: The Politics of Race and Nation* (Boulder, CO: Lynne Rienner Publishers, 1996), 49.

[13]"Can the G7 Ride Again?" *The Economist*, June 22, 1996, 76.

[14]"India Survey," 4.

TABLE 9–1	Comparative Wealth	
Country	**GDP**	**GDP per Capita**
Afghanistan	$21.5 billion	$800
Argentina	483.5 billion	12,400
Canada*	1.023 trillion	31,500
Denmark	174.4 billion	32,000
France*	1.737 trillion	28,700
Germany*	2.362 trillion	28,700
India	3.319 trillion	3,100
Iraq	89.8 billion	3,500
Italy*	1.609 trillion	27,100
Japan*	3.745 trillion	29,400
Mexico	1.006 trillion	9,600
Nepal	39.53 billion	1,500
New Zealand	92.51 billion	23,200
Poland	463 billion	12,000
Russia*	1.408 trillion	9,800
Switzerland	251.9 billion	33,800
Taiwan	576.2 billion	25,300
UK*	1.782 trillion	29,600
U.S.*	11.75 trillion	40,100
Vietnam	227.2 billion	2,700

*G7 + Russia—known as the G8—countries are indicated by an asterisk.
Source: Selected Countries' 2004 GDPs from Infoplease Almanac online at http://www.infoplease.com/ipa/A0874911.html

Of course, every society in the end must find its own (sometimes tortuous) path to prosperity. Obviously, some do better than others when it comes to finding the most suitable path. The factors that work well in an ethnically homogeneous and geographically compact society of three million people, as in Singapore, are unlikely to work in a heterogeneous and huge society of nearly one billion, as in India. Such a comparison can be extended: Singapore is no doubt a prosperous place, but its democracy is hardly the sort normally found in Western countries. In fact, Americans would be hard put to recognize Singapore as a democracy at all. People in Singapore are well off because they work hard. They are, however, legally obligated to be neat, tidy, industrious, and thin—whether they want to or not.

To make sure,

> ... police keep watch from the rooftops of Singapore to catch people committing such crimes as littering or chewing gum. Parents of schoolchildren deemed to be overweight receive letters ordering them to change the family menus. The government tells people how much of their money to save.[15]

The Asian model of development is a complicated one, assuming a particular model exists. Singapore may be self-righteously clean, but South Koreans chew gum and do worse things in their streets.[16] Moreover, at this point none of the participants in the "Asian miracle" can be considered full-fledged democracies. China, a decidedly undemocratic country, has experienced nearly unprecedented economic expansion in the 1990s and early 2000s based on the free market currently operating in the eastern regions of the country. Since the early 1990s China's economy has consistently grown near or in the double digits and averaged 12 percent

---

[15]T.R. Reid, "Confucius Says: Go East, Young Man," *The Washington Post Weekly Edition*, November 27–December 3, 1995, 21.
[16]Ibid.

annually. At the same time, though, human rights protection in China remains an issue of serious concern. The kidnapping of young women by Chinese men because of a shortage of women in some regions has basically produced a widespread form of sexual slavery.[17] China also sells human organs abroad, "harvested" from executed criminals. India, a practitioner of democracy for the last six decades, is still reluctant to relinquish government-maintained barriers to market-based economic reforms, though less so than the 1980s. India has become a prized destination of the outsourcing of jobs that numerous American corporations are engaged in.[18]

Obviously, some cultures possess an antimarket bias that seems to override or direct the political climate. Before communism came to power in Russia, a collective perspective prevailed in rural villages. Now, even with democratic institutions in place, many Russians are unsure of the benefits of the market economy. The outcome of the 2000 and 2004 presidential elections, which presented an option to return the communists to power, suggests that a firm majority of voting Russians, about 60 percent, still have confidence in economic reforms that emphasize the free market.

South Korea for centuries was both poor and contemptuous of entrepreneurs, and South Koreans were deeply respectful of the Confucian-inspired scholar-bureaucrat.[19] The country had to overcome its cultural bias against making individual fortunes before it could advance economically. Once this happened, the cap on economic development was removed, probably for good. However, after the Korean War (1950–1953) a younger generation of South Koreans gradually emerged. This generation was better educated than their predecessors and determined to emulate the success of nearby Japan, a country that rapidly emerged from military defeat and economic devastation by employing carefully selected Western economic models.

It cannot be blithely assumed that free markets and democracy go hand in hand, even though it is tempting to do so. Free markets in the modern world can't be entirely free. The public sector plays a necessary role because the government is expected to engage in regulatory activities and, in deference to its traditional role, guarantee personal security.

What, then, does it take for a society to achieve both a prosperous economy and democratic polity? Apparently, the same sorts of conditions apply to both. An economist with international repute suggests that economist Adam Smith stated the answer quite simply nearly two-and-a-half centuries ago:

> Little else is requisite to carry a state to the highest degrees of opulence from the lowest barbarism, but peace, easy taxes, and tolerable administration of justice.[20]

Successful democracies contain these three elements, although they may fall somewhat short of perfection. Figure 9–1 suggests that the quality of life, as measured by the Human Development Index, is higher in democracies, though some democracies are simply more democratic than others. Singapore, for example, has a high quality of life but is far less concerned about individual rights than is the United States or the United Kingdom.

Ironically, the world's fastest growing economies in the 1990s and early 2000s have turned out to be in East Asia, where governments are involved in a "strategic-growth" model.[21] Under this model, governments don't interfere in the free market so much as they monitor where they might help promote certain aspects of the market. This is done by bureaucrats who behave as though they are entrepreneurs, but only when no one else does. In Singapore, one of the top success stories in

---

[17]Melanie Kirkpatrick, "The New Underground Railroad," *The Wall Street Journal*, May 12, 2006, A12.

[18]"Tread Carefully," *The Economist*, June 29, 1996, 33.

[19]Michael Prowse, "Miracles Beyond the Free Market," *Financial Times*, April 26, 1993, 15.

[20]Quoted in Jeffrey Sachs, "Growth in Africa: It Can Be Done," *The Economist*, June 29, 1996, 20.

[21]Prowse, "Miracles Beyond the Free Market," 15.

FIGURE 9–1   **Quality of Life Worldwide**

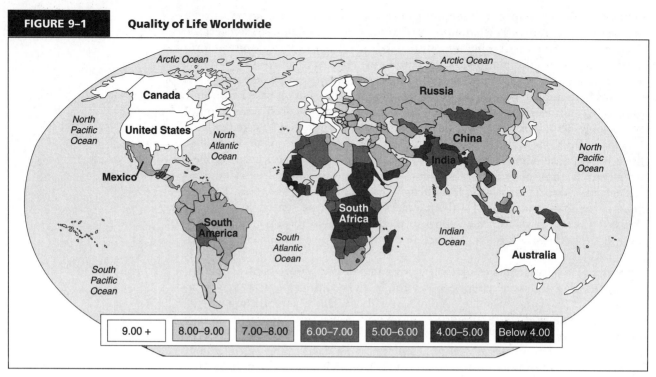

9.00 +	8.00–9.00	7.00–8.00	6.00–7.00	5.00–6.00	4.00–5.00	Below 4.00

Source: UN Development Report, 2001.

East Asia, when private companies "failed to respond to opportunities identified by bureaucrats, state-owned or controlled groups were often pushed to the fore ..."[22]

There are certainly varying paths to prosperity. According to an important study published since the early 1990s, the more individual freedom government provides, the greater the economic growth.[23] This finding makes sense by simply considering the fact that in traditional dictatorships, even those that encourage entrepreneurship, the government can arbitrarily take away anything a citizen has at any time. This hardly creates an incentive to work hard, accumulate wealth, and invest. The government must ensure that contracts between parties will be honored and property secured for its owner. The Chinese communist political elite, however, has revised this concept to mean that greater *economic* freedom is all that is required. So far the Chinese leadership has successfully managed to avoid a parallel emphasis on political freedom.

9-3 The Globalizing Economy

There is a certain sense in which the world's economy is really global: More than ever before, most people are living in an increasingly interdependent world economy. This interdependence is, if anything, accelerating because of new information technology and the linking and internationalization of financial markets.

Economic prosperity and the enjoyment of a decent lifestyle have been exclusionary for most of modern history: They were confined for the most part to the "First World." Even there, substantial portions of the population had to struggle before they gained the opportunities available to the prosperous majority. Prosperity is spreading and growing, though it is still confined to a minority of countries and peoples.

Still, prosperity is often considered a mixed blessing. It almost always means that traditional lifestyles will change; some beyond recognition. For some

---

[22]Ibid.

[23]"Democracy and Growth: Why Voting Is Good for You," *The Economist*, August 27, 1994, 17.

traditionalists, prosperity is sometimes perceived as threatening because it is often associated with American traits. In fact, the global economy is frequently criticized because of its "Americanization." In part, this is because the American economy is unrivaled in its success and scope and because Americans are so good at selling their products. As the global economy expands, "American consumer goods are likely to be first choice for millions of new consumers in the Third World, who want to drink Coke, smoke Marlboro cigarettes, and watch Hollywood films."[24]

Americanization is definitely going on, but it is most noticeable in selected locations. Many people in developing nations are migrating from rural areas to quickly developing urban centers to find work and a better life. In the process, they often find poverty and unhealthy environments, too. Yet if a global economy exists or is emerging, it will most likely be found in cities, where both the advantages and disadvantages of development are most pronounced.

The growth of urban communities over the last half of the twentieth century was relentless. In 1950, only two urban areas had populations over ten million—London and New York. Forty-five years later, fourteen urban areas had populations that ranged from eleven million in Tianjin, China, to twenty-six million in Tokyo, Japan. London's population has remained steady at ten million so the only Western city with a population over eleven million is New York. The other thirteen large cities are non-Western.[25] Clearly, economic growth focuses on urban centers regardless of culture or country.

9-4 Economic Regionalism

There is probably no such thing as smooth and even economic development in any country. For example, if the American South had succeeded in becoming an independent country in 1861, it would have been at that time the wealthiest country in the world, but by 1865, its primarily agriculture-based economy was devastated. It took nearly a century for the region to again become the most prosperous area in the United States.[26] In the meantime, the northeastern and midwestern parts of the country moved rapidly ahead as industries and commercial centers expanded onto world centers.

Not only can a country's geographical regions develop unevenly, but race, religion, and ethnicity may also cause uneven economic growth. In the United States, for example, African Americans do not generally enjoy the same quality of life as white Americans. The former die sooner, are less educated, and are in poorer health than the latter. In many urban areas, economic and social decay is in ample evidence in the inner cities, while suburbs contain a thriving middle class. Whites have fled to the suburbs, taking their education, skills, and money with them, while blacks, who tend to possess none of these advantages, have been trapped in places such as Chicago's Southside and New York City's Harlem.

It is a truism that young people hear all the time: Staying in school and getting an education is the only way to a better life. And it is true: "Since 1970, the incomes of the least educated 10 percent have fallen, while those of the best educated 10 percent have surged."[27] More broadly, the gap between the rich and the poor has widened:

> Globally, the situation isn't any better. During the middle 1960s, the poorest 20 percent of the world's people used to have 2.3 percent of the world's income but now have only 1.4 percent, while the richest 20 percent have increased their share from 70 percent to 85 percent.[28]

---

[24]"The Global Economy," *The Economist*, October 1, 1994, 38.

[25]"Cities," *The Economist*, July 29, 1996, 5.

[26]"The American South," *The Economist*, December 10, 1994.

[27]"The Impossible Dream," *The Economist*, July 13, 1996, 89.

[28]"A Global Poverty Trap?" *The Economist*, July 20, 1996, 34.

To use other revealing numbers, 1.2 billion people—nearly a fourth of whom live in the United States—enjoy 85 percent of the world's income, while more than five billion people have to scrape by (if they can) with only 15 percent.

Development seems to get underway in a few locations and, if all goes well, spreads (or at least acts as a catalyst). In the seventeenth and eighteenth centuries, London and Paris became the financial and industrial centers of Britain and France. They remain so today, though several other urban areas have established themselves as critical components of the national economy in each country. Other industrial powers, such as the United States and Germany, have economies that developed in several major urban areas, partly because both the economic and political systems were relatively decentralized.

Many developing countries lack the leisure the established economies of the First World enjoyed as they developed. Cities in Western Europe and North America grew steadily as people left their farms and small towns and moved to urban areas for a better quality of life (a pattern that reversed in the last years of the twentieth century in the United States as increasing numbers of Americans, desperate for peace and quiet, returned to smaller towns). Cities in developing countries, by contrast, are growing quickly—too quickly—as millions stream into them from outlying areas. Earlier urban expansion proceeded with a more or less adequate accompaniment of public service infrastructure. Today, cities such as Cairo, Mexico City, and Dacca lack the resources to cope with the rush of added residents who are overwhelming public services. Thus, while economic development can proceed at a suitable pace in some aspects such as business zones, where industries as disparate as diamond cutting and tourism provide jobs, the avalanche of people precludes the possibility of anything close to full employment.

Often, a developing country's government spends its limited resources in a futile attempt to simply maintain order in the capital. It then faces the difficult task of trying to extend its authority to the country's hinterland and build an economic infrastructure: transportation and communication systems, educational and health facilities, and guaranteed civil order.

Other serious problems are associated with developing economies. Not the least is the character of the political system: Dictatorships are not as plentiful as they were in the 1970s and 1980s, but they remain numerous, particularly in Africa and the Middle East. These regions also experience the greatest difficulties in economic development. Economic development is stymied by corrupt practices on behalf of the ruling elite (who typically tend to store a good part of the national wealth in personal Swiss bank accounts) and the ravenous appetite of top military officers who divert much of the national budget to the acquisition of the newest weapon systems.

Even in some Middle East countries that are wealthy according to many indices, overall development may be minimal. This is because wealth is concentrated rather than dispersed. In several cases, especially in the Persian Gulf states, national wealth is typically controlled by a ruling family who uses it to sustain political domination and discourage competition. It is very difficult for a broad-based middle class to emerge. Much of the national wealth, which may be considerable, is sent overseas for safety's sake—to those Swiss bank accounts, for example—or is directed away from building the country's infrastructure to the private pleasures of the ruling family and its retainers.

9-4a A Global Underclass

A global or globalizing economy has a generally positive connotation. Its advocates tend to ignore possible negative consequences, such as the often destructive influence globalization has on local traditions and values. Lives are disrupted as a rapidly changing technology and marketplace force people to retrain or acquire new skills. Soon, it will be rare for an individual in any economy to remain in the same job for his or her entire working career.[29]

Social dislocations are inevitable as a truly global economy evolves. The "downsizing" large corporations have undertaken since the late 1980s in the United States and Western Europe and the stagnant standard of living millions of families in these areas have experienced are indications that global transitions do not occur without substantial difficulties. The dislocations, not surprisingly, are far more serious and widespread in developing economies, where the infrastructure may not even have existed, let alone be capable of revision. Where poverty is extreme and widespread, there is little hope of progress: investment, transportation and communication systems, and skill and education levels are often very primitive and always inadequate. Just as importantly, political coherence is frequently absent if the government lacks the will and capability to extend its authority throughout the country.

In fact, the government's authority may be so minimal that other political agents usurp it. Some may be openly hostile to the regime. In Egypt, religious organizations such as the Muslim Brotherhood and the Islamic Jihad deliver public services including health clinics, food stations, and educational facilities. Hamas did much the same in Palestine. When it contested and won parliamentary elections in 2006 Hamas as well as nearly everyone else was surprised at the disgust most Palestinians felt toward the government thrown out of power that was known for its corruption and ineptness. These organizations have filled a void in places where governmental authority has broken down, never had a significant presence, or is viewed for all practical purposes as military occupation.

It is unclear what can be done to alleviate the conditions of the global poor. Governments, as just suggested, are often helpless to act. Much of the time they are incapable of imposing or collecting taxes from those in a position to pay them. Without an adequate tax base, a government cannot provide stimuli for economic development or even take back neighborhoods from nongovernmental organizations that provide public services.

Even if a government can acquire the resources to improve upon an economic infrastructure, **corruption**—the practice of bribing officials to secure government contracts—remains an important and probably permanent problem. While corruption occurs everywhere, it is most pervasive where one would expect it be: in developing societies where laws against it are lax, nonexistent, or safely ignored because they are unenforced.

corruption
The practice of bribing government officials to receive contracts for economic projects. Corruption is considered a way to do business in many societies.

Developing democracies have little to be smug about. Competing political parties in countries as different as India and Russia have concentrated on promising giveaways to large numbers of people. (One presidential candidate in Russia promised free vodka. The current Russian president in 2006, worried about the low Russian birthrate, announced cash benefits for Russians who had babies.) When a successful party comes to power, it must make good on at least some of its promises. In doing so, it can bankrupt the state or, at a minimum, discourage foreign investment in an economy whose leaders exhibit no self-discipline.[30]

One argument holds that corruption is actually good for development: Simply pay the appropriate individual to override red tape, saving money and time. Unfortunately, such a formula is actually too simple. Evidence suggests that the higher the level of corruption, the lower the rate of investment.[31]

The gap between rich and poor is tremendous and growing. One estimate suggests that the average GDP per person in the Organization of Economic Cooperation and Development (OECD)[32] is fifty-five times that of the poorest countries.[33]

---

[29]See Ralf Dahrendorf, "Preserving Prosperity," *New Statesman and Society*, December 15–29, 1995, 36–41.

[30]"Road to Ruin," *The Economist*, August 17, 1996, 32.

[31]Paul Blustein, "Pssst. Here's a Little Something That Seems to Slow Growth," *The Washington Post*, sec. D, July 17, 1996.

[32]OECD is a group of the most industrially developed countries in the world, and focuses on eliminating trade barriers and acting on issues of mutual concern, such as taxing international corporations.

[33]*The Economist Book of Vital Statistics* (New York: Random House, 1990), 34.

Rich countries are confronted with a dilemma: whether to commit substantial resources to struggling societies, or simply let them continue to flounder.

9-5 Development and Demographics

This text has maintained that government is both a necessary and permanent fixture in citizens' lives, usually for better, occasionally for worse. Government can do a great deal to encourage economic development. It can even encourage or discourage what is arguably the most important determinant of development: the quality and quantity of the population.

A government can encourage or discourage population growth by establishing a set of incentives or disincentives. At one extreme, for example, China's government strenuously pursues a **zero-population growth (ZPG)** policy. Chinese authorities will often pressure a pregnant woman to undergo an abortion if she already has one child. At the other extreme, governments can encourage population growth by prohibiting or severely restricting not only abortion, but all family planning efforts.

Government economic policy in developing societies often confronts severe demographic pressures. The most serious include a very large proportion of young people and an increasing population that is outstripping any economic progress. These are two interrelated problems, but let's consider them one at a time:

1. In most developing countries, as much as half of the population is under the age of fifteen or at least under eighteen. The under-fifteens require educational facilities as well as proper nutrition and health care if they are to become productive working adults who will make durable contributions to the economy. It is expensive to provide such services, though, and the infrastructure needed to do so is often lacking or inadequate. Millions of children reach adulthood every year without preparation for employment and become a constraint on rather than an asset to economic progress.
2. The under-fifteens, for reasons just indicated, aren't economically viable; they can't be until they possess necessary work skills. Unemployment can reach high levels, perhaps a third of the work force, and underemployment—part-time or seasonal employment—also skyrockets. Young people without jobs or prospects may become prey for political or religious extremists who offer solutions and hope. Political instability is a frequent consequence of economic underdevelopment.

Figure 9–2 suggests the problem developing societies face. Notice that First World countries have the opposite problem: a bulge of older people. There are proportionally three to four times as many older people in developed societies as in underdeveloped societies. As people live longer, a country's labor force faces the possibility of paying higher taxes to provide entitlement programs such as social security for older people. In developing economies, the labor force is too big for the number of available jobs; in established and industrialized economies, the labor force is often too small, at least as far as skilled workers, to support government programs.

In France, 20.2 percent of the population is under age fifteen, about the average of 20.5 percent for the developed economies of the OECD. The United States is slightly over the average at 21.5 percent. Contrast those numbers with sub-Saharan Africa, where the percentage is 46.2 percent or the Middle East, where the average is 42.3 percent. The under-fifteens increase to between 48 and 52 percent in countries such as Kenya, Kuwait, Nigeria, Palestine, and Yemen. Most of the young are also among the poorest members of these societies. These are depressing numbers for countries seeking economic modernization.

Trends for the future are not especially encouraging. By 2010, the world will add at least another billion to the over six billion recorded in 2000. Almost all of

zero-population growth (ZPG)
A policy that promotes a controlled birth rate, encouraging no more than two offspring per set of parents. Germans and Italians, for example, are barely replacing themselves and are only modestly increasing their populations because of immigration.

FIGURE 9–2   **Demographics: Developed versus Developing Worlds**

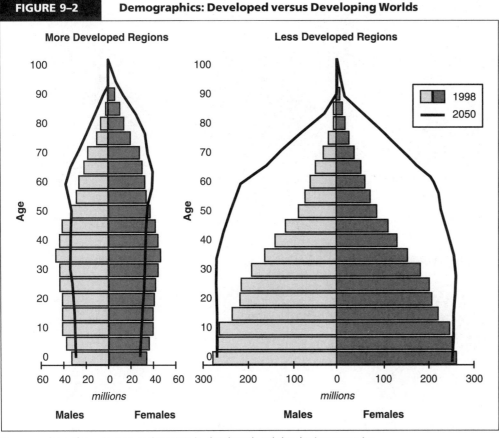

Demographics of age in men and women in developed and developing countries.
Source: United Nations Population Division, *World Population Prospects: The 1998 Revision.*

the population growth will occur in the developing areas. (See population distributions and projected trends in Figure 9–3.) This trend is expected to continue for the better part of the twenty-first century.

In 1950, the developed world included about a third of the planet's total population. By 1985, this proportion was down to one-quarter, by 1995 one-fifth, and by 2025, it will be around one-sixth. Significant population growth, in other words, is occurring precisely in the parts of the world that need it least. Moreover, in the developing regions of Latin America, the Middle East, and sub-Saharan Africa, nearly 50 percent of the population is under the age of fifteen, an age category that is too young and too unskilled to be productive.[34]

Of course, at some point, the world's population will level off. Estimates vary widely and range between eight billion by the middle of the twenty-first century to twelve billion at the end of the century. Even in the fastest growing areas of Africa and the Middle East, the percentage increase is declining, though the growth in absolute numbers is still substantial. In the meantime, though, the world's population is gaining more than ninety million members annually, mostly in regions where poverty remains endemic. Moreover, human beings are remarkably resilient. Europe lost at least a third of its total population of sixty million during the mid-fourteenth century to the Black Death plague. In some areas the death rate was 50 percent. Europe easily made a demographic comeback within a couple of generations. The AIDS epidemic in Africa is destroying millions of lives, but the continent's population still increases each year.

---

[34]John Allen, *Student Atlas of Economic Development* (Dushkin/McGraw-Hill, 1999), 63.

FIGURE 9–3   **Projected Population Growth**

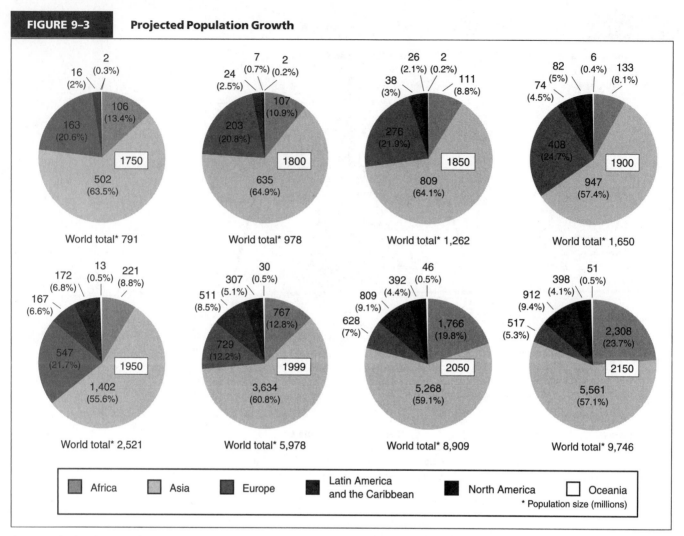

Source: United Nations Population Division.

9-6 Promoting and Sustaining Economic Development

Why does one country have a growing economy that benefits most of the population while another is mired in poverty? There is no completely satisfactory answer. It may be just as useful to suggest how government can help as well as how it can destroy economic development by doing the wrong thing or by sheer negligence:

1. It is up to government to guarantee that the *rule of law* is fully applied. Imagine, for example, the consternation of foreign investors when, in 1995, the Chinese government disavowed the twenty-year lease it had given to McDonald's on a piece of property in Beijing because there was more money in building a $2.1 billion Oriental Plaza for commercial and residential development.[35] Unless a government can guarantee that both citizens and bureaucratic agencies will live up to contracts and respect the law, others will have little confidence in a country's long-term prospects. A decade later, little progress had occurred.

2. The first point argues persuasively for the second: Democracy and successful and prosperous economies tend to go together (though the tendency is not an absolute rule). A few dictatorships have managed to move national economies

---

[35]Orville Schell, "China—the End of an Era," *The Nation*, July 17–24, 1995, 85.

along. Chile during the Augusto Pinochet military regime of 1970–1989 and China since 1979 have demonstrated that both rightist and leftist governments can foster economic growth. They did this by reaching an unwritten accord with their respective citizenries: As long as citizens put politics aside they would be allowed and even encouraged to pursue individual economic goals. However, democracy was restored to Chile during the 1990s as a growing middle class increasingly demanded entrance into the political decision-making process. Whether a similar phenomenon will occur in China remains to be seen. Most dictatorships, however, destroy economic development. There are numerous kleptomaniac dictators who systematically loot a country's wealth. Investors naturally prefer to deal with governments that depend on durable legal institutions rather than political personalities who may tear up past agreements.

3. Government is the only institution that can effectively intervene in the economy, but it must do so wisely. For example, it does not benefit society to rush headlong into development with no consideration of the effect on the physical environment. The Soviet Union's economic policies ignored ecological concerns with catastrophic results. Industrialization was considered so important that lakes and rivers were terribly polluted. Nuclear waste was buried in public parks in Moscow. Leaded gasoline is still used in developing countries, including several in East Asia. All of these policies have long-term negative health effects on populations that insist on achieving modernity regardless of the cost to themselves or to future generations.

4. Rapid modernization is often the goal of a government that feels it must move quickly to satisfy a population tired of austerity and deprivation. This rapidity frequently destroys traditional values and customs that have the sanctity of past centuries. In many developing societies, remember, amassing wealth is considered to be a vice rather than a virtue. People frown on commercial activities, preferring less development and more civility. Even the third American president, Thomas Jefferson (1801–1809), expressed doubts about those who made their livings from banking and mercantile activities and lived and worked in bustling cities whose inhabitants, Jefferson opined, led less wholesome and moral lives than their rural counterparts.

   Government can't do much about changing values, especially if it is committed to promoting and encouraging modernization. The late Chinese leader Deng Xiaoping (1904–1997) made a noncommunist remark when he proclaimed that "to get rich is glorious," perhaps the Chinese equivalent of the "greed is good" notion that developed during the 1980s in the United States. Deng's comments were also non-Confucian in stressing opportunism over obedience and harmony. Although Deng was going against much of Chinese tradition, he knew what he was doing. The Confucian system did not prohibit wealth or its accumulation. The Chinese could be safely coaxed into being profit-minded without abandoning Confucianism in the rest of their lives.[36]

   China isn't the only country subject to such contradictions. Even in the very modern country of the United States, incongruities crop up. As indicated earlier, the American South at the beginning of the twenty-first century is probably the most economically advanced region of the country. Its economic progress is most noticeable in the "boomtown" of Atlanta. Other southern cities, such as Savannah and Charleston, have preferred to conserve their historical qualities even at the cost of curtailed economic expansion. Atlanta's local government has consistently and enthusiastically encouraged economic growth since Reconstruction in the 1860s and 1870s.[37]

5. The size of the role government plays in economic development may be difficult to balance. Making government the sole coordinator of the economy is a

---

[36]Ibid., 93.

[37]Alexander Stille, "Who Burned Atlanta: The Real Story of the All-New City," *The New Yorker*, July 29, 1996, 52–58.

prescription for disaster. At the same time, economic development is almost inconceivable without the presence of the public sector. Governmental agencies provide and usually help maintain an infrastructure critical for national development—public education, public health delivery systems, and public transportation systems are all essential.

6. Government may have to intervene in delicate social issues if an economy is to move forward. This is not always easy, but on occasion a government is able to preserve tradition while still building a modern society. One of the most traditionalist societies in the world, Saudi Arabia, insists on keeping women hidden by veils and segregated from men. At the same time, though, the Saudi government, consistent with orthodox Islam, permits and even encourages women to pursue their educations through the doctoral level and to enter the professions as long as they continue to appear in public veiled, with only their eyes showing. At workplaces, where they usually are removed from contact with any men who aren't family members, they may wear lab coats or business attire. Most Westerners of both sexes would find such a social system far-fetched and intolerable, but different cultures travel different paths to modernization.

While few seriously dispute that government has a role in the economy, public confidence that government always knows what it is doing has diminished. Every developed society has a large governmental presence and substantial social programs, but it also has increasingly severe restraints as populations age and taxes are increased to take care of the aged. Ironically, the poorer societies envy these problems because they can't even dream of providing luxuries such as public housing and national health insurance. Although the economies of the world may be globalizing, a truly integrated global economy is a long way off.

There is an anti-globalization movement that has been active in several countries. The anti-globalists view globalization as an unfortunate process that has wreaked havoc with some national economies even while it has improved others. They have occasionally joined forces with environmentalist movements who see aspects of globalization as destructive of a pristine ecology. Governments themselves can be anti-globalist, as in North Korea and Cuba, where regimes habitually seek to isolate their citizenries from outside influence. Yet, for good or ill, anti-globalists may be too late. The process of globalization began about five centuries ago as technology helped commerce and trade to expand.

As additional trade routes were developed and new markets opened (sometimes reluctantly or forcibly as in the cases of nineteenth-century China and Japan), it was increasingly difficult to remain immune from or ignore the impact of foreign cultures. By the twentieth century it was nearly impossible. The train, the car, the plane, the telephone, and more recently the Internet link variant parts of a global community. Of course, not all of globalization has been beneficial because of some job relocation and the occasional exploitation of cheap labor in much of East Asia and Latin America.

That said, government still has an important role to play but it now must play a more refined or serious role because it is not immune from criticism or the flow of information across the globe. In the past a government could act unilaterally and arbitrarily and get away with it. Currently, however, all of its deeds, good and bad, receive early and careful public scrutiny. Because of global communications it is extremely difficult for a government to hide its abuse of human rights or its economic mistakes.

Chapter Summary

1. The world is increasingly becoming a global economy. This economy includes both advantages and disadvantages; substantial regions of the world are extremely poor, while other countries are achieving unprecedented economic advances.

2. The three-world model of the First, Second, and Third Worlds developed during the Cold War applies far less these days, but it does highlight some of the more important discrepancies between countries that have and have not established viable free-market economies in a democratic context.

3. Even a country fortunate enough to possess substantial natural resources may not have a developed economy that enables the growth of a strong middle class or provides most members of the society access to economic opportunities and benefits. Even in progressing countries, economic development rarely occurs evenly or smoothly across the society.

4. The relationship between free-market economies and political democracy seems inevitable, but there are important exceptions. In some cases, economic development has stimulated a desire on the part of a rising middle class to gain access to the political process.

5. The world economy is still in the process of globalizing. As prosperity increases, large elements within traditionalist societies perceive modernization as a mixed blessing.

6. A global underclass may be developing as dozens of poor countries lag farther and farther behind the countries that have taken off economically. In poor regions, the government may have minimal authority or may even be replaced by nongovernmental organizations that provide services to the populace that the government is unable to provide.

7. Economic development in some countries is racing against population increases that threaten to overwhelm both the economic and social infrastructures.

8. Government has a permanent role in promoting and sustaining economic development. The role takes on different dimensions in different societies, and governments must know when and how much to intervene in economic development.

Chapter 9 Quiz

1. Some of the most impressive economic gains made during the last few decades were in
   a. the Middle East.
   b. southern Africa.
   c. eastern Europe.
   d. East Asia.

2. The term "Third World" refers generally to
   a. North America.
   b. Soviet Union and Eastern Europe.
   c. the "underdeveloped" regions of Africa, the Middle East, and Latin America.
   d. Australia and New Zealand.

3. "Tiger cubs" is a reference to
   a. the former communist states of Eastern Europe.
   b. Central American republics.
   c. Asian countries such as Malaysia, Indonesia, and Thailand.
   d. the Persian Gulf states.

4. The G7 is a reference to
   a. the world's seven largest national economies.
   b. the European Union.
   c. North African countries.
   d. East Asia's largest economies.

5. Autarky can be described as
   a. synonymous with capitalism.
   b. the economic system that prevails in Singapore.
   c. national economic self-sufficiency.
   d. the Chinese version of foreign trade.

6. The "strategic-growth" model includes
   a. dominance of the public sector in the economy.
   b. a strongly stated Bill of Rights.
   c. complete governmental absence from the workings of the economy.
   d. bureaucratic monitoring of selected economic enterprises when deemed necessary by the government.

7. In Egypt, the Muslim Brotherhood and Islamic Jihad have replaced the government in some areas of the country by
   a. providing public services.
   b. terrorizing poor Egyptians.
   c. acquiring a parliamentary majority.
   d. taking over the military.

8. Zero-population growth (ZPG) is a policy that is most aggressively pursued by
   a. Japan.
   b. China.
   c. Russia.
   d. Indonesia.

9. By 2010, the world's population is expected to reach
   a. two billion.
   b. ten billion.
   c. four billion.
   d. seven billion.

10. The phrase "to get rich is glorious" is attributed to
   a. Joseph Stalin.
   b. Deng Xiaoping.
   c. Thomas Jefferson.
   d. Alexander Hamilton.

Political Geography and Demography

KEY TERMS

living space   partition
manifest destiny   political implosion

Human beings have, in a relatively brief time, populated the entire planet and established themselves as the earth's dominant species. Human populations did not multiply substantially until the last few centuries, as the Industrial Revolution and the development of medical science and health care delivery systems gradually lowered infant mortality and lengthened the life span. Around 1800, the world's population reached the one billion mark for the first time; by 1900, it crossed two billion; in 2000 more than six billion people were living on the planet and in 2006 6.5 billion people inhabited planet earth. In round numbers the world's population total will increase to around 6.8 billion in 2010 and 7.5 billion by 2020. Projections vary, but most tend to agree that the planet's population will be in the neighborhood of nine to ten billion by 2050 and will then level off. In many countries, such as Italy and Japan, the leveling off has already begun and population growth has been either flat or even negative.

This chapter examines how geography and population affect a country's political process. Geographical location—whether a country is an island, surrounded by mountain ranges, or located in an exceptionally hot or cold climate—is important because it helps determine a country's political history and culture. The chapter also studies what impact the quality and quantity of a population have on a country's domestic and foreign policies. It considers various demographic features, including the impact of ethnic and racial minorities, and examines how geographical setting, location, and natural resources combine with demographics to influence a country's participation in international politics.

10-1 Demography, Geography, and Politics

The influence of demography and geography on politics can hardly be overestimated. Demography's impact, though gradual, adds up to a substantial determinant: Slow changes in demography, hardly noticed at the time, often influence the great events of history. Population changes can have a drastic effect on a country's world standing, its future, and even its survival. For example, in one part of the world, the West and several Westernized countries, the population is "aging" because people are having smaller families, so a greater portion of the population is adult. Fewer children means more individual wealth, but it also means that a smaller labor force takes on a greater burden to support people who are too old to work and are living far longer than their ancestors. By contrast, in non-Western areas, economically speaking, there are more young people than available jobs; this translates into less individual wealth because a smaller portion of the population can be productive economically.

Population pressures have been used to explain the explosion of Islam during the early decades of the seventh century in Arabia. In Arabia at that time perhaps six million people were in residence, a large population for the time and place; this number placed great strains on the available water and food supplies. Early Muslims were motivated by their faith but also by the need to relieve harsh living conditions and some overcrowding.

For the sake of convenience, the world is often divided into distinct political blocs. During World War II (1939–1945), two blocs of countries, the Allies and the Axis powers, confronted one another. During the Cold War (roughly 1945–1990), the Western democracies competed with communist states for political and economic influence across the globe. Some world maps used in public high schools and libraries portrayed the communist countries in red during this period. If there was uncertainty about a country's ideological allegiances, the country was often colored pink. Today's maps evidence no particular pattern of colors. Today's maps also include a great many more sovereign states (going from about sixty in 1950 to nearly 200 by 2000) and the previous political geography is no longer relevant. The Department of State has applied the label "rogue states" to countries such as Cuba, Syria, Iran, the Democratic People's Republic of (North) Korea (DPRK), Sudan, and Libya.

After the Castro regime was established in Cuba in 1959, and Castro declared himself to be a Communist, Cuba became "red." The island is only ninety miles from Key West, Florida, a geographical fact disconcerting not only to many Americans who made their homes in southern Florida, but also to those further away who had not thought about Cuba previously. Suddenly, geography became a key factor in the Cold War. Because of its proximity to the American homeland and the emplacement of ICBMs (intercontinental ballistic missiles) by the Soviet Union in Cuba, the Castro regime was viewed as a dire threat to American national security. Yet, Cuba is not any longer considered a major threat. There are greater dangers on the international horizon: The American government and its allies after 9-11 began to prepare for the terrorist threat of chemical and biological attacks. Moreover, the North Koreans during 2002 and 2003 became more of a focus for American attention because of their insistence on developing nuclear weapons and the ability to deliver them. In October, 2006, the DPRK announced it had tested a nuclear device underground and was threatening to test more. The possibility of nuclear weapons in North Korea alarmed the country's immediate neighbors, particularly Japan and South Korea, but the United States was most concerned. In the foreseeable future, North Korean missiles could be developed with a range that could reach Alaska and Hawaii. During the same time period, Iran also became a focus of attention of both the United States and several European countries that felt concern over nuclear weapons being developed in a country sworn to "wipe Israel off the map" and determined to become a major regional power.

Where people are located often helps to determine their perspective on world events. During World War II, Americans on the West Coast felt that the United States should try to defeat the Japanese first. Americans on the East Coast were convinced it was in the national interest to concentrate on the Germans first. World events also have an effect on people's knowledge of geography: Few Americans could have identified Korea, Vietnam, Somalia, Bosnia, Kuwait, or Iraq on a blank world map before American soldiers were sent to these countries.

Both history and politics are determined to a great extent by geography. Where people live is a tremendous determinant of who they are and how they view the world and their place in it. Russians, for example, see the world much differently than Americans. With the exception of the American Civil War (1861–1865), no military conflict has been fought on American soil—the attacks of 9-11 are viewed as an exception—since the republic was established (although British soldiers briefly turned up in 1814 in what was then the new capital of Washington City during the War of 1812, to burn down the White House and other public buildings). Surrounded by vast oceans and bordered by two friendly, relatively stable countries, Canada and Mexico, both incapable of and disinterested in doing harm to the United States, Americans have enjoyed peace and security through more than two centuries.

In contrast, the Russians have not been as fortunate. Sweden (once a more significant European power with a small but well-trained army) in the early eighteenth century, France in the early nineteenth century, and Germany in the first half of the twentieth century all invaded Russia (Germany did so twice in less than three decades). The invasions were unsuccessful, but they caused terrible losses of life and property. The Russians remember them as examples of heroic and desperate struggles in their national history, and they find it difficult to trust countries that have repeatedly invaded them.

Countries that are well-established and rich dominate the global economy. Several of these countries—including Germany, Italy, Spain, and France—invited young immigrants from the Third World to join their labor forces during the 1960s, further changing world demographics. The immigrants, for the most part, stayed and started families. In some major European cities they have become a substantial proportion of the population. Yet, the Europeans were doing what was necessary. Their low birth rates meant that fewer young people were entering the labor markets. Most of the immigrants came from Africa and the Middle East. Both their ethnicity (black African or of Semitic ancestry) and their religion (the majority are Islamic) clearly marked them apart from the Europeans already in place.

The governments of these more wealthy societies fear that a recession would make immigrants a natural target for popular resentment. Ironically, until a half century ago, governments didn't have to worry about taking care of older people because there weren't very many, and immigrants, documented or undocumented, had not become a factor in the labor force. Technology has changed and even reversed these situations. Especially in the West, the number of people over age sixty-five is increasing faster than the number of people under the age of fifteen, and governments are grappling with immigration policy. Germany and, to a somewhat lesser extent, Italy actively recruited unskilled and semi-skilled workers from developing areas geographically close to Europe. Germany imported tens of thousands of young Turkish workers during the 1950s and 1960s. The Turks were willing to come and many ended up staying in Germany to enjoy its high standard of living. During this period Germany actually had more jobs than it could fill. Germans by then were having smaller families and increasingly early retirements. The Turks filled the gap. By the 1980s, however, the economic situation had changed and Germans began to experience a high unemployment rate. The integration of East Germany into the federal republic after 1989 only aggravated the situation because the East German economy was substantially underdeveloped compared to its western counterpart. Still the Turkish community, around two million strong at this point, has evidenced no desire to leave.

The United States became the world's greatest economy in substantial part because of immigration. Each new wave of immigrants—the Irish in the 1840s, Eastern Europeans in the 1880s and 1890s, Cubans in the 1960s, and Southeast Asians in the 1980s, to name just a few—brought with them their own peculiar economic skills and ambitions that contributed to the growth of a modern economy. In 2006, illegal immigration, principally from Mexico, became a major political issue.[1] Estimates of twelve million undocumented workers in the United States caught the attention of the media, the public, and the politicians. The states that border Mexico—California, Arizona, New Mexico, and Texas—were especially concerned over the matter. Even studies that revealed the economic advantages of immigration did not convince many Americans who were concerned about rapidly changing cultural aspects such as language, ethnicity, and religion.

10-2 The Political Importance of Settled Populations

The earliest large populations settled in river valleys such as the Nile, Tigris-Euphrates, Indus, and Yangtze, where fertile soil provided sufficient food for

---

[1]Elisabeth Bumiller, "Behind Bush's Address Lies a Deep History," http://www.nytimes.com, May 16, 2006.

communities that sometimes numbered in the millions. The Egyptian, Sumerian, Indian, and Chinese cultures and states developed in these regions. The first governments most likely appeared in these areas to manage extensive agricultural systems and secure them against occasional marauders. During these times, government took on the qualities familiar to any current resident in a political system: a central place of authority, representatives in various regions of the country, a bureaucracy to collect taxes, a judicial system to interpret laws and resolve disputes, and a military formation to maintain order, discourage foreign invasion, and perhaps do some invading of its own. Egypt has the most durable record in these respects: For three and a half millennia that experienced only a very few interruptions, the Egyptian Empire maintained a bureaucracy and a military that guaranteed political stability within and allowed conquest for centuries beyond the homeland's borders.

Governments in ancient states such as Persia and Babylonia did not provide many services to the population—they collected taxes, conscripted youths into the army, and maintained a haphazard network of roads. Even this latter activity was unnecessary in the political societies that were little more than small city-states, as during the classical period in ancient Greece. Tradition rather than government encouraged large families, but governments were grateful: Large numbers of people were, until recent times, widely considered a crucial ingredient of political power. Yet the greater the population, the more governments felt the need to expand. The Roman Empire was by far the largest and richest of the ancient empires. Its government was able to provide "bread and circuses" for the general population in order to keep people amused (usually by watching gladiatorial events) and well fed. The Romans were also great builders who constructed aqueducts and roads to provide fresh water to millions of citizens and to transport armies wherever they needed to go to quell rebellions or ensure the collection of taxes to continue building aqueducts and roads.

Population therefore became an early and critically important determinant of both economic and political power. To a substantial extent it still is, but the emphasis has changed: The *quality* of the population has become the main criterion of national success, in part but certainly not completely supplanting the *quantity* of the population. Not that quantity is totally unimportant. A country with political ambitions must have enough people to be taken seriously, although the absolute number itself will differ from region to region. A country with a population of around twenty-five million, such as Iraq, for example, is almost automatically a serious regional power in the Middle East, where most countries have populations under fifteen to twenty million, while a similar population in Western Europe or East Asia is considered modest. In Europe several countries—Britain, France, Italy, Germany, Russia—all have populations well over sixty million. In Asia, several countries have populations easily over 200 million—China, India, and Indonesia are examples. In the Middle East the giants are Turkey, Egypt, and Iran, all of whom top seventy million and one of which, Egypt, is approaching the eighty million mark, but few of the other countries in that region have over twenty million.

Quality of population can prevail over quantity in both an economic and a military sense. Consider the two neighboring countries of Egypt and Israel. In the quarter century between 1948 and 1973, these two countries fought four major wars with one another. Egypt's population is about ten times that of Israel's (see Table 10–1), yet Israel won these wars. The real advantages were Israel's: Its soldiers were better motivated (convinced they were fighting for their country's very survival), better fed, educated, trained, and equipped with first-rate military technology. Numbers, of course, do matter. Yet, at least in the short run (Israel can't afford to fight a major conflict for more than a few weeks), quality prevailed over quantity.

Quantity of population can actually become a great disadvantage when it comes to a country's expression of political power. Robert Malthus, an eighteenth-century scientist and demographer, warned that increasing populations were outgrowing the resources available to them in most countries. It was easy to understand

TABLE 10–1	**Egypt and Israel: A Brief Demographic Comparison**	
	Egypt	**Israel**
Average life span	71.3 years	79.5 years
Literacy rate	57.7%*	95.4%
Infant mortality	31.33 per 1,000 live births	6.89 per 1,000 live births
GDP per capita	$4,400	$22,300
Total population	79 million	6.4 million

*Male literacy is about 50 percent higher than the rate of female literacy.
Source: Adapted from *The World Factbook* (Washington, DC: Central Intelligence Agency, 2006).

why he came to this conclusion: The Industrial Revolution was beginning to take off in central and Western Europe, and the population, especially in the urban areas, was increasing dramatically as sanitation and medical science made remarkable advances. Malthus argued that populations increase geometrically—in other words, they keep doubling every generation or so until some disaster occurs. A plague such as the Black Death that killed a third of Europe's population (then estimated at around sixty million people) in the middle of the fourteenth century is certainly a memorable disaster. Yet, history strongly suggests that wars, famine, diseases, and other lethal events only briefly blunt population growth. Within a few generations after the scourge of the Black Death, Europe had more than recovered, experienced the Reformation and the Renaissance, and begun an economic and political domination of the globe that would not diminish until well into the twentieth century.

Malthusian fears have simply not been realized—at least, not yet. Malthus underestimated the ability of societies and technologies to care for the needs of several billion people. This is not to say that some countries aren't heeding the admonition to discourage population growth. China has a rigorously advocated if incompletely enforced one-child-per-family policy. Couples who insist on having more than one child sometimes face economic sanctions imposed on them by their own government. In other countries, particularly economically advanced ones, the government doesn't have to establish a population policy. Large numbers of children used to provide "social security" in old age—children and grandchildren provided for elderly family members who were unable to work any longer. The grim reality of high infant mortality rates also encouraged parents to produce large numbers of children in the hope that most of them would survive to adulthood. Modern medicine has alleviated this tragic scourge in most countries. In addition, as economic prosperity has grown, so have government-sponsored old-age security plans. There is simply much less economic reason than there used to be to have large families.

Malthus still may prove right in some places. Populations are doubling precisely in societies where they shouldn't. Many African countries see their populations double every twenty to twenty-five years. In true Malthusian fashion, Africa's rapid population growth made it the world's only region to experience a decline in food production per person during the last three decades of the twentieth century. Just as one example, live births per 1,000 women ages fifteen to nineteen are the highest in the world in Liberia, Uganda, and Nigeria. These countries also contained some of the poorest populations in the developing world that are kept that way because of meager natural resources and/or corrupt governments. Some African countries, such as Nigeria, have substantial natural resources. Yet they also tend to have unstable political regimes where rulership is often based on and justified by regional or tribal associations. The low standard of living in most of Africa impacts on other important aspects of lifestyle as well. A typical woman in Liberia receives very little if any prenatal care: She is 600 times more likely to die giving birth than her American counterpart.[2]

10-3 Demography and Political Stability

The ethnic and religious features of a population are frequently very powerful determinants of political stability and overall social harmony. A community with a history of ethnic and/or religious conflict can be severely detrimental to the entire society. An already tense situation can erupt into violence when, over a few generations, it is possible for a majority to become a minority. A case in point is that of Northern Ireland. Most of the Irish received political independence from the United Kingdom in 1922. However, the six northern counties remained within the UK because of the desires expressed by their Protestant majority. Religious affiliation in this small region is important because of the long history of religious conflict. When the "time of troubles" began (or, perhaps more accurately, continued a conflict between militant Catholics and Protestants that was already at least 300 years old) in 1969 in Northern Ireland, Protestants outnumbered Catholics two to one. In 2000, the proportion was reduced to three to two. By 2030, Protestants and Catholics may be approximately equal in number.

Catholics, if current trends continue, could eventually outnumber Protestants. This prospect concerns many Protestants, who have long been a minority elsewhere on this overwhelmingly Catholic island. Two main Protestant fears have substantially governed their political attitudes. Realistically or not, they fear becoming a religious minority in their own country (Northern Ireland) and suffering discrimination accordingly; as well as being annexed by the Republic of Ireland and its dominant Catholic majority, and therefore becoming a small and probably permanent religious minority in a newly united Ireland.

Israeli Jews during the 1980s experienced similar anxieties when the Arab population of Israel began increasing at a much faster rate than the Jewish population. If Israeli Arabs combined with the Arab population of Israeli-occupied West Bank, Arabs could outnumber Jews in Israel in the foreseeable future. This anxiety was markedly reduced when hundreds of thousands of Russian Jews were allowed to migrate to Israel during the late 1980s and the Israeli government began to withdraw its presence in selected portions of the West Bank and, in 2005, all of Gaza. It planned by 2010 to complete its withdrawal from most of the West Bank.

The Irish and Israeli examples are only two of many such scenarios. Governments have throughout history used population as a tool to change demographic features in regions and even in entire countries. China, for example, has since the 1960s systematically moved large numbers of its citizens into Tibet (which it annexed in 1958) to ensure that Tibet will remain a Chinese province. Indigenous Tibetans are gradually becoming a minority in their own country. Governments who use demographics to further their political ends often cause much human suffering. During the early 1990s Serbs, the largest community in a disintegrating Yugoslavia, attempted to engage in "ethnic cleansing" by either forcing Bosnian Muslims and Croatian Catholics to leave their ancestral homes or murdering them. There were strong efforts in Iraq, for example, to absorb the Assyrian community that is not Arab and is one of the oldest Christian populations in the world.[3] Armenians continue to accuse Turks of conducting a policy of genocide during 1915–1916 in which as many as 1.5 million Armenians were slaughtered by the Turkish army. Turkey has yet to admit that any such thing occurred. The suffering or its legacy from persecution can endure for generations, causing political consequences that in themselves have significant potential for tragedy.

---

[2]"Sub-Saharan Africa," *The Economist*, September 7, 1996, 3. See also "Fertility," *The Economist*, December 7, 2002, 100, and "Huddled against the Masses," *The Economist*, October 14, 2006, 58–59.

[3]Vivienne Walt, "Iraqi Christians Fear Invasion Backlash," *USA Today*, sec. A, December 20, 2002, 15A.

It is important to note also that some countries actually have more land than people available to fill it. The population of the Russian Federated Republic, for example, has been dropping precipitously. It dropped from 148.7 million in 1994 to 143.5 million in 2006.[4] Unless current trends are reversed or at least slowed, Russia's population by 2050 could fall to 101.5 million. Population decline or stagnation in several western European countries is in great part because people are simply having fewer children. In Russia, population decline is occurring for that reason but also because people, particularly men, have a low life expectancy as the result of alcoholism, suicide, and accidents.[5]

10-4 Politics, Policy, and Population

The frequent drawing and redrawing of political boundary lines has created all manner and sizes of countries. The largest countries in the world, in terms of population, tend to include some with huge territories, but also several of relatively modest geographical size. (India, for example, has more than three times the population of the United States in one-third the territory.) The pressure of population growth has sometimes persuaded governments to expand their jurisdictions at the expense of their neighbors. Governments encourage large numbers of people to move for several reasons. The most important are:

1. Moving population into sparsely settled regions strengthens the claim of a government to the territories in question, an especially helpful policy if a territory is partially or wholly claimed by a neighboring country. For many years, for example, the Soviet government enticed Russians to move to western Siberia, offering all kinds of material benefits. They pursued this policy vigorously because of a not unjustified fear that China was interested in claiming parts of Siberia—parts that belonged to China for centuries before the Russians seized them in the eighteenth and nineteenth centuries. And if Russia wants its citizens to move east, China wants some of its citizens to move into the westernmost provinces where the current population is of modest size, mostly Muslim, and/or non-Chinese. Similarly, the Israeli government provided tempting tax advantages to motivate thousands of its citizens to establish homes in the West Bank. They reason that the more territory Israelis settle, the less territory they will have to surrender to the Palestinians in any final peace settlement.
2. A government may sincerely desire to settle "virgin territory." During the nineteenth century, the United States government, seeking to expand to the West Coast, sold land very cheaply to Americans willing to go and settle the West. Brazil currently offers incentives to its citizens to move into the Amazon River valley, including some places where nonindigenous peoples have never gone. As they encounter indigenous populations they were previously unaware of, these Brazilians repeat history: Five centuries ago, Europeans spread diseases to indigenous peoples who had built up no immunity against them, and Brazilians are doing the same today.

The expansionist tendencies of Germany, Italy, and Japan in the years leading up to and including World War II (roughly 1931–1945) were in part motivated by the desire to acquire natural resources and **living space** for their rapidly growing populations. Unlike the United States and Russia, these countries did not possess vast, untapped resources. They felt compelled to seek these resources elsewhere, and their solution was to expand across borders. Obviously, one political problem's resolution created many more. Germany's expansion into much of Europe and

living space
The German term, popularized during the 1930s, describing the goal used to justify acquiring territory in eastern Europe, removing the indigenous populations, and sending Germans to replace them—the Germans needed "living space."

---

[4]Padma Desai, "Running Out of Russians," *The Wall Street Journal*, May 22, 2006, A13.

[5]Ibid.

FIGURE 10–1   **German Map Showing Czechoslovakia as a Threat, 1938**

Japan's into Asia made a lot of enemies for both countries. Even today, neighbors still view both countries rather apprehensively, feeling they have reason to be suspicious.

A government may also implement an expansionist policy because of real or perceived threats to its sovereignty or even its continued existence. Consider, for example, a 1938 German-produced map that illustrates Germany's fictitious fear of Czechoslovakia (Figure 10–1). The message was simple: If Germany did not dismember Czechoslovakia, it would have no choice but to live in the shadow of attack by a Czech air force that was in theory able to strike anywhere in Germany.

How real was the Czech threat? It wasn't very real at all. Czechoslovakia's population and military forces were one-sixth the size of Germany's, and its overall military capacity was certainly inferior. Objectively, Czechoslovakia had neither a reason nor the ability to threaten its neighbor. But even brutally aggressive states feel compelled to somehow rationalize their ambitions. They can do so, as Germany did, by portraying the intended victim as a capable predatory force with evil designs. The intended victim must therefore attack in self-defense.

Within a country, the government may exercise policies that blunt economic growth, cutting off portions of the population from participating fully in the economy. The most blatant example concerns gender. As Figure 10–2 suggests, women experience severe discrimination in much of the world starting early in life, especially (and ironically) in countries that need every available and qualified person to contribute. Women are often excluded from gaining access to educational facilities and training programs for skilled and well-paid jobs.

It is clear that the quality of demographics impacts substantially on economic growth. Discrimination based on gender, ethnicity, and/or religion is usually a prescription for economic disaster because a lot of people aren't allowed to be fully productive. However, there are governments that prefer economic stagnation or worse to losing control over a population. In fact, as bizarre and inhumane as it sounds, governments have been known to pursue economic policies that they know are likely to result in stagnation. Giving up control enforced by ideology or tradition is difficult for a political elite to do.

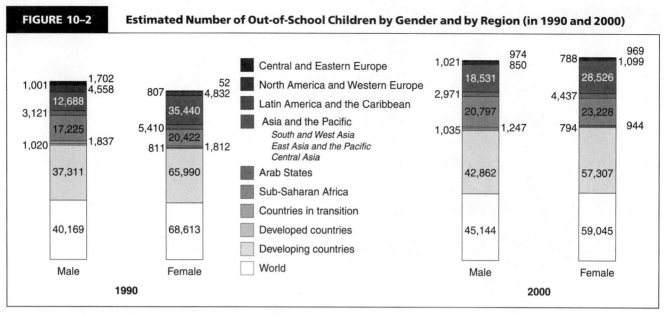

FIGURE 10–2 **Estimated Number of Out-of-School Children by Gender and by Region (in 1990 and 2000)**

Source: UNESCO Institute for Statistics (UIS) estimates, 2003 revision.

10-5 Political Geography, Political Dissolution, and the International Constellation

A major power usually achieves its distinction by going through a period of expansion. The expansion is often not terribly considerate of people who are in the way. The Empire of Japan, for example, decided to acquire territory and concomitant natural resources by pursuing military strategies. A political elite with modernizing tendencies came to power in Japan in 1868 and almost immediately set out to establish Japan as a world contender. Japan occupied Taiwan in 1895, Korea in 1910, Manchuria in 1931, and kept expanding into the western Pacific region until its territorial ambitions collided with the interests of the United States in 1941.

At times, though, a country may become excessively ambitious. Just as Japan began its expansion in East Asia during the last third of the nineteenth century, the United States was beginning to exert its influence beyond the Pacific Coast of North America. Only a year before the modernizing elite—a combination of economic and military enthusiasts who wanted Japan to join the international mainstream as a great power—launched Japan's territorial conquests, the United States acquired Alaska from Russia. American and Japanese goals in the Pacific were destined to conflict. In the closing years of the nineteenth century, the United States annexed several Pacific islands, extending American influence as far west as the Philippines, which it wrested from Spain in a three-month war in 1898. From that point on, it was only a matter of time before Japan and the United States collided with one another to determine which would be the supreme power in the Pacific region.

Both the government and the people of a country may sincerely believe in their nation's destiny. Many nineteenth-century Americans were convinced that the United States had a **manifest destiny** to expand across the continent from the Atlantic to the Pacific Ocean and beyond. The expansion led Americans into conflict with indigenous tribes that were in their way and with Mexico, which the United States eliminated as a serious rival in the Mexican-American War of 1846–1848. The Japanese possessed a similar feeling about themselves, genuinely

manifest destiny
The term used to describe and justify the American expansion from ocean to ocean.

believing they were the natural leaders of East Asia. To prove it, the Japanese for nearly half a century followed an aggressive military policy that led them to occupy Taiwan in 1895, wage a successful war against Russia in 1904 and 1905 that won the Japanese several strategic Pacific islands, colonize Korea beginning in 1910, and invade China beginning in 1931. Japan's goal was to become the greatest economic and military power in East Asia, in the process securing the natural resources and cheap (sometimes slave) labor required to maintain its great power and status. Japanese ambitions almost inevitably led them to Pearl Harbor and Hiroshima. By the 1930s Japan had singled out the United States as the most serious threat to its hegemony in East Asia and sought to eliminate America as a power in the region. The Japanese had long believed that most of East Asia was in their sphere of influence whereas the United States as well as the United Kingdom were interlopers in a region they didn't belong in. By 1941 only the United States remained as a serious obstacle to Japanese expansion in the western Pacific. Japan attacked the American Pacific Fleet at Pearl Harbor in order to eliminate the United States as a hindrance. The Japanese underestimated the American reaction that was determined to destroy Japan's military. Yet the Japanese, even after it was clear they were losing the war, continued to resist until the destruction of the cities of Hiroshima and Nagasaki by atomic bombs on August 6 and 9, 1945.

Almost every major country has an expansionist past. From the sixteenth through the nineteenth centuries, Britain and France, for example, established far-flung colonial empires that were global in scope. Nor did Britain and France go unchallenged. Germany, Italy, and Japan were latecomers in the colonizing game, but they were still able to acquire extensive holdings of their own in the late nineteenth and early twentieth centuries. The rapacious nature of the territorial acquisitions of several countries helped produce World War I as great powers with global interests competed for the territory, population, and vast natural resources required to sustain industrial economies.

Expanding powers that eventually collide with one another provide only one example of how changing political lines and spheres of influence affect the international constellation. A **political implosion**, or total political collapse, within a country represents another. Whenever a political breakdown occurs, the impact can drastically change the entire international situation. When the Roman Empire dissolved over 1,500 years ago, for example, the map of the ancient world changed both drastically and irrevocably, creating opportunities for new and innovative political configurations.

political implosion
The collapse of a political system from within, usually caused by a breakdown in public confidence in the economic and political institutions.

More recently, the Soviet Union offers an example of what happens when a major global power first retreats from superpower status and then simply disappears as a political entity. By the end of 1991, the Soviet Union had not only ceased to exist but had been replaced by fifteen sovereign states, the former Soviet republics (FSRs). International politics, for four decades characterized by the Cold War between the Soviet Union and the United States, would now need to be described by a new paradigm. The United States is well into the second decade of the post–Cold War era, but Americans have not yet found an acceptable descriptive title for it. What is clear, though, is that the Cold War is long over. This dawning era was first described as the "new world order" but some have more recently entitled it as the "new world *dis*order" because of the dissolution of several countries and the nonstate violence and terrorism that is increasingly a dominating feature in the international arena.

International politics became characterized by several complicated features after communism's collapse:

1. Instead of one Soviet nuclear superpower, four lesser ones now existed: Russia, Belorussia, Ukraine, and Kazakhstan.
2. Several of the new or renewed FSRs have themselves been in danger of dissolving as secessionist movements appeared and challenged the central government.

3. The new states have often engaged in territorial disputes—Russia and Ukraine, for example, have argued about who possesses Crimea. In 1954, then Soviet leader Nikita Khrushchev "gave" Crimea to Ukraine as a gesture. This did not pose any special problem because Russia, Ukraine, and Crimea were all under the jurisdiction of the Soviet Union. While Crimea is still under Ukrainian authority, this region features a Russian majority that accounts for two-thirds of the total population. To further complicate matters, Crimea is the homeland of the Tatars, hundreds of thousands of whom Stalin exiled thousands of miles east to "Tatarstan" because he considered them untrustworthy. Many of these Tatars and their descendants want to go home to Crimea.

Even within the current-day Russian Federated Republic there are tensions between the Russian majority and the nearly twenty million residents (about a seventh of the population of around 140 million) who are not ethnically Russian. A foremost example of the difficulty is the region of Chechnya, a small non-Russian territory of no more than 1.2 million people. The Chechens are not Russian or Slavic. Moreover, Chechens are Muslims who have been battling the "infidel" Russian occupation since the nineteenth century. They declared their independence from Russia in 1991 and have been fighting for it ever since.[6]

The collapse of one political system, even one as little lamented as the Soviet Union, can cause severe dislocations both internally and in the international arena. Public services, for example, may deteriorate or disappear completely. The Soviet health care delivery system at its best was far from equal to that of any Western country, and the system grew worse after the Soviet collapse as services deteriorated. In the meantime, Russians who had grown accustomed to being a superpower now saw their empire quickly unravel. The twenty-five million Russians in the non-Russian FSRs were no longer a privileged elite, and non-Russian regions within the Russian Federated Republic itself began to question Russian sovereignty. The end of the Soviet state and the Cold War did not mean an end to friction and conflict, but simply created a new and unfamiliar international arena with its own problems. In some respects, it is also a more dangerous arena.

In this sense, the absence of a second superpower is noticeable. Without two nuclear superpowers counterbalancing one another, the world may be a good deal less safe than people would hope. The Middle East region is an illustrative example. Syria and Iraq were once client states of the Soviet Union while the United States favored countries such as Israel and Saudi Arabia. In the vacuum left by the departure of Soviet influence, former clients are less controllable. The Syrians and Iraqis, for example, were considered by the American government to be supporters of international terrorism that targets Americans, Israelis, and other Westerners. Iraq under Saddam Hussein tried for many years to develop (and hide) weapons of mass destruction. By early 2003, American patience with the Iraqi leader had reached its end. The American military during the spring of 2003 successfully proceeded to destroy the Hussein regime.

10-6 Demography and Political Partition

It is no secret that different kinds of people sometimes don't get along. In the same vein, some countries prefer not having to tolerate the company of those they don't like. This intolerance is frequently based on the way people look and speak, their religious convictions (whether perceived as the wrong ones or entirely lacking), or their ethnic backgrounds. Toleration or its absence has tremendous implications for a nation's political history and culture. In literally dozens if not hundreds of current examples, diverse populations resolve their difficulties by simply drawing new boundary lines to replace those they don't like—a remedy known as **partition**.

partition
The political remedy of dividing a territory among two or more antagonistic communities without much likelihood of satisfying any of the parties.

---

[6]"The Conflict in Chechnya: A Chance of Peace?" *The Economist*, November 23, 2002, 49.

Some partitions are *de facto* (actually, or by fact)—that is, they are the result of an armed conflict. Bosnia and Lebanon, for example, are partitioned into various religious communities for this reason. These separate political entities may or may not be recognized by the international community, though with the passage of time they usually gain at least tacit acceptance. Other partitions are *de jure* (by right), officially arranged by the contending parties or perhaps imposed by an international organization such as the United Nations. De facto and de jure partitions have at least one feature in common: They rarely satisfy any of the parties involved, all of whom are convinced that someone else got the better deal. Partition was a solution frequently resorted to in the aftermath of World War II, as major colonial powers withdrew from their possessions. The Middle East and South Asia had endured conflicts between such implacable foes that partition presented the only sensible way out. Thus, the British divided the Asian subcontinent in 1947 into India and Pakistan, creating states that were predominantly either Hindu or Muslim. Although the partition was not intended to hurt anyone, it caused great human suffering on both sides. As millions of people, Hindus and Muslims, moved (or were ordered to move by the British) hundreds of miles, mostly on foot, they suffered great hardship—the result of lack of adequate planning, poor sanitation, and thieves and murderers along the way. These two countries then fought several wars over disputed territory. More than half a century later, Kashmir, on the border between India and Pakistan, is still the territorial prize in a dispute between the two countries.

In another region, the British became completely frustrated with their mandate in Palestine, originally provided by the League of Nations, after World War II. They turned the matter over to the United Nations (UN). The UN partitioned Palestine in 1947 into Palestinian Arab and Jewish states (Figure 10–3). The partition was agreeable only to the Jewish community; the Arab leadership involved refused to recognize the authority of the United Nations to impose a partition. In the resulting war, the UN partition plan was never implemented. Six decades and several wars later, the Jewish state of Israel is working out its own form of partition, mostly without Palestinian counterparts in the area of the West Bank.

The British more or less brokered the India-Pakistani partition, and the UN tried to broker one in Palestine after the British gave up on the country. In both cases, an outside agent was involved in the partition process in a mostly nonmilitary fashion. In a third case, in Cyprus, an outside agent with ethnic interests militarily imposed a partition. When Cyprus received independence in 1960, four-fifths of the population was Greek and the remainder was Turkish, two communities with a centuries-old tradition of hostility toward one another. The Turkish minority felt that the Greeks were exploiting and discriminating against them. In 1974, Turkey decided to come to the assistance of its kindred souls in Cyprus. Turkish soldiers invaded and occupied the northern (and more economically developed) third of the island, where they remain to ensure continued Turkish-Cypriot autonomy.

Partitions aren't necessarily in place forever, of course. After World War II, Germany was partitioned into East and West Germany. Forty-five years later, the two parts reunited peacefully as communism collapsed in Eastern Europe. Nor are partitions always violent. Occasionally two antagonists agree to what is called a "velvet divorce," the term applied to the peaceful and orderly dissolution of Czechoslovakia into the Czech Republic and Slovakia in 1993.

Unplanned and even accidental partitions also occur. Lebanon is a small country (about four million people in an area smaller than the state of Connecticut) with a remarkable number of religious sects. Several sects possess their own well-armed militias and have carved out their own tiny political enclaves that may consist of only a few square miles. It is difficult for the official Lebanese government[7] to exert its authority beyond the confines of the capital city of Beirut. Lebanon

---

[7]The government of Lebanon is official only because Syria recognizes it and guarantees it exists. Syria has a long-standing interest in Lebanon and regards the country as part of a greater Syria.

| FIGURE 10–3 | The United Nations' Partition Plan for Palestine, 1947 |

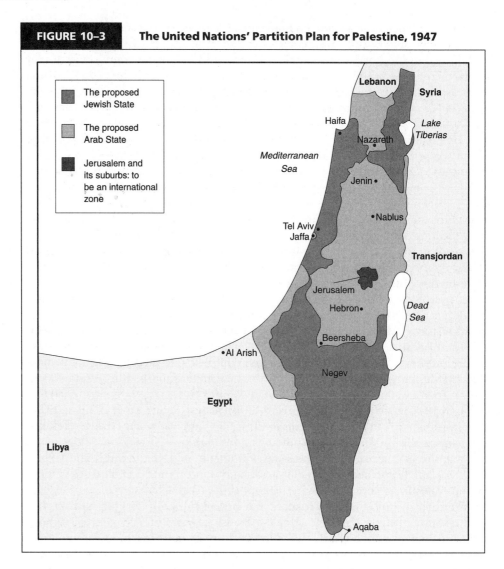

appears to be a country in name only—its inherent and historical disunity has resulted in a number of *de facto* partitions. Lebanon experienced an Israeli military invasion in 2006 in great part because the central government could not control the southern part of its own country that was being used by a terrorist organization, Hizbollah, to attack Israelis on the other side of the border.

Political partitions and dissolutions are not confined to the non-Western parts of the world. In 1996, a large proportion of Quebec's French-speaking community almost passed a referendum that would have amounted to the province's secession from Canada. Canada may still be partitioned sometime in the near future. Almost certainly, another referendum will arise and could pass, especially if more and more English speakers leave the province and settle in other parts of Canada.

Italy may offer an even more precarious example; it is not the successfully united country it seems. During the 1980s, a strong movement appeared in the northern and most economically prosperous part of the country to partition Italy into two parts.[8] The Northern League's political program is innovative. The League plainly suggests that the way to end excessive taxation is to get rid of the central government and its penchant to take from the rich (north) and give to the poor (middle and south). It calls for ejecting the southern part of the country from Italy because it considers the south economically backward and overly dependent on

---

[8]Lara Santoro, "Flamboyant Politician Would March the North Out of Italy," *The Christian Science Monitor*, September 13, 1996, 7.

welfare. The Northern League wants to establish a new state in the north and even has a name picked out—Pandania.

What do these partitions and potential partitions portend? Over the last decade or so, countries have been multiplying at an unprecedented rate, mostly because other countries, like the Soviet Union, have dissolved, or because competing ethnic and religious communities have separated, as in India and Pakistan.

Are more partitions on the horizon? Probably. Large and diverse countries such as India, Canada, and even China are all potential candidates, with substantial and disaffected minority populations concentrated in various regions. Smaller countries, though, may take the opposite tack and take the opportunity to merge rather than divide. Sometimes neighboring countries or regions within countries have more in common with people just across the border than they do with people in other regions of the same country. Consider, for example, Estonia and Finland: Their languages are almost identical (Estonians are fond of watching Finnish television) and their cultures and ethnic backgrounds are very similar. Azerbaijan and Turkey are another possible combination of countries that share similar or identical languages, religion, culture, and ethnic heritage.[9]

Even seemingly solid countries such as the United States and Canada may have regions that see natural partners across the border. Many residents of Washington state and Oregon feel a certain commonality with Canadians living in British Columbia and Alberta. By the same token, Americans along the country's southwestern border may develop an increasing economic and cultural overlap across the frontier with Mexico even if difficulties with illegal immigration persist. If northern Italians feel disaffected with Rome, Quebeçois with Ottawa, and Chechens with Moscow, it is not unreasonable to conclude that some Americans living in the westernmost states (or anywhere, for that matter) might have less than maximum loyalty to Washington.

This is not to say that the United States is close to unraveling—it isn't. Extremists on both sides of the issue of immigration have expressed the possibility that the United States might even see part or all of the southwestern states revert to Mexican control. This is far-fetched, of course, but helps to fuel the argument. Very few countries in the world enjoy permanent frontiers that can be traced back more than a few generations. In any event, there is no reason to believe that after centuries of constantly shifting national boundary lines, there are no changes yet to come. Very few countries currently in existence have the same national borders they had fifty or 100 years ago. The next chapter will briefly examine the impact partitions have on the conduct of international politics.

Chapter Summary

1. A country's geographical location and the size and quality of its population are crucial determinants of a society's history, culture, and political processes and institutions.
2. Political power once depended heavily upon the numerical size of a nation's population. Today, the quality of a population—its health, education, and skill level—is increasingly the most important demographic aspect.
3. Population growth is rapidly increasing in relatively poor countries. Economic development is not keeping up and in many instances may even be regressing.
4. Powerful countries usually have a history of territorial expansion. Their expansions were designed to secure additional land for a growing population, to acquire needed natural resources, or both. Expansionist countries can eventually collide, as Japan and the United States did in 1941.
5. Colonial empires built on expansionist agendas inevitably seem to collapse. The last to do so was the Russian-dominated Soviet Union.
6. Political partition is a common if less than satisfactory solution to historical conflict between communities of people. The differences that cause partition may be ethnic, religious, linguistic, and/or cultural in nature.

---

[9]"Mergers and Acquisitions," *The Economist*, August 31, 1996, 44.

7. While partitioning is one way to resolve disputes between different communities, forging economic mergers between like-minded regions in different countries may become a new way.

Chapter 10 Quiz

1. The number of sovereign states in the world between 1950 and 2000
   a. increased from around sixty to nearly 200.
   b. were mostly communized.
   c. grew mostly because of Islamic radical movements.
   d. decreased to the number available in 1900.

2. In previous times, Russia has been militarily invaded by
   a. Sweden.
   b. Germany.
   c. France.
   d. all of the above.

3. There is a very substantial overseas Turkish community of about two million people in
   a. France.
   b. Italy.
   c. Germany.
   d. Britain.

4. During the Middle Ages, a third of Europe's population was killed by
   a. Mongol invaders.
   b. earthquakes.
   c. the Black Death.
   d. religious persecution.

5. The "time of troubles" is a reference to hostility between
   a. Catholics and Protestants in Northern Ireland.
   b. Hindus and Muslims in India.
   c. Arabs and Jews in Israel.
   d. Christians and Muslims in Lebanon.

6. The Chinese government has moved large numbers of its citizens in recent decades to
   a. Taiwan.
   b. North Korea.
   c. Tibet.
   d. Vietnam.

7. In 1938, Germany claimed that it was being threatened by
   a. Austria.
   b. Czechoslovakia.
   c. Belgium.
   d. Denmark.

8. Manifest destiny can be described as a doctrine that
   a. justified slavery in the American South.
   b. justified war against Iraq.
   c. was synonymous with isolationism.
   d. extended United States territory from coast to coast.

9. The Asian subcontinent was partitioned in 1947 into
   a. India and Pakistan.
   b. Israel and Palestine.
   c. Greek and Turkish enclaves.
   d. Shia and Sunni Muslims.

10. The term "velvet divorce" is a reference to the dissolution of
    a. East Germany.
    b. Soviet Union.
    c. Yugoslavia.
    d. Czechoslovakia.

Political Violence

If one even glances at human history, it is easy to conclude that humans are a species with a disposition toward violence, and perhaps escalating violence at that. The first half of the twentieth century saw two world wars and numerous other conflicts that visited unprecedented violence on large civilian populations in meticulously planned and purposefully pursued endeavors.

The United States is a comparatively violent country, but with the exception of the Civil War, most of the violence has thus far been criminal rather than political. Not that this makes much difference to the victims of violence. Nearly all European countries are less violent than the United States. Some theories about human evolution suggest humans descended from violent apelike predecessors. Perhaps, the reasoning continues, the United States is an unusually violent country because "most of the killer-apes migrated to America over the centuries."[1] Moreover, most of these killers were apparently men, because males are much more violent than females and kill twenty times as often.[2]

There is little doubt that the United States has a great deal of crime and that much of the crime is violent, although the annual murder rate has declined in recent years.[3] Political violence is not unknown in the United States or other democracies, but the fact that most people worry more about criminal than political violence is instructive. In most nondemocratic societies, political violence exceeds criminal violence. Sometimes it is difficult to tell the difference. Criminals, too, can be more afraid of a government with minimal or no concern about legal rights and processes. Criminals are less likely to commit crimes because the government is more brutal than they are. Driven to desperation, normally law-abiding citizens, even in a country such as North Korea under Kim Jong Il, would commit violent crimes if their families were hungry. This chapter examines various dimensions of political violence. Topics include legal as well as illegal violence, the sometimes conflictive and adversarial relationship between state and citizen, and the kinds of violence—wars, government brutality, and terrorism—that often characterize the international constellation and frequently define relations between specific states.

11-1 Government, People, and Violence

Do human beings really possess a genetic disposition toward violence? Most people live their lives without ever committing violent acts, and many are fortunate enough to never suffer a serious violent act committed against their persons or even witness harm done to others. A certain proportion of people cause their fellow humans pain throughout their lives.

In Western societies, most people confine any violent expressions to officially sanctioned channels and usually express violence in a vicarious fashion—for

---

[1]Peter C. Sederberg, *Fires Within: Political Violence and Revolutionary Change* (New York: HarperCollins, 1994), p. 103.

[2]See Richard Wrangham and Dale Peterson, *Demonic Males: Apes and the Origins of Human Violence* (Boston: Houghton Mifflin, 1996).

[3]By 2006, around two million Americans were serving jail terms or prison times.

instance, at a football game. People understand that the opposing side is their political equal and is guaranteed the same rights they enjoy. Yet for a few hours

> ... there is only one side that's created equal—yours. The rest are misshapen, mutant bastards, who deserve to suffer horribly because they are so ugly.[4]

Perhaps this is a slight overstatement but, except for occasional aberrations, violence is normally constrained and kept within bounds at a sporting event.

Political violence is a different matter. Those who live in stable polities where government discharges its obligation to protect human rights enjoy wonderful benefits—personal security, enriched lifestyles, and material comfort. Citizens in democratic states believe it is the government's responsibility to create and sustain a secure environment. Many nondemocratic governments will not guarantee such rights. Argentina during the 1970s and 1980s, for example, was ruled by a military regime that caused thousands of its own citizens to permanently disappear. It is now known that many of these people were political prisoners who were arrested, drugged, and pushed out of airplanes over the Atlantic Ocean.[5] North Korea keeps much of the population on the edge of starvation and condemns millions to perpetual malnutrition by devoting resources to the army and the Communist party elite and developing weapons of mass destruction. Since 1995, North Korea has endured food shortages that are occasionally alleviated by food shipments from international donors.[6] The regime believes that the pursuit of nuclear weapons with precious national resources is a higher priority than a well-norished population. A government is, by common agreement, established to protect its citizenry from harm. The potential for harm may come from outside sources or from elements within the citizenry itself. When its political authority is widely respected and accepted, a government can do a fairly solid job of providing the physical security each citizen requires. A citizen need not worry about the government itself doing harm because its agents are subject to the same laws that apply to the rest of society. Governments that carry this out are usually (but not exclusively) democratic.

Some societies have decidedly undemocratic governments who nevertheless protect individuals from crime. The streets of Riyadh and Beijing are a lot safer at night than those of New York and Washington, D.C.—unless, that is, a Saudi citizen is overheard expressing a religious viewpoint that contradicts or is opposed to strict Islamic doctrine, or a resident of Beijing suggests that competitive and free elections would be a good idea for China. In these instances, the government infringes on rather than protects personal security.

However, government all too often is the source of, rather than the resolver of, political conflict. The government monitors all other social agents for potential violence. Violence is considered legitimate only when it is applied by an authorized agency of the government (the police or a national militia, for example). This aspect of political violence, though, becomes controversial when a sizable number of citizens or the international community considers the government itself to be illegitimate. This happens when a government commits arbitrary acts of violence that are injurious to basic human rights.

Unfortunately, examples of this kind of political violence are abundant. In the Russian Federated Republic, Chechens (residents of the region called Chechnya) do not accept political control from Moscow. During the last half of the nineteenth century the Russian government occupied Chechnya, a non-Russian region populated mostly by Muslims, and forcibly annexed the region to its empire. Nothing changed when the communist regime took power in 1917. Some Chechens during World War II (1941–1945) even sided with German invaders against the Soviet regime, an episode that made Chechens even more suspect to Russians. With good

---

[4]Bill Buford, "Un-American Activities," *The New Yorker*, July 8, 1996, 90.

[5]Horacio Verbitsky, *The Flight: Confessions of an Argentine Dirty Warrior*, trans. Esther Allen (New York: New Press, 1996).

[6]*CIA Factbook, 2006.*

reason, Kurds in northern Iraq under Saddam Hussein were convinced that the central government wished to destroy them. The efforts of the Hussein regime to destroy Kurdish settlements with chemical weapons were terribly effective during the early 1990s before the United States established a no-fly zone in northern Iraq where most of the country's Kurds live. Hussein did not hesitate to murder thousands of Kurdish men, women, and children. He considered them to be opponents of his regime and his way of dealing with opponents was through extreme violent brutality.

legal violence

Violence the state commits in keeping with the law. The state sometimes has the responsibility to apply violence to maintain order in the society, to protect its citizens, or to remove from society those who have injured others.

Still, while violence is always unpleasant, it may not always be legally wrong. **Legal violence** is the prerogative of the state. This means the state must apply violence in a fashion that the law sanctions and the public voluntarily supports. In democracies, legal violence is applied with restraint and, usually, only as a last resort. The United States unleashed a remarkable amount of violence on Afghanistan after September 11, 2001, when the American armed forces used modern military technology against the Taliban government and al-Qaeda terrorist strongholds. Most of the world viewed this violence as reasonable and legal because the United States was reacting to attacks that murdered nearly 3,000 American citizens. Targeting and assassinating individual al-Qaeda leaders and operatives is a gray area and much more controversial. Critics ask whether this sort of action is simply state-authorized murder or still in the realm of self-defense.[7] **Illegal violence** is violence inflicted by unauthorized agents. To turn the previous example around, terrorists characteristically commit violent acts against normally defenseless civilians as a part of their political agenda. The terrorist attacks on the World Trade Center in 1993 and 2001 are cases in point. The wanton destruction of human life was as immoral as it was illegal according to most international norms because the target was defenseless civilians.

illegal violence

Violence that violates the law and that is exercised by unlawful and unconstitutional agents. Sometimes illegal violence causes the deterioration of a political regime. At other times, it surfaces after the breakdown of a regime.

It is occasionally difficult to separate criminal from political violence. Sometimes the two overlap, as criminal organizations become increasingly powerful while governmental authority weakens and law enforcement deteriorates or ceases to exist altogether. This happened in Somalia in the early 1990s when the central government completely disintegrated. By the middle 1990s, Bosnia was deteriorating as criminal gangs competed with one another to purchase government concessions being privatized. Ruthless tactics quickly retired honest businesses endeavors from the competition.[8] Large parts of Bosnia fell under gang control as different criminal organizations carved out their own fiefdoms. Ironically, such criminal organizations can become the only source of stability and order in a region.

death squads

Murderous gangs that execute a regime's political opponents, even though the death squad is not an official agent of the state.

Violence is normally considered illegal whenever non-state agents commit it. Yet the state can be the greatest perpetrator of political violence. **Death squads** in several Central American countries, though not official agents of the state, have murdered people opposed to the policies of the government. Many of the murderers were off-duty police officers who were moonlighting for cash payments, supplements to the low salaries endemic in most of Latin America for police personnel. During the 1980s in El Salvador, for example, off-duty police officers murdered civilians who the government considered a threat to the regime. For the most part they did so with impunity because there was no real chance they would be pursued and arrested by their own colleagues or tried by a judiciary that was completely controlled by the executive.

This is not to say that democracies are immune from illegitimate political violence. In August 1968, a police riot occurred during the Democratic Party Convention in Chicago. Officers freely swung their nightsticks at the heads of Vietnam War protesters who were calling them names and raining plastic bags of excrement on them from the upper stories of nearby buildings. Chicago was a brief and dreadful but instructive exception to the normal activities of police officers in large cities. Most police personnel most of the time are not violent and do their utmost to refrain from being violent. The exceptions make the news.

---

[7]See Seymour M. Hersh, "Manhunt: The Bush Administration's New Strategy in the War Against Terrorism," *The New Yorker*, December 23 and 30, 2002, 66–74.

[8]Chris Hedges, "Gangs Descend to Pick Bosnia's Carcass Clean," *The New York Times*, sec. A, October 7, 1996, A4.

Clearly, a historical and often intimate association exists between violence and the political process. This association, though, is sporadic. Most governments are actually nonviolent most of the time. A large proportion is altogether loath to invoke violent methods to preserve order except as a last resort.

Yet there is no denying that political violence characterizes many modern governments. Perhaps the greatest current example is in sub-Saharan Africa. Several states in this region have not experienced sustained, peaceful political change since they became independent countries in the 1950s and 1960s. Government turnover was infrequently peaceful and often the result of a military coup. African politicians are in a profession that has an incredibly high mortality rate. For the first three decades after most African countries received their political independence, more than two dozen presidents and prime ministers lost their lives through assassination or mistreatment after a coup overthrew the government.[9]

Political Violence at the 1968 Democratic Convention in Chicago

© Bettman/CORBIS

The political violence that plagues Africa is at least in part related to the pronounced economic misery of most of the population. Much of the developed world has lost interest in Africa. Moreover, some countries that had an interest did the region little good. Soviet economic advisors, for example, ruined every African economy they influenced. By collectivizing industries and inducing the government to curtail or even eliminate the private sector, productivity declined or stagnated. There was little appreciation of the successful economic model of having in place both the private and public sector. The virtual elimination of the private sector in these countries caused many members of the business establishment to simply leave. They took their capital with them.[10] Nigeria, for example, should be a wealthy country. It has the largest population of any country in Africa and huge reserves of oil and other natural resources. But Nigeria also has tribal, ethnic, and religious divisions and hostilities, features that have kept the country in or close to civil war since it received independence in the 1960s. Moreover, Soviet-inspired

---

[9]"Sub-Saharan Africa," *The Economist*, September 7, 1996, 4.

[10]Ibid.

collectivized economies worked no better in Africa than they did anywhere else. Economic despair and tribal conflicts have combined to make political violence the rule rather than the exception in many African countries.

11-2 The Phenomenon and Uncertainty of State Violence

enforcement violence
The ability of a political regime to sustain itself by applying force whenever necessary to both maintain its existence and secure social order.

The ability of the state to sustain itself and its institutions is described as **enforcement violence**. The term sounds ominous, yet both democratic and nondemocratic regimes assume they must maintain order and enforce legal resolutions to social problems. Very few regimes have ever had an interest in fomenting chaos.

But in politics there are always exceptions, and some of the exceptions are critically important. In China during the Great Cultural Revolution (approximately 1966–1976), mobs of ideologically inspired youths, with the government's encouragement, became a law unto themselves as they rampaged through the streets of China's major cities and throughout the countryside. The Chinese Communist leadership had reasoned that after two decades of quiet, it was necessary to renew the revolution that had brought it to power in 1949. A generation with no personal memory of prerevolutionary China seemed the perfect vehicle. Members of the older generation whose revolutionary fervor was considered inadequate were paraded through the streets with dunce caps on their heads. Others were exiled from the cities to rural areas to learn humility by working with their hands in open fields. Some were merely beaten, and more than a few people lost their lives from mistreatment.

During this period, China provided an excellent example of the dysfunctional aspects of political violence. Violence, when it becomes commonplace and is sanctioned by political authorities, easily gets out of hand and causes long-term havoc on a society's level of economic as well as social development. Millions of Chinese teenagers who should have been in school learning to become engineers and scientists were instead encouraged by the government to torment their fellow citizens who seemed to lack revolutionary fervor. It is difficult to be sure how much talent and productivity were lost because of this self-defeating policy. Perhaps even more frightening, though, was another lesson—how easily even a strong totalitarian government can lose control of events, sometimes rather quickly, even when it instigated those events itself. The violence the leadership had encouraged quickly got out of hand. In the end, the state had to call out army units in some regions to insist that the students return to their homes and schools.

It is disconcerting to realize how quickly a government can lose control of events in a territory and population it supposedly has jurisdiction over. When the government loses control or simply disappears from the scene, criminal and political violence tend to blend. Along the border between the United States and Mexico, for example, drug-trafficking gangs have acquired so much power, wealth, and organization that citizens on both sides of the border are moving away, selling their homes and ranches to representatives of the gangs at low prices.[11] In recent years, however, some gangs have taken to smuggling Mexicans into the United States, a risky venture because many of the smuggled Mexicans are often left to fend for themselves in the desert after they've paid the smugglers a considerable amount of money.

States, of course, can be exceptionally violent toward one another. Wars in the twentieth century involved entire populations, usually as victims, but also as willing and even enthusiastic participants who were convinced that they are fighting for their lives. (Sometimes they were.) Prior to modern times, major wars were more often confined to battlefields safely removed from civilian population centers. By the

---

[11]William Branigin, "Drug Gangs' Terror on the Texas Border," *The Washington Post National Weekly Edition*, September 30–October 6, 1996, 17–18.

1930s, though, armies in Europe and Asia were occupying entire countries and systematically abusing local populations. Violence by the middle third of the twentieth century became technologically enabled to assume global proportions and capable of ending the lives of tens of millions of people. In fact, armies received a new duty: They were to help eliminate populations considered dangerous or unwanted by the occupying regime. Armed forces now became collaborators and participants in political violence rather than merely the military arm of a regime's policy.

11-3 Slavery as Political Violence

If government is the protector of individual security and property, then problems abound when government is insufficiently filling the role. Take the deplorable institution of slavery, for instance. Though outlawed by every government on earth, it flourishes on three continents. In the African republic of Mauritania, which in 1980 outlawed slavery for the third time, one out of every twenty residents is a "full-time" slave. Many more are "semi-free"—people who aren't allowed to marry or own property without the permission of those who, in effect, own their labor.[12]

Most slaves are children and women, and black Africans still furnish the greatest number of slaves. Women of all races in many countries are treated as chattel and endure a great deal of abuse. In fact, women can be bought or sold like cattle and even for cattle—in Sudan, five cows is the going rate for a young and healthy female.[13] For a summary of global slavery, see Figure 11–1. Slavery still flourishes in some remote regions in the Middle East, especially on the Arabian Peninsula,[14] while in the West women tend to outlive men, and the reverse is true in numerous African and Middle Eastern countries.

Some governments attempting to encourage the growth of the free market ignore certain forms of slavery. In China, young women are kidnapped and forced into slavery. An unmarried man can purchase a woman for between $250 and $500 from a kidnapper, no questions asked,[15] though by the early 2000s the price had escalated to $2,500 because of a shortage of females. Enslavement is nearly unknown in the cities, but it is a familiar activity in the rural areas of China, where three-quarters of the population still lives and works[16] and where women are valued as cheap farm labor.

Slavery is not the only form of violence governments fail to reduce. Sometimes a government tolerates violence because it diverts the attention of masses of people from their problems and from their dissatisfaction with the government. Two millennia ago, unknown thousands were slaughtered by wild animals or by one another in the Roman coliseum. Government employees financed and even choreographed these activities for the "amusement" of spectators. An emperor remained popular as long as he could provide imaginative and spectacular ways to kill people or animals or have one kill the other. Football or hockey games may be indirect descendants of Roman gladiatorial sports because there is occasional violence, some intended, some not, between opposing teams.

Violence or the threat of violence is an effective political tool in a variety of ways. The United States and its allies threatened, for example, to go to war against Iraq in 2003 in order to force Saddam Hussein to disarm weapons of mass destruction he said he didn't possess. Secretary of State William Seward (1861–1869) advised President Abraham Lincoln at the beginning of the Civil War to ask Congress to declare war on both Britain and France as a way to unite the country and keep the North and South from one another's throats. Lincoln wisely dismissed the

---

[12]"The Flourishing Business of Slavery," *The Economist*, September 21, 1996, 44.

[13]Ibid., p. 43.

[14]See Bruce S. Feiler, *Abraham: A Journey to the Heart of Three Faiths* (New York: William Morrow, 2001).

[15]Seth Faison, "Women as Chattel: In China, Slavery Rises," *The New York Times*, sec. A, September 6, 1995, A1 and A4.

[16]Ibid.

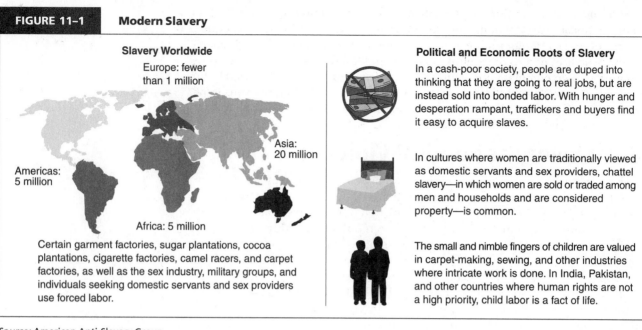

| FIGURE 11–1 | Modern Slavery |

Slavery Worldwide

Europe: fewer than 1 million

Asia: 20 million

Americas: 5 million

Africa: 5 million

Certain garment factories, sugar plantations, cocoa plantations, cigarette factories, camel racers, and carpet factories, as well as the sex industry, military groups, and individuals seeking domestic servants and sex providers use forced labor.

Political and Economic Roots of Slavery

In a cash-poor society, people are duped into thinking that they are going to real jobs, but are instead sold into bonded labor. With hunger and desperation rampant, traffickers and buyers find it easy to acquire slaves.

In cultures where women are traditionally viewed as domestic servants and sex providers, chattel slavery—in which women are sold or traded among men and households and are considered property—is common.

The small and nimble fingers of children are valued in carpet-making, sewing, and other industries where intricate work is done. In India, Pakistan, and other countries where human rights are not a high priority, child labor is a fact of life.

Source: American Anti-Slavery Group.

advice. At the time, though, the idea was not completely without merit. A foreign war against two major powers would certainly have concentrated the entire country's focus.

Mao Tse-Tung, founder and longtime ruler of the People's Republic of China (1949–1976), is remembered for his statement that "political power comes out of the barrel of a gun." In his case, this was no exaggeration. Mao apparently had few qualms about using violence both before and after he came to power and like Hitler and Stalin, the two other preeminent mass murderers of the twentieth century, was rather indifferent to widespread human misery and death. He proved this observation by overseeing the deaths of some seventy million people during his rule. Nor is this atypical. In both the Soviet Union and China, many times more people perished *after* the revolution brought totalitarian regimes to power than *during* the revolution itself.

11-4 Ideologically Driven Violence

As discussed in an earlier chapter, a fascist or communist movement usually has the capacity and the will to violently campaign for political power. Once in power, an ideologically motivated regime can become more rather than less violent. It now has, after all, an entire state apparatus—secret police, intelligence services, and the army—available for violence. Those who don't fit a regime's definition of loyal citizen often find themselves in serious trouble. The Gestapo in Nazi Germany and the KGB (secret police) in the Soviet Union encouraged students to report teachers, children to report parents, and employees to report bosses who may have made an aside or a joke about the regime or dictator. In Iraq Saddam Hussein employed several security and intelligence agencies to spy on Iraqi citizens and even on one another. In such societies people are literally afraid to say what they believe and generally tow the prevailing government line.

For millions of people and dozens of regimes, ideology is a convenient way to relate to the world, though not necessarily a realistic way. The trouble begins when some do not, or because of race or ethnic background cannot, subscribe to the prevailing ideology. Ideologies frequently have their own logic. Those who don't accept the ideology must be removed either through internal exile and isolation in a work camp or, in extreme situations, death in a concentration camp. During the Stalinist period in the Soviet Union, individuals were often rudely awakened in the middle of the night and simply disappeared into a work camp in Siberia. In most cases, they were not seen by their families or friends again.

Ideologically based regimes are intent on building or returning to a golden age in which disapproved minorities have no place and no future. The Nazis wanted to create a "New Germany." The Soviet communists wanted to create the "new Soviet man." In each case, society had to be purged of those the government considered totally irredeemable. Jews and Roma (or gypsies) in Germany, and "counterrevolutionaries" and, occasionally, Jews and other ethnic minorities in the Soviet Union and, later, in China, were believed unfit to live in the new society each regime was about to construct. The Germans probably had the longest list of undesirables: In addition to Jews and Roma, homosexuals, Communist party members, and the mentally deficient were often murdered en masse by the authorities. Others who escaped with their lives were sometimes sterilized. Millions were murdered or mutilated simply because they were of the wrong religion, ethnicity, gender preference, political affiliation, or because they were deemed unfit to live under a regime determined to create a "master race."

Much the same happens with regimes that base their legitimacy on theocratic or religious pillars. In Iran and Sudan, for example, holding a religious conviction inconsistent with the government-endorsed theology, or holding no conviction at all, can draw officially sanctioned reprisals, some of them involving physical penalties. Blasphemy is, for example, a capital crime in these countries. In Afghanistan under the Taliban (1996–2001), blasphemers were frequently and publicly executed in a former soccer field by being "gutted."

Ideologically based violence, when the state apparatus applies it, is political violence with practically no chance of being moderated. In fact, moderates are often

BIOGRAPHY

Ayann Hirsi Ali

Ayann Hirsi Ali (b. 1970) has a remarkable story. She was born in Somalia into a traditional Islamic family. At the age of eleven she was chosen by her parents to marry a young man she barely knew. She fled her arranged marriage and Somalia at the age of twenty-two and found her way to the Netherlands, a country with a long history of toleration and welcome to refugees fleeing religious or political persecution. This is, after all, a place where it's easy to purchase a cup of coffee and marijuana in the same shop because both, like prostitution, are perfectly legal.

Hirsi Ali learned Dutch and eventually became successfully involved in politics. She is fond of saying that she lived the "American dream" in Holland. She won a parliamentary seat in 2003 as a member of a mainstream liberal party. In 2004 she collaborated with Theo Van Gogh, a great-great nephew of the famous painter, to produce a twelve-minute documentary movie entitled "Submission." The movie focused on the demand of female obedience Islam and the penalties, including beatings by the husband if the wife performed any task in an unsatisfactory manner. The movie was considered by some Dutch Muslims, a little over 6 percent of the total population, to be critical of Islam. One of them, Mohammed Bouyeri, murdered Van Gogh and left a note on the body threatening to destroy Hirsi Ali (who went into hiding for the next three months), the Netherlands, and the United States. Van Gogh himself was a Dutch gadfly who had satirized Christianity and Judaism as well as Islam. Dutch Islamic leaders said they were not surprised that Van Gogh had been killed because of his provocative exposés of numerous controversial subjects, including religion. In a free society this sort of activity was both accepted and expected by the overwhelming majority of the population. In the Netherlands, nothing is considered above criticism or mockery.

The Dutch government immediately provided Hirsi Ali with around-the-clock security at home and at work. However, in 2006 she was deprived of her Dutch citizenship because it was determined that she had not been completely truthful on forms completed when she was admitted to the Netherlands. Hirsi Ali resigned her parliamentary seat and accepted a visiting fellowship at the American Enterprise Institute in Washington, D.C. She remained defiant and, during her remaining months in the Netherlands, gave interviews in which she stated that she would continue to work on a script for a sequel to "Submission." Hirsi Ali considers herself to be completely estranged from Islam, though she is viewed as a traitor by many of her former co-religionists. She continues to receive death threats on almost a daily basis.

among the first victims of violence. Such violence has frequently worked against the very interests of the regime producing it. During World War II, the German government was intent on exterminating all the Jews it could find. Even after 1943, when it was clear that Germany was losing the war, the extermination continued and often increased. During the last year of the war (1944–1945), the extermination actually accelerated in an effort to finish the job before defeat arrived. German authorities were so ideologically devoted to the physical elimination of men, women, and children, that they were considered a threat to Germany's existence because they allowed resources that were desperately needed by the army to be diverted to the extermination camps and guard those they wanted dead.[17] Another genocidal example is the Pol Pot regime in Cambodia (1975–1979), which caused the deaths of nearly two million people out of a population of seven million by executing them or by enforcing government-sanctioned and coordinated starvation. The goal of this madness was to create a new agriculturally based society by cleansing the old society of useless people such as physicians, teachers, engineers, and intellectuals—in short, anyone who couldn't easily become a farmer. Before it was overturned, Pol Pot's government had concluded it might be worth killing nearly everyone over the age of eighteen to achieve an agricultural commonwealth free of anyone who might retain memories of the previous "corrupt" society. In Cambodia, for a few years it seemed that if anyone besides top officials wanted to survive to old age it would be necessary to murder those who had left their teen years.

These examples are far from atypical. When a regime that is strongly motivated by ideology comes to power, it is almost certain to be insecure because of its correct perception that large segments of the population may not endorse the ideology. Such a regime almost always comes to power through a revolution and is usually especially insecure in the immediate aftermath. Upon achieving power, such a revolutionary regime often engages in a "reign of terror" to eradicate all known opposition.[18]

reign of terror
Arbitrary violence institutionalized by a newly installed revolutionary regime that is both insecure and ideologically driven.

The term **reign of terror** originated with the French Revolution (1789–1799); wholesale and state-sanctioned terror occurred from 1792 to 1794. Thousands of people, many of whom were apparently guilty of no crime and who had no interest in politics, were publicly executed. To the revolutionary regime, it didn't matter—the goal was to rid society of a social class, in this case the landed aristocracy, and anyone viewed as the aristocracy's retainers, sympathizers, or supporters. Similar phenomena occurred after the revolutions in Russia, China, Cuba, and numerous other countries that have come under the sway of self-righteous and remarkably brutal regimes.

Of course, the installation of a democratic political structure doesn't necessarily mean the end of a country's ideologically inspired violence. The newer democracies that appeared in the early 1990s in places as diverse as Russia and Nicaragua are instructive examples. Both countries have democratically elected executives and legislatures, yet plenty of nondemocratic residues remain in both countries.[19] Look at these countries closely and one can see plenty of ideologically minded individuals in the bureaucracy, police, and army who have not given up on restoring their preferred political system.[20] Moreover, both countries are continually faced with regional insurrections among people uninterested in accepting and deeply resentful of authority from the political center, regardless of whether the authority was earned through the democratic process. In 2006, the Palestinians electorate voted overwhelmingly to elect Hamas, a primarily terrorist organization with a political apparatus, to run their government. This was perhaps the one of few

---

[17]Max Hastings, *Armageddon: The Battle for Germany, 1944–1945*.

[18]For a well-written and readable analysis of what happens after a successful revolution, see the classic work by Crane Brinton, *The Anatomy of Revolution* (New York: Vintage Books, 1965).

[19]Hendrick Hertzberg, "Nicaragua's Second Act," *The New Yorker*, September 23, 1996, 7–8.

[20]Ibid.

democratically held elections in which the party sworn to the destruction of another country was popularly chosen to form a government to carry out its policy.

Nor are countries that have developed a solid tradition of democratic processes immune from ideologically based violence. Many ethnic, religious, and linguistic minorities in India violently expressed their desire for increased autonomy or outright independence frequently during the first half-century of the country's independence.[21] It is still possible that India could disintegrate into several smaller states. The perennial conflict the country has with Pakistan could provoke such disintegration. For example, several of India's states have large Islamic communities that are majorities of the population in those states. Those near the frontier with Pakistan, such as Kashmir, may want to secede from predominantly Hindu India and join a predominantly Islamic country. The Kurdish communities in Turkey, Iraq, and Iran are geographically contiguous and could conceivably desire to form their own state by seceding from the others.[22]

A small country can disintegrate into fiefdoms controlled by warlords who vary between being politically violent themselves and exerting a force for stability. For twenty-five years after 1975, Lebanon's central government, for example, had minimal or no control over much of the country. The neighboring powers Israel and Syria, whose agents controlled the southern half and northeastern parts of the country, respectively, haphazardly replaced some of the authority of the Lebanese government. Much of the country, though, was divided by local sectarian militias, each of which controls anywhere from a few square city blocks in Beirut, the capital city, to a few hundred square miles in the country's outlying lands. Each militia subscribed to a radical ideology or belongs to a radical religious sect that does not tend to favor political compromise or the peaceful resolution of disputes. The Lebanese are reclaiming their sovereignty since Israel departed in 2001 (though it briefly returned in August–September 2006 to confront attacks by Hezbollah, a terrorist organization) and Syria left in 2005.

11-5 The Virtue of Minimal Political Violence

A political regime that can govern with minimal or no violence is an effective one. It is either a regime that has so ruthlessly suppressed its opposition that it has little need to invoke violence or, more preferably, a regime whose political institutions enjoy such widespread and voluntary support that violence becomes totally unnecessary. Neither extreme model exists in reality.

Political and social order is what nearly all regimes strive for and sincerely desire. But democratic and nondemocratic regimes go about achieving this goal in different ways. One scholar of the subject has suggested that order is achieved through either **coercion** or **consensus theory of order**.[23] In the coercion theory of order, might makes right, whereas in the consensus theory, widely accepted and institutionalized norms and values maintain order. Democracies such as the United States, according to consensus theory, have satisfactorily resolved the issues strong enough to threaten or destroy the national consensus that has taken generations to establish. Issues such as abortion may still detract from the overall consensus, but they aren't able to destroy the public's confidence in the generally accepted institutions available to deal with the issue.

Coercive theory often assumes that a large part of the country must be subdued to create order. The regime may enforce a value system, with violence if necessary, on an unwilling or resistant segment of the population, persecuting or forcibly

coercion theory of order
A theory stating that a political regime can maintain order by forcing its values on a resistant or unwilling population that is unlikely to voluntarily accept them.

consensus theory of order
A theory stating that a political regime can maintain order with minimal or nonexistent political violence when it has established a widespread acceptance of political values and norms.

---

[21]"The State We're In," *The Economist*, September 14, 1996, 40.

[22]Dexter Filkins, "Turkey to Allow U.S. to Use Bases under a Smaller Plan," *The New York Times*, sec. A, January 20, 2003, A10.

[23]Sederberg, *Fires Within*, 14–15.

converting religious, ethnic, economic, or sociocultural minorities to another value system or ideology. The regime might choose to leave them alone if they simply keep quiet and tacitly accept a less-than-equal place in the political system.

Order, however achieved, is not always the most desirable quality. In societies where slavery was a thriving institution, such as ancient Rome or the American South of the eighteenth and nineteenth centuries, there was usually order, but the order actually oppressed a large proportion of the population. More recently, millions of former Soviet citizens enjoyed reasonably comfortable, orderly lives even though they lived under a stagnant bureaucratic system that gave them little personal liberty. Some Russians actually miss the order that is now missing from their lives. The Chinese Communist regime, in contrast, has provided enough economic excitement through its advocacy of the free market[24] to sustain its preferred form of totalitarian stability.

11-6 Terror: The Fullest Expression of Political Violence

In the last third of the twentieth century, political terrorism became the most explicit form of political violence. It is a phenomenon that has existed for centuries, tracing back to Roman times.[25] Modern versions of terrorism are many times more horrific because of the availability of increasingly lethal weapon systems. No longer are terrorists simply political assassins or isolated bomb throwers. Nor are their targets individual, if important, officeholders. Terrorism terrifies because, in its modern version, anyone and everyone is a potential target.

Terrorism has many characteristics and forms. This chapter will introduce two of the most general expressions of terror: state and non-state. While the two occasionally overlap, each has distinct features and activities. The next section will examine the basic essentials of each.

11-6a Non-State Terrorism

Non-state terrorists are usually individuals who have determined it is no longer worthwhile to try to accomplish political objectives within the law, a law which to them represents the power of an immoral and/or illegitimate regime. They are contemptuous of the society's political institutions and practices. While such characteristics could simply make someone politically apathetic or a disillusioned but harmless recluse, a minority of those who feel politically alienated also consider themselves at war with not only the prevailing power structure, but the structure of the entire society. Before someone becomes a terrorist, he or she must first believe that society is so corrupt it is irredeemable; it must instead be destroyed, root and branch. If this sounds harsh and unreasonable to most people, it is because people generally prefer the society they live in, with its faults, to an unknown and perhaps worse environment.

Nineteenth-century terrorists confined themselves to shooting or bombing high-ranking government officials, including U.S. President William McKinley (1897–1901), who was shot to death just after taking office to serve a second term of office. The current age of political terrorism is generally considered to have begun in 1968 as airplane hijackings reached almost epidemic proportions. Remarkably few people were seriously injured or lost their lives in these hijackings, and as airport security improved (at least in most places), hijackings rapidly decreased in frequency.

---

[24]The Chinese leader, Deng Yao-ping (1904–1907), has stated that "it is glorious to get rich," a radical opinion for a communist, but an excellent one for a politician.

[25]David C. Rapoport, "Fear and Trembling: Terrorism in Three Religious Traditions," *The American Political Science Review*, vol. 78, no. 3 (September 1984), 658–76.

Unfortunately, as terrorists become frustrated in one area, they tend to develop newer, progressively more lethal methods in others. They also learn from one another:

> Analysis of terrorist incidents indicates that many groups consciously apply lessons learned from previous terrorist incidents. For example, terrorist tactics are changing constantly in response to changes and improvements in the ability of the authorities to manage particular types of terrorist incidents.[26]

Pan Am flight 103's destruction in 1988, caused by a bomb placed in its cargo bin, is a frightening example of escalating terrorism. The bombing of a federal facility in Oklahoma City in 1995 is another. Hundreds of completely defenseless people died in these attacks. During the 9-11 attacks, thousands of people perished in a few hours. Moreover, a disconcerting number of religiously inspired terrorists, convinced they will immediately enter paradise upon physical **martyrdom**, are willingly and happily dying for their causes. In Israel beginning in September 2000, Arab suicide bombers carrying explosives climb aboard public buses, killing themselves and dozens of other people. After a lull, more suicide bombers appeared, blowing themselves up along with unsuspecting Israeli shoppers in crowded marketplaces.

martyrdom
The willing death of an individual in order to further a radical ideological or theological message.

There are several critical and somewhat interrelated differences between the older and newer forms of terrorism:

1. *Civilians are now the target of choice.* Many terrorist organizations no longer consider civilians innocent bystanders. Instead, no one is innocent in a depraved society. If a terrorist views a society as corrupt or immoral, he or she is likely to view everyone in that society as contributing to the corruption and immorality, or at least as a willing collaborator. Because individuals are as bad as the system, individuals should be destroyed along with it. Thus, civilian aircraft, department stores (a favorite target of the Irish Republican Army), or public buses (a target of the Hamas operatives in Israel) have become legitimate targets. In this view, the only really innocent people are those self-righteously terrorizing the rest of the population. Murdering random civilians also has a practical aspect. In doing so, terrorists demonstrate that no one is safe and no government is capable of protecting its own citizenry from their violence.

2. *Terrorist organizations believe in and practice maximum lethality.* Because terrorists now go after civilian populations, it is inevitable (and, from the terrorist's standpoint, desirable) that people of all genders and ages will be killed or injured. The terrorist's objective is to ensure that no one feels secure going to work, going shopping, or attending school, because there are no safe places. Making people afraid to venture from their homes and even making them feel insecure inside their homes is the ultimate goal.

Most successful terrorist organizations tend to enjoy at least a degree of state sponsorship. Iran, North Korea, Libya, and Syria are countries that have often been linked to terrorist organizations. State sponsors are often much like the terrorists themselves: self-righteous in the face of the international community's condemnation. Some organizations have actually enlisted several states as sponsors. Why does any government support known terrorists? Several reasons apply:

1. *State sponsorship is financially inexpensive.* A government can provide a terrorist organization with relatively low-cost assistance by supporting training camps and providing safe houses and financing. Moreover, a government can withdraw its support at any time. It need not provide explanations. Once a government decides continuing support is no longer in its best interests, it can eliminate its relationship with the organization.

---

[26]Grant Wardlaw, *Political Terrorism: Theory, Tactics, and Countermeasures*, 2nd ed. (Cambridge: Cambridge University Press, 1989), 172.

2. *State sponsorship serves a government's foreign policy objectives.* The Iranian government, for example, has provided support to organizations such as Hezbollah in Lebanon as part of its quest to extend both Iranian influence and the Shiite Muslim faith. Syria for decades has sponsored terrorist groups that attack Israeli civilian targets. It has also used terrorism to pressure Israel to comply with the Syrian government's foreign policy goals, including removal of the Israeli presence in the Golan Heights, located on the Syrian-Israeli frontier.

3. *State sponsorship can be denied or withdrawn.* It is difficult to demonstrate links between a government and the terrorist organizations it sponsors, and no government prefers to make its support of terrorism public. A few governments may actually acknowledge a link, but they deny that they are sponsoring terrorism, arguing instead that they are supporting "freedom fighters" in their just struggle against a powerful enemy. [27]

With the passage of time, many terrorist organizations have come and gone. It is difficult to be sure at any given time how many terrorist organizations exist or how threatening they are to the governments and societies they have targeted. To confuse the authorities, some organizations commit an outrage and then simply reassemble under a new name. Some have been known to claim credit for the acts of others.

During the 1960s and 1970s, the most visible terrorist organizations were motivated by secular ideologies on the extreme left and, to a somewhat lesser extent, on the extreme right. The Baader-Meinhoff gang in Germany, for example, targeted members of both the business and political establishments, arguing that their leaders were conspiring to exploit and abuse the masses of working people under their control. The Red Brigades in Italy took a similar approach, singling the same kinds of people out for kidnapping and extortion and shooting public figures in the kneecaps and groin. (A former Italian prime minister, Aldo Moro, was kidnapped and eventually murdered in the most famous case of Italian terrorism.) Most of these groups have either faded from the scene or have seen their members apprehended and imprisoned.

The winding down of the Cold War helped curtail the activities of many of the ideologically driven groups. Moreover, the arrival of radical religious regimes, first in Iran in 1979 and several years later in Sudan and Afghanistan, to an appreciable extent shifted the focus of terrorism. Most if not all major religions have extremist movements: Shiite Muslims in Iran, Hindu nationalists in India, Jewish settlers in the West Bank, and a few Christian sects in North America have inspired some terrorist activities.

These movements often target democratic societies they view as corrupt and decadent. The clerical regime in Iran, for example, constantly refers to the United States as the "great Satan" (Israel is the "little Satan"). Religiously inspired terrorists are, it seems, even less likely to object to dying than their secular cohorts. Devout Muslims, for example, who perish while attacking an enemy of Islam believe that they go immediately to paradise. Martyrdom is encouraged in this life and rewarded in the next. Iran is an example of a theocratic regime that firmly believes in martyrdom and encouraged its soldiers during its war with Iraq (1980–1988) to be unafraid of dying in a just cause. The regime even ordered fourteen-year-olds to clear minefields with their bodies, assuring them and their parents that dying nobly for the sake of Islam entitled them to immediate entrance to paradise. See Table 11–1 for examples of terrorist events over the last three decades. The September 11, 2001, attacks by al-Qaeda on the United States reports a new and even more frightening escalation of terrorism by non-state actor.

---

[27]None of this necessarily removes state sponsorship from responsibility for terrorism. The "axis of evil" reference to Iraq, Iran, and the Democratic Peoples' Republic of (North) Korea given in President Bush's 2002 State of the Union Address clarified the notion that no state can remain immune from retaliation if it sponsors terrorist attacks. See Elisabeth Bumiller, "Axis of Evil: First Birthday for a Famous Phrase," *The New York Times*, sec. A, January 20, 2003, A17.

TABLE 11–1	Selected Terrorist Events since 1972

Date and Location	Event
September 1972—Munich, Germany	PLO-sponsored terrorists abduct and murder 13 Israeli athletes and a German policeman during the Olympic Games.
January 1975—New York City	Puerto Rican group FALN detonates a bomb in a tavern, killing four.
April and October 1983—Beirut, Lebanon	Suicide bombers kill 309 U.S. Marines and 58 French paratroopers.
June 1985—India	Sikh terrorists blow up an Air India plane, killing 329.
December 1988—Lockerbie, Scotland	Libyan terrorists blow up a Pan Am plane, killing 441 people in the plane and on the ground.
February 1993—New York City	A bomb placed in the basement garage of the World Trade Center goes off, killing six.
April 1995—Oklahoma City	American terrorists use a truck bomb to destroy the Murrah Federal Building, killing 168.
June 1996—Saudia Arabia	Terrorist group Hezbollah kills 19 U.S. servicemen at the Khobar Towers military complex.
June 1997—Luxor, Egypt	The Islamic Group kills 58 foreign tourists on holiday visiting Luxor.
August 1998—Nairobi, Kenya Dar es Salaam, Tanzania	Truck bombs at U. S. embassies kill 244 military personnel.
October 2000—Aden, Yemen	Seventeen sailors on the USS Cole are killed by a boat bomb.
September 2001—New York City, NY; Arlington, VA; Shanksville, PA	Al-Qaeda terrorists hijack and crash airliners into the World Trade Center, the Pentagon, and a field, killing 3,044 people.
October and December 2001—India	JeM terrorist group attacks the Kashmir legislative building and Indian Parliament, killing nine.

11-6b State Terrorism

A government may have some very practical reasons for imposing a violent regime on its citizenry. The more brutal and sustained features of state terrorism are areas of concern that until recently represented an underdeveloped area of research. The events of September 11, 2001, have encouraged students of terrorism to renew their efforts to understand and analyze the phenomenon.[28]

There is a growing awareness that a government that commands a bureaucracy, secret police, and armed forces is capable of committing all sorts of crimes, often with impunity. This may be changing. Surviving German Nazi leaders after World War II were placed on trial for crimes against humanity. Several of them were hanged or imprisoned. The former Serbian leader, Slobodan Milosevic, was on trial by an international court in The Hague until he died in 2006.

Terrorism was practically institutionalized under the Nazi regime in Germany and the Stalinist regime in the Soviet Union. Both succeeded in ridding themselves of anyone suspected of less than loyal support and even encouraged children to inform on their parents if they displayed any lack of enthusiasm for the regime. Terror in a totalitarian regime is a politically useful tool to maintain the regime's power.

The state as terrorist is neither a new concept nor a new phenomenon. The state is obviously capable of doing substantial harm for long periods of time. This gives the state a great advantage over non-state terrorists, who have to keep shooting people and blowing up buildings to ensure they have the attention of the public and the authorities. The state, in contrast, is a permanent fixture whose agencies are constantly in the public eye.

A government that perpetuates a policy of political violence by imprisoning or executing people for their political opinions and/or religious and racial

---

[28]See, for example, Cindy C. Combs and Martin Slann, *Encyclopedia of Terrorism* (New York: Facts on File, Inc., 2002).

backgrounds can get away with it for a long time and can commit more violence than any other social agent. After all, a government typically commands and often monopolizes the resources required for perpetuating violence. Moreover, some governments that have an active policy of terror count on a degree of popular support or at least neutral acquiescence, as both the Nazis and communists did.

State terror can assume different versions and intensities. At least three general gradations of terror can be identified:

1. *Intimidation:* This usually occurs through the state's control of the electronic and print media and security forces. The media provide instructions for proper political behavior and ruthlessly discourage dissent. They also make the penalties for misbehavior clear. In China, for example, those who protest loudly against government policies may well be shipped off for a three-year visit to a labor camp. If a labor camp inmate can be "re-educated," that person may return to society.

2. *Coerced conversion:* A revolutionary organization such as the Bolsheviks in Russia or communists in China may take power and call for a complete overhaul of the national economy and social lifestyle. Those who don't or won't fit in are frequently sent to "re-education camps." They often don't return. Iran provides another recent example of coerced conversion. In 1979, the regime of clerics instituted and still enforces restrictive dress codes for all females. It has also applied criminal penalties to the entire population for immoral behavior as defined by the Koran: For example, those guilty of adultery or blasphemy are stoned to death.

3. *Selective genocide or autogenocide:* The most serious and frightening policy of state terrorism is the elimination of entire communities within a national population. The genocidal activities the Nazi regime undertook against the Jewish population of Europe (1939–1945) and the Stalinist purge of the peasant class of kulaks, mostly independent and successful farmers, in Ukraine (during most of the 1930s) caused the deaths of millions of civilians. Autogenocide—extermination of one's own people—occurred during the Pol Pot regime in Cambodia from 1975 to 1979.

These three categories often overlap. Intimidation can eventually lead to genocide. Before the Nazis decided to physically destroy the German Jews and eventually all of the European Jews, they first barred them from professions such as law, medicine, and teaching. Eventually, Jews were forbidden to purchase milk, own pets, or cultivate private vegetable gardens. Finally, they were forbidden to live. Misery and humiliation preceded and prepared them for extermination.

State terrorism challenges the Western political and philosophical traditions of humanitarianism, toleration, and protection of individual and natural rights. The terrorist state may simply be a new formulation of the old conflict between despotism and democracy; between the point of view that the state precedes and is superior to the individual, and the classical concept of individual sovereignty. Most terrorist regimes commit atrocities against their own citizens or confine themselves to oppressing selected ethnic or religious communities. Others are more ambitious and support terrorism beyond their own borders. Several, such as Sudan, Syria, and North Korea have been known to do both by making life miserable for their own people as well as supporting or hosting terrorist organizations that committed atrocities on particular targets. By the 1990s, though, non-state terrorist agents were beginning to appear that did not necessarily require the apparatus of the state to carry out their atrocities. The Taliban regime in Afghanistan (1996–2001), after all, was greatly influenced by the al-Qaeda operatives within its borders. Osama bin Laden brought with him both fighters to support the Taliban and hordes of money to purchase weapons. In the African country of Sudan, a policy was implemented by a radical government to murder and rape non-Muslims and non-Arab Muslims in the western province of Darfur. Despite international protests, the brutality has continued with only occasional interruptions since early 2003.

The traditional constraints of the state no longer are working well as information becomes more easily available wherever computers can be accessed. Neither are the old prohibitions or tactics. Non-state terrorist actors are making their own rules. Today's fanatical terrorists aren't as interested in staying alive as the previous generation was and are a lot more devoted to murdering large numbers of people. They are motivated less by ideological appeals or political agendas and more by a vision of the purity of wholesale destruction that is required before they can impose their version of spiritual justice. A new and more ominous phase of terrorism has apparently begun. The democracies have become increasingly focused on dealing with the threat posed by more lethal kinds of terrorist activity since the events of September 11. Terrorism has become a defining international feature in the early twenty-first century. For that reason we will devote a later chapter to its character and impact on the international scene.

Chapter Summary

1. Important differences separate criminal and political violence. Political violence is minimized in the Western or Western-style democracies, while criminal behavior is often minimized in systems whose governments are capable of the worst forms of violence for any infraction of the law.
2. Democracies tend to have governments that subject themselves to the laws they have legislated. Nondemocratic governments tend to enforce the law fairly and consistently except when it comes to political crimes—opposition, dissent, or belonging to a distrusted minority community.
3. State-sponsored violence exists in a number of countries. Yet, as in China during the Great Proletarian Cultural Revolution, even a totalitarian government can lose control of its own systematic violence once it develops an overly enthusiastic following.
4. State authorities may ignore or even sanction gender violence, and the institution of slavery is alive and well in several countries. In such instances, the state, even if it wishes to end a horrific practice, may be reluctant to pursue the matter because it doesn't want to confront time-honored and entrenched traditions.
5. Ideologically driven violence is perhaps the most lethal when perpetuated by a political regime. Even citizens willing to completely subscribe to the government's policies may not be allowed to do so if they belong to a racial, religious, or social grouping the government wants to eliminate.
6. Non-state political terrorism in its most contemporary form assumes that no one in a "corrupt" society has a right to claim innocence. Therefore, anyone is liable to become a terrorist target.
7. Non-state terrorists often have substantial longevity and lethal capabilities because they enjoy state sponsorship. If supported by a state, terrorists can forcefully and indirectly express the state's foreign policy agenda.
8. State terrorism can produce incredible misery for a population. It can manifest itself in several ways, ranging from intimidation of selected minorities or entire populations to their physical extermination.

Chapter 11 Quiz

1. During the 1970s and 1980s, Argentina
   a. enjoyed democratic government.
   b. experienced military occupation by the United Kingdom.
   c. was ruled by a military regime that regularly violated human rights.
   d. established a monarchy.

2. Chechens are
   a. close allies of the Kurds.
   b. Christians.
   c. unaccepting of control by Russia.
   d. a rock band.

3. During the 1980s, death squads most notoriously operated in
   a. El Salvador.
   b. Iran.
   c. Palestinian-controlled territories.
   d. Chicago.

4. During China's Great Cultural Revolution
   a. the rule of law prevailed.
   b. there was substantial economic development.
   c. ideologically inspired youths committed acts of violence throughout the country.
   d. orthodox communists lost power.

5. In some African countries, China, and parts of the Middle East
   a. Islam is winning mass conversions.
   b. slavery is still flourishing.
   c. democracy is making rapid strides.
   d. regimes are adopting strictly free market economic systems.

6. The author of the observation, "political power comes out of the barrel of a gun," is
   a. William Seward.
   b. Mao Tse-Tung.
   c. Saddam Hussein.
   d. the Chicago Police Department.

7. The Pol Pot regime in Cambodia during 1975–1979 produced
   a. a prosperous economy.
   b. good relations with the United States.
   c. an evolving democracy.
   d. genocide against its own people.

8. Lebanon is a country that is an example of
   a. theocratic governance.
   b. an aggressive foreign policy.
   c. strong authoritarian governance by the central government.
   d. the power of sectarian militias.

9. Martyrdom, the willingness to give one's life for a cause, is enthusiastically and frequently practiced against
   a. Israel.
   b. Chechnya.
   c. Japan.
   d. Spain.

10. The reference of "great Satan" is directed by the clerical regime in Iran against
    a. Israel.
    b. Russia.
    c. the United States.
    d. Saudi Arabia.

11. Coerced conversion has been practiced by
    a. Russian Bolsheviks.
    b. Chinese communists.
    c. Iranian clergy.
    d. all of the above.

PART 5

The International Situation at the Beginning of the Century

These two chapters review the current status of international politics as well as what immediately preceded it (Chapter 12) and pinpoint ethnicity and ethnic conflict (Chapter 13) as a feature that seems destined to characterize international relations well into the twenty-first century. Both chapters examine the aftermath and residues of the Cold War. In addition, international terrorism (Chapter 14) has become a serious threat to global political stability and economic development. A new paradigm is being developed that questions old assumptions about the nation-state system and may devise new definitions of what really constitutes sovereignty. Non-state actors such as terrorist organizations are creating new formulations of foreign policy on the part of not just the United States, but other countries that either impact on or are supportive of terrorism. The international constellation also faces in the early years of the twenty-first century new and often unprecedented challenges by non-state actors, particularly religious fanatics, whose political agendas are based on ethnic, tribal, or singularly theological motivations. Many of these actors do not seek to resolve disputes or grievances through diplomatic or otherwise peaceful channels. Instead, they see no alternative to obliterating the current international system.

The International Constellation

From the end of the Napoleonic Wars in 1815 to the beginning of World War I in 1914, the world was a remarkably stable place compared to the century that followed. For the most part, the major European powers stopped (temporarily) making war on one another and busied themselves carving out huge colonial empires in Africa, the Middle East, and East Asia. After the end of World War I in 1918 the French and British, militarily victorious in the war, installed several governments in newly independent Arab states to protect their oil interests. Even before World War II ended in 1945, the main features of the postwar international system were becoming very clear. Major European powers such as Britain, France, Germany, and to a somewhat lesser extent, Italy, along with Japan, had dominated international politics for about a century. But they had so exhausted themselves in the conflict that their entire economies had been devastated and their populations decimated. Moreover, nationalist movements in several Middle Eastern and south Asian countries emerged that had little patience with old regimes, mostly monarchies that supported and were supported by Western regimes. Of the major participants in the war, only the United States had escaped becoming a battleground and emerged with its economy intact. Nor did the United States have an extensive colonial empire that engendered resentment by subject peoples. Even before the end of World War II the United States was emerging as the only democracy capable of standing up to and thwarting Soviet ambitions.

The British had successfully resisted the German desire for conquest on the European continent in the early years of World War II. Yet, for all of their courage the British probably would not have survived without American economic and military assistance. Britain had not endured a German occupation but was economically exhausted nonetheless and certainly in no position to compete with the United States for global leadership or stand up to the Soviet Union's territorial expanse in eastern and central Europe. Within two years, Britain would ask the United States to accept traditional British responsibilities to protect the Middle East and southeastern Europe. This request soon led to the **Truman Doctrine**, a strategy for containing Soviet expansion.

France had experienced a four-year German occupation (1940–1944); no sooner had it begun its recovery than its colonial empire in southeast Asia and north Africa began to unravel. The French re-established their own political institutions in 1946 under a new constitution that inaugurated their Fourth Republic. A weak economy, social and political conflicts, and the disintegration of their colonial empire kept France a bitterly divided country. In the twelve-year history of the Fourth Republic, the French saw twenty-three governments come and go. A multiparty system and a constitutionally weak executive created other problems for the French. Not until 1958, with the advent of the Fifth Republic, would the French again achieve political stability under a strong and centralized executive structure.

The Nazi regime's excesses had alienated most of the European peoples. The Germans faced the future as a country divided into East and West, despised and distrusted by millions of their neighbors, and with the daunting task of becoming a sovereign state again. Japan, like Germany, was in shambles and faced deep-seated hostility from the countries it had conquered and abused. Although Japan had never before lost a war, it was now militarily occupied after becoming the only country in history to experience nuclear warfare.

Truman Doctrine
Promulgated in 1947, this plan provided a strategy for containing Soviet communist expansion in southeastern Europe and the Near East. Later it was extended to Western Europe through NATO.

The collapse of so many great powers in such a short period of time marked the end of an age. Two superpowers, the Soviet Union and the United States, emerged as the only countries able to exert power on a global scale. For most of the next half century, international politics would be characterized by superpower rivalry. The status of superpower was reserved for the Soviet Union and the United States because only they had the resources—huge territory, large population and economy, and a nuclear arsenal available to destroy the world—to warrant that title. Then, rather suddenly and almost quietly, one of the superpowers disintegrated. The United States, for the time being at least, remains the sole superpower in the early years of the twenty-first century. This could change in the future. China is rapidly becoming an economic powerhouse with an annual growth rate of 10–12 percent. It already has a nuclear arsenal and the largest population in the world. Moreover, if Europe continues to economically and politically integrate (a process that began in the 1950s) under the auspices of the European Union, it too could conceivably achieve superpower status. A united Europe would have a larger population and more skilled workforce than the United States.

This chapter will explore the immediate and potential consequences of an unprecedented situation: the United States as the sole superpower without serious rivals, but not without problems and challenges. It will try to identify some of these challenges as well as explore their possible consequences and outcomes. The international constellation of the first few decades of the twenty-first century will look very different from its counterpart in the last decades of the twentieth, but will still grow out of the dominant features that characterize the global picture of today.

12-1 The International Arena

About three and a half centuries ago, the Treaty of Westphalia (1648) ended the Thirty Years' War in Europe. It was in Europe that the modern state system first took form. The rough outlines of the system developed during and immediately after this period. Of course, Europe in 1648 looked quite different from the Europe of 1945; even the Europe of 2005 barely resembled the Europe of 1945. Many current states did not exist 350 years ago after the Thirty Years' War or even a century ago just before World War I. Some that did exist no longer do. Moreover, the rest of the world virtually exploded with new countries in the post–World War II period, particularly in Africa (see Figure 12–1).

Very few countries that existed in 1914 when World War I began had the same national boundaries at the end of the twentieth century. Losing or winning a major conflict can cause noticeable changes in a country's borders—in fact, the change can be so severe that the country is literally wiped off the map. Poland, for example, disappeared at the end of the eighteenth century after its predatory neighbors, Austria, Prussia, and Russia, partitioned it, only to reappear at the beginning of the twentieth century.

Today, people live in a world with nations that are or were "stateless," as well as with nations that live within a state and are often in conflict with it. Kurds and Palestinians in the Middle East and the Karen people in Myanmar (Burma) are excellent examples. The Kurds have been in conflict with and within four states—Iraq, Iran, and Turkey—because their nation spills over several borders. Still, the world today lives in essentially a **nation-state system** because there is no part of the globe that some sovereign state hasn't claimed jurisdiction over. In other words, there is no reprieve or escape from a state's presence no matter where one goes. A nation-state

> . . . may decree that a person dies; with no less effort, it may offer the protection that enables a person to live. . . . Whether it be to be born, to live, or to die, no one can do so without official recognition—the recognition of the nation-state.[1]

nation-state system
While many nations do not have their own states and many states are composed of numerous nations, some type of sovereign jurisdiction has extended to the entire earth's surface, creating a network of nation-states.

---

[1]John D. Stoessinger, *The Might of Nations: World Politics in Our Time*, 10th ed. (New York: McGraw-Hill, 1993), 6.

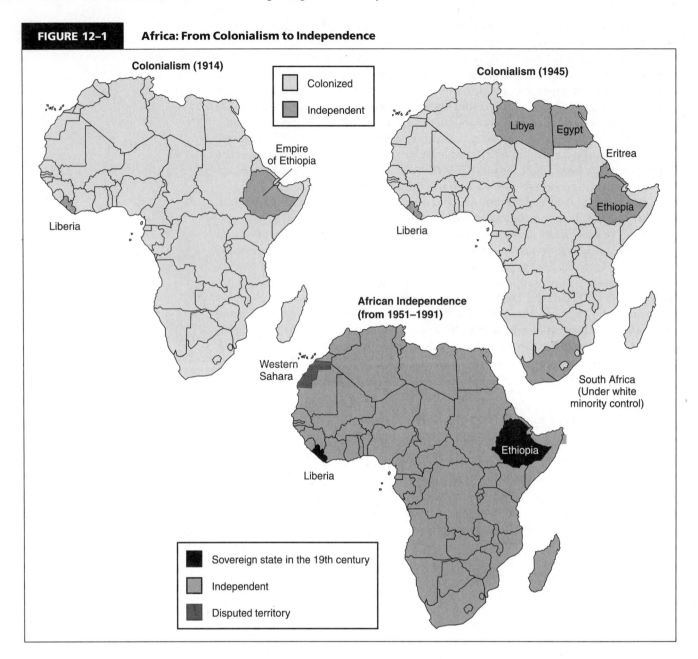

FIGURE 12–1   **Africa: From Colonialism to Independence**

Notice that in all of these life events, the *state* is the final arbiter. There simply is no higher secular authority. States create and enforce laws and mete out punishments for misconduct. But what governs the relationships *between* sovereign states?

A body of international regulations and laws suggest how governments ought to behave toward one another. Interestingly, most countries regularly and voluntarily adhere to these standards. For example, health regulations offered by the World Health Organization (WHO) and aircraft security, landing, and takeoff facilities coordinated by the International Air Transport Association (IATA) are nearly universally accepted. Many of these governing and regulating organizations are under the auspices of the United Nations. Others, including environmental organizations, are independent, but they often publish widely agreed-upon regulations.

With rare exception, the world's nearly 200 countries work within international guidelines because it makes sense for them to do so. International understandings facilitate trade and commerce, encourage multilateral cooperation, and generally make life easier for untold millions of people in numerous countries. This is not to say that this is the beginning of the end of the sovereign state. In fact, it could be argued that international cooperation actually helps to sustain sovereignty, because cooperation must serve the national interest of the cooperating state or it wouldn't be involved.

Cooperative measures work only as long as participants see advantages. Volunteerism goes a long way, but once it stops, what happens? No sovereign authority is available to enforce compliance with an international law or practice. The International Court of Justice, for example, can hand down a judicial decision against a particular country, but the country, especially if it is a strong one, can completely and safely ignore the decision.

The United Nations General Assembly can also pass resolutions against a particular regime, but these resolutions achieve little practical effect. The UN can even expel a member, but, short of taking collective military action against a renegade regime—an infrequent event—the UN cannot do much to change the behavior of any government. In 1950, the United Nations authorized a multinational military force (under American leadership) to resist North Korea's invasion of South Korea by undertaking a "police action." Such decisions usually have restrained goals; in Korea, the UN settled for the North's expulsion from the South rather than an occupation of the North. Similarly, in 1990 and 1991, a twenty-eight-member coalition (again under American leadership) aligned to remove the Iraqis from Kuwait, but the coalition did not attempt to get rid of the regime of Iraqi leader Saddam Hussein altogether. That would not happen until 2003.

The revolution in communications technology has critically influenced the international arena and the foreign policy expressions of individual states. The United States during the Vietnam conflict provided the first nationally televised war in history. Watching the news during the dinner hour became for millions of American families the decisive factor in determining whether they supported their country's presence in Vietnam. Increasingly, in great part because of television, Americans found themselves questioning what the United States was doing in Vietnam and why it was necessary to send young soldiers to endanger themselves there.

Image matters in international politics, as do perception and misperception. World War I cost perhaps twenty-five million lives and unfurled as governments developed different perceptions about their neighbors. The war began with the assassination of the designated successor to the emperorship of Austria-Hungary; this caused the Austrian armed forces to mobilize against Serbia, Austria's age-old enemy, whom the Austrians suspected of complicity in the assassination. Germany felt honor-bound to mobilize on behalf of its ally, Austria. Likewise, Russia felt morally obligated to come to the aid of a fellow Slavic country, Serbia. Then France and Britain decided to mobilize because Germany was threatening the neutrality of Belgium. Hardly any believed that a European war would last for four and a half years. The German Kaiser told his soldiers in August 1914 that they would be home before the leaves fell in autumn. Millions of them never saw home again. Some of this may sound disconcertingly familiar. In the 1990s and early 2000s, Russia was still supportive of Serbia, while Germany supported Croatia, both regions of the former Yugoslavia long at odds with one another.

No government that ordered military mobilization in the late summer of 1914 anticipated the horrific casualties that followed over the next four-and-a-half years. In the end, no one was sure why the war happened at all.[2] The most murderous century in history was well underway.

To avoid a repetition of 1914, the Western democracies attempted to placate Germany as it undertook a military and economic revival during the 1930s. A small democratic state on Germany's southern border fell victim to German aggression. The aggression was based on the pretext that Czechoslovakia's German minority

---

[2]For an excellent treatment of this subject, see Barbara, Tuchman, *The Guns of August* (New York: Macmillan, 1962).

appeasement
The idea that a hostile nation can be persuaded to maintain peaceful relations if other countries give in to some of its demands. The British and French governments' attempt to placate German territorial ambitions enjoyed substantial popular support in the late 1930s. The guiding notion was that it was only fair to meet at least some German demands because Germany had been so harshly treated by the Versailles Treaty at the end of World War I.

required protection from a hostile Czechoslovak majority. Czechoslovakia was absorbed by Germany piecemeal during 1938–1939. The sacrifice of this country was sanctioned by the British and French governments who thought that by doing so Germany would be appeased and desist from further aggression. This policy of **appeasement** didn't work, and Europe fell headlong into another war. The bad memories of appeasement endured well into the 1960s as those who were young soldiers during World War II came to power in the United States and Western Europe. American foreign policymakers in the 1960s accordingly decried concessions to communism in southeast Asia. The result was an extended land war in Vietnam and stark divisions within American society over whether the war was necessary. The "Vietnam syndrome" was still around a generation later: The first President Bush in 1990 and 1991 went out of his way to assure the American people that the U.S. involvement in the Persian Gulf conflict would not result in "another Vietnam." After the occupation of Iraq in 2003, mostly by American forces, critics of the war began to compare the prolonged insurgency against the occupation to Vietnam.

Foreign policy formulation is guided, then, by past failures and successes and occasionally by failures perceived as successes. The problem is that international politics, like so much else in life, is constantly changing. If contesting powers possess nuclear weapons, it is important to prevent an international crisis from flaring to the point that no one feels able to back down (in other words, to avoid a possible replay of 1914). Simply put, any prevailing country must give an opponent a face-saving way to avoid conflict. President John Kennedy (1961–1963) did this in 1962 when he allowed Soviet leader Nikita Khrushchev to gracefully retreat from a decision to ship Soviet missiles to Cuba to aim at the United States. This moment was as close as the two superpowers actually came to nuclear war.

12-2 Prerequisites of State Power

Becoming a superpower is a rare occurrence. Because, as indicated earlier, it was one of the few countries in the world that possessed nearly everything required to be a superpower, the United States achieved the status in relatively short order and without the terrible sacrifices required of the Soviet population during World War II. Most countries with ambitions to become a "great power" need what one would expect: a fairly large and skilled population, a goodly amount of natural resources, including those resources required for a substantial industrial infrastructure, and able political leadership. A certain amount of good luck doesn't hurt, either. Being left alone to exploit and develop natural resources during the first two centuries of its existence certainly helped the United States become a global power. Until the nuclear age, the geographical location of the United States guaranteed its insulation from foreign attack until well into the twentieth century.

Suppose, though, that a country lacks many of these advantages and still wants to be a power, at least in its own region, or is convinced it must become a power to guarantee its own survival—what can it do? Consider two impressive if sometimes controversial examples:

1. *Israel:* By nearly all accounts, Israel is a country with a serious shortage of natural resources. Israel is a small country of only 8,000 square miles (about the size of New Jersey). During most of its first half century of political independence, Israel was surrounded and vastly outnumbered by countries sworn to its destruction. Forced by circumstances to rely primarily on itself for survival, Israel developed the strongest and most efficient armed forces in the Middle East and positioned itself as a center of agricultural and technological innovation. Israel also acquired the ability to deliver at least 200 nuclear missiles to their targets. (The Israelis consistently deny this last point, but military experts believe they have this capability.)

2. *Japan:* Defeated in World War II and deprived of the East Asian empire that provided it with vital resources, including oil and rubber, Japan from 1945 on was reduced to its home islands. Japan has always been incapable of feeding itself—it is a country the size of California with four times the population. Land is in such short supply that rice is grown on mountainsides and in-ground burials are not permitted. And Japan is completely dependent on overseas sources to supply 95 percent of its energy needs. The Japanese understood that to recover from a disastrous war and retrieve their status as a regional power, the country would have to excel in trade and the efficient manufacture of affordable, good-quality products. One of the earliest examples of Japanese efforts to regain economic importance after World War II's devastation occurred with the appearance of the radio transistor. The Japanese did not invent the radio or the car or the computer, but they developed the techniques required to make them better, more efficient, and very reliable. Even without its own supply of raw materials for its growing industries, Japan still achieved a rapid economic resurgence. It now has the largest skilled labor force of any democracy outside the United States.

12-3 Multipolarity, Bipolarity, and Unipolarity

Nearly everyone who lives on this planet is, for better or worse, a part of the nation-state system. It therefore seems natural to want to understand how the system works. Over the last several decades, the world has become increasingly complicated. In 1945, just over two billion people lived in fewer than sixty countries and several extensive colonial empires. Half a century later, the colonial empires were gone, replaced by more than 100 sovereign countries (later to grow to nearly 200), and the global population had exploded to nearly six billion people. With the significant exception of the Soviet Union, the major participants in World War II had more than recovered and were again among the economic and political leaders of the world. Japan and Germany reconstituted themselves as democracies and developed the world's second- and third-largest economies, respectively, while the Soviet Union stagnated economically and politically before its final collapse as a hopelessly incompetent and corrupt system in 1991. This phenomenon occurred primarily because these countries created or re-established political democracies that contained strong private sector economies that were mostly independent from but remained influenced by a significant government presence that guaranteed such things as pensions, health benefits, and a safe banking system.

The current international system is a product of processes that trace back perhaps as far as the Congress of Vienna (1814–1815) when the political foundations of modern Europe began to appear and Britain became the world's wealthiest power. Possessing the world's largest navy, economy, and colonial empire, the British also kept the international system in balance, assuring that no continental power could achieve overwhelming hegemony in Europe. Britain allied itself with Russia to defeat the French during the Napoleonic Wars (1799–1814), joined the French to defeat Russia in the Crimean War (1853–1856) and united with both the French and the Russians to defeat Germany in World Wars I and II (1914–1918 and 1939–1945). Britain was thus widely viewed as the balance in a situation characterized by **multipolarity**, or competition between several nations for regional supremacy. The major European countries, however, took increasing notice of rising powers such as Japan and the United States that, by the beginning of the twentieth century, had acquired significant global status. As World War II ended, it was clear that only the United States and the Soviet Union could project national power on a global scale. The international system had transformed into a situation characterized by **bipolarity**, or competition between two superpowers for global supremacy.

multipolarity
An international situation in which several powers compete against one another for regional supremacy. Multipolarity may divide countries into various contending coalitions.

bipolarity
An international situation in which two superpowers challenge each other for global supremacy. Usually, each is too strong for one to eliminate the other or to be challenged by any other power.

unipolarity
An international situation in which a single superpower has unchallenged global supremacy, commanding a disproportionate share of military force and economic dominance.

With the dissolution of the Soviet Union, it is tempting to conclude that during the early 1990s the world entered an era of **unipolarity**, with an unchallengeable United States taking the role of sole superpower. In one sense, of course, this has happened. The United States is the world's premier military power, its largest economic power, and monitors numerous countries to ensure that international predators, such as Iran, North Korea, and Serbia, don't aggress against their neighbors. Such states are considered by much of the international community to be dangerous to their entire regions as well as to their neighbors because of their desire to secure weapons of mass destruction (WMD) that include nuclear arsenals. Moreover, their regimes tend to brutalize their own citizenries in order to devote resources to acquiring often expensive weapons systems.

At the same time, the world seems to be returning, at least partially, to a multipolar situation. The United States faces no plausible military challengers, but Japan and Western Europe pose impressive long-term economic competition. On the horizon, China, and to a lesser extent, India, are rapidly modernizing their economies. It is difficult to predict the international constellation of the future, but it is almost impossible to imagine its composition without the presence of a European Union, China, India, and perhaps Brazil and Nigeria, all of these important or emerging economic and political powerful entities.

One of the most serious problems facing the United States—one that promises to have significant staying power well into the next century—is nearly the opposite of the challenge to American foreign policy during the Cold War. Instead of confronting monolithic communism, the United States now faces the political disintegration of a number of supposedly sovereign states. This deterioration has especially affected Eastern Europe and the former Soviet republics (FSRs), as well as Third World regions in which conflicting ethnic groups commit violence against one another. This much more complex and unpredictable picture may present more problems for the United States than communism did.

Political disintegration is an issue even in the First World. The two countries bordering the United States, for example, are contending with separatist movements. A majority of French-speaking Quebeçois may secede from the Canadian federation. In Mexico, a rebellion that began in 1995 among indigenous peoples in the southern part of the country provided a wake-up call that signaled Mexico's incomplete national unity.

Of course, if Quebec leaves Canada, it will do so in a peaceful secession (many English-speaking as well as French-speaking Canadians favor Quebec's secession). The breakup of Czechoslovakia into the Czech Republic and Slovakia in 1993 was a quiet "velvet divorce." Yet most of the three dozen or so wars going on at any given time are within rather than between countries. Iraq in the Middle East, Sudan in Africa, and Sri Lanka in South Asia are all examples of countries in which ethnic and religious feuding has partitioned states, possibly on a permanent basis.

What does seem to be certain is that the international arena is not an inactive place. By the early years of the twenty-first century, there was increasing realization that China and India, the two largest countries in the world, were rapidly becoming economic heavyweights. And, at least in China's case, a military power as well. Together, these two countries represent two-fifths of the entire world's population. Much of the increase in energy prices experienced during 2005 and 2006 in most of the world was traceable to the fact that Chinese and Indians were consuming more energy as their economies grew and as their middle classes expanded.

12-4 Collective Security

In the end, there is good reason to conclude that no one country, regardless of how strong or how committed it is to using its power in the global arena, can control world events. When the United States decided to dislodge Iraq's occupation of Kuwait in 1990, it did so in concert with a coalition of twenty-eight countries, including most Arab states. While a superpower may find it natural and even expected to lead, it must do so with the cooperation of its allies and, preferably, international organizations.

The notion of **collective security** has existed for a long time. The idea is simply this: A number of countries interested in preserving the international status quo combine efforts to stop the one or two countries interested in challenging it. Most of Europe joined forces against France from 1799 to 1814 to achieve collective security, and the same sort of phenomenon occurred in World War II. During the Cold War period much the same notion was in place because of the threat many believed the Soviet Union represented. NATO, for example, was intended to be a security arrangement of the North Atlantic democracies in Europe and North America to thwart Soviet aggression. An attack on one member would be considered by all the others as an attack on them. The United States adopted a version of this policy in 2006 when its allies, Japan and South Korea, understandably felt threatened by North Korea's insistence on nuclear bomb testing.

Iraq supplies a more recent example. Saddam Hussein's regime in 1990 threatened the existence of several countries in the Persian Gulf region, none of whom were capable of repelling an Iraqi invasion (Saddam's army had more soldiers than the entire population of Kuwait). The industrialized democracies dependent upon the flow of oil and natural gas from the Gulf could not abide Iraqi dominance of a huge proportion of these valuable natural resources.

The objectives in actions taken to achieve collective security can differ. Nazi Germany was so thoroughly evil, it was persuasively argued, that its regime had to be destroyed and its leadership permanently removed from power. However, during the early part of the war, the death camps built by the Germans were still largely unknown. Britain and the Soviet Union were simply fighting for their national existence. In Iraq's case, the Saddam Hussein regime was also considered evil, but the coalition that fought it did not consider it as menacing an evil as the Nazis. Thus, while it was necessary to evict Saddam from Kuwait, it was unnecessary to oust him from power, however desirable the international community (and probably most Iraqis) might find the prospect. This perspective, however, began to dissolve during 2002 and 2003.

The notion of "safety in numbers" can apply to international relations. A dominant regional or global power does not take kindly to challengers. Neither do lesser powers that have carved a comfortable and respectable niche for themselves in the international arena and that have a cordial relationship with the one or two major powers around. Following are some telling examples of each of these situations:

1. *France (1789–1815):* The 1789 French Revolution shook every throne in Europe. The execution of the royal family, the declaration of radical revolutionary themes such as liberty and equality, and the rise of Napoleon united most of Europe against France. The coalition was so strong that in the end it defeated Napoleon, a leader widely regarded even by his enemies as a military genius. France at one point was fighting against the combined forces of Austria, Britain (the unofficially acknowledged leader of the coalition), Prussia, Russia, Spain, and Sweden. None of these countries were prepared to tolerate the domination of much of the continent by a single power, but none alone could have defeated France.

2. *Germany (1914–1918 and 1939–1945):* Germany made two attempts to dominate Europe during the first half of the twentieth century. In both cases, the United States had to assume the leadership of the coalition that prevented German supremacy in Europe, especially during the second conflict when the German army occupied most of the continent. In effect, the United States replaced Britain as the power most capable of coordinating collective security arrangements and leading a coalition against any country attempting to upset the balance of power.

collective security
The idea that countries interested in preserving the status quo can ally to defeat a country trying to challenge it.

3. *Soviet Union (1945–1990):* Germany lost its bid for continental hegemony but upset the balance of power anyway. During the Cold War, the intention was not to defeat the Soviet Union in a military conflict—an insane notion in the nuclear age. Instead, the United States and its allies strove to contain Soviet expansion in the hope (not unrealistic, as it turned out) that the communist state would mellow or eventually collapse under its own self-defeating ideology. During the Cold War, the United States became the "leader of the Free World" and busied itself with building containment coalitions such as **NATO**, or the North Atlantic Treaty Organization.

NATO

The North Atlantic Treaty Organization was created in 1949 to thwart any Soviet designs on Western Europe. NATO was part of the containment strategy formulated in the Truman Doctrine.

Following the end of the Napoleonic Wars in 1815, Britain emerged as what passed in those days for a superpower. No other country could compete at that moment in history with British military and economic strength. The century that followed, from 1815 to 1914, was known as the *Pax Britannica,* or British peace. Remarkably few wars broke out during this period. Of course, old habits are hard to break, and European countries fought one another occasionally, but these conflicts did not threaten to destroy Europe's overall balance of power. Most of the time, the larger countries were involved in building colonial empires and violently eliminating opposition to their authority in their colonies. From 1914 through 1945, though, tensions produced two world wars, followed by a haphazard and incomplete *Pax Americana.* Unlike other major powers that preceded its predominance, the United States was a reluctant global player, a reflection of its historical desire to be left alone. In fact, some of the criticism of the American presence in Iraq is traceable to a traditional American isolationist strain in the political culture to remain removed from conflicts beyond our shores.

Long before the Cold War ended, the world realized that collective security would have to be modified. During its last years, the Soviet Union had too many problems to threaten other countries. In all likelihood, it no longer had any desire to do so. Collective security now focused on local or regional threats to the status quo, as in the Persian Gulf conflict.

12-5 The New World Order

Think for a moment about how the Cold War simplified international relations. The United States had a menacing enemy available at all times that it could blame for problems in the world or even at home. In many ways, the Soviet Union was a perfect focus for American foreign policy:

1. It was a totalitarian system equipped with an ideology that predicted and actively worked toward the doom of the capitalist economy.
2. The Soviet system was nondemocratic and therefore the opposite of the type of system admired in American political culture.
3. The Soviet Union was a nuclear power that posed the first mortal challenge to the United States in its history.
4. The Soviets were devoted to challenging and damaging American interests on a global scale.

When the Soviet Union dissolved, Americans no longer had an adversary to fear and loathe. For decades, the Soviet Union had provided Americans with simplicity and certainty; everyone knew that the Soviet Union was a competitor and a threat. Americans also enjoyed a confidence that the Soviet system was evil and the American system was good and right. In other words, it was reassuring for both sides in the Cold War to have a worldview that divided people and cultures into irredeemably good and bad sides: Each side saw itself as pure and noble and the other as corrupt and antagonistic to the best interests of the human race. Such a dichotomy is difficult to replace.

| FIGURE 12–2 | Post–World War II European Alliances |

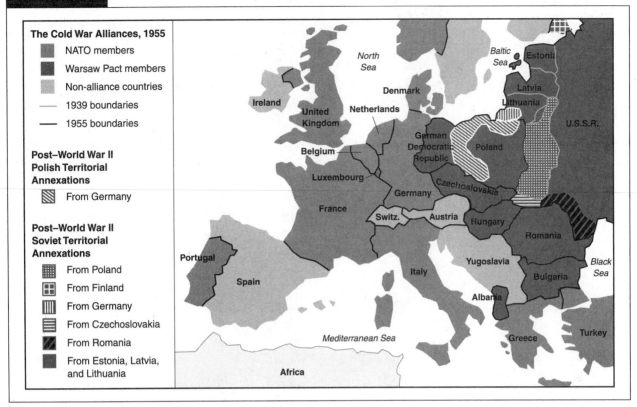

The challenge facing the United States when the Soviet Union dissolved was how to respond to a world without challenges, or at least none that were life-threatening. That perspective ended suddenly and unexpectedly on September 11, 2001. The uncertainty of the previous decade as to where the United States should focus its attention was over with the occurrence of terrorist attacks on American soil and the promise of more to come. Despite the fact that currently, and for the foreseeable future, the United States is "in a class of its own economically and perhaps militarily,"[3] it will face continuing and serious challenges. A fast-changing world will continue to provide unanticipated problems.

During the next few decades the United States will probably remain a superpower with serious competitors. Regional power blocs have already appeared, disappeared, and may reappear (see Figures 12–2 and 12–3). A sizable power bloc could compete with the United States. The possible emergence of a politically and economically (and probably militarily) united Europe is the strongest consideration.[4] The war on terrorism revealed a wide dislike of the United States in several countries, though it is uncertain how widespread or durable the dislike is. It is certainly disconcerting to learn that thousands of parents in the Middle East and elsewhere are naming their children after Osama bin Laden.[5] But this does not in itself necessarily make the world a more dangerous place.[6]

Since the Soviet demise in 1991, the assurances the Cold War provided—neither the Soviet Union nor the United States would risk annihilation in an attempt to destroy each other—have been absent. They have been replaced by

---

[3]Paul Kennedy, *The Rise and Fall of the Great Powers* (New Haven: Yale University Press, 1982), 514.

[4]Richard L. Hudson, "Europe's Great Expectations," *The Wall Street Journal*, sec. A, January 24, 2003, A10g.

[5]Ehud Ya-ari, "Bin Ladenism: The Cult of Death," *The Jerusalem Report*, September 23, 2002, 14–15.

[6]Mark Memmott, "Are These Really Years of Living Dangerously?" *USA Today*, sec. A, November 1, 2002, 18A.

FIGURE 12–3	Post–Cold War Europe

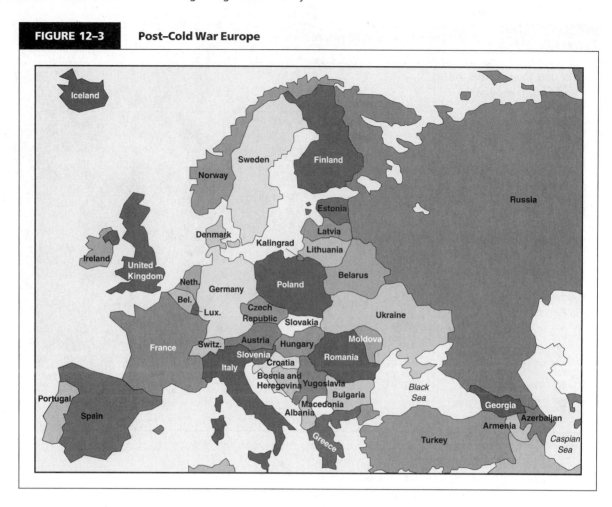

threats posed by hostile and unpredictable regimes such as Iran and North Korea. It is also increasingly difficult to be sure who is an ally and who is the enemy. Certainly, the goals of Iran and North Korea are decidedly counter to Western interests. Yet, even here there is uncertainty: Two seemingly reliable American allies, France and Germany, in the early weeks of 2003 severely criticized the United States for moving too quickly to war, ignoring the opportunity to appeal to the United Nations. And Saudi Arabia, long considered friendly to American and Western interests, is now viewed skeptically by numerous Americans because of the suspicion that Saudis sponsor and encourage terrorists in their own country and enable them to wreak havoc elsewhere. Fifteen of the nineteen 9-11 hijackers were Saudi citizens as was Osama bin Laden before his citizenship was revoked in 1998 by Saudi officials. **Wahabist Islam**, a version of Islam that nurtured in Arabia for 300 years, has relentlessly encouraged violence against Western powers considered to be infidels and other more moderate Muslims considered to be heretics.[7]

The United States and the international system have entered a new and different era. While no monolithic superpower challenges and competes with the United States, current and potential movements can easily guarantee sleepless nights for policymakers. Even before the Soviet collapse, both superpowers had begun to appreciate the limits of their substantial power. The United States from 1965 to 1975 experienced tremendous frustration in the Vietnam War as the determination and ruthlessness of a Third World military force finally induced an American

Wahhabi Islam
An extremist form of Islam established by ibn Abd al-Wahhab, (1703–1792). Wahhabism is Islam's most rigid and puritanical branch, totally and violently opposed to any breach of what it considers to be orthodox Islamic doctrine.

[7]For a critical examination of the extremist elements within Islam, see Ibn Warraq, *Why I Am Not a Muslim* (Amherst, New York: Prometheus Books, 2003). See also Jeff Stein, "Can You Tell a Sunni from a Shiite?" *The New York Times*, October 17, 2006, A12.

BIOGRAPHY

Muhammad ibn Abdul Wahab

Muhammad ibn Abdul Wahab (1703?–1792) founded a radical and puritanical sect of Islam that has been a cornerstone of the Saudi Arabian regime since the Saud family took power during the 1920s. Wahab lived at a time when the Islamic world was clearly declining in terms of influence and power. The largest Islamic power at the time, the Ottoman Turkish Empire, had experience severe military setbacks and its presence in Central Europe and southern Russia was diminishing, a process that would end with the termination of the empire in the 1920s. Wahab determined that Islam's rollback and weakening was because of a departure from orthodox Islamic practices and the growing influence of non-Islamic cultural and scientific strains that he believed were diluting and corrupting the true faith. He believed that the return to pristine Islam would also enable a return to Islamic power and greatness.

Wahab inspired a long list of groups he considered to be enemies of Islam that included Christians, Jews, pagans, and polytheists. He pursued and advocated their complete eradication, particularly on the Arabian peninsula because non-Muslims should not be present in the Islamic homeland. He believed quite literally in the Quranic injunction that Christians and Jews either are or are descended from swine and apes. He also indicated that the Quran should be the only legal authority in Islamic society. In present-day Saudi Arabia, it is. The Quran is strictly enforced along the lines Wahab would approve of including the application of the death penalty for adultery. Wahab was also an enthusiast for the physical elimination of anyone, including moderate Muslims, whose theological views differed from his own.

Ibn Wahab formed an alliance with a local tribal chieftain, the leader of the Saud clan. The deal included the marriage of Saud to a Wahhabi daughter. To the present day this alliance, cemented by blood ties, continues and reinforces the harsh application of Islamic orthodoxy throughout the country of Saudi Arabia.

withdrawal. A decade later, the Soviets withdrew from a similarly disastrous conflict in Afghanistan, another Third World country. The invasion had relentlessly drained military personnel and resources. Neither the United States nor the Soviet Union risked the full level of military commitment each possessed, probably for lack of popular support at home and because each country had no clear objectives for fighting the war in the first place.

The international system that seemed to solidify in the early 1800s began to show signs of wear by the time the twentieth century dawned. It may still be unraveling. For at least a century, European powers had energetically planted their flags across the globe. While most of the British, Spanish, and Portuguese empires in the western hemisphere secured their political independence from Europe during the late eighteenth and early nineteenth centuries, they were not yet in a position to compete with their former colonial masters, who still dominated the eastern hemisphere.

However, some interesting signs of change cropped up. The United States and Japan were definitely rising powers by 1900, and Europe itself was still precariously divided into rival blocs that seemed to be daily coming closer to an armed continental conflict. The two world wars toppled Europe as the most important and powerful political force in the world, but only temporarily. Combined, the countries of Western Europe have as large a population and as skilled a labor force as the United States and Japan together. Moreover, Europe may be through fighting wars, except for occasional but contained conflicts such as the one in Bosnia. The European Union is anticipated to eventually include most if not all of the countries of Eastern Europe. Germany, France, Italy, and Britain represent the third-, fourth-, fifth-, and sixth-largest national economies in the world. With the threat of Soviet communism gone, Europe may once again come into its own, especially if it can maintain the peace and achieve the political unity many Europeans desire. Whether it can is uncertain. It hasn't been able to do so since the Roman Empire collapsed 1,500 years ago. The long history of European wars and mutual distrust is unlikely to be forgotten for many generations to come.

12-6 International Politics in the Twenty-First Century

No one knows the future. By the same token, no wise person ignores the lessons of the past. The history of international politics can be viewed as a long story of great economic and military powers that rise and fall, sometimes unpredictably.

Paul Kennedy's thesis in *The Rise and Fall of the Great Powers* is that "imperial overstretch" ruined the chances of great powers to remain great. A global presence through colonial empire (Britain) or through unprecedented military expenditures (United States) can simply be too costly for any country to sustain. The cost for the Soviet Union, which may have devoted as much as 50 percent of its economy to military preparedness (a factor that no doubt helped cause its demise), became overwhelming after several decades for an economy that was already in serious decline.

Potential powers always loom on the horizon. Large countries with substantial resources, such as China, Brazil, Indonesia, and Nigeria could become dominant regional powers. However, able political leadership, usually in short supply even in the most powerful countries, may not be available when needed. China's political elite is known to be seriously split over future political and economic directions. Brazil has a history of sliding away from its focus on development. Indonesia was governed for a third of a century by one family, guaranteeing a lack of solid political institutions and enhancing institutionalized corruption. And Nigeria, where one in five Africans lives, remains deeply divided along ethnic and tribal lines unlikely to evaporate very soon.

While it can be treacherous to make predictions, it is not unreasonable to assume that in the next century governments will still compete with one another on regional and global scales for the resources necessary to improve the material welfare of their citizenries. Governments seem almost programmed to compete against one another for the necessities they are obligated to provide for their citizenries. Both governments and their capabilities as well as the resources they command may change over time. In the Middle Ages, wars were fought in the Near East over religion. The twentieth century witnessed much competition and more than a few wars over oil. During the next century, it is hardly rash to assume that Near Eastern countries with exploding populations and ambitious plans for economic development could violently compete for the resource of water, an even more precious commodity in the desert than oil. And religious motivations have been exacerbated by the advent of modernization. Islamic radicals refer to some of their enemies as "Crusaders," a term obviously reminiscent of the military expeditions Christian Europe sent during the Middle Ages to invade and occupy Islamic lands, though they neglect to consider that the Crusades were in part prompted by earlier Islamic invasions of southern Europe.

12-7 The Nuclear Nightmare

The end of the Cold War was not the end of international dilemmas and dangers. The next chapter will briefly explore the renewal of ethnic and religious conflicts and the problems these conflicts pose for world peace and stability. The collapse of communism was a dream come true for most advocates of democracy. Yet the resolution of one problem inevitably produces others. Several international difficulties resulted from the Cold War's demise.

Rather suddenly, "loose nukes" arrived on the scene. Instead of two presumably responsible superpowers who supposedly knew better than to go to war controlling the world's nuclear arsenal, nuclear weaponry was dispersed into the hands of several governments. After the Soviet collapse, four former Soviet republics— Russia, Ukraine, Kazakhstan, and Belarus—inherited nuclear installations. Most weapons were transferred to Russian control. Occasional lapses in security, though, could cause one to conjure up images of terrorists stealing (or even buying from an impoverished Russian government) nuclear devices. This scenario is, of course,

FIGURE 12–4   **Countries with Nuclear Capabilities**

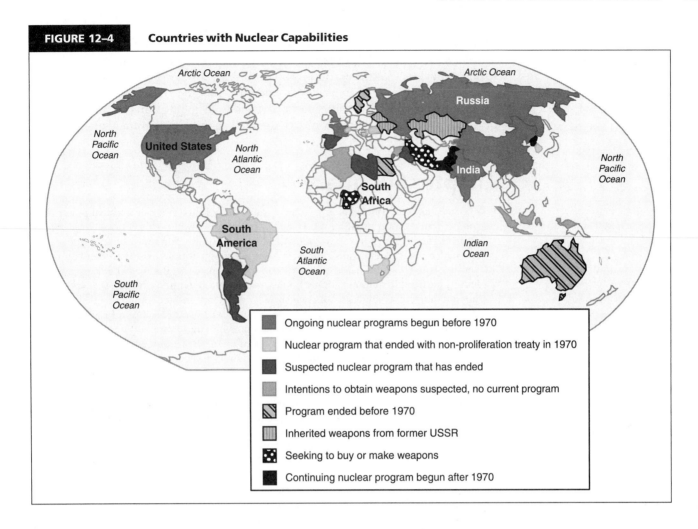

Legend:
- ■ Ongoing nuclear programs begun before 1970
- ▨ Nuclear program that ended with non-proliferation treaty in 1970
- ■ Suspected nuclear program that has ended
- ■ Intentions to obtain weapons suspected, no current program
- ▨ Program ended before 1970
- ▥ Inherited weapons from former USSR
- ▦ Seeking to buy or make weapons
- ■ Continuing nuclear program begun after 1970

unlikely to materialize, but as one bumper sticker has suggested, "One nuclear explosion can ruin your whole day." One imaginative smuggler was able to hide a substantial amount of uranium in his underwear, taking it from Moscow all the way to Prague before he was discovered and detained.[8]

A second and more realistic danger concerns governments who develop their own nuclear technology. As Figure 12–4 suggests, nuclear technology is already widely available. It is probably futile to hope that earth will one day be completely rid of nuclear weapons and the potential for self-destruction. North Korea and Iran have eagerly pursued the acquisition of nuclear weaponry. By 2003 North Korea, in the opinion of close observers, was already building nuclear bombs. Saddam Hussein in Iraq acquired chemical weapons and used them on his own citizens, the Kurds, in the northern third of the country. He also readily used them during the long war with Iran (1980–1988) against enemy combatants. To compound the nuclear dilemma, India and Pakistan have their own nuclear arsenals aimed at one another. There has been unrelenting hostility resulting in several wars already between the two countries since they achieved independence in 1947.

American officials were anxious after 9-11 that terrorists might try to attack the United States with biological weapons such as smallpox. A national debate ensued during 2002 over whether and who to vaccinate against the smallpox virus.[9]

---

[8]Walter Goodman, "Worrying About Russia's Uranium," *The New York Times*, sec. B, November 19, 1996, B3.

[9]"Scientists Favoring Cautious Approach to Smallpox Shots," *The New York Times*, sec. A, December 20, 2002, A1 and A4. See also Elizabeth M. Whelan, "Smallpox Questions," *The Wall Street Journal*, sec. A, October 3, 2002, A14. One immediate problem is weighing the risk of immunizations. For each one million vaccinations, between two and three people will die just from the vaccine itself. Another two to three dozen will become seriously ill.

Successful political leaders traditionally work toward having and furthering political stability. The accelerating phenomenon of suicidal terrorists (and perhaps even suicidal or, at least, possibly self-destructive national elites in Iran and North Korea) strongly suggests that the world is not consistently influenced by what Westerners would regard as rational behavior. In addition, non-state actors such as al-Qaeda are threatening to disrupt international stability in their efforts to advance their own political agenda through violence directed against men, women, and children who are viewed as hostile.

Chapter Summary

1. The international constellation is in a constant state of flux as major national powers rise and fall. The current situation is no exception; a seemingly permanent post–World War II confrontation ended peacefully when one of two superpowers disappeared from the scene.
2. The nation-state system is alive and well. More sovereign entities exist than ever before.
3. Though countries still jealously guard their sovereign status, the overwhelming majority actively participate in international bodies, including the United Nations, that are crucial in regulating increasingly global areas such as commerce and technology.
4. Most countries are not as fortunate as the United States and lack a number of resources that can make them great powers. Many accept their roles as second-tier countries, and others feel compelled to make the most efficient use of the resources they do possess.
5. Through the twentieth century, international politics has been characterized by multipolar, bipolar, and perhaps unipolar situations. It is unclear whether the world is now in a unipolar climate or is reverting to multipolarity.
6. Collective security is an important and defining feature of international stability. When it is working well, collective security helps to guarantee that no country or group of countries can threaten international peace and the balance of power.
7. The immediate future of international politics is fraught with uncertainty now that the Cold War has ended. New powers are almost sure to emerge at some point, as they always have in the past. Even new democracies may pose challenges to the United States.
8. The demise of the Cold War did not mean the end of the nuclear threat to civilization. The threat may have even increased because of the real possibility that more governments and perhaps terrorist organizations will acquire nuclear technology, along with the ability to deliver nuclear weapons to designated targets.

Chapter 12 Quiz

1. The Truman Doctrine was a strategy to
    a. re-establish the French colonial empire.
    b. contain Soviet expansionism.
    c. continue to militarily occupy Germany after World War II.
    d. establish democracy in Japan.

2. Stateless nations include all except which of the following?
    a. Kurds
    b. Palestinians
    c. Karen people
    d. Poles

3. In 1950 the United Nations undertook a police action against
    a. Iraq.
    b. North Korea.
    c. Afghanistan.
    d. Vietnam.

4. The policy of appeasement was an attempt by Britain and France in 1938 to placate ——— by surrendering a huge portion of Czechoslovakian territory.
    a. the Soviet Union
    b. Switzerland
    c. Germany
    d. Poland

5. Two countries that have done well economically despite a lack of substantial resources include
   a. Israel and Japan.
   b. Germany and Russia.
   c. Britain and France.
   d. Iran and Pakistan.

6. The international situation that prevailed between 1945 and 1990 can be characterized as one of
   a. multipolarity.
   b. bipolarity.
   c. unipolarity.
   d. regional supremacy.

7. The Canadian province most desirous of secession from the federation is
   a. Ontario.
   b. Alberta.
   c. Quebec.
   d. Saskatchewan.

8. Most of the 9-11 hijackers were citizens of
   a. North Korea.
   b. Iraq.
   c. Saudi Arabia.
   d. Iran.

9. Islamic radicals generally refer to their perceived enemies as
   a. Crusaders.
   b. Communists.
   c. Shiites.
   d. Pagans.

10. All of the following have nuclear powers except
    a. Japan.
    b. United States.
    c. France.
    d. India.

13

Ethnic Conflict and
the International Constellation

KEY TERMS

ethnics   nationalism
failed states

As discussed previously, the collapse of Soviet and East European communism brought new problems and challenges to the international scene. It seemed like an opportune time for democracy to spread across the globe without interference. Moreover, as the American military learned in Afghanistan during 2001–2002, many countries in the world are not politically coherent but are divided by strong and often politically dominant regional associations and tribal allegiances. Ethnic divisions within a single political system can include religious, linguistic, and other cultural features that tend to work against a central government's ability to unite a population into a full-fledged nation-state. In 2003, as the United States prepared to go to war with Iraq, similar concerns were considered because of deep ethnic and religious divisions within Iraqi society. Iraq has three main demographic groupings—non-Arab Kurds in the north, Sunni Muslims in the center third of the country, and Shia Muslims in the south and in and around Baghdad—as well as several smaller ones including Assyrians, Turkomans, and Arab Christians.

The various ethnic conflicts flaring up across the globe are defining and characterizing future international politics. The effects of nationalism, subnationalism, and ethnicity on the political process will be reviewed in this chapter. The chapter will also discuss the difficulties so commonly found between nation and state.

13-1 The New World Order Revisited

Ethnic divisions have not been the only phenomenon to threaten international harmony. They may not be the last. In any case, it will be helpful to first explore the history of actual or potential challenges to international stability:

1. Between 1800 and 1945, the number of sovereign states in the international community increased from about twenty-five to sixty. During the half century between the end of World War II in 1945 and the collapse of the Soviet Union in 1991, the number tripled to more than 180. Many of the newer states were former colonies of the British, French, Dutch, and Portuguese. The Soviet Union could be considered the last colonial empire to dissolve because it was succeeded by fifteen independent states. In the early years of the twenty-first century, several sizeable groups still desired to create their own states. Many Kurds in Iraq, Turkey, and Iran speak of an independent Kurdistan; Tamils in Sri Lanka want the island-state partitioned so that they may have their own country; many members of the Palestinian Diaspora in the Middle East, in Europe, and elsewhere want to "go home" to reclaim their land. The earth's territory is finite, but the claims upon it seem almost infinite. More and more new states are territorially and demographically small, and many, perhaps most, are not economically viable. Some lack established or permanent political institutions. A few states exist in name only, completely lacking any effective political institutions. This raises the question of to what degree they may contribute to or detract from overall instability in their respective regions. **Failed states** are disconcertingly numerous in parts of the Middle East and Africa.

2. The multiplication of sovereign states takes into account only a tiny fraction of the hundreds of ethnic communities that are either clamoring for a stronger degree of political independence—for example, Chechens in Russia, Basques in

failed states
A political entity in which the central government either does not exist or lacks an ability to impose adequate control over the entire country.

Spain, Kurds in Iraq, Tamils in Sri Lanka, and Baluchis and Arabs in Iran—or at least a greater degree of autonomy, both cultural and political. These communities generally desire more separation from a political center they feel is controlled by a rival or ineffective ethnic community.

3. National boundaries the international community has long assumed are fixed in concrete may no longer be regarded by ethnic minorities as legitimate. These ethnic minorities often consider the central government's presence invasive, uninvited, and alien.

4. The Soviet empire's collapse has produced a largely unexpected impact: an unsettling of the state system as ethnic minorities assert or reassert their desire to control their own political destinies. Simultaneously, a lack of global leadership has developed; other countries are unable to fill this role. Some major powers, such as France and Germany, are sometimes dismayed that the United States is willing to accept global leadership. At other times powers such as France, Germany, and Russia resent the United States acting in what these countries perceive as a unilateral mission to exercise or increase its influence in various regions. Ironically, the United States, for most of its history, was an isolationist country. Isolationism was no longer tenable after the United States was attacked in 1941 by Japan, and military technology made such a policy totally impractical by the 1950s. The dawning of the nuclear age in 1945 allowed no country anywhere to remove itself from world events. By the early 2000s, terrorists had demonstrated that not even the United States, as remote and powerful as it is, was immune from attack by dedicated and ruthless fanatics.

5. The territorial state is itself a questionable entity. It is misleading to look at a multi-colored map of the world and assume that the boundary lines always imply central government control. A government, by virtue of its military and the support of its population, may indeed control all the territory its borders outline. But that isn't the entire story. As one scholar has pointed out: "The distinction between *power over people and power over territory* is a useful one to make, for it singles out two aspects of sovereignty that are best addressed separately: disputes involving the right of peoples to self-determination and territorial disputes among them."[1]

Put another way, political situations are not always what they seem. Earlier chapters stressed the point that there are important differences between terms such as *nation* and *state*. This chapter highlights the idea that these differences can be so substantial that conflicts occur as often between nations *within* states as they do between different sovereign states.

13-2 Competing Nationalisms

The disagreeable truth of ethnic conflict is that **ethnics**, or ethnic communities, often clash because two or more of them turn up at about the same time on the same land and then disagree as to who really owns the territory or who has the right to remain on it. This reality has been in ample evidence for centuries. When Europeans "discovered" America five centuries ago, they also discovered long-settled inhabitants.

ethnics
A term of abbreviation applied to ethnic communities. An ethnic is simply an ethnic group distinguished and united by its religion, culture, language, or common history of suffering.

The Amerindians were the indigenous peoples of the Americas. They numbered in the neighborhood of seventy-five million, considerably more than Europe's total population at the time. These were the descendants of the original inhabitants of the western hemisphere who had first crossed over from Asia 15,000 to 20,000 years ago. The Amerindians were quickly decimated, mostly by diseases such as smallpox that the European settlers brought with them. Not until the last decades of the twentieth century did these indigenous peoples begin to make a

[1]Gidon Gottlieb, *Nation Against State: A New Approach to Ethnic Conflicts and the Decline of Sovereignty* (New York: Council on Foreign Relations Press, 1993), 15.

demographic comeback. In 2006, Bolivia became the first country in the western hemisphere to democratically elect a head of government whose ancestry was almost purely from indigenous people.

When two cultures collide, one inevitably and arrogantly thinks of itself as superior, and sometimes they both do. Technologically speaking, one culture usually is superior. As a rule, Europe was able to subdue a good part of the world for several centuries because of its technological advancement in military weaponry. This is not to say that non-European societies weren't technologically proficient. China, after all, apparently invented gunpowder, but used it as a form of amusement in firecrackers. Europeans seized on the technology as a means to militarily intimidate enemies. European hegemony ended partially as modernization and nationalist aspirations progressed in the developing world and partly because the Europeans themselves found it too expensive and unproductive to continue to exercise control over societies in Asia and Africa.

Ethnic conflict was not simply a case of white European Christians versus everyone else, even during Europe's dominant period. Ethnic conflict has often prevailed within Europe itself. (World War II itself could be considered a huge ethnic conflict and certainly provided an example of "ethnic cleansing.") As the Soviet Union dissolved, long-subdued mutual loathing among various ethnic communities came quickly to the surface. As a seasoned observer of Soviet and Russian affairs put it:

> In Tallinn, I heard Estonians describe Russians as cretins and brutes, and Russians describe Estonians as Nazi collaborators. In Yerevan, Armenians were sure that Azerbaijanis had deliberately "set off" the earthquake that killed at least 25,000 people with an underground nuclear test and were about to carry out an Islamic crusade against them more bloody than the Turkish massacre of Armenians in 1915. In Baku, Azerbaijanis knew with absolute certainty that the Yerevan government was preparing to grab all its territory and assert an Armenian kingdom with the help of émigré millionaires in Los Angeles.[2]

Even the territorial integrity of the Russian Federated Republic, which contains about half the population and two-thirds of the territory of the old Soviet Union, is constantly beset by non-Russian ethnic minorities in various regions of the country. During the mid-1990s, Chechnya had a strong separatist movement even though Russia physically surrounds Chechnya on three sides. Nor is Chechnya alone. As the map in Figure 13–1 suggests, the Russian Federated Republic contains numerous non-Russian communities.

Even the more than 1.2 million Chechens are divided: The separatist movement enjoyed popular support only in the southern third of the country. Russia's presence was actually welcomed in the northern third, while the middle third of the country was mixed. Though a small country, Chechnya is divided into regions under 100 teips, or clan leaders, who fight for control of 400 villages.[3] The Russian government must contend with an unruly province, while the Chechen government has little control over a good part of its legal jurisdiction.[4]

Few countries are completely immune from at least occasional ethnic tensions. Frequently considered the most successful story of ethnic integration, the United States reveals signs of being something less than a melting pot. As noted American historian Arthur M. Schlesinger, Jr., has incisively written,

> The cult of ethnicity has reversed the movement of American history, producing a nation of minorities—or at least of minority spokesmen—less interested in joining with

---

[2]David Remnick, *Lenin's Tomb: The Last Days of the Soviet Empire* (New York: Random House, 1993), 89.

[3]"Chechnya, No Man's Land," *The Economist*, October 7, 1995, 56.

[4]Russians and Chechen nationalists may hate each other, but both have to contend with the "English myth" that has been transmitted between generations since sometime in the eighteenth century. Somehow, a number of Chechens are convinced that sooner or later they are destined to come under the jurisdiction of the British crown. Thus far, no one in the British government has suggested that the country is ready to annex Chechnya. "Weekend Edition," National Public Radio, December 8, 1996.

FIGURE 13–1   **Russia's Ethnic Republics**

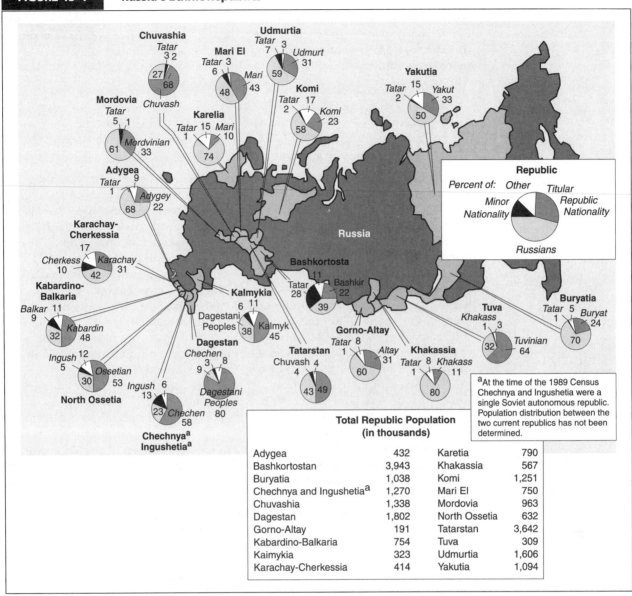

Total Republic Population (in thousands)			
Adygea	432	Karetia	790
Bashkortostan	3,943	Khakassia	567
Buryatia	1,038	Komi	1,251
Chechnya and Ingushetia[a]	1,270	Mari El	750
Chuvashia	1,338	Mordovia	963
Dagestan	1,802	North Ossetia	632
Gorno-Altay	191	Tatarstan	3,642
Kabardino-Balkaria	754	Tuva	309
Kaimykia	323	Udmurtia	1,606
Karachay-Cherkessia	414	Yakutia	1,094

[a]At the time of the 1989 Census Chechnya and Ingushetia were a single Soviet autonomous republic. Population distribution between the two current republics has not been determined.

the majority in common endeavor than in declaring their alienation from an oppressive, white, patriarchal, racist, sexist, classist society. The ethnic ideology inculcates the illusion that membership in one or another ethnic group is the basic American experience.[5]

Ethnicity is an undeniable and critically important feature of the modern state system because ethnic affiliation frequently challenges or replaces national loyalties. It may even prove to be the instrument of the system's future alteration into more and smaller states in which political stability and consensual regimes may be rarities.

13-3 Nationalism and Ethnicity

Nationalism—one's identification with a politically or culturally distinct group of people—has for generations been a crucial determinant of international politics as

Nationalism
A people's psychological bonding with symbols of a common ancestry or of other identifiable links with one another, usually accompanied by a widespread pride in a nation's accomplishments.

[5]Arthur M. Schlesinger, Jr., *The Disuniting of America* (New York and London: W. W. Norton, 1992), 112.

well as a defining feature of who and what an individual is. Even if people do not individually think of themselves as Americans, for example, many non-Americans regard them as such. It's not unreasonable: If people speak a particular language, live in a particular geographical area, and belong to a particular political economy, they are most likely to affiliate with other people who share the same traits. Even more importantly,

> nations exist much more in time than in space. The history of common triumphs and suffering evokes powerful bonds of solidarity for nations large and small. Common suffering seems to be more important in this respect than are victories. The Civil War was probably the most tragic experience of the American nation. Yet both North and South have come to regard this grim American tragedy as a period of glory.[6]

It is possible that the United States would be a less unified country had the Civil War never occurred. The war's unforeseen length and wholesale devastation gave both sides a common if horrific reference point for national coherence. The viability of nationalism apparently depends a great deal on widespread, shared suffering.

National coherence is frequently based on a country's "finest hour," to use Winston Churchill's famous phrase. Russia still memorializes its defeat of Nazi Germany at the cost of at least twenty-eight million Russian lives; Israel maintains the memory of six million Holocaust victims; and China continues to officially honor the surviving veterans of the Long March during the 1930s, which cost hundreds of thousands of lives but saved the communist cause. It may be trite, but it is still accurate to conclude that a people who endure great privation together tend to remain an integrated group. There is nothing like a mortal danger to a country (or the lingering memory of one) to keep a people unified.

Nationalism frequently invokes a "heroic age" that comes close to deifying a country's founders. In a dictatorship, deification is actually insisted upon—huge statues and banners as big as city blocks display images of the country's current or past leaders. Democracies are hardly immune from this practice, though it is usually both more dignified and more modest. The United States, for example, inculcates respect for its founders, the wise assemblage of persons who created the country's successful political and legal institutions. Those who met in Philadelphia in 1787 and formulated the U.S. Constitution, for example, are respectfully referred to as the "Founding Fathers" (not very dissimilar to the "Fathers of Rome" title given to Roman senators during the period of the Republic). Yet these individuals, while well versed in political philosophy, were also rather good politicians. Many of them went on to hold high office. Some also had their lesser attributes. Alexander Hamilton, a prime mover for adoption of the Constitution and the first Secretary of the Treasury, was embarrassed by the public exposure of an extramarital affair and was later killed in 1803 in a duel with the then third vice president of the United States, Aaron Burr. All in all, though, Americans have been fortunate and usually well served by their political leadership. Other countries may have a problem in this regard: The Russian tsarist regime that ended in 1917, for example, was characterized by a royal family uninterested in and totally out of touch with the people and thus is not a period Russians would regard nostalgically; nor did the early communist leaders such as Lenin provide enduring idols.

Nationalism has great staying power. Both communists and democrats have been monumentally wrong about nationalism, for similar reasons. Each assumed that nationalistic fervor would gradually and quietly dissipate as economic prosperity increased and was more equitably distributed. Once widespread prosperity was achieved, the thinking went, loyalties to one's ethnic community would be reduced to insignificant and peaceful levels. Leaders expected that parochial boundaries based on ethnicity or religion would gradually dissolve as economic and technological improvements became available to more and more people.

---

[6]John G. Stoessinger, *The Might of Nations: World Politics in Our Time*, 10th ed. (New York: McGraw-Hill, 1995), 8.

To some extent and in several places, this phenomenon did occur. Many individuals have become more concerned with their stock portfolios than with the skin pigmentation, accents, or religious beliefs of their neighbors. The difficulty, of course, is that economic progress is not a given. Once an economic downturn occurs, as it did in several West European countries during the 1990s and into the early 2000s when unemployment accelerated to and stubbornly remained at 10 or 12 percent, there is rarely a shortage of political opportunists to blame the economic problems on any newly arrived immigrants, especially those of a different color or religion. Economic motivations partly explained German and French reluctance in 2003 to support American determination to disarm Saddam Hussein's regime by force. A war might mean a cutoff or rationing of oil, an event that Germans and French would find more inconvenient than Americans. Moreover, one out of every eight inhabitants of France is a Muslim, a high enough proportion to give the government pause.[7]

The idea that people who achieve material prosperity tend to forget their nationalist attachments can be pervasive, but it is also wrong.[8] Part of the delay in fully integrating the member states of the European Union is the reluctance of several countries to accept what they view as infringements on their national sovereignty. There is substantial opposition to European integration in several countries, including the United Kingdom. The resentment is based on the fear that national concerns would be relegated as inferior to continental concerns.

13-3a Ethnicity's Revenge

In coming years, the 1990s may be recalled as a decade when nationalism intensely asserted itself as soon as it had the chance. Hundreds of ethnic groups, seemingly dormant for long periods of time, loudly insisted that their entire communities accord them ultimate loyalty. It's all rather ironic: The global economy is relentlessly expanding, and countries are becoming increasingly interdependent through commerce and trade; yet the countries and the ethnic communities within them work all the harder to emphasize their distinctiveness, protect their special traditions, and separate themselves from what they regard as unwarranted interference.

A global society has both advantages and disadvantages. However, some ethnic communities interpret the advantages and disadvantages differently. For example, some communities might regard integrated and interrelated communities and global development in technology as benefits; others view them as encroachments and sources of instability. Instead of breaking down ethnic cultures, modernization is in a curious way reinforcing them. Millions of people throughout the world, most noticeably in the developing countries, are unnerved by the sudden technological penetrations into their lives. Their reaction is personal and visceral: They cling steadfastly to the core of their community's defining features. The ties to community become the ultimate loyalty, while the outside world is viewed with hostility and suspicion. Legal as well as illegal immigration from Mexico to the United States, a trend that is at least a century old, is obviously and substantially influencing American demography.[9]

An ethnic group's desire for recognition and autonomy is both natural and understandable. Unfortunately, it is also provocative and unnerving to a national government fearful of dismemberment. Even worse, ethnic aspirations may destroy international stability and raise some disturbing questions. How many sovereign entities can the international system comfortably or reasonably support? How far

---

[7]Richard W. Stevenson, "Antiwar Protests Fail to Sway Bush on Plans for Iraq," *The New York Times*, sec. A, February 19, 2003, 1A and 12A; and Christopher Hitchens, "The Rat That Roared," *The Wall Street Journal*, sec. A, February 6, 2003, A18.

[8]For a superb explanation of how wrong, see Isaiah Berlin, "The Bent Twig: A Note on Nationalism," *Foreign Affairs*, vol. 51 (October 1972), 30–36.

[9]John M. Broder, "Immigration, From a Simmer to a Scream," *The New York Times*, Section 4, p. 1, May 21, 2006.

TABLE 13–1	Economic Differences in Italy	
Region	**Population**	**GDP per Head**
All Italy	58.1 million	$17,099
Northern Italy (north of Florence)	25.9 million	$20,573
Southern Italy (Florence and southward, including Sicily)	32.2 million	$14,308

can the widespread desire for sovereignty be taken? How big should an ethnic community be to possess a territorial state? One scholar suggests that:

> The emergence of states like Slovakia, the collapse of other states, like Somalia, and the continued existence of insignificant ministates confirm that statehood is no longer a "big deal."[10]

At the same time, it is clearly impractical for thousands of identifiable ethnics to establish their own territorial states. There is some doubt that all or even most of them really want one. Many do because they feel uncomfortable in their current political situation. Iraq, India, China, Canada, and Sri Lanka, for example, all have ethnic minorities distinct from the majorities in terms of language, religion, and overall culture. In all of these places, an ethnic or religious minority is struggling to preserve its identity.

These are only three of perhaps dozens of states that face or have already endured partition. A previous chapter examined the problems associated with partition. What alternatives to partition exist?

1. *Failed states:* Somalia in eastern Africa unraveled in the early 1990s as clannish loyalties, always stronger than state loyalties in Somalia, became undisputed first attachments. A state fails when a central authority no longer exists, or does not receive much attention or respect if it does exist. By 2006 the central government in Somalia controlled less population and territory than its opponents.

2. *Regional secession:* The breakup of Czechoslovakia in 1993 into the Czech Republic and Slovakia was a peaceful process as was the secession of Singapore from Malaysia in the 1970s; Quebec's possible departure from Canada may become another one. These are exceptions, though; most secessions involve a prolonged conflict. The secession of Bangladesh from Pakistan in 1971 was ultimately successful but success was in great part facilitated by a war. A regional secession occurs most often because the region's ethnic community is distinct from the rest of the country in culture, religion, language, history, and possibly all of these. Even long-standing and relatively stable democracies such as Italy's have strong separatist movements. In Italy's case, the Lombard League is determined to peacefully separate the northern and most prosperous third of the country from the rest (Table 13–1).

   Cyprus represents another possible secession. Turkey occupied the northern third of the country in 1974 to protect the Islamic Turkish minority living there from what they perceived as the political and economic domination of the Christian Greek majority. Cyprus has been a divided country ever since and shows no likelihood of reuniting (Figure 13–2).

3. *State dissolution and "refederation":* It is possible that a state's disintegration makes good sense over the long term. Nothing engraved in stone says that every state must have a single center of political authority. Local jurisdictions often manage their affairs well, and arbitrarily drawn frontiers—say, those in Africa that Europeans designed—aren't always considerate of tribal or regional divisions.

---

[10]Gidon Gottlieb, *Nation Against State*, 19.

FIGURE 13–2   **Division of Cyprus**

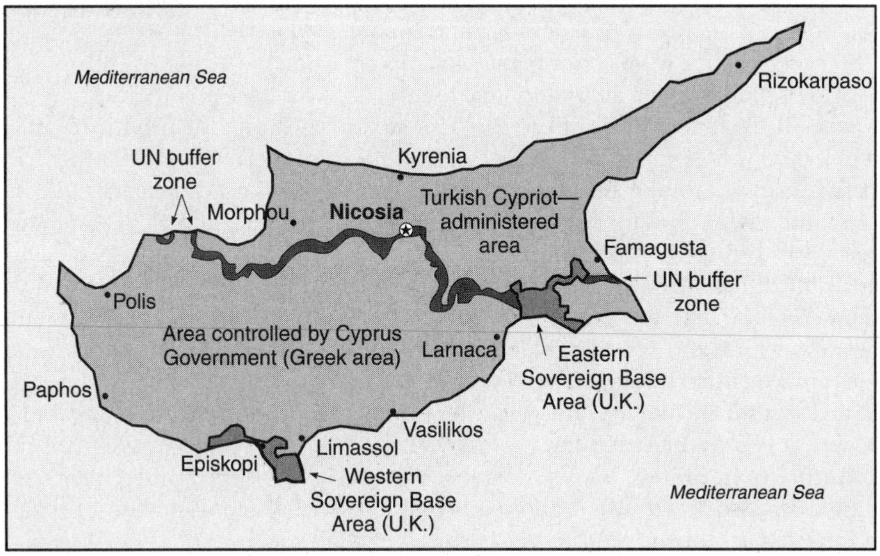

Osama bin Laden is officially a wanted criminal in both Afghanistan and Pakistan, but apparently he is enjoying the protection of regional warlords who in effect control portions of the country in which the central government is not effective or even in evidence. Despite the destruction of much of his al-Qaeda terrorist network and the effectiveness of the American military's attack on its strongholds in Afghanistan, bin Laden has been neither captured nor killed. His survivability is apparently dependent upon the fact that he is hiding in an area on the border between Afghanistan and Pakistan that is in reality controlled by neither country's government.[11] Instead, tribal leaders with whom bin Laden is friendly control these regions and are, for all practical purposes, the law.

Local leadership is not a perfect situation. In the best scenario, local leaders are indigenous to the areas they control with paramilitary personnel (whose loyalty is usually to these particular leaders rather than to an overall political regime or set of institutions). This is not exactly the sort of environment conducive to political democracy, but local chieftains do tend to provide the people with helpful things, such as public schools and medical services, that the central government, often not a beacon of democracy itself, either will not or cannot provide. Considering that there must be stability before democracy has a chance, this may not be a bad compromise.

13-3b Ethnicity and Religion

Most ethnic communities are characterized by a particular religious doctrine. However, one must be careful not to succumb to what can be a stereotype. Plenty of Israelis aren't Jewish, many Irish aren't Catholic, and lots of Egyptians aren't Islamic. While Westerners usually assume that Indians are Hindu, India's 150 million Muslims (about a seventh of the total population) make it the second largest Islamic country in the world. Darfur, a region in western Sudan, is a humanitarian disaster with millions of people practically helpless with the daily threats of rape, slaughter, and starvation making their lives miserable or violently ending them.[12] In great

---

[11]Gerald F. Steib, "The Osama File: What He's Doing, Why It Matters," *The New York Times*, sec. A, February 19, 2003, A6. Nevertheless, a third of al-Qaeda's top two dozen leaders have apparently been eliminated since the September 11 attacks.

[12]Anthony Lake and Francis Fukuyama, "Darfur's Fleeting Moment," *The New York Times*, Section. 4, p. 15, May 21, 2006. By fall of 2006, at least 200,000 Darfuris had been murdered. See "The Arab World," *The Economist*, October 21, 2006, 27.

part, all of this is occurring because of the racial and religious composition of Darfur, black and Christian, and the designs of the quasi-government forces such as the Janjaweed to subjugate or destroy entire communities that are opposed to or different from the mostly Arab and Islamic Sudanese majority.

Stereotypes can sometimes persist no matter what the reality is. Ethnics who belong to a religion that the state finds disagreeable can face severe discrimination or worse. In fact, religious differences are capable not only of producing ethnic conflict, but even of spawning ethnic communities themselves. Consider the dreadfully familiar example of Bosnia, in which powerful religious differences have created ethnic divisions. The reason Bosnian Croats, Muslims, and Serbs tend to be physically indistinguishable from one another is because they aren't very racially or historically different. All three "speak the same language and share the same land and much of the same history,"[13] but it is their religious differences that cause their separation within the Bosnian society. Given the right set of circumstances, usually engineered by unscrupulous, ruthless, and manipulative political leaders, religion can furnish a sort of artificial but pervasive ethnicity that can be every bit as competitive and violent as the real thing.

Ethnic communities, even in pluralist societies such as the United States, tend to be closely associated with a dominant religious faith. A combination of religion and ethnicity is not in itself necessarily or inevitably violent. The religious factor though, has the potential to aggravate perceived or real differences between ethnic groups. Fear of "the other"[14] intensifies when the other's religious practices *and* ethnic background differ from those of the prevailing majority.

It is far from a coincidence that ethnic conflicts usually have a religious dimension. Israeli Jews versus Palestinian Muslims and Christians, and Bosnian Muslims versus Serb Orthodox and Croatian Catholics are only two of many prominent examples. The Egyptian Coptic Christian community, increasingly under attack from radical Muslims, considers itself ethnically as well as religiously separate from the country's Islamic majority. Many Copts, perhaps a tenth of Egypt's population (and a higher proportion in some of the country's southernmost regions) believe themselves the only authentic Egyptians, take pride in the fact that Egypt was the first country to convert to Christianity, and consider themselves the direct descendants of the country's ancient inhabitants. They regard Muslims as invading Arabs and latecomers, unwelcome and uninvited arrivals.

From all of this, some tentative conclusions about the links between religion and ethnic revivalism can be drawn:

1. In the overwhelming majority of cases, religion reinforces and, on occasion, even predominates ethnic perspectives on the world. India may be the largest and most important example of this phenomenon. India and Hinduism preceded Christianity by at least 1,500 years and Islam by 2,000. India's cultural and, later, its national character developed in tandem with the ethical and social features of Hinduism. Indian nationalism is inseparable from Hinduism, as far as India's more conservative Hindu elements are concerned.

2. Religion and ethnicity reinforce one another both culturally and politically. If one is attacked, the other is, too. European Christians crusading against Arab Muslims certainly demonstrated this phenomenon during the Middle Ages. At the same time that European Christians and Arab Muslims were attacking one another, Turkish Muslims were attacking Indian Hindus. In each case, the objective was nothing less than the destruction of a faith and culture.

3. Whenever one religion is fighting to expand, another feels it is under negative and perhaps violent attack. Indian Hindus justifiably felt persecuted by Muslims in much the same way Arab Muslims believed European Christians were

---

[13]William Finnegan, "Salt City," *The New Yorker,* February 12, 1996, 48.

[14]"The Pope Speaks at U.N.: Human Rights and the 'Risk of Freedom,'" *The New York Times,* sec. A, October 6, 1995, A16.

unjustifiably aggressive during the Crusades. Entire civilizations consider themselves in a fight for their very survival, even today.

4. Religion combined with ethnicity can become a catalyst for civil war if a minority feels it is put upon or abused by a country's political center. A minority is often not a minority in certain sections of the country. In some Indian states, for instance, Muslims are a numerical majority; in the western Chinese province of Xinxiang, Turkish Muslims are a numerical majority. The Indian and Chinese governments worry with reason that these communities may attempt to secede, a prospect that often receives encouragement from kindred peoples on the other side of the border.

Of course, different religions that feel beleaguered can find it convenient to support a common cause. In the southernmost region of Lebanon, until 2000 in Israel's "security zone," Lebanese Christians joined with the Israeli Defense Forces to fight Shia Muslims.[15] Even aside from this conflict, Lebanon is a country divided and subdivided into sectarian communities, as discussed in a previous chapter. Lebanese Christians and Israelis alike are convinced that the military expression of the radical Shiites, the Hezbollah, is a mortal threat, an assumption that prompted the Israeli incursion into southern Lebanon during the summer of 2006. Lebanon is a country politically defined by its religious divisions (Figure 13–3). The southern Lebanese conflict indicates how durable religious conflicts can be: This particular war has been going on and off since the middle 1970s, and no end is in sight after three decades of fighting. The roots of the conflict, of course, go even further back, perhaps to the Middle Ages.

13-3c Ethnic Conflict and Migrations

National borders are more porous than they have been in much of modern history. Citizens of the fifteen European Union member states are moving with greater ease across borders than ever before. Hundreds of thousands of Americans and Canadians cross their 3,000-mile frontier daily. Yet these examples pertain to western countries, many of which have taken strong measures to seal these same frontiers against anyone they don't want to let in. At the same time, the numbers of people who desire to emigrate (or whose governments have "encouraged" them to leave) have exploded, along with their levels of desperation.

During the eighteenth century, British courts exiled criminals and prostitutes to sparsely inhabited and economically backward places such as Australia and parts of America, both to get rid of them and to help settle vast stretches of territory. While this model has little to do with ethnicity, other governments have applied it in a selective and often vindictive fashion; during the summer of 1980, the Cuban government sent hundreds of its most violent criminals to a place the Castro regime felt richly deserved them—the United States. Similarly, shortly before World War II, the Nazis practiced ethnic cleansing and sought to remove Jews and others they considered undesirable from Germany. Other countries were not eager to take in these refugees. The German government placed nearly 1,000 unwanted persons—mostly Jews—on a "ship of the damned" in 1938 that no country allowed to dock, including the United States, where the Coast Guard turned the ship away at the border of American waters.

Whether they are expelled or sincerely desire to leave a country, immigrants have sometimes become a remarkable asset to a country and have other times presented a serious social and economic problem. The movement of so many people exposes reluctant or hostile governments unprepared to receive them. Extensive migration in the closing years of the twentieth century influences both the domestic and foreign policies of numerous governments.

---

[15]"Israel's Forgotten War in South Lebanon," *The Economist*, July 15, 1995, 27.

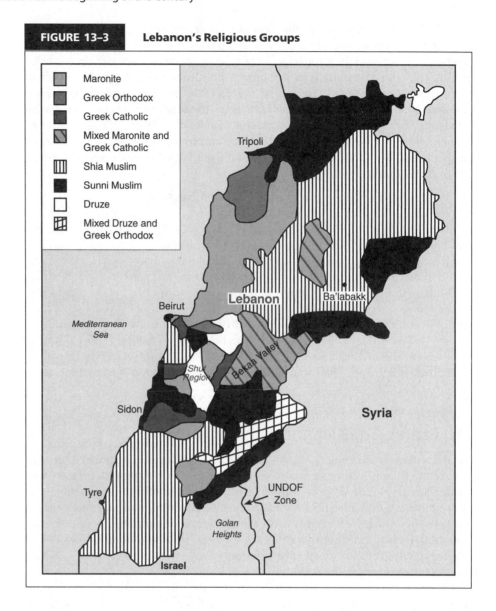

FIGURE 13–3   **Lebanon's Religious Groups**

What is causing the movement of so many people—perhaps as many as twenty million each year since 2000—across borders around the globe? The numbers are perhaps unprecedented since the fall of the Roman Empire 1,500 years ago. The complete answer is a complicated one.

The most persuasive response is that the international state system is and always has been incomplete. There are probably hundreds of ethnic communities of substantial size that are unhappy with, feel trapped by, or are violently opposed to national boundary lines that the global community officially recognizes. The farther one is removed from the more familiar and oldest part of this system (Europe, North America, and a few other areas), the less certain the state system becomes. Take Central Asia, composed of countries most Americans are unfamiliar with and, unless they hurry, may not get a chance to know. As one observer has pointed out:

> Central Asia looks more like a medieval map, in which geography and ethnicity—defined by highly ambiguous and ever-shifting centers of power—will matter increasingly more and fixed borders will matter less.[16]

[16]Robert Kaplan, "Countries Without Borders," *The New York Times*, October 16, 1996, A14.

Central Asia contains the six former Soviet republics that are predominantly Muslim. American ignorance of the region is even more astounding considering the amount of natural wealth it possesses. These republics are experiencing turmoil based on ethnicity, while conflict is also arising over tribal attachments.

The resultant civil wars have created a form of forced migration as large numbers of refugees flee from warring sides and the usually simultaneous collapse of the central government. Numerous states from Turkey to India are in peril.[17] Some are experiencing a decline in stability as central governments lose control of large stretches of territory and population. Northwestern Turkey, for example, is the home to several million Kurds who have resisted the encroachment of Turkish culture and language and political authority for decades. This is a community the Turkish government refuses to refer to by name; instead they are officially called "mountain Turks," as though refusing to recognize the problem will make it go away. The Indian state of Kashmir has been disputed territory since India and Pakistan became independent in 1947. A mostly Hindu India insists on retaining control of a state that is mostly Islamic and whose population might want to join Pakistan if given the opportunity.

Trouble is brewing even in supposedly stable countries. Previous discussions have mentioned the separatist tendencies in safely democratic countries such as Germany, Canada, and Italy. The situation in Germany is especially volatile. East and West Germany were separated for about forty-five years along ideological and political lines. West Germany grew to become the third biggest economy in the world, while East Germany languished as a communist society. When the two parts reunited in 1990, West Germany undertook to rebuild the eastern economy. East Germans have resented what they see as condescension on the part of West Germans. West Germans have resented the resentment of the *Ossis,* as the East Germans are called.

It seems safe to say that after a period of adjustment, Germany will eventually become a thoroughly united country. But the Germans demonstrate that even very similar cultures can, over a period of time, become very distinct communities. When the Berlin Wall was standing (from 1961 to 1989), Ossis used to risk their lives to escape to the West. Since the Wall came down, Ossis have grown apprehensive about the West's rampant materialism and accelerated pace of life. Unity quite understandably ended migration but, unpredictably, created other difficulties.

What conclusions can safely be drawn about ethnicity and migration?

1. Migratory patterns since the 1970s have acquired an increasingly ethnic character. Millions of North Africans have moved to France and Italy, West Indians and South Asians have moved to the United Kingdom, Turks and other Middle Easterners have gone to Germany, and Latin Americans have migrated to the United States, often because they were officially or unofficially encouraged to do so. Menial jobs were available in the new homeland, and within a generation or two, the children and grandchildren of these immigrants rose in economic and social status to white-collar professions.

2. By the mid-1990s, a sort of reverse immigration began. This one was again ethnic in nature, but the pattern was to move *away from* Western countries, an idea nearly unheard of a generation earlier. Well-educated individuals from Europe and North America who possessed "transferable skills"—usually computer and financial expertise—were on the move to East Asia and other rising economic and technological powers. A wave of blue-collar migration also began around this time. British skilled and semiskilled workers, for example, began moving to places such as Hong Kong to accept relatively good-paying jobs that the indigenous Chinese labor force didn't want.[18] The immigration of skilled people in substantial numbers is probably a healthy sign for the global economy. Unfortunately, these are the exceptions rather than the rule of migration—at least, so far.

---

[17]Ibid.

[18]"Marketplace," National Public Radio, October 14, 1996.

No matter which migration patterns prevail, hospitable welcomes can become scarce, especially in times of economic hardship. The long-held notion that Americans (with the exception of indigenous communities) would always welcome immigrants in the United States—where almost all citizens are themselves the descendants of immigrants, where immigrants have historically strengthened and vitalized the economy, and where newcomers have made useful social contributions—was in serious jeopardy by the 1990s. Many people began concluding that the United States had received all the immigrants it could handle and that their presence was straining public services. This idea gained momentum during the 1990s, especially in states like California that had accommodated a large proportion of the new residents.[19]

In sum, ethnicity definitely plays an important role in a substantial and growing anti-immigrant bias. By 2006, Germany had about eight million foreign residents within its borders, nearly 10 percent of the total population and the largest number of any west European country. The steadily increasing community of non-Germans had been growing since the 1960s when Germany was experiencing an economic revival and there was a need to import foreign workers. The explosion of the immigrant community coincided with a period of rising unemployment. This combination predictably increased expressions of intolerance toward foreigners. Some of these expressions became violent and evoked disconcerting reminders of Germany's Nazi era.[20]

After September 11, 2001, Americans came to the conclusion that they are the target of choice of Islamist terrorists. The prevailing American view of terrorists, though, quickly became one of stereotyping: Terrorists were assumed to be from the Middle East and were radical Islamists. Certainly, this observation was true of the perpetrators of 9-11. However, the United States also has homegrown or domestic terrorism to deal with as well. Yet those who originate from or present an appearance of Middle Eastern origins have become suspect in the minds of many Americans. This is a pity because most immigrants from the Middle East are law-abiding citizens. Indeed, many of the Middle Eastern immigrants live in the United States because they sought to escape persecution and even death in their own countries.[21] In other words, they are in the United States because they, similar to the earlier arrivals that began around 1620, seek to save their lives and protect their freedoms.

Compared to France and Germany, which have seen anti-immigrant biases erupt into violence, the United States suffers a mild case of anti-immigrant feelings. French and German youths, mostly unemployed and often inspired by racist ideology, have occasionally resorted to beating up foreign workers from North Africa and the Middle East. These outbursts are probably at least partially traceable to economic conditions. During the mid-1990s, France and Germany experienced double-digit unemployment rates, while the United States maintained a rate of only 5 percent. These rates lasted into the 2000s, and in the United States worsened to about 6 percent because of the bursting of the dotcom bubble and a domestic recession.

Some ethnic communities are integrated into a society's political economy more easily than others. In countries such as Canada and the United States, integration occurred with a minimum of acrimony. In places such as Japan or Iceland, integration doesn't occur at all because foreigners are not encouraged to migrate there (Japan) or because few people want to immigrate (the extremely cold climate of Iceland is an example). The political impact immigrants make can be severe and enduring. Authoritarian regimes are often unhesitatingly brutal in throwing out or even committing genocidal acts against unwanted ethnic and religious communities.

---

[19]"Welcome and Stay Out," *The Economist*, May 14, 1996, 55.

[20]Ibid.

[21]Ibid.

Finally, immigration will almost certainly be a permanent component in considerations of ethnicity and one that worries several countries. Governments opposed to the United States going to war with Iraq in 2003 based some of their reluctance on the fear that wartime dislocations would create yet another refugee problem. Actually, most Iraqis who left their country did so before 2003 because they were afraid of the violent excesses of the Saddam Hussein regime. With millions of people on the move, either as legal immigrants or as refugees fleeing war zones, economic impoverishment, or natural catastrophes, it is inevitable that the most developed parts of the world will have to deal with the impact. National debates on immigration will increasingly take on an ethnic flavor as large groups of people from Third World and destabilized countries attempt to improve or save their lives.

Chapter Summary

1. The international state system has expanded rapidly since 1945, multiplying the number of states in the world. Some countries have arisen without establishing reliable political institutions.
2. Mutual fear and loathing between different ethnic groups surfaced dramatically as the Soviet Union collapsed. The recent conflict between Russians and Chechens is actually a renewal of a conflict that dates back to the 1850s when Russians began to occupy Chechnya.
3. A nation often is unified by a people's history of common suffering. Once nationalism is firmly established, it tends to override a society's other considerations, including economic self-interest.
4. In the post–Cold War era, a state's collapse is no longer unusual. Countries with no viable government, such as Somalia, are countries in name only. Other countries with competing ethnic communities may survive in partitioned or fragmented form.
5. Religion plays a significant role in the division of people into groups. Many of these groups perceive themselves and others as different ethnic groups, even though physically and historically belonging to the same ethnic background.
6. Ethnic conflicts have caused increasing numbers of people to migrate. Millions of people are on the move across the planet.
7. In modern times (since about 1500), migratory patterns have chiefly emphasized the movement of Europeans to the Americas. Current migratory patterns still emphasize the movement of migrants from developing nations to both Western Europe and North America. However there is noticeable migration of skilled workers who find tempting opportunities in selected developing countries such as Kuwait, Taiwan, and South Korea.
8. The influx of large numbers of nonwhite and non-Christian immigrants is significantly changing the demographics of several Western countries. Extremist and nationalist political elements resent this development and are quick to take political advantage of an unfavorable economic environment, blaming economic woes on immigrants.
9. The immigration patterns of the 1990s will likely continue well into the twenty-first century.

Chapter 13 Quiz

1. By 2003, the United Nations included member states that numbered around
   a. 200.
   b. 150.
   c. 75.
   d. 25.

2. Each of the following ethnic groups has its own state except
   a. Turks.
   b. Kurds.
   c. Tamils.
   d. Poles.

3. Isolationism was a policy practiced for most of its history by
   a. Canada.
   b. Germany.
   c. Russia.
   d. the United States.

4. An example of ethnic cleansing occurred during
   a. genocidal acts of Turks against Armenians.
   b. the Serbian occupation of Bosnia.
   c. German-orchestrated mass murder of European Jews.
   d. all of the above.

5. An example of a country's "heroic age" is
   a. China's "Long March."
   b. America's "Founding Fathers."
   c. Britain's "finest hour."
   d. all of the above.

6. The east African country of Somalia is an example of
   a. the collapse of a state.
   b. peaceful secession.
   c. successful entrance into the global economy.
   d. model democratic processes.

7. The second largest Islamic country in the world is
   a. Indonesia.
   b. India.
   c. Iran.
   d. Iraq.

8. In the western Chinese province of Xinxiang, the majority of the population is
   a. Han Chinese.
   b. Indian.
   c. Turkish Muslims.
   d. Coptic Christians.

9. The six Islamic republics of Central Asia were formerly a part of
   a. China.
   b. the Soviet Union.
   c. the Middle East.
   d. northern India.

10. Immigrants from north Africa have tended to move to
    a. Britain and Germany.
    b. Scandinavia.
    c. France and Italy.
    d. Syria and Portugal.

Political Terrorism

As was indicated in a previous chapter, terrorism is a viable threat to the political status quo. The events of September 11, 2001 (9-11), were traumatic not only for the United States but for most of the world. It should be noted, however, that terrorism's targets increasingly included the United States as the kidnappings, imprisonments, and murders of American citizens during the preceding two decades testify. September 11 conclusively demonstrated that terrorism could organize and sustain a global reach that involved systematic planning over a long period of time. It also revealed that terrorism could be effective without the covert support of a major or superpower. Finally, 9-11 showed that the tactics of terrorism had significantly changed. The old adage that terrorism's intent was to kill a few and frighten thousands had transitioned into simply killing thousands and that its further intent was to kill thousands more if at all possible in order to destroy the United States.

The major change in terrorism's tactics, targets, and impacts did not occur suddenly. Some of the more radical forms of terrorism that have become daily references in the electronic and print media over the last several years have in fact been apparent to students of terrorism over many decades. The 9-11 tragedy was long preceded by extreme pronouncements and episodes of violence in several countries characterized by a marked radicalization of Islam in the Middle East and elsewhere. The manifestations of this radicalism can be traced back nearly a century; they were ignored or downplayed, for the most part, because of the more pressing threats of fascism and communism to the Western democracies.

A surge of the literature on terrorism, terrorists, and counterterrorism began appearing by the late 1960s and has accelerated since 9-11. The literature evolved from analyses of terrorism on the extremes of left and right, ideological and often physical attacks on symbols of Western-style capitalism and culture, and political democracy. During this period, the literature understandably treated terrorism as an annoyance and inconvenience more than a threat to overall public safety. Hostage-taking, airplane hijackings, and occasional kidnappings sometimes resulted in lost lives. However, most victims of acts of terrorism could reasonably expect to survive the experience. Terrorism was accepted as another potential hazard in modern life before it became perceived as a serious challenge to the existing order and at war with the United States representing either the West or a superpower in particular and democracy in general. Islamic radicalism emerged as the most serious manifestation of disgust with and revulsion to what were considered the shortcomings of the western global economic and political hegemony. Its ultimate goal was nothing less than to establish a global caliphate or orthodox Islamic theocracy.

14-1 Introduction to and Definitions of Terrorism

It is probably easier to characterize terrorism than to define it. We will try to discuss main characteristics as we work our way toward a satisfactory definition. As a society, Americans have become consumed with the subject since 9-11. Many of us are also fearful that destruction at the level of 9-11 or worse is a real possibility. We deplore and condemn terrorism but find it difficult to formulate an objective definition of the phenomenon. We are confused and angered when we learn that other societies regard the United States as a perpetrator of terrorism and that the planners and perpetrators of 9-11 are widely regarded as heroes in their own and other countries.

Since 9-11, most of the attention of both the public and terrorism experts has been upon the terrorism produced by Islamic radicalism. A critical focus of this brief work will also concentrate on the steadily increasing violence planned and caused by Islamic extremists. However, we do this while noting that "Islamism" is far from being the only source of terrorism currently, in the past, and, in all likelihood, in the future. There are active terrorist organizations in Nepal, Bolivia, Sri Lanka, Northern Ireland, and Spain that have recently caused or are currently causing politically inspired terrorism that has nothing to do with Islam, though on occasion quite a bit to do with religious radicalism.

One source of the difficulty to accurately defining terrorism is that terrorism itself is a constantly changing and evolving activity. Its ideological influences ebb and flow; the radicalism of the extreme political left during the 1960s, for example, encouraged what is by today's standards regarded as modest forms of terror. Planes were hijacked with great frequency, but the passengers had excellent chances of survival. Even the more violent groups, such as the **Red Brigades** in Italy or the **Baader-Meinhof gang** in Germany, tended to carefully select their targets for kidnapping or assassination or, in the case of the Red Brigades, "kneecapping." These groups were convinced that the society they were attacking was evil, corrupt, and decadent, but they displayed an appreciated reluctance to slaughter thousands of people to make their point.[1]

The issue of defining terrorism is itself one that leads to other complications. Defining the concept and the activity one way or another could determine whether terrorists should be dealt with as legitimate fighters for a cause and therefore entitled to be treated as "lawful combatants" under the Geneva Convention for the Treatment of Prisoners of War. To this day, the United Nations has not been able to formulate a definition that would satisfy all of its members (in great part because some of them represent regimes that support terrorism).[2] Different governments treat terrorism in different ways. Some European countries regard terrorists as criminals while the United States regards them as thugs and murderers who should be eliminated as a threat to international society much the same way governments dealt with pirates three centuries ago. However, the American government has assumed since 9-11 that the United States is engaged in a full-scale war with "jihadists" or "Islamists" who are determined to destroy democracy and then turn North America into an Islamic state.

Terrorism's lethality has accelerated dramatically over the last several decades. However, terrorism's primary features and goals remain essentially the same. Terrorists are frequently individuals who are dissatisfied with and/or vehemently opposed to the prevailing political and social order. Yet, the reverse can also occur in which a government may apply terrorism to protect the kind of society it is seeking to create or sustain. In fact, the term terror is derived from its first appearance in France during what we now commonly refer to as the **Reign of Terror** during that country's first revolution that began in 1789. The reign of terror reached its peak during 1792–1794 when the radical elements of the revolutionary regime took power and initiated drastic policies to prevent the restoration of the monarchy it had just overthrown and keep itself in power. The regime desired to create a completely different society from the one it regarded as decadent and corrupt in which society's members addressed one another as "citizen" and in which equality was stressed and social class eliminated. Those who were opposed to this change or who were leftovers from the old regime and considered bad fits for the new one had to go. Many went into exile, but others were executed during the Reign of Terror.

Red Brigades
Founded in 1970, the Red Brigades became the most notorious left wing terrorist group in Italy. Its most notorious activity was carried out in 1978 when it kidnapped and murdered a former Italian prime minister. Popular support quickly diminished following this event.

Baader-Meinhof gang
Also known as the Red Army Faction, this group was formed in 1970 and was violently opposed to the then West German government's supportive relationship with Israel. Andreas Baader and Ursula Meinhof both died in prison and the gang gradually dissolved by the late 1990s.

---

[1]Grant Wardlaw, *Political Terrorism: Theory, Tactics, and Counter-Measures*, 2nd ed. (Cambridge: Cambridge University Press, 1989), p. 16.

[2]See, for example, Jed Babbin, *Inside the Asylum: Why the UN and Old Europe Are Worse Than You Think* (Washington, DC: Regnery Publishing, 2004). See also Irshad Manji, *The Trouble with Islam Today: A Muslim's Call for Reform in Her Faith* (New York: St. Martin's Press, 2003).

It should be noted that terrorism is an old activity that by many centuries precedes the appearance of the term. Some scholars have traced terrorism back centuries, even millennia. During the first century of the Common Era, for example, those opposed to Roman rule in the province of Palestine often resorted to violent acts. The *sicarii* were assassins who would stab to death those who cooperated or collaborated with the Roman authorities.[3]

One scholar who has studied the terrorism phenomenon for decades concluded that "political terrorism is the use, or threat of use, of violence by an individual or a group, whether acting for or in opposition to established authority, when such action is designed to create extreme anxiety and/or fear-inducing effects in a target group larger than the immediate victims with the purpose of coercing that group into acceding to the political demands of the perpetrators."[4] This definition is somewhat incomplete because it does not mention religiously inspired terrorism. However, radical religious beliefs tend to include a political agenda that usually includes the utter destruction of the current social system and its political institutions. Certainly, the desire of, for example, al-Qaeda, to replace American international influence with a global caliphate contains both political and religious influences.

Another student of terrorism has aptly described the phenomenon as follows:

> Terrorism, then, is an act composed of at least four crucial elements: (1) It is an act of violence, (2) it has a political motive or goal, (3) it is perpetrated against innocent persons, and (4) it is staged to be played before an audience whose reaction of fear and terror is the desired result. This definition eliminates football players, lunatics on a killing spree, and the assassin who tries to kill a bad ruler, from the label of terrorist. All acts of violence are not terrorist acts, however heinous the acts may be.[5]

Of course, terrorists can be and occasionally are sociopaths, but they are nearly always a great deal more than that. Terrorists have a political/religious agenda that they are relentlessly pursuing and that takes priority over most if not all other considerations. They consider themselves therefore to be above the laws the rest of us normally subscribe to. They have moral justifications for their proclivity of violence. Americans, for example, who remain bewildered about why al-Qaeda chose to target the World Trade Center and the Pentagon in 2001 simply, according to this mantra, do not understand. They belong to an irredeemably evil system that has caused great harm in the world and whose rapacity threatens to destroy the lives of those devoted to spiritual pursuits as decreed in holy writ.

14-2 Causes of Terrorism

Terrorism is an equal opportunity employer. While it is true that poverty, oppression, and national as well as individual humiliation can encourage the recourse to terrorism, it is also accurate that terrorists are sometimes recruited from comfortable circumstances. Some terrorists have been engineers, physicians, and technicians; many of these were married with young children. Ilich Ramirez Sanchez (aka "Carlos the Jackal") was a notorious terrorist during the 1970s and 1980s when his group attacked various Western personnel and installations. Sanchez, though, came from a prosperous upper-middle-class background in Venezuela and could have led a comfortable life. He chose, instead, to pursue a career as an extremist leftist that was characterized by violence and murder.[6] Many of the 9-11 hijackers

---

[3]David Rapaport, "Fear and Trembling: Three Religious Traditions," *American Political Science Review*, 78, no. 3 (September, 1984), 658–676.

[4]Wardlaw, p. 16.

[5]Cindy C. Combs, *Terrorism in the Twenty-First Century*, 4th ed. (Upper Saddle River, New Jersey: Pearson Prentice-Hall, 2006), p. 19.

[6]Sanchez was arrested in 1994 by the French while being prepped for a liposuction procedure. Apparently, terrorists care about their appearance as much as the rest of us. In 1997, he was tried in France for capital crimes and sentenced to life imprisonment in 1997.

TABLE 14–1	Examples of Terrorism Organizations and Causes	

Organization	Causes for Existence	Ideology
ETA (Basque nationalist group)	Desired separate and sovereign existence independent of Spain	Nationalism
(IRA) Irish Republican Army	Remove British influence in Northern Ireland	Irish Catholic nationalism
Stern Gang (Israel nationalist group)	Forced removal of British and Arab presence in Palestine during 1950s	Jewish nationalism
Sendero Luminoso (shining path)	Desire to establish communist commonwealth in Peru	Radical Marxism
al-Qaeda (the base)	Remove non-Western influence in the Middle East and re-establish Islamic caliphate	Radical form of Islam

were young men who seemed to have bright and prosperous futures in exciting and productive professions.

One common denominator for terrorists is that they generally are young and idealistic. It is most unusual for terrorists to get to be middle-aged or retire. Only a few survive to become "elders of terrorism." Terrorists are mostly men, but, increasingly, women are involved in terrorist acts. Very often female terrorists are relatives of men who have already died committing terrorist acts.

Entire volumes have been published on terrorism's causes and it is almost certain that more will be. (Table 14–1 shows a summary of some outstanding terrorism representations.) The causes themselves change with the times. The political fanatics of the extreme right and left in the 1960s and 1970s have given way to the religious fanatics of Islam as well as other religious belief systems. Sometimes, economic desperation can drive young men and women into the ranks of terrorist organizations, especially if they conclude they have nothing to live for and have no prospect of leading a meaningful life. Suicide bombers in Israel and Iraq, for example, kill themselves in the hope that they will attain paradise and that their families will take pride in their accomplishment. In some cases, though, terrorists destroy themselves and others because they have been intimidated into doing so by organizations intent on creating as much destruction as possible to achieve their ends.

In all of these examples, the terrorist organizations firmly believed that only through violence would their goals be secured.

Religious doctrine itself can encourage and sustain martyrdom. The determination of (mostly) young men and women to murder and die is having a profound impact on the Western democracies, their primary target of choice. The impact on the global economy, our social institutions, and widespread bewilderment about why people hate others so much that they are willing to die to kill them all became issues that, since 9-11, have become part of American and European culture. After 9-11 many Americans immediately asked, "Why do they hate us, and by the way, who are they?"[7] Even now we are uncertain about the answer. But the question is an important one. Understanding the sources of terrorism is critical to blunting its effect or defeating it. It is important to keep in mind that rational behavior is in the eyes of the beholder. Our view of fanatical and often suicidal terrorists is usually influenced by another question: Why in the world do people want to behave this way?

Much has been made of the observation that terrorists are unafraid to die because they are willing to sacrifice themselves for a cause that is greater than their individual lives. However, Islamic extremists are the only current major group that has made death into a desirable outcome for the perpetrator. Suicide bombers are

[7]Walid Phares, *Future Jihad: Terrorist Strategies against America* (New York: Palgrave MacMillan, 2005), p. 144. See also, Daniel Chirot and Clark McCauley, *Why Not Kill Them All? The Logic and Prevention of Mass Political Murder* (Princeton, NJ: Princeton University Press, 2006.)

really martyrs (or *shaheed* in Arabic) enthusiastically desirous to perish for their just cause. The 9-11 hijackers were convinced that their deaths would enable them to enter paradise where all sorts of delightful awards awaited the result of their noble deed. Moreover, in the process of attaining martyrdom, they would destroy symbols of American arrogance and decadence: the World Trade Center and the Pentagon. The loss of other lives in the process was apparently immaterial to them or, they reasoned, 3,000 Americans who worked for or were somehow involved with the financial and military arrogance of the United States deserved to die. The perpetrators felt a sense of moral urgency to kill.

Terrorism, of course, is an emotionally charged term and activity. And most terrorists possess a large amount of resentment of and hostility to the societies and institutions they are determined to destroy. Indeed, terrorism has evolved in its lethality to its ultimate agenda: the complete destruction of an existing social order. Nineteenth- and early twentieth-century terrorists frequently concluded that the society they despised was and would remain beyond redemption. But they also understood that they had neither the means nor, in most cases, the will to act on that conclusion. Many operated under the assumption that killing a head of state or a group of government ministers would suffice to make their point. Few civilians had to worry about their lives. "Kill one, frighten 10,000" was a strategy that made a good deal of sense to most terrorists, most of whom, in any event, were uninterested in killing people on an indiscriminant and massive scale.

The globalization of the world economy increasingly and rapidly changed terrorism's perspective. While much of terrorism remains local or regional, a decidedly apocalyptic school of terrorism sees opportunities for wholesale destruction of entire populations. Until recently, however, only states with autocratic regimes and at least semimodern bureaucracies had the ability commit genocide, the ultimate terror.[8] The twentieth century's rapid advancements in technology and science enabled exceptionally brutal governments to destroy entire ethnic, religious, social, or national communities either in their own countries, such as the Stalinist regime in the Soviet Union (1924–1953), or the Maoist regime in China (1949–1976), or in countries occupied by a state's military as the National Socialist regime in Germany (1933–1945) did to a good part of Europe during the early 1940s. It is worth noting that horrific regimes such as those indicated above systematically murdered or indirectly caused the deaths of at least fifty million people, most of them defenseless civilians. Mao Tse-Tung, the founder of the Communist state in China in 1949, and his regime may have been responsible for seventy million deaths over less than thirty years, the largest number of deaths caused by any government in peacetime, because of unrealistic economic and military goals that blunted agricultural as well as industrial production for decades.[9] Millions of farmer-peasant families were forced to "lend" food to the Red Army. The loan was not one that farmers could afford and it was never repaid, an issue that encouraged widespread hunger in China and actual starvation in several Chinese provinces.

The newest and most current phase of terror doesn't distinguish between men and women or old and young. In this sense, all members of a particular society are guilty of either religious or political sin. The Palestinian terrorist organization Hamas,[10] for example, approves the killing of Israeli children because they will, if allowed to live, grow up to become soldiers who will continue the oppression of the Palestinian people. Al-Qaeda did not consider the World Trade Center or the Pentagon on September 11, 2001, to be full of innocent people merely going to

---

[8]The term "genocide" was coined in 1944 during the Holocaust or mass murder of European Jews. It comes from the Greek word *genos*, a reference to tribe or family, and from *cide*, the Latin term for kill. See Lewis M. Simons, "Genocide and the Science of Proof," *National Geographic* (January 2006), 28–35.

[9]For some fascinating documentation of this number, see Jung Chang, *Mao: The Unknown Story* (New York: Alfred A. Knopf, 2005).

[10]Hamas is an Arabic acronym for "resistance movement." It has operated against Israeli targets since the later 1980s and has itself been a target of choice by the Israeli government and military.

their places of work: rather the nearly 3,000 who perished were considered to be an integral part of the American system of avarice, exploitation, military imperialism, and immorality that was afflicting much of the rest of the world in general and the Islamic world in particular.

Few terrorists consider themselves to be terrorists. Many argue that they are freedom fighters or martyrs for a cause. A radical Islamist cleric, for example, argues that "The meaning of the term 'terror' that is used by the media . . . is the jihad for the sake of Allah. Jihad is the peak of Islam."[11] Holy warriors therefore strike terror in the hearts of their enemies. In fact, victims of Jihad deserve to be terrorized in this sense because they refuse to recognize the supremacy of Islam. Jihadists are not, in other words, killing people out of a misguided ideology that encourages a fight for equality or liberty or the dignity of the individual. Quite the contrary; they are fighting against those things. They do not believe that Islam is struggling to reach parity with other faiths; they are convinced that Islam is supreme to others and that non-Muslims must acknowledge their inferiority and allow themselves to be exploited and discriminated against.

This is not to say that the old standbys that encourage terrorism are lacking. The sense of exploitation, humiliation, and impoverishment help to explain the decision to become a terrorist. It is accurate to suggest that terrorist organizations experience a substantial success rate by targeting impressionable youth, usually men and women in their late teens and early twenties, who at the same time feel as though their lives are without much or any meaning and see little future improvement in either their material or spiritual conditions. We also know that there are many exceptions to all of these features. An individual becomes a terrorist often for very personal and unique reasons. We can't underestimate the emotion of hatred either. It is a strong phenomenon that in most people is short-lived, but in others can inspire a lasting and relentless desire to "get even" or to somehow attain justice. Certainly, we know entire communities of people who have historic memories of horrific episodes that frequently engender violence. Armenians recall the massacre of perhaps as many as 1.5 million of their people during the later stages of World War I (1914–1918) by the Ottoman Turks nearly a century ago. Armenians still occasionally do bad things to Turks, even though today's Turks have no apparent interest in Armenians one way or another. In the Balkans, the Serb, Croat, and Muslim communities each hold grudges against one another that can be traced back several hundred years. As recently as the 1990s, each of the three competed to commit outrages against the other two in Bosnia. On occasion, two of them, usually Serbian Orthodox and Croatian Catholics, would combine to slaughter the third, usually Bosnian Muslims.

Other traumas are more recent but still consume generations and have no foreseeable end. Many Palestinians, for example, recall what they refer to as the *Nakba*, or catastrophe, in which hundreds of thousands lost their homes and property during the first Arab-Israeli War during 1948–1949 and became refugees. Ironically, the Palestinian *Nakba* is also the Israeli great moment when the first Jewish state in 1,900 years came into existence. Different views of history as well as different historical experiences can induce people to turn to terrorism. Northern Irish Catholics and Protestants committed terrorist acts against one another off and on for three centuries that saw no end until late into the twentieth century.

Most terrorist organizations do have finite objectives. The Irish Republican Army (IRA) in Northern Ireland sought to re-unify the five northeastern counties of the island to the Republic of Ireland to the south and west. In other words, the IRA sought to reduce the Protestant majority in Northern Ireland to a permanent minority in a united island. During the 1960s and 1970s, small groups of Quebecois sought the opposite: to violently remove the province of Quebec from Canada

Nakba
An Arabic word for disaster and since 1948 applied to the plight of Palestinians who perceive the establishment of Israel on parts of traditional Palestine to be their own tragedy.

---

[11]Quoted in Bat Ye'Or, *Eurabia: The Euro-Arab Axis* (Madison and Teaneck: Fairleigh Dickinson University Press, 2005), p. 119.

rather than have its six million citizens surrounded by a culture and a nationality that was essentially English. In Sri Lanka, the separatist Tamil community has produced extremists who desire to politically separate Tamils from the Singhalese majority population.

Terrorists are serious individuals who must be totally committed to the cause they serve. It is difficult for anyone to adopt terrorism as anything less than a full lifestyle. An infiltrator of the IRA remembered a conversation with an IRA veteran who told him, "You cannot pretend to be a terrorist. I had to be to do the exact same thing as the IRA man next to me. Otherwise I wouldn't be here."[12]

Does terrorism ever really end? Not really, but there is some hope that at least some terrorist organizations finally get tired of plotting to murder people, if only because nothing substantial seems to be achieved. After four decades of violent acts against the Spanish government in which more than 200 defenseless civilians died, the ETA, the Basque separatist group in northwestern Spain, announced in March 2006 that it was laying down its arms. Since the Madrid train bombings on March 11, 2004, ironically committed by al-Qaeda-linked operatives, revulsion against terrorism had grown so much in Spain that ETA decided it would seek greater autonomy for the Basque region peacefully perhaps because of an immediate and unfounded suspicion that the ETA had caused the outrage. (It had been quick to deny involvement in 3-11, as the date quickly became known.)

Nor do twenty-first-century terrorists limit themselves simply to conventional-type bombs or airplane hijackings. Biological, chemical, and even nuclear weapons are considered by some (though not all) terrorist groups as legitimate weapons with which they can maximize casualties. Biological weapons are nothing new. The plague known as the Black Death that killed off a third of Europe's population during the middle 1300s may have been started by the Tartars who used catapults to hurl infected corpses into the cities they were besieging. The British apparently used biological weaponry during the American Revolution against the colonists in the form of smallpox decades before inoculations against the disease became available.[13] The Japanese during World War II experimented with human subjects and various lethal biological agents. Both the Soviet Union and United States during the Cold War possessed large arsenals of biological weapons. Fortunately, they never used them on any kind of large scale.

Chemical weapons were used in World War I (1914–1918). Chlorine gas was introduced by the Germans in 1915. Two dozen different kinds of poison gases killed hundreds of thousands of Allied and German soldiers. The results were so frightening that poison gas wasn't employed by either side in World War II. However, Saddam Hussein was fond of using poison gas (mustard and nerve gases) against his own citizens (the Kurds) and during the Iraqi-Iranian War (1980–1988) against Iranian military forces. In the case of the Kurds, Saddam Hussein's warplanes simply sprayed toxins during 1986–1987 over Kurdish villages, killing thousands of men, women, and children.

Probably the most fearful weapon of mass destruction (WMD) is the nuclear option. At least nine countries are known to have such weapons because they have admitted possessing nuclear arsenals, but the number could easily be a dozen or more. Israel, for example, probably possesses at least 200 nuclear devices but has not ever admitted that it does. Each arsenal includes anywhere from around a dozen nuclear devices (North Korea) to several thousand (United States and the Russian Federated Republic). Other countries, such as Iran, are known to be actively engaged in attempting to acquire such weapons by either building their own systems or purchasing them elsewhere.

---

[12]Matthew Teague, "Double Bind: The Untold Story of How British Intelligence Infiltrated and Undermined the IRA," *The Atlantic Monthly* (April 2006), 53–58, 60, and 62.

[13]See Elizabeth Anne Fenn, *Pox Americana: The Great Smallpox Epidemic of 1775–82* (New York: Hill and Wang, 2001).

The great fear, of course, is and remains that a terrorist organization might be able to purchase or even build a nuclear weapon on its own and then use it against a large civilian population center.

14-3 Reactions to Terrorism

Terrorism has plenty of advocates as well as practitioners, and terrorists sometimes have popular support for their actions: Palestinian suicide bombers can almost always achieve celebrity status after their deaths. The institutionalized hatred of Israel has resulted in majority support of Palestinians for martyrs, an endorsement that both mystifies and horrifies Israelis and many Western observers. Support for terrorism can be so widespread that terrorist organizations can effectively compete in and even win free democratic elections. This happened in the case of Hamas in January 2006 when it won parliamentary elections held in the Palestinian areas of the West Bank and the Gaza Strip.[14] There was also joyful celebration by many Palestinians in the streets of their cities upon hearing of the carnage caused by the 9-11 hijackers in the United States; Palestinian adults happily distributed sweets to children.

Terrorism, though, can be confusing. Actual or intended victims frequently do not understand why they have been attacked. Because they are almost always perfectly innocent people simply going about their lives, this reaction is understandable. What is not fully or even minimally understood by targeted audiences is the amount of animosity terrorists have toward their victims. The very perception that Westerners, for example, can simply proceed with their lives, usually pursued in relative comfort and security, while others consider themselves to be brutalized is repugnant, for example, to Islamist terrorists.

Democratic societies in particular have all kinds of difficulties in formulating policies to deal with terrorism. Great care is usually taken to be respectful of individual rights including the rights of those who are suspected of or in prison because of terrorist activities.

It's also discomforting to be around targets of terrorism. Understandably, most people would prefer to be somewhere else. Death threats issued against Ayaan Hirsi Ali, a woman born in Somalia in 1970, reared as a Muslim, and a former member of the Dutch parliament, was pressured by her neighbors in an apartment complex in

---

A Note On   HAMAS

Hamas (an acronym in Arabic for the Movement of the Islamic Resistance) was founded in 1987, at the beginning of an uprising (*intifada*) by the Palestinians against the Israeli occupation of the Gaza Strip and the West Bank that had gone on for the previous two decades. The next year, Hamas issued a covenant that stated the solution for the Israeli-Palestinian conflict is the elimination of Israel as a sovereign state and the creation of an Islamic state in Palestine through the means of a holy war. The war would be conducted against Israel and, if necessary, against various secular factions of Palestinians. That Hamas won a free election in Palestinian-controlled areas of Gaza and the West Bank in March 2006 was a shock to nearly everyone, including Hamas. Since then, there have been divisions within Hamas itself on how to deal with Israel and how much Islamic doctrine to implement. In the meantime, Hamas refers to Israel as a terrorist state because of the attacks its military makes on Palestinian installations and has sponsored suicide attacks on Israeli public places.[15] Israel, for its part, has pursued a policy of "focused preventive actions" (targeted killings) to eliminate those Hamas leaders who plan terrorist attacks on Israeli towns and cities, usually in the form of suicide bombers.

---

[14]Hamas won a total of seventy-six seats out of 132, a solid majority that surprised everyone including Hamas itself.

[15]John Kifner, "Islamic Fundamentalist Group Splitting Palestinian Uprising," *The New York Times*, September 18, 1988, A13.

Amsterdam to leave. They feared that Islamic radicals, many of whom have called for Ali's death because of her public comments condemning the treatment of women in Islamic societies and remarks that questioned the basic tenets of Islam, would blow up the entire complex to be sure they killed her.[16] After her departure, Ali's neighbors were relieved to learn that their property values increased.

Terrorism can also influence public opinion in very substantial ways. A May 2006 poll, for example, reported that half of the Dutch people wanted Hirsi Ali stripped of her citizenship and removed from the country.[17] They got their wish when she went into hiding elsewhere in Europe and then the United States. The fear of terrorism and/or the desire to placate a religious or ethnic minority can induce a population and its political leadership to make very substantial concessions. Whether this tactic achieves a desired result—the return to and perpetuation of peace and quiet—is doubtful.[18] What seems to be apparent is that concessions to terrorists are usually regarded as signs of weakness by them. This is more than a casual observation or cliché. When Israelis left the Gaza Strip in 2005, some Palestinians simply regarded this move as tangible proof that Israel was on the run and expected to achieve similar results with continued violence in the West Bank.[19] They assumed it was another sign, like the earlier Israeli withdrawal from southern Lebanon a few years earlier, that Israel had been worn down by the casualties the country had sustained to maintain its presence in these places.

Some governments, particularly the United States and Israel, early on announced that they would not under any circumstances negotiate with terrorists or accede to their demands. The idea of negotiating with terrorist organizations is basically a repugnant one to those governments that are genuinely persuaded that talking to terrorists is immoral and no different than negotiating with criminals. Of course, the reverse is also true: Many terrorist organizations have absolutely no interest in talking to a regime that it considers evil. Thus, for example, Hamas will not recognize Israel or any treaties other countries have formed with it while Israel will have nothing to do with Hamas until it recognizes Israel's right to exist and ceases violent activities against the country's citizenry. These diametrically opposed views became very apparent after Hamas won the Palestinian parliamentary elections in 2006 and became the constitutionally chosen government for Palestinian residents of the Gaza Strip and parts of the West Bank.

It's important to note that debates over how to respond to the threat of terrorism can become a national pastime and can also be a point of divisiveness between otherwise like-minded countries, especially democratic ones. For example, internal and foreign critics of American foreign policy have suggested that the 9-11 attacks might have been avoided if the United States had developed greater sensitivity and more understanding when it came to dealing with the Islamic world. American support for Israel that has been continuous since Israel's establishment in 1948 has been often cited as a policy that has provoked outrage in the Arab and Islamic world[20] that has led to radical and violent initiatives against the United States. This school of thought also posits that by taking a more conciliatory stance toward the Palestinians, there would be less rancor toward the United States.

---

[16]Marlise Simons, "Muslim's Loss of Dutch Citizenship," www.nytimes.com/2006/05/18/world/europe/18 dutch.html?pagewanted=print. Ms. Ali was also asked to leave the Netherlands because she had lied to gain refugee status. She accepted an appointment with the American Enterprise Institute in Washington, DC, and moved there in 2006. Ali had also collaborated with Theo van Gogh, a Dutch movie producer, to bring out a ten-minute documentary entitled "Submission," on the exploitation of women in Islam, another reason many radicals wanted her dead. Van Gogh was indeed murdered by an Islamic radical who shot and then stabbed him to death; Ali, after receiving death threats, got around-the-clock security from the Dutch government. Ali is regarded by Islamists as an apostate and blasphemer, both offenses punishable by death according to the Quran. During the same year, the aftermath of this episode eventually led to the resignation of the government.

[17]Daniel Schwammenthal, "Dutch Courage," *The Wall Street Journal*, May 20–21, 2006, A8.

[18]R. James Woolsey, "West Bank Terrorist State," *The Wall Street Journal*, May 23, 2006, A16.

[19]Ibid.

[20]The most recent example of this criticism is the controversial publication by John Mearsheimer and Stephen Walt, "The Israel Lobby," http://www.1rb.co.uk/v28/n06/mear01_.html, which itself has been severely criticized as a one-sided and unreasonable condemnation of a reliable American military and political ally.

When democracies react to terrorism events, there are usually legal and constitutional restraints. The American government during the Bush administration has
been cited by its critics as employing extra-constitutional means in its efforts to
monitor telephone conversations and inspect financial records of those considered
to be current or potential terrorists and their supporters. Overall, however, it has
become increasingly important to keep track of international money transfers inso-
far as they are supportive of terrorist plans to kill and destroy people and buildings
met with nearly universal endorsement.[21]

Other reactions to terrorism are more divisive. Israel has applied a policy of
what is widely referred to as **targeted killings** in its efforts to blunt attacks of terrorism against its citizens. Targeted killings are sometimes referred to as "focused preventive actions" by the Israelis, a euphemism for assassinations. Regardless of what
they are called such activities are considered, at least by the Israelis, as part and par-
cel of an effective counterterrorism strategy. Targeted killings are normally implemented to leaders of terrorist groups and cells. Israel isn't the only country that
employs the policy of targeted killings, but it is the country that has probably used
them the most and has not attempted to in any way hide the fact.[22] Basically, the
idea behind targeted killings is to terrorize the terrorists. The logic runs along the
lines that if a terrorist is too busy watching out for her or himself, the terrorist will
have little or no time to plan attacks against others. Targeted killings have been an
Israeli staple of government policy since the early 1970s when Israeli hit teams were
dispatched to kill the organizers of the Munich Olympics massacre of eleven Israeli
athletes in 1972. Members of the hit teams themselves were in turn targeted by the
same Palestinians they were trying to assassinate, but the designated targets were
eliminated.

Perhaps the most principled (though not necessarily the most realistic)
response to terrorism is to pursue its destruction by implementing a thorough-
going democratic political process in a society that is under siege from terrorists.
This has been a strong component of the American policy in Iraq since 2003 after
the Saddam Hussein regime was kicked out of power by the United States and its
allies. However, the tensions among the Sunni, Shiite, and Kurdish communities in
Iraq have made the democratic art of political compromise both difficult and
dangerous.

Sunni Arab Iraqis under the Hussein regime dominated the government, bureaucracy, military, and economy even though they were no more than a fifth of
the total population and naturally miss the substantial benefits that their privileged
positions provided. Because of their country's demographics many Sunni Arabs in
Iraq view the construction of a democratic state as their undoing even if they aren't
particularly sympathetic to the efforts of terrorists.[23] An uncertain number of them
have resorted to incredibly indiscriminate violence against the Shiite Arabs in an
attempt to intimidate them back to the subservient status they were kept in under
the regime of Saddam Hussein and his family.[24]

By 2006, there was in ample evidence the phenomenon of what can be referred
to as "reciprocal terrorism" among Iraqi sectarian communities. Shiites and Sunnis
demonstrated that each could be every bit as murderous toward completely
defenseless noncombatants as the other. Sunni terrorists even murdered Shiites on
the way to the funeral of a friend or relative who had been murdered by Sunnis earlier. Shiites retaliated by killing Sunnis in rather indiscriminate ways. Neither side
spared women and children. The cycle continues in Iraq and elsewhere as each side
becomes more and more reluctant to acknowledge the right of the other to exist.

targeted killings
For decades, Israel has pursued a policy
of assassinating leaders of terrorist groups
to demonstrate that no one is immune
from retaliation. Targeted killings have
become a favorite method of counterterrorism that has also been adopted by the
United States in Afghanistan and Iraq.

[21]"Patriotism and the Press," http://www.nytimes.com/2006/06/28/opinion/28Wed1.html?hp=&pagewanted=print.

[22]Gal Luft, "The Logic of Israel's Targeted Killings," *The Middle East Quarterly* (Winter 2003), Volume X, No. 1.

[23]Fouad Ajami, "Heart of Darkness," *The Wall Street Journal*, September 28, 2005, A16.

[24]"The Death of Abu Musab al-Zarqawi," *The Economist*, June 10, 2006, 43.

BIOGRAPHY

Osama bin Laden (b. 1957)

Since September 11, 2001, Osama bin Laden has been the world's most wanted terrorist. Although his name was well known to American and other countries' intelligence agencies before 9-11, it was mostly unfamiliar outside of those organizations. Bin Laden first came to public notice when he fought against the Soviet occupation of Afghanistan during the 1980s. The Soviet military was forced out of the country by 1988 and bin Laden as well as others was given credit for the Soviet defeat. He established al-Qaeda in the same year. The Soviet Union dissolved three years later. Bin Laden assumed from this victory that if the Soviet Union could be defeated so could the United States. When Iraqi forces occupied Kuwait, bin Laden offered the Saudi monarchy his services in protecting the kingdom from Iraqi aggression, but was turned down. He was outraged when, in 1991, American forces were stationed in Saudi Arabia to launch an attack on Iraq to remove Saddam Hussein's forces from Kuwait. In 1996, he declared war on the United States, but was mostly ignored by his intended victims until 9-11. Two years later, bin Laden declared the formation of a coalition, the International Islamic Front for Jihad Against the Jews and Crusaders, to fight the United States and its allies. In 1998, al-Qaeda also bombed two American embassies in East Africa. The most devastating attack organized and executed under bin Laden's auspices to date was 9-11 three years later. Bin Laden's hatred of Western culture in general and American society in particular, their values and religious beliefs is implacable. Most experts agree that he is planning another and even more horrific attack on American personnel and installations that may involve a weapon of mass destruction. He remains determined to completely remove the American presence in and influence from the Middle East. Ultimately, bin Laden desires to re-establish the caliphate that appeared after Mohammad's lifetime (570–632 A.D.) and was dissolved in the 1920s and Islam overall as the predominant political and religious force on the planet.

14-4 Assessing and Addressing the Current Threat of Terrorism

Throughout the modern history of terrorism, there has been substantial debate over whether the phenomenon should be considered simply as criminal activities or as a very real threat to political and social stability. For many the debate was resolved on 9-11. To an appreciable extent, terrorism and its potential were maximized that day. Some observers clarified the event as analogous to the December 7, 1941, attack by the Japanese on Pearl Harbor that forced the United States into World War II. However, it is important to point out that terrorism is a global curse that occurs, for the most part, outside of the United States and has impacted the lives of millions of people. Russia, for example, has experienced several horrific episodes, including one in its capital city of Moscow that resulted in the deaths of hundreds of people. As is well known, Israel fights terrorism literally everyday. And hundreds of millions of people are regularly terrorized by their own governments that arbitrarily incarcerates and tortures them (Syria), dictates a prescribed and brutally enforced morality (Saudi Arabia), or even starves them (North Korea).

We began this chapter by acknowledging how difficult it is to define terrorism. We also aren't very sure about how much damage terrorism can do to us. The 9-11 episode in the United States, the March 11, 2004, attacks on public trains in Spain, the July 7, 2005, attacks on the London subway system in the United Kingdom, and the September 2004 Beslan school massacre in Russia each killed dozens or hundreds of people, and the daily carnage in Iraq are cruel reminders that terrorism's threat is serious and can be ignored only at great peril. At the same time, we know that terrorists make mistakes and that with the use and sharing of intelligence, most terrorist activities can be thwarted and the damage done by successful attacks can be at least minimized.

All that said, the world remains a dangerous place.[25] Those who study terrorism generally agree that an attack with a weapon of mass destruction (WMD) must be

---

[25]Terror targets can now be anywhere. See, for example, Eric Lipton, "U.S. Terror Targets: Petting Zoo and Flea Market?" http:www.nytimes.com/2006/07/12/Washington/12assets.html.

anticipated and preparations made for its eventuality. A WMD attack is not inevitable, but it is certainly feasible. The AUM Shinrikyo (Supreme Truth) cult was established in Japan in 1987 and, by 1995, had the ability to carry out a sarin gas attack on the Tokyo subway system that killed several passengers and required hundreds of others to be hospitalized.[26] The sarin was produced in the cult's own state-of-the-art laboratories. Terrorism is an increasingly sophisticated phenomenon that has shown itself capable of attracting quite talented technicians and scientists who, provided the proper resources are available, can produce a biological, chemical, or nuclear weapon that can kill hundreds of thousands or millions of people.

We know that regardless of how strong and pervasive it is, military power alone will not thwart or detour terrorists from pursuing their agendas. Many terrorists are willing, sometimes even eager, to die for their cause, particularly if they can destroy the lives of their enemies in the process. Several have stated that they have a supreme advantage because they love death and will receive wonderful rewards when they arrive in paradise. Military power is necessary, but it is only part of a solution. Moreover, because terrorists can operate from virtually any location, there are no safe zones. Everyone is a potential target, an environment that terrorism purposely creates, sustains, and uses to create an atmosphere of uncertainty that terrorists hope will lead to social unrest and breakdown. One of the most important goals for terrorism is to demonstrate that a national government cannot adequately protect its own people from attack. In this way, the government's credibility is weakened because it fails in its first and most essential responsibility to ensure the physical security of its citizens.

Moreover, terrorism is often employed in a cause that has a substantial amount of popular support. One reason terrorism from the ideological extremes of left and right in western Europe during the 1960s and 1970s ultimately failed and dissolved was in great part because the terrorist groups, mostly small in size ranging from a few dozen to a few hundred operatives, never developed any real connection to the society they were trying to dismantle. Many of these groups were infiltrated by police and government intelligence units and all of them were, in any case, widely deplored across the political spectrum.

The terrorism of the early 2000s is very different, especially when considering Islamic radicalism. After the London transport bombings that were perpetrated by Islamic radicals in July 2005, several surveys to gain insight into the feelings of British Muslims were taken.[27] The findings were disturbing to British authorities: 20 percent of British Muslims felt sympathy for the attackers and 13 percent suggested the bombers should be regarded as martyrs in a holy cause. One percent, or almost 20,000 Muslims living in areas of London, expressed their willingness to embrace violence themselves to bring an end to a "decadent and immoral" Western society.[28] All of this suggests that terrorists can live quite comfortably in a "nurturing community"[29] that sympathizes with and is supportive of their goals, including those that may be only achieved through violence.

There is little doubt that the struggle against terrorism will be a long and difficult one and will most likely consume decades. Experts doubt that terrorism will ever be completely eliminated. It has, in fact, become yet another challenge to the overwhelming majority of people of all religious faiths and ethnic backgrounds who simply want to be left alone to pursue their individual lives. To effectively deal with terrorism, it is often advised that its causes must be rooted out: poverty, religious prejudice, ethnic persecution, the Arab-Israeli conflict, the dislocations caused by the expanding global economy, and autocratic regimes that have enjoyed

---

[26]See Michael Dasher, "AUM Shinrikyo," in Cindy Combs and Martin Slann, eds., *Encyclopedia of Terrorism* (New York: Facts on File, 2002), pp. 21–23.

[27]Nearly two million Muslims, the bulk of the Islamic community in the United Kingdom, live in or around London. The overwhelming proportion of these are British citizens.

[28]Daniel Pipes, "The State of Islam in Britain," http://www.jpost.com/servlet/Satellite?cid=1150885973186&pagename=JPost%2FJPArtic . . . , July 12, 2006.

[29]Ibid.

degrees of support from democracies that require essential natural resources to sustain and enhance their economies.

Even if all of these issues were successfully addressed, however, terrorism would continue in some form. There will always be disconsolate groups that resort to indiscriminant violence and, in their rage, hatred, and resentment, spare no one. To contain the worst impacts of terrorism will require international vigilance and an ability by national governments to act in concert to share intelligence while working cooperatively to address the complicated issues from which terrorism is issued.

Chapter Summary

1. Until the early years of the twenty-first century most terrorists were content with murdering a few people to simply intimidate the vast majority who were unharmed. This policy has changed to one in which radical terrorists desire and plan to destroy thousands or even millions of people to accomplish their goals.
2. Terrorism has been perpetrated from the extreme political left and right as well as by agents of religious radicalism.
3. State terror was institutionalized by several regimes during the twentieth century and several political, racial, religious, and ethnic minorities were singled out as dangerous elements that had to be destroyed.
4. Terrorism isn't simply perpetrated by individuals who live in impoverished conditions and have little or nothing to lose; increasingly, terrorism is an avenue taken by educated and relatively well off individuals who consider their targets an abomination.
5. Counterterrorism can be and sometimes is as violent and destructive of innocent life as terrorism itself in part because terrorists often seek shelter within civilian populations.
6. Radical Islamic terrorism is currently the most violent and determined expression of terrorism; its ultimate goal is to establish a global caliphate.
7. Genocide is frequently used by violent regimes that engage in state terror to completely eliminate a community of people considered alien or somehow a threat to the society.
8. Radical Islamists have become the most dangerous terrorists of all because of their interest in acquire weapons of mass destruction and using them to attack large population centers.

Chapter 14 Quiz

1. The current surge of modern terrorism is generally agreed to have began roughly during
    a. World War I.
    b. The American Revolutionary War.
    c. The late 1960s.
    d. September 11, 2001.

2. Jihadists are
    a. similar to Rotarians.
    b. reform-minded Republicans.
    c. a peaceful religious sect.
    d. radical Muslims intent on making war against the United States.

3. The term, "Reign of Terror" was first applied during the
    a. French Revolution.
    b. Russian Revolution.
    c. period of time in the United States when disco dancing was extremely popular.
    d. height of gangland violence in Los Angeles.

4. The two widely recognizable American buildings attacked by terrorists were
    a. the Empire State Building and the New York Stock Exchange.
    b. Mall of America and the Sears Tower.
    c. Wrigley Field and Comiskey Park.

    d. World Trade Center and the Pentagon.

5. Acts of terrorism are very often committed by
    a. men and women.
    b. well educated and employable people.
    c. religious fanatics.
    d. all of the above.

6. The ultimate goal of al-Qaeda is to
    a. work for Arab civil rights in Israel.
    b. live in harmony with Christianity and Judaism.
    c. re-establish the Islamic caliphate.
    d. secularize Arab society.

7. In the Islamic world, a suicide bomber is generally known as a
    a. martyr.
    b. fool.
    c. scholar.
    d. humanitarian.

8. Genocide is a reference to
    a. the complete annihilation of a community of people.
    b. drastic economic reform.
    c. the arrival of the millennium.
    d. the advent of a new political party.

9. Hamas is a terrorist organization headquartered in
    a. Washington, DC.
    b. New York City.
    c. Gaza.
    d. Ankara, Turkey.

10. In 1915, the Armenian people were apparently massacred by the
    a. Chinese.
    b. Turks.
    c. Arabs.
    d. Persians.

11. Saddam Hussein used chemical weapons against the
    a. Kurds.
    b. Syrians.
    c. Palestinians.
    d. Baha'i.

12. Ayaan Hirsi Ali is a
    a. terrorist.
    b. former member of the Dutch parliament.
    c. fervent member of an obscure Islamic sect.
    d. Palestinian refugee.

13. The 1972 Munich Olympics are infamous because
    a. most of the participating athletes cheated by taking steroids.
    b. the German organizers were on illegal drugs.
    c. eleven members of the Israeli delegation were murdered by Palestinian terrorists.
    d. Hezbollah members took several gold medals.

14. All of the following are practitioners of state terror except
    a. Saudi Arabia.
    b. Syria.
    c. Japan.
    d. North Korea.

CHAPTER 15

Summary and Conclusions

KEY TERMS

nuclear threshold
political implosion
pragmatism

supranationalism
universal nation

The issues raised in this text are likely to be around for a long time. The United States and much of the rest of the world are constantly reinventing themselves. During the Cold War, two nuclear superpowers, each having its phalanx of allies and military treaties, competed for influence across the planet, a situation that dominated the international landscape during 1945–1990. When that period ended, there was a brief optimistic surge of hope and even conviction that because a great totalitarian menace was gone, democracy would make tremendous strides. There were very few obvious international predators that could challenge or injure the large democracies. Independent countries that had been Soviet republics—Belarus, Ukraine, and Kazakhstan—inherited and then voluntarily gave up their nuclear arsenals. Things seemed under control. However, the emerging reality was something different: Rogue states such as Iran, and North Korea were bent on acquiring weapons of mass destruction. The North Koreans, by 2003, had already acquired a small number of nuclear weapons, perhaps half a dozen or so, had tested one in 2006, and were determined to build more of them.

Terrorism, a serious problem during the last decades of the Cold War, became more murderous and more daring during the 1990s and early 2000s. It developed and exercised a global reach and has become more sophisticated and technologically proficient. Much of contemporary terrorism is also influenced and motivated by religious fervor that cannot be placated with compromise or concessions. The aim of major terrorist organizations today is nothing less than the total upheaval of modern democratic societies they regard as decadent, immoral, and unworthy of survival.

Politics is itself a manifestation of reinvention; it has to be because of the nature of humankind. Just over half a century ago, Americans regarded Germans and Japanese as monsters and murdering psychopaths. Today, these two nations have stable democracies and have become military and political allies of the United States, as well as economic partners and competitors. Similarly, two generations of Americans viewed Russians as menacing and malevolent adversaries. Now they are generally seen as people in need of encouragement and help to democratize their political system and modernize and privatize their economy. This list of contrasts could easily go on.

This chapter offers some concluding remarks and observations about the overall themes of this text—democratization, ethnic conflict, authoritarian and democratic political institutions, political ideology, and the American role in the global political economy. The chapter also tries to make some projections. Given the less-than-predictable nature of human endeavors, making projections may be risky. But one thing can be said with certainty: The pace of political change is increasing on a global scale, and interesting and unprecedented times are undoubtedly ahead of us.

15-1 American Democracy in a Nondemocratic World

During the half century between 1939, when World War II began, and 1989, when the Berlin Wall came down, signaling the end of the Cold War and the collapse of European communism, the world changed in drastic ways. A hundred or more new states appeared during these five decades. Several others—East Germany, the Soviet Union, Yugoslavia—dissolved. The decade that followed the end of the Cold War has been a period of transition that poses both challenges and opportunities for democracy.

Once democratic institutions and processes are solidly in place, they tend to stay that way. Several chapters, for example, reviewed how executive, legislative, and judicial structures can work to enhance democracy once their integrity is established. Yet it is also apparent that even political leaders who sincerely desire to institutionalize democracy can put off doing so if they are unsure whether they or their country will be around in a few years. For all of that, though, democracy—or at least varying forms of democratization—has made noticeable progress over the last decade and more.

The political and overall culture plays an important role in firmly establishing and sustaining democratic institutions and processes. At times, these processes can all go terribly wrong. In 1848, a strong reformist movement in much of Europe led to modest but durable democratization in several Western European countries. In the German states, however, many reformers were driven underground or emigrated to America, where they were quickly integrated. Some political historians view this dismissal of political reformers in Germany as an important factor in the absence of strong democratic traditions, the Nazi experience, and, in Eastern Germany, nearly half a century of communism.

Individuals affect the world whether they live in democratic or nondemocratic countries. British Prime Minister Winston Churchill (1874–1965), for example, was struck by a taxi cab in December 1936 while crossing a street in New York—a challenging activity then as now, but made even riskier by Churchill's habit of jaywalking. The cab was going only 35 mph; Churchill might well have been killed had the cab been zooming along at 45 or 50 mph. Who, then, would have led Britain through its darkest days in World War II? And what if Churchill's great enemy, the German dictator Adolf Hitler, had died in 1938, before launching World War II? Would he be remembered as a leader who restored the German economy and national morale, even if in a brutal fashion, rather than as a mass murderer and sociopath who committed suicide at the end of World War II in 1945 in preference to surrender and almost certain trial as a war criminal?

Former Egyptian President Anwar Sadat's trip to Jerusalem in 1977 ended thirty years of hostility between Egypt and Israel. Richard Nixon's visit to China in 1972 helped begin the improvement and normalization of relations between that country and the United States. The fact that the last leader of the Soviet Union, Mikhail Gorbachev, and President Ronald Reagan personally liked each other helped trust grow in the relationship between the two nuclear superpowers just as the current friendship between Alexander Putin and George W. Bush has helped ease tensions between the two countries. The friendship overcame Reagan's view of the Soviet Union as the "evil empire"; Reagan discovered that Gorbachev was not himself particularly evil. Together, they helped end the Cold War and consequently helped produce a somewhat safer world.

A personalized style of diplomacy doesn't always work, but that doesn't mean that two sides can't reach some agreement. National leaders may thoroughly detest each other—Ariel Sharon of Israel and Yasser Arafat of Palestine are a good example—but still work out mutually satisfactory arrangements. The trick is to exercise **pragmatism**—experimenting with solutions that benefit both sides—rather than try to fulfill an ideological mission. Personalities matter: While Gorbachev was neither an ideological fanatic nor a paranoid, one of his predecessors, Joseph Stalin, was both—and each left an indelible mark on his country's history.

Political democratization remains an incomplete and far from global process. In fact, there is not even universal agreement that democracy, especially the Western variety, is always a good thing. In December 1996, Chinese government officials escorted a group of American journalists on a visit to a newly built dam the Chinese

pragmatism
A practical approach to politics and diplomacy as opposed to an ideological style. Pragmatists often experiment to see what works and what doesn't.

were particularly proud of. The Chinese wanted to brag about the benefits the dam would bring, such as less seasonal flooding and better irrigated agricultural systems. The American journalists were more interested in asking questions about the amount of environmental damage ecologists said the dam was causing as well as about the more than one million people who were given no choice but to leave their homes to make way for the dam's construction. The Chinese authorities had not considered or taken an interest in these issues, and they certainly didn't want to respond to questions about them. One official abruptly ended the discussion by suggesting to the journalists that "you Americans have too much freedom."[1]

The discussion is instructive—it reveals the great disparity between two very distinct political cultures. The Americans were shocked because no governmental agency in the United States would have had the authority, let alone the nerve, to move large numbers of people without their consent. The Chinese were chagrined that outsiders were questioning their effort to modernize on moral or legal grounds. The remark that Americans have too much freedom was not simply a casual or isolated observation. Clearly, the Chinese believed the American journalists had a lot of gall to make judgments about their actions, and the journalists were incredulous that the Chinese would pursue modernization at the cost of the environment and their own people.

China has the biggest population in the world and one of the fastest growing economies. Over the last decade or so, it has become an increasingly substantial American trading partner. But it also has shown no discernible interest in any political reform that would lead to democratization and its inevitable result—the diminishing of Communist party control (and the power and privileges such control provides) in China. These factors pose a dilemma for an American democracy whose consumers are eager to purchase Chinese products, but who also object to the slave labor system used to produce those goods.

The United States, as the world's military superpower and still the largest economic power, will continue to have to make some morally difficult choices: Is it more important to have an economically healthy relationship with China or to use economic incentives to wean the Chinese government from its less-than-humane policies regarding economic development? Both positions tug at the foundation of American foreign and economic policy and at the essence of America's political culture.

15-2 On the Horizon

The end of superpower rivalry did not mean the beginning of boredom in international politics. This text has already reviewed the challenges that such critical and widespread phenomena as ethnic conflict and the rise of religious radicalism pose to stability. These phenomena are not usually conducive to either democratization or to economic development. In some cases, though, neither of these processes is a priority to movements and governments that desire ethnic cleansing, the installation of a religiously orthodox regime, or both.

Very little is static in international relations. The Cold War's termination is not the end of history, but simply the start of a new and quite different epoch. To begin with, some disconcerting and rather durable aftereffects have trailed the Cold War and the new age of rogue states and terrorism:

1. The menace of nuclear war has been considerably reduced but is far from eliminated. The United States and Russia, for example, had each reduced its nuclear weapons inventory from 27,000 in 1990 to 12,000 by 2000, but this was still more than enough to destroy the world several times over.[2] While

---

[1]"Weekend Edition," *National Public Radio*, December 14, 1996.

[2]Edward L. Rowny, "A New START with Russia," *The Wall Street Journal*, sec. A, December 11, 1996, A22.

neither country wants a nuclear confrontation, both still have an abundance of weaponry.

2. Unpredictable groups or governments have the potential to acquire nuclear weapons, perhaps from a cash-strapped Russia known to lack top-of-the-line security at its nuclear installations. Moreover, a disconcerting number of countries are already on the **nuclear threshold**, on the verge of acquiring nuclear weapons or the ability to build them. Some of these countries—Iran and North Korea, for example—are governed by regimes with long and demonstrative records of irrational and aggressive behavior in the international arena. Some also support political terrorists who would be keenly interested in acquiring a nuclear option.

nuclear threshold
On the verge of acquiring nuclear weapons or the technical ability to build them.

3. While the larger industrial democracies, known as the G7,[3] currently dominate the global economy and possess unquestionable military and technological superiority over any combination of adversaries, they are far from unanimous in their concerns and objectives. For example, France and the United States are often at odds in their foreign policy expressions. The French in 2003 weren't even sure who, the United States or Iraq, should win the conflict. In 1996, each tried to block the other's preference for the United Nations Secretary-General. Even more seriously, the two governments argue over the post-Soviet role NATO will play. The French want NATO to focus more on the Mediterranean theater because of their understandable concern with the political instability and economic difficulties of North African countries. France and other NATO members such as Italy fear that a large influx of illegal immigrants will precipitate economic dislocations and increase political terrorism.[4] The United States, in contrast, focuses more on the possibility of political instability in Eastern Europe and the former Soviet republics and the resultant opportunities for communists or extreme nationalists to come to power. Former communist states such as Bulgaria are strong candidates for **political implosion**, or complete governmental collapse, as the economy continually deteriorates and democracy has not gained enough of a foothold to offer alternatives. Yet, several former communist states, such as Poland and the Czech Republic, were considered success stories by the early 2000s and had both reviving economies and increasingly democratic political systems. More and more attention was by this time being focused on the Middle East because of the decidedly undemocratic and often brutal nature of most of the region's regimes and as a source of political terrorism. Ironically, tyrannical government may be all that is keeping some Middle Eastern states coherent.

political implosion
The collapse of a political system from within, usually caused by a breakdown in public confidence in the economic and political institutions.

4. Political fragmentation as the result of ethnic and/or religious divisions will continue to require American attention and, on some occasions, American intervention. Consider the example of Bosnia. Only a few hundred miles away from a mostly stable, democratic, and prosperous Western Europe, Bosnia is a place where violence still lurks despite the fact that in the last several years the area has been relatively peaceful because of the presence of NATO military forces. A NATO official on duty in Bosnia once observed, "If you need combat soldiers to escort you to your residence, it's not the kind of place where you're really going to feel at home."[5]

5. As the months that led up to the military effort to disarm and dislodge Saddam Hussein from power demonstrated, there is hardly a consensus on how to deal with difficult and predatory regimes. Both France and Germany as well as China and Russia vociferously disagreed with the American policy to forcibly disarm Iraq and preferred instead to pursue diplomacy through the United Nations

---

[3]As indicated in the chapter on the political economy, the G7 includes the United States, Japan, Germany, France, the United Kingdom, Italy, and Canada.

[4]Gail Russell Chaddock, "Paris Tries to Direct NATO's Club Med," *The Christian Science Monitor*, December 9, 1996, 6. See also Lorenzo Vidino, *Al Qaeda in Europe: The New Battleground of International Jihad* (Amherst, New York: Prometheus Books, 2006). For an interesting history of the traditional hostility between France and the United States, see John J. Miller and Mark Molesky, *Our Oldest Enemy: A History of America's Disastrous Relationship with France* (New York: Doubleday, 2004).

[5]Colin Woodward, "Bosnia's Uneasy Peace: One-Year Report Card Shows Gains, Failures," *The Christian Science Monitor*, December 4, 1996, 7.

during the early months of 2003. The United Kingdom, Italy, and Spain, however, were very vocal in their support of United States actions. Interestingly, several of the newer democracies in Eastern Europe such as Poland and the Baltic states also supported the United States.

This list is far from all inclusive. It does suggest, though, at least some of the difficulties that will confront and challenge the United States as it formulates and implements foreign policy in the near future.

15-3 Perception versus Reality

The perceptions one group of people has of other groups make history and drive both national and international politics. Between 1933 and 1945, Germans tortured and murdered millions of Jews, even to the detriment of Germany's national interest, because they were convinced that Jews were an evil scourge that had to be eliminated regardless of the cost.[6] The conviction was a complete fantasy, but it was also one that had a history stretching back to the Middle Ages. Unless people perceive reality with some sense of rationality, individuals as well as entire nations can become victims of dangerous misconceptions.

Millions of Americans during the early decades of the Cold War assumed that Soviet communism was a pervasive threat to their way of life. In this case, a Soviet challenge to American military power actually did exist (although there was never a viable threat that the Soviet economic system would catch up to the American standard of living). This was a containable challenge, yet the perception that communists were somehow able to subvert and destroy American society persisted for decades. Paranoia overcame common sense for a time as not a few Americans stocked canned goods in fallout shelters in case of communist attack. Some even convinced themselves that the fluoridation of water was part of a communist conspiracy to weaken the physiology of American citizens.

There are often significant divides between perception and reality. One expert considers the division a serious component in the conduct of international politics. He defines this component as

> . . . a vital dimension of international relations: the frequent and highly significant differences between the way nations perceive one another and the way they really are. For the titanic struggles among the nations of our time are not only waged on the basis of objective realities. They are also fought out in the realm of imagery and imagination.[7]

Images matter, and they can linger for a long time. When NATO was created in 1949, its purpose, as its first Secretary General explained, was "to keep the Russians out, the Americans in, and the Germans down."[8] Six decades later, the concerns are much the same but less intense. Western Europeans still occasionally worry that an economically desperate Russia might strike out, that the Americans will recover their isolationist perspective and remove their military units from Europe, and that the Germans, with the region's largest economy, will again become predominant and militaristic. However, as the new century opened, Europeans, Russians, and Americans were all beginning to focus on the rise of Islamic radicalism in the Middle East, South Asia, and in their own countries.

Certainly, real differences existed between the United States and the Soviet Union during the Cold War. These differences reflected a division in ideology, military and political rivalry, and national interest—all objective and understandable realities. But many perceptions magnified and distorted these realities. Soviet

[6]To read more on this example of self-destructive national hatred, see the controversial study by Daniel Jonah Goldhagen, *Hitler's Willing Executioners: Ordinary Germans and the Holocaust* (New York: Alfred A. Knopf, 1996).

[7]John G. Stoessinger, *The Might of Nations: World Politics in Our Time*, 10th ed. (New York: McGraw-Hill, 1996), 402.

[8]Quoted in A. Hyde-Price, "Future Security Systems for Europe," in C. McInnes ed., *Strategy and Security in the New Europe* (London: Routledge, 1992), 42.

dictator Joseph Stalin who ruled for thirty years between 1923 and 1953 was a political paranoid who assumed that the United States was striving to destroy him. For their part, Americans during the 1950s needed to become better educated about the goals and history of the Soviet Union to more accurately evaluate the Soviet challenge, rather than spend their time searching for communist infiltrators in American industries.

Perception does indeed have a way of becoming reality. Millions of Americans in 2003 were angry enough at the French over their reluctance to support American policy in the Middle East to announce their boycott of France's wine and cheese imports. From being longtime American allies, the French quickly became associated with defending the morally bankrupt regime of Saddam Hussein. Others, including many Americans, considered the attention given to Iraq to be misplaced. After all, it was the North Koreans who, by early 2003, were developing nuclear weapons and the ability to deliver them to targets.[9] Iraq was still confined to manufacturing, and hiding from United Nations' inspections teams, biological and chemical weapons.

Stereotypes can influence people and nations and can even gradually be transformed into reality. The Arab-Israeli conflict is an excellent case study. For many years after Israel's establishment in 1948, Arab governments accused Israel of conspiring to seize Arab territory and threatened to "drive the Israelis into the sea" before this could happen. The Israelis, unreceptive to the idea of being destroyed, launched successful pre-emptive wars in 1956 and 1967 to forestall an Arab attack. The result was that Israel did come to occupy more Arab territory—exactly what the Arabs feared and what, ironically, might not have happened had the Arabs not threatened Israel. Several decades later, Israel is still in the process of gradually returning Arab lands. This is a perfect if rather depressing case of a self-fulfilling prophecy.

15-4 Integration and Fragmentation

It is safe to assume that the international situation will continue to change, substantially and rapidly, in the early years of the twenty-first century. The impact of such change will strongly influence the process of American politics. As the one remaining superpower, the United States will be expected to fully participate in the global economy, the continuing and expanding technological revolution, and democratization. Problems that are difficult to resolve and that in fact may not be completely or permanently resolvable will continue to challenge the United States, including ethnic conflict, religious nationalism, and the rise of innovative forms of political sovereignty. The world may be in the midst of a lengthy era of collapsing empires that began a century ago—the latest being the Soviet empire—and may continue to watch as new (or renewed) states come into being.

The United States and much of the rest of the world may find themselves in a situation characterized by a dynamic contradiction. On the one hand, a strong **supranationalism** appears to be rising, in which countries voluntarily compromise national sovereignty for the mutual benefits of pooling their economic and political resources. The European Union is thus far the most successful example of this process, but it is confined to Western European politics. In some of these countries, such as Denmark and the United Kingdom, large segments of the population are hesitant about full involvement in a movement that may diminish national sovereignty. Others, such as the Czech Republic and Slovenia, are enthusiastically applying to be admitted to what they regard as an exclusive and prosperous club.

Countering supranationalism are the fragmentation and disintegration occurring elsewhere. Instead of becoming more unified, some countries are falling apart.

supranationalism
A phenomenon in which several countries in a region pool their resources and agree to be monitored by the same institutions. Some believe supranationalism will succeed nationalism in global politics.

---

[9]"Don't Forget Mr. Kim," *The Economist*, March 1, 2003, 42.

Instead of becoming more integrated into an economic or political region, some countries strongly guard their peculiar forms of ethnocentrism and isolationism. North Korea's regime, for example, prefers to remain removed from the mainstream of the global economy rather than open the country up to economic and political changes that would undermine the government's control.

During the 1990s, it became apparent that these two opposite political phenomena were occurring across much of the world. Organizations such as the North American Free Trade Association (NAFTA) and the European Union (EU) were enabling countries to affordably trade with one another to mutual advantage as tariff barriers were eliminated. The EU, as discussed in an earlier chapter, is working toward political as well as economic integration, highlighted by a functioning though limited European Parliament that since the 1980s has gradually acquired more and more authority.[10] Both NAFTA and the EU seem poised to expand as more countries who qualify economically and politically (that is, possess workable democratic processes) apply for membership. This kind of integration has enabled economies to grow and technologies to expand for mutual benefit.

At the same time, fragmentation is increasingly commonplace. Some countries are either dissolving into smaller sovereign units or are trying to avoid dissolution by granting more autonomy to various regions. India, for example, divided its ethnically troubled northeastern state of Assam into five separate states. The division ultimately satisfied no one, and elements of the largest ethnic group in Assam (there is no majority) want to secede from India altogether.[11] India is only one of several sizable and diverse countries that may experience partial or total disintegration in the future.

Neither integration nor fragmentation has any end in sight. Each process is destined to be a strong dimension of international politics in the early decades of the twenty-first century. Both phenomena will impact and be influenced by the United States. As the first (and so far the only) **universal nation**, with peoples from all over the globe integrated into society, Americans will continue to be viewed by both admirers and adversaries as the cornerstone of political change.

universal nation
A collection of diverse peoples from throughout the world who have migrated to one country and made a place for themselves and their descendants. The United States is the first (and at present, only) universal nation.

When it comes to integration and fragmentation, the American experience remains instructive and perhaps even prophetic. During most of the last half of the twentieth century, the United States was caught up in a sometimes painful effort to achieve racial integration and harmony. Technically, virtually no remaining legal barriers to integration exist. Yet, disconcerting signs indicate that a "disuniting of America"[12] may actually be occurring and that some ethnic communities in the United States may welcome it.[13]

The aftermath of September 11 challenged the integrative process of the United States. Many Americans looked with suspicion on a variety of groups—American Muslims, people of Middle Eastern extraction, women who wear headscarves—though these groups are filled with law-abiding citizens. The United States is a universal nation, but it is an unfinished one. From time to time, international events impact on the process and disturb or delay it. During the early 1980s, many Iranian university students were sent home by an American government that faced hostility from Tehran. During the early 1940s, as mentioned earlier, Japanese Americans were incarcerated in an overwhelming act of injustice after the Empire of Japan attacked Pearl Harbor on December 7, 1941. There is nothing to suggest that interruptions in the integrative process are avoidable.

---

[10]"Looking for Legitimacy," *The Economist,* January 11, 1997, 49–50.

[11]"Beyond the Brahmaputra," *The Economist,* January 4, 1997, 38.

[12]Arthur M. Schlesinger, Jr., *The Disuniting of America* (New York and London: W. W. Norton, 1992).

[13]"The Ebonics Virus," *The Economist,* January 4, 1997, 26–27. It's interesting to note that in October 2006 the United States became a country of 300 million people and was expected to grow to 400 million within the next four decades. The pressures of population increase suggest we have more to worry about than being disliked or disunified, including global warming and drinkable water. See, for example, Michael Specter, "The Last Drop: Confronting the Possibility of Global Catastrophe, " *The New Yorker,* October 23, 2006, pp. 60–71.

The American purpose is not always received with great enthusiasm outside of the country, either. The United States often and sometimes blatantly views itself as a moral nation. This view grew out of a philosophy Americans adopted at the beginning of the country's history that the United States was the "New Jerusalem" where the corrupt and autocratic habits of the old countries would never take root. Instead, America was a special place. In the colonial period,

> Common expressions such as "New-English Jerusalem," "American Jerusalem," "God's American Israel," "American Canaan" connoted from the superior virtue of the people of the colonies and their superior well-being, a sure sign of their election.[14]

Many Americans also don't understand why any country is reluctant to be like America if it has the opportunity to do so:

> While few countries would take issue with the tenets of democracy, many have balked at U.S. insistence that their systems should resemble American-style democracy in order to be legitimate. U.S. emphasis on multiparty elections, a pristine human-rights record, and a free-market economy becomes a point of resentment, if not contention.[15]

Still, the United States remains the most critical player in international politics. As former Secretary of State Madeline Albright once observed, the United States is the "indispensable nation," whose role in international politics must be "between disengagement, which is not possible, and overextension, which is not sustainable."[16]

Since the American military occupation of Iraq in 2003, several traditional allies of as well as internal critics within the United States have expressed the criticism that America is too quick to demonstrate its military power. The United States is also the most successful democratic experiment in history. It will almost certainly be called upon to support democratic movements wherever they occur. American support may be what makes the difference between stability and implosion for some fledgling democracies. This text ends with a brief emphasis on the American role because America's prevailing presence in world affairs will likely continue, and because democracy, for all the perils that lie ahead of it, is moving forward. Today's college students may be the generation that sees the firm establishment of democracy across the globe.

Chapter Summary

1. The end of the superpower rivalry between the United States and Soviet Union created an uncertain world that offered both opportunities for the expansion of democracy and challenges to its continuance.
2. Non-state actors such as terrorist organizations provided a sense of urgency to getting local conflicts resolved since non-state actors can commit outrageous and violent acts without risking their existence.
3. The American democracy remains the decisive element in the international constellation; it is viewed by some as the world's greatest hope and by others as its most serious threat.
4. Another dichotomy with global implications has to do with whether we are becoming more integrated or fragmented as a global society. While the global economy grows and steadily expands to include more and more people ethnic and religious differences continue to divide nations and communities within nations.
5. The United States remains the world's first and, so far, only universal nation. Its economic strength, military superiority, and political influence will continue to characterize, for better or worse, the relations between states for the foreseeable future.

---

[14]Liah Greenfield, *Nationalism: Five Roads to Modernity* (Cambridge, Massachusetts: Harvard University Press, 1992), 407.

[15]Adonis Hoffman, "Increasingly, U.S. Finds Itself Whistling Alone," *The Christian Science Monitor*, December 13, 1996, 18.

[16]"Albright's Perch," *The Economist*, January 11, 1997, 30.

Chapter 15 Quiz

1. After the Cold War's conclusion, all of the following countries voluntarily surrendered their nuclear arsenals except for
   a. Belarus.
   b. North Korea.
   c. Ukraine.
   d. Kazakhstan.

2. After the end of the Cold War, all of the following countries dissolved except for
   a. East Germany.
   b. the Soviet Union.
   c. Estonia.
   d. Yugoslavia.

3. The dismantling of the Berlin Wall in 1989 signaled the end of
   a. World War I.
   b. World War II.
   c. the Cold War.
   d. democracy in Germany.

4. Countries known to be pursuing nuclear weapons or programs include all except which of the following?
   a. Iran
   b. North Korea
   c. Libya
   d. South Korea

5. Bosnia is an example of
   a. political fragmentation.
   b. religious harmony.
   c. a rapidly advancing economy.
   d. the resilience of the country's communist movement.

6. The explanation "to keep the Russians out, the Americans in, and the Germans down," was applied to
   a. the United Nations.
   b. the formation of NATO.
   c. Central Asia.
   d. the Balkans.

7. The European Union is an example of
   a. internationalism.
   b. nationalism.
   c. supranationalism.
   d. ethnonationalism.

8. NAFTA is a
   a. military alliance.
   b. hemispheric parliament.
   c. peace-keeping organization.
   d. trade association that eliminates trade barriers among countries in North America.

9. The term "universal nation" applies to
   a. the European Union.
   b. the United States.
   c. the United Nations.
   d. international trade.

10. The term "indispensable nation" applies to
    a. Saudi Arabia.
    b. France.
    c. the United States.
    d. the United Kingdom.

Political Atlas

Order of Maps

| FIGURE A–1 | Demographic Shifts in the United States, 1950–2020* |

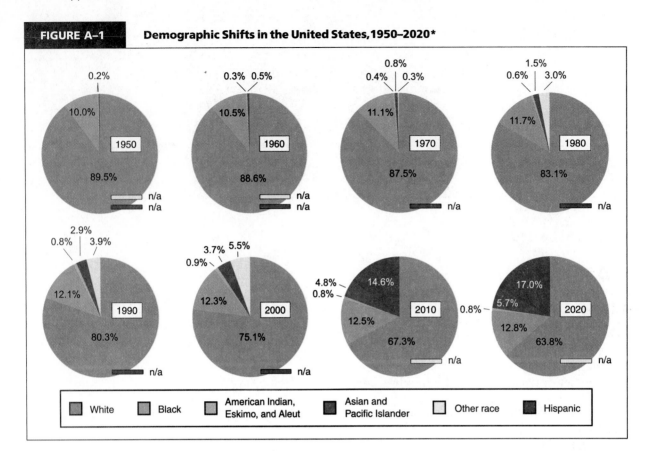

*The data indicated in this illustration do not provide proportions for the Hispanic population because the opportunity to identify oneself explicitly as Hispanic or Latino is a recent one. The Bureau of the Census allowed Hispanic or Latino designations but such information was considered a subset of the more traditional categories such as black and white. Future censuses will enable respondents to identify themselves as Hispanic.

| FIGURE A–2 | Ethno-Linguistic Boundaries |

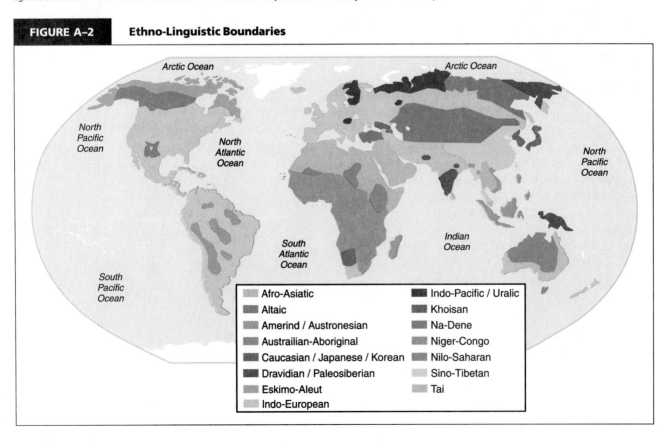

FIGURE A–3   Quality of Life Worldwide

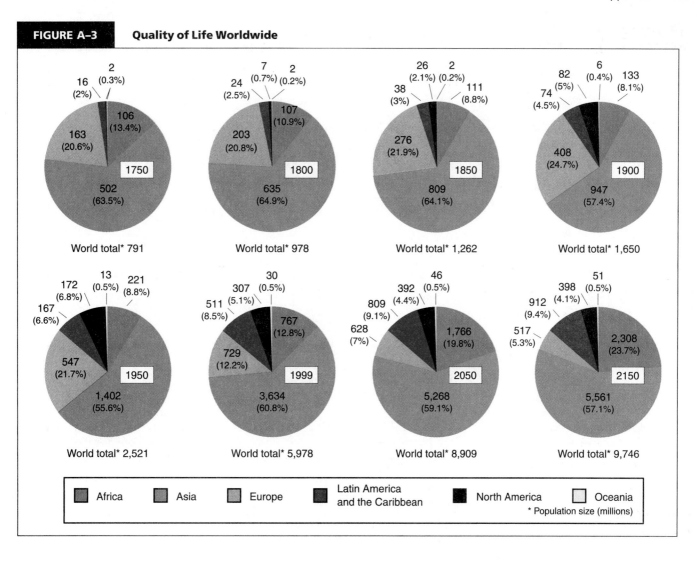

World total* 791

World total* 978

World total* 1,262

World total* 1,650

World total* 2,521

World total* 5,978

World total* 8,909

World total* 9,746

Africa   Asia   Europe   Latin America and the Caribbean   North America   Oceania

* Population size (millions)

FIGURE A–4   Estimated Number of Out-of-School Children by Gender and by Region (in 1990 and 2000)

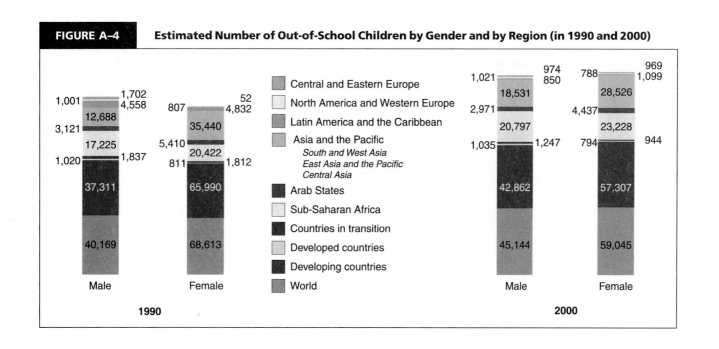

Central and Eastern Europe
North America and Western Europe
Latin America and the Caribbean
Asia and the Pacific
    South and West Asia
    East Asia and the Pacific
    Central Asia
Arab States
Sub-Saharan Africa
Countries in transition
Developed countries
Developing countries
World

Male   Female

1990

Male   Female

2000

FIGURE A–5	**Gun Control in Selected Countries**
	Imagine the reaction if the U.S. government tried to become a Type 1 country

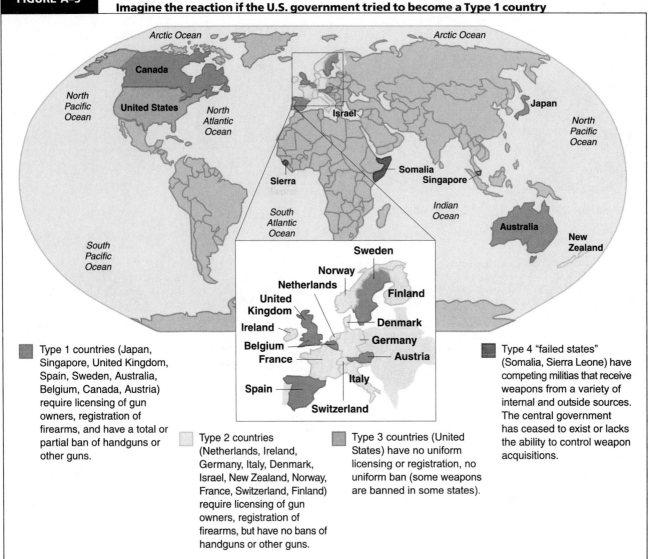

Type 1 countries (Japan, Singapore, United Kingdom, Spain, Sweden, Australia, Belgium, Canada, Austria) require licensing of gun owners, registration of firearms, and have a total or partial ban of handguns or other guns.

Type 4 "failed states" (Somalia, Sierra Leone) have competing militias that receive weapons from a variety of internal and outside sources. The central government has ceased to exist or lacks the ability to control weapon acquisitions.

Type 2 countries (Netherlands, Ireland, Germany, Italy, Denmark, Israel, New Zealand, Norway, France, Switzerland, Finland) require licensing of gun owners, registration of firearms, but have no bans of handguns or other guns.

Type 3 countries (United States) have no uniform licensing or registration, no uniform ban (some weapons are banned in some states).

FIGURE A–6	**Division of Cyprus**

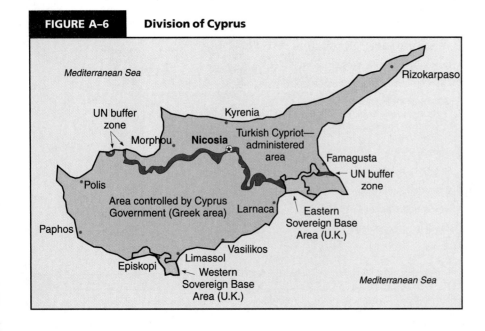

FIGURE A–7

Military Actions by U.S. Presidents
Presidents have often used their authority as commander-in-chief of the armed forces to take military action in places thousands of miles from the United States in order to secure and protect American personnel and property

United States— Lincoln called forth the militias of the several states on April 15, 1861, approximately three months before Congress convened.

Mexico— By sending U.S. troops into a disputed area claimed by both Texas and Mexico, Polk, in 1846, encouraged an enemy attack. He then asked Congress to recognize that a state of war existed, which it did.

Iraq— President George H.W. Bush ordered U.S. troops to Saudi Arabia and Iraq in the Gulf War, which, like Korea and Vietnam involvements, was approved by Congress, but Congress did not officially declare war, instead authorizing use of all necessary force, based on the auspices of existing UN treaties.

Afghanistan and Iraq— Congress gave its approval of President George W. Bush's War on Terrorism and his sending of troops to Afghanistan, but while it authorized all necessary force, it stopped short of declaring war on the country. Congress then authorized the use of force against Iraq.

Vietnam— Like Korea, U.S. presence in Vietnam was never an officially declared war. As commander-in-chief, Lyndon Johnson, and later Richard Nixon, overstepped legal boundaries by sending military personnel to the country.

Korea— Truman's conceptualization of his authority was tested when Chinese troops invaded Korean soil. Instead of asking Congress to declare war, Truman, on the advice of Secretary of State Dean Acheson, decided that Korea was not technically a war—it was a police action justified under UN treaty obligations.

FIGURE A–8   **Code Law Versus Case Law**

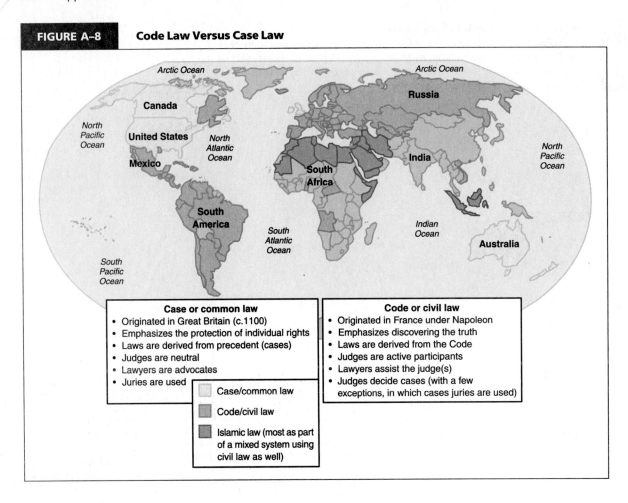

Case or common law
- Originated in Great Britain (c.1100)
- Emphasizes the protection of individual rights
- Laws are derived from precedent (cases)
- Judges are neutral
- Lawyers are advocates
- Juries are used

Code or civil law
- Originated in France under Napoleon
- Emphasizes discovering the truth
- Laws are derived from the Code
- Judges are active participants
- Lawyers assist the judge(s)
- Judges decide cases (with a few exceptions, in which cases juries are used)

- Case/common law
- Code/civil law
- Islamic law (most as part of a mixed system using civil law as well)

FIGURE A–9   **Quality of Life Worldwide**

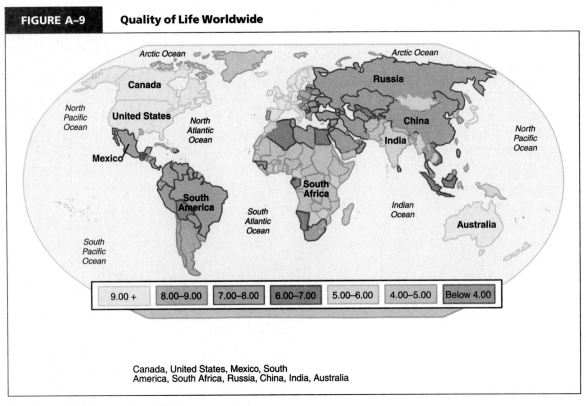

| 9.00 + | 8.00–9.00 | 7.00–8.00 | 6.00–7.00 | 5.00–6.00 | 4.00–5.00 | Below 4.00 |

Canada, United States, Mexico, South America, South Africa, Russia, China, India, Australia

Source: UN Development Report, 2001.

FIGURE A–10 Afghanistan: Ethnic Communities

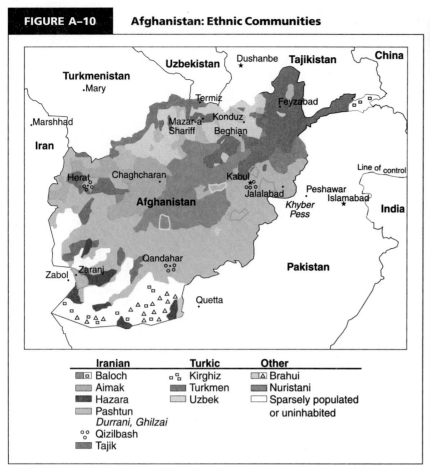

Iranian
- Baloch
- Aimak
- Hazara
- Pashtun
  Durrani, Ghilzai
- Qizilbash
- Tajik

Turkic
- Kirghiz
- Turkmen
- Uzbek

Other
- Brahui
- Nuristani
- Sparsely populated or uninhabited

FIGURE A–11 Democratic Peoples' Republic of (North) Korea and the Republic of (South) Korea

FIGURE A–12 The United Nations' Partition Plan for Palestine, 1947

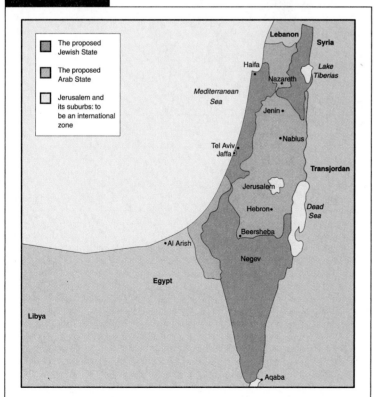

- The proposed Jewish State
- The proposed Arab State
- Jerusalem and its suburbs: to be an international zone

FIGURE A–13   **Africa: From Colonialism to Independence**

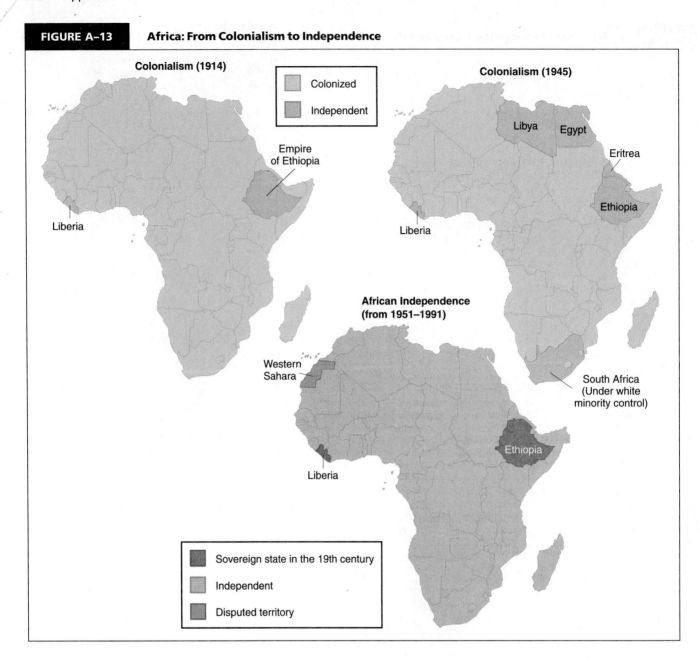

FIGURE A–14   Post–World War II European Alliances

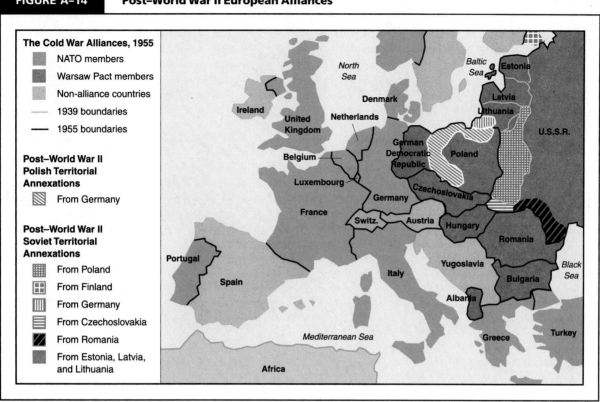

The Cold War Alliances, 1955
- NATO members
- Warsaw Pact members
- Non-alliance countries
- 1939 boundaries
- 1955 boundaries

Post–World War II Polish Territorial Annexations
- From Germany

Post–World War II Soviet Territorial Annexations
- From Poland
- From Finland
- From Germany
- From Czechoslovakia
- From Romania
- From Estonia, Latvia, and Lithuania

FIGURE A–15   Post–Cold War Europe

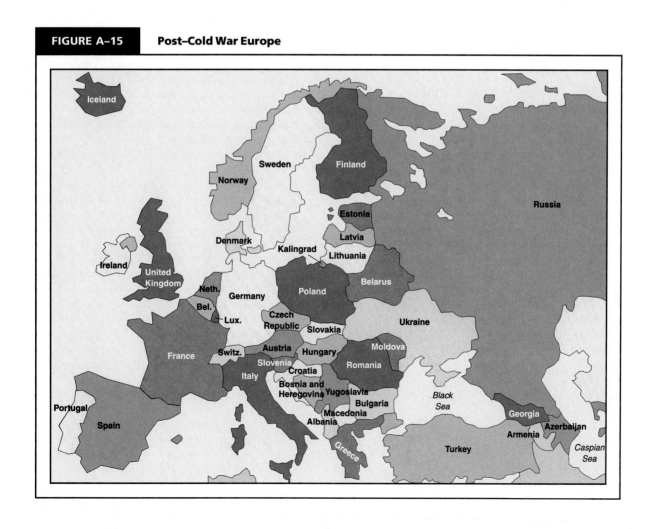

Russia (including Chechnya)
Incidents 102
Injuries 113
Fatalities 51

Nepal
Incidents 100
Injuries 104
Fatalities 33

Thailand
Incidents 359
Injuries 584
Fatalities 148

India (including Kashmir)
Incidents 272
Injuries 1,051
Fatalities 398

Pakistan
Incidents 163
Injuries 398
Fatalities 160

Afghanistan
Incidents 207
Injuries 328
Fatalities 298

West Bank/Gaza
Incidents 479
Injuries 302
Fatalities 74

Iraq
Incidents 2336
Injuries 9399
Fatalities 6234

Colombia
Incidents 101
Injuries 208
Fatalities 112

10 Most Active Terrorist Groups: 2005
(incidents)

1. al-Qaeda Organization in the Land of the Two Rivers (190)
2. Hamas (183)
3. Taliban (100)
4. Communist Party of Nepal– Maoist (93)
5. Communist Party of India– Maoist (90)
6. Liberation Tigers of Tamil Eelam (62)
7. Revolutionary Armed Forces of Colombia (61)
8. Palestinian Islamic Jihad (53)
9. Ansar al-Sunnah Army (42)
10. al-Fatah (33)

10 Most Frequent Targets: 2005
(incidents)

1. Police (1166)
2. Government (1160)
3. Private citizens & property (901)
4. Other (351)
5. Business (242)
6. Utilities (221)
7. Educational institutions (185)
8. Religious figures & institutions (176)
9. Transportation (140)
10. Unknown (88)

5 Most Frequent Tactics: 2005
(incidents)

1. Bombing (2650)
2. Armed attack (1532)
3. Kidnapping (310)
4. Assassination (159)
5. Arson (114)

10 Most Lethal Attacks: 2005

1. al-Qaeda Organization in the Land of the Two Rivers
   Suicide bombing
   February 28: Al-Hillah, Iraq
   125 fatalities

2. al-Qaeda Organization in the Land of the Two Rivers
   Suicide bombing
   September 29: Balad, Iraq
   102 fatalities

3. al-Qaeda Organization in the Land of the Two Rivers
   Suicide bombing
   July 16: Musayyb, Iraq
   98 fatalities

4. al-Qaeda Organization in the Land of the Two Rivers
   Suicide bombing
   September 14: Baghdad, Iraq
   88 fatalities

5. Unknown group
   Suicide bombing
   November 18: Khanaqin, Iraq
   77 fatalities

6. al-Qaeda Organization in the Land of the Two Rivers
   Suicide bombing
   November 9: Amman, Jordan
   63 fatalities

7. Ansar al-Sunnah Army
   Suicide bombing
   May 4: Arbil, Iraq
   60 fatalities

8. Abu Hafs Al-Masri Brigade and Secret Organization of al-Qaeda in Europe
   Suicide bombing
   July 7: London, England
   total 56 fatalities**

9. Soldiers of the Prophet's Companions
   Suicide bombing,
   March 10: Mosul, Iraq
   53 fatalities

10. al-Qaeda Organization in the Land of the Two Rivers
    Suicide bombing
    July 29: Rabiah, Iraq
    52 fatalities

**listed as four separate, but coordinated incidents

FIGURE A–17   Countries with Nuclear Capabilities

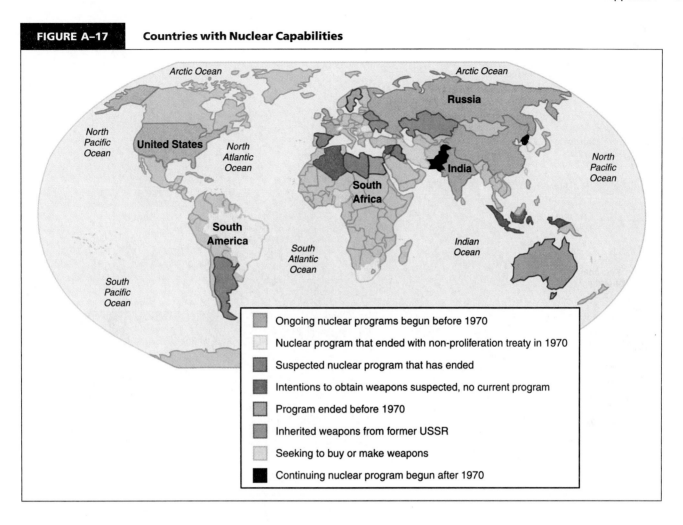

Ongoing nuclear programs begun before 1970

Nuclear program that ended with non-proliferation treaty in 1970

Suspected nuclear program that has ended

Intentions to obtain weapons suspected, no current program

Program ended before 1970

Inherited weapons from former USSR

Seeking to buy or make weapons

Continuing nuclear program begun after 1970

FIGURE A–18   The Dissolution of Yugoslavia

An example of ethnic divisions.

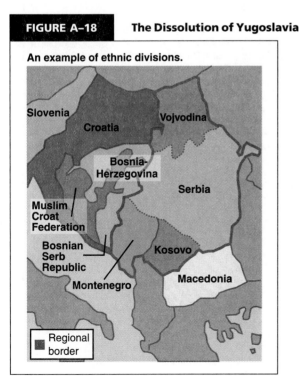

Regional border

FIGURE A–19   **Russia's Ethnic Republics**

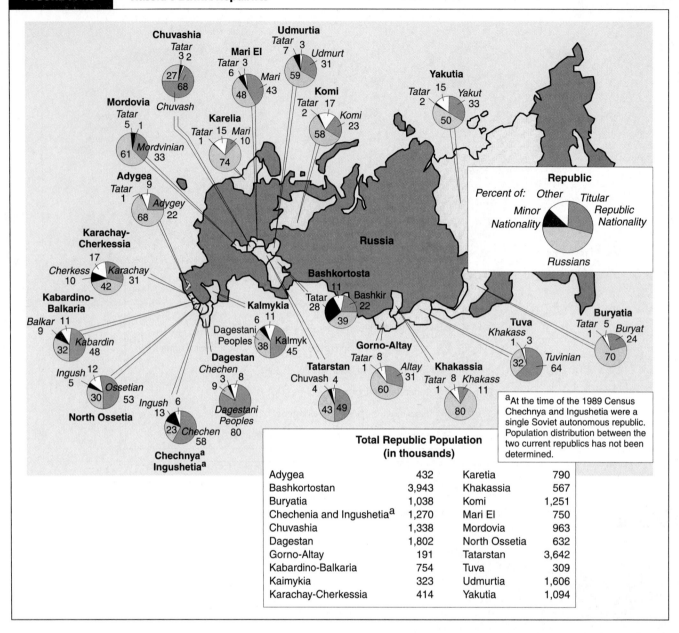

Chuvashia
Tatar
3 2
27
68
Chuvash

Mari El
Tatar 3
6
Mari
48   43

Udmurtia
Tatar 3
7   Udmurt
59   31

Komi
Tatar 17
2   Komi
58   23

Yakutia
Tatar 15
2   Yakut
50   33

Mordovia
Tatar
5 1
Mordvinian
61   33

Karelia
Tatar 15 Mari
1   10
74

Adygea
Tatar 9
1   Adygey
68   22

Karachay-
Cherkessia
17
Cherkess Karachay
10   31
42

Kabardino-
Balkaria
Balkar 11
9   Kabardin
32   48

Ingush 12
5   Ossetian
30   53
North Ossetia

Kalmykia
6   11
Dagestani
Peoples 38 Kalmyk
45

Dagestan
Chechen
3   8
9   Dagestani
Peoples 80

Ingush 6
13
23 Chechen
58
Chechnya[a]
Ingushetia[a]

Russia

Bashkortosta
11
Tatar   Bashkir
28   22
39

Gorno-Altay
Tatar 8
1   Altay
31
60

Tatarstan
Chuvash 4
4
43 49

Khakassia
Tatar 8 Khakass
1   11
80

Tuva
Khakass
1   3
32   Tuvinian
64

Buryatia
Tatar 5   Buryat
1   24
70

Republic

Percent of: Other   Titular
Minor   Republic
Nationality   Nationality

Russians

[a]At the time of the 1989 Census
Chechnya and Ingushetia were a
single Soviet autonomous republic.
Population distribution between the
two current republics has not been
determined.

Total Republic Population (in thousands)			
Adygea	432	Karetia	790
Bashkortostan	3,943	Khakassia	567
Buryatia	1,038	Komi	1,251
Chechenia and Ingushetia[a]	1,270	Mari El	750
Chuvashia	1,338	Mordovia	963
Dagestan	1,802	North Ossetia	632
Gorno-Altay	191	Tatarstan	3,642
Kabardino-Balkaria	754	Tuva	309
Kaimykia	323	Udmurtia	1,606
Karachay-Cherkessia	414	Yakutia	1,094

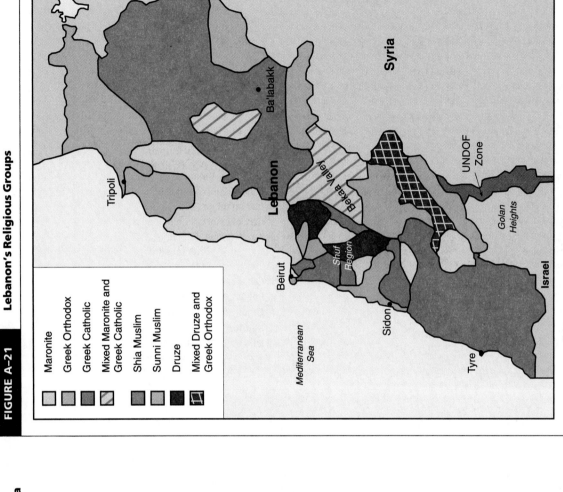

FIGURE A–21   Lebanon's Religious Groups

Legend:
- Maronite
- Greek Orthodox
- Greek Catholic
- Mixed Maronite and Greek Catholic
- Shia Muslim
- Sunni Muslim
- Druze
- Mixed Druze and Greek Orthodox

FIGURE A–20   Israel Proper and Palestinian Territories of the West Bank and Gaza

*Israeli-occupied with current status subject to the Israeli-Palestinian Interim Agreement—Israelis to leave Gaza Strip by the end of 2005.

FIGURE A–22   **Iran: Ethnic and Religious Communities**

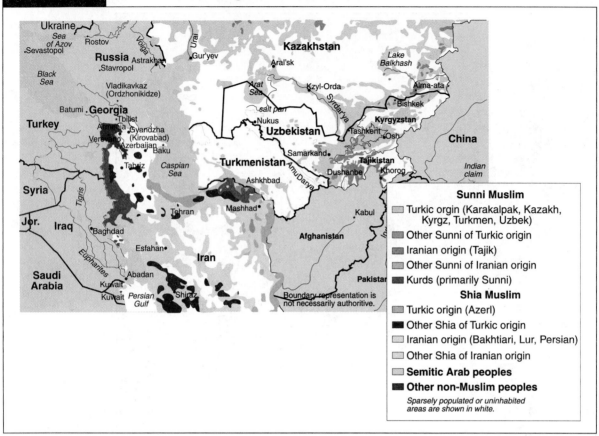

Sunni Muslim
- Turkic orgin (Karakalpak, Kazakh, Kyrgz, Turkmen, Uzbek)
- Other Sunni of Turkic origin
- Iranian origin (Tajik)
- Other Sunni of Iranian origin
- Kurds (primarily Sunni)

Shia Muslim
- Turkic origin (Azerl)
- Other Shia of Turkic origin
- Iranian origin (Bakhtiari, Lur, Persian)
- Other Shia of Iranian origin
- **Semitic Arab peoples**
- **Other non-Muslim peoples**

Sparsely populated or uninhabited areas are shown in white.

Boundary representation is not necessarily authoritive.

FIGURE A–23   **Kurdistan**

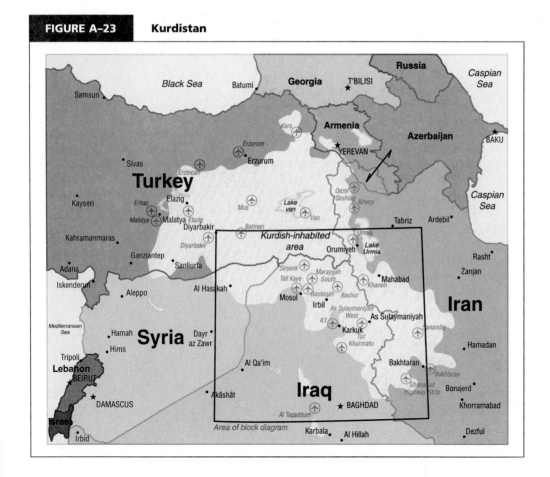

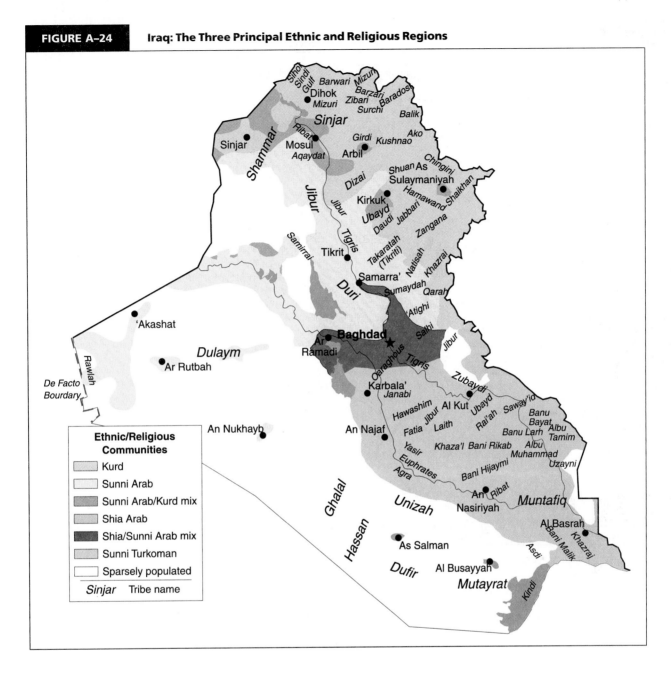

FIGURE A–24   **Iraq: The Three Principal Ethnic and Religious Regions**

FIGURE A–25   **Sudan (including Darfur)**

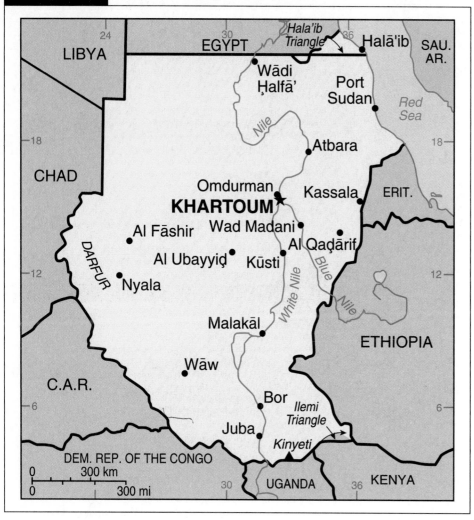

GLOSSARY

A

absolute monarchy A system in which the chief executive holds all significant political powers and transfers power to his or her heirs.

accidental president A phenomenon in American politics: the sudden and unexpected ascension of a vice president to the presidency.

antiparasite laws Instituted by the Soviet government, these laws discouraged laziness by requiring all members of Soviet society to work.

appeasement The idea that a hostile nation can be persuaded to maintain peaceful relations if other countries give in to some of its demands. The British and French governments' attempt to placate German territorial ambitions enjoyed substantial popular support in the late 1930s. The guiding notion was that it was only fair to meet at least some German demands because Germany had been so harshly treated by the Versailles Treaty at the end of World War I.

autarky An economic system in which a society strives to achieve economic self-sufficiency within its own borders and become independent of foreign markets and international commerce.

B

Baader-Meinhof gang Also known as the Red Army Faction, this group was formed in 1970 and was violently opposed to the then West German government's supportive relationship with Israel. Andreas Baader and Ursula Meinhof both died in prison and the gang gradually dissolved by the late 1990s.

Baltic states The three small republics (Latvia, Lithuania, and Estonia, with a combined population of about eight million) that were forcibly annexed by the Soviet Union in 1940 and, in 1989, became the first of the Soviet republics to secede, leading to the eventual collapse of the entire Soviet system.

bipolarity An international situation in which two superpowers challenge each other for global supremacy. Usually, each is too strong for one to eliminate the other or to be challenged by any other power.

bureaucracy The machinery of government that carries out the policies that the executive and legislative branches have formulated.

C

cabinet government In a parliamentary system, the cabinet is composed of party leaders who stand or fall together, creating a cabinet government. Cabinet members must publicly agree and must maintain a parliamentary majority to retain power.

case law Law based on judicial interpretations of existing laws and statutes. Court decisions become law themselves.

code law Law based on written codes that give judges little leeway in interpreting established laws.

coercion theory of order A theory stating that a political regime can maintain order by forcing its values on a resistant or unwilling population that is unlikely to voluntarily accept them.

collective responsibility Once a policy is formulated, all of the cabinet ministers in a parliamentary system assume responsibility for its defense and implementation.

collective security The idea that countries interested in preserving the status quo can ally to defeat a country trying to challenge it.

command economy The total control and bureaucratization of a national economy from the political capital, which makes often arbitrary economic decisions without consideration of either need or quality.

common law Law based on judicial decisions that trace back to the Middle Ages in Britain. Common law is the antecedent of case law.

consensus theory of order A theory stating that a political regime can maintain order with minimal or nonexistent political violence when it has established a widespread acceptance of political values and norms.

constitutional monarchy A system in which a nondemocratic institution, the monarchy, is preserved by transferring any substantive decision-making power from the monarch to the parliament.

corruption The practice of bribing government officials to receive contracts for economic projects. Corruption is considered a way to do business in many societies.

D

death squads Murderous gangs that execute a regime's political opponents, even though the death squad is not an official agent of the state.

devolution The decentralization of the roles of a national government with a gradual and usually peaceful transfer of domestic authority to regional jurisdictions.

dialectical materialism The Marxist notion of history as a series of class struggles culminating in a classless society of workers.

dictatorship of the proletariat In Marxist theory, a condition occurring at the end of history, in which the actual producers in society seize control of the apparatus of the state, abolishing class distinctions and allowing producers to enjoy the fruit of their labors.

divine right A monarch's assumption that he or she has spiritual justification for exercising complete power, with minimal or no constitutional restraints.

E

East Asian dragons (or tigers) The East Asian countries of South Korea, Taiwan, and Singapore whose economies and standards of living are approaching those of the West and Japan. Other countries such as Indonesia, Malaysia, and Thailand may soon be included in this group.

economic miracle The rapid economic recovery of a country militarily defeated and economically devastated. Germany and Japan, the defeated Axis powers in World War II, are generally regarded as case studies of countries that fully recovered both their economic importance and global standing in just a few short decades.

economic rights The right to a pension and guaranteed medical treatment, earned by each able-bodied individual who fulfills the duty to work in a socialist or communist system.

electronic democracy An electoral system in which each participant or voter can register direct approval or disapproval on issues through a computer or other electronic device.

elite A privileged minority in society, usually composed of no more than 10 percent of the population, that controls the political decision-making process.

enforcement violence The ability of a political regime to sustain itself by applying force whenever necessary to both maintain its existence and secure social order.

ethnics A term of abbreviation applied to ethnic communities. An ethnic is simply an ethnic group distinguished and united by its religion, culture, language, or common history of suffering.

ethnocentrism A population's almost paranoid aversion to "foreign" minorities and their commitment to a special destiny that justifies maltreatment of other nations.

extremist (political) party A political organization on the radical left or right that espouses an ideological viewpoint that usually (but not always) lacks popular support at election time. The party may also express an extremist religious point of view.

F

failed states A political entity in which the central government either does not exist or lacks an ability to impose adequate control over the entire country.

free market An economic system characterized by minimal government regulation and opportunities for every member of society to acquire material wealth.

G

G7 The top seven economies of the world—the United States, Japan, Germany, France, Italy, United Kingdom, and Canada. These countries may be joined in the near future by rapidly advancing economies such as China's. The G7 is sometimes expanded to G8 as a courtesy to Russia.

genocide The systematic murder, usually planned or at least sponsored by the government, of an entire community or nation of people based on its religion, ethnicity, and/or social status.

H

head of government The top government officer who exercises actual political power.

head of state The ceremonial leader who *symbolizes* national sovereignty and political legitimacy.

I

illegal violence Violence that violates the law and that is exercised by unlawful and unconstitutional agents. Sometimes illegal violence causes the deterioration of a political regime. At other times, it surfaces after the breakdown of a regime.

impeachment The process in place in presidential systems that allows legislatures to charge officeholders with wrongdoing and remove them from office if they are found guilty.

J

judicial review The court's ability to declare an act of the executive or the legislature unconstitutional, whether on the state or national level.

K

Kremlin The physical and political center of the Russian government in Moscow through the czarist and communist periods for most of Russian history, except when the capital was located in St. Petersburg during the eighteenth and nineteenth centuries.

L

laws Rules that formalize and reinforce patterns of social behavior that the overwhelming majority of society's members consider acceptable and beneficial.

left A common reference to ideologies that tend to be liberal or socialist in nature.

legal violence Violence the state commits in keeping with the law. The state sometimes has the responsibility to apply violence to maintain order in the society, to protect its citizens, or to remove from society those who have injured others.

legislative councils Advisory bodies that monarchs in Persian Gulf states and other traditionalist regimes choose and maintain.

legitimacy The determination through one or more means—by divine right, or through electoral or ideological processes—that a regime has the right to govern for a precise or indefinite period of time.

"little tigers" Smaller countries located in East Asia with strong and growing modern economies, specifically South Korea, Singapore, and Taiwan.

living space The German term, popularized during the 1930s, describing the goal used to justify acquiring territory in eastern Europe, removing the indigenous populations, and sending Germans to replace them—the Germans needed "living space."

loyal opposition In democratic regimes, the "loyal opposition" is usually the minority party in the legislature. The minority will challenge the government on various issues while awaiting the opportunity to become the majority in the next election.

M

mainstream (political) party A political organization that strives to win elections by appealing to moderate, centrist voters and, when necessary, playing down its ideological bases by emphasizing pragmatism and flexibility.

manifest destiny The term used to describe and justify the American expansion from ocean to ocean.

martyrdom The willing death of an individual in order to further a radical ideological or theological message.

minority government Occurs in a parliamentary system when no party or coalition of parties can secure a numerical majority of legislative seats; a minority government functions only until a new election, which often occurs within several months.

minority president A phenomenon that characterizes American presidential politics: A candidate can win an election without acquiring either a majority or plurality of the popular vote.

multimember districts A region in which the constituency elects two or more representatives who may or may not be from the same political party.

multipolarity An international situation in which several powers compete against one another for regional supremacy. Multipolarity may divide countries into various contending coalitions.

N

Nakba An Arabic word for disaster and since 1948 applied to the plight of Palestinians who perceive the establishment of Israel on parts of traditional Palestine to be their own tragedy.

Napoleonic Code The first legal code to be established in a country with a civil law legal system.

nation A community of people who possess distinctive ethnic, linguistic, religious, geographical, and cultural and historical commonalities. These features do not have to all be simultaneously present.

Nationalism A people's psychological bonding with symbols of a common ancestry or of other identifiable links with one another, usually accompanied by a widespread pride in a nation's accomplishments.

nation-state system While many nations do not have their own states and many states are composed of numerous nations, some type of sovereign jurisdiction has extended to the entire earth's surface, creating a network of nation-states.

NATO The North Atlantic Treaty Organization was created in 1949 to thwart any Soviet designs on Western Europe. NATO was part of the containment strategy formulated in the Truman Doctrine.

natural law Law that is universal and absolute: It applies to and prevails over all peoples throughout time.

Nazism The ideology officially expressed in Germany from 1933 to 1945 that practiced racism and genocide.

nepotism The practice of appointing one's close relatives to high political office to ensure maximum support and loyalty.

NICs The acronym for *newly industrialized countries*, most of which are located in East Asia and Latin America.

nuclear threshold On the verge of acquiring nuclear weapons or the technical ability to build them.

P

parliamentary majority The majority party in a parliamentary system. The executive must receive consistent support from a numerical majority of legislators to continue in office and to secure the passage of its legislative program.

parliamentary party Those members of a political party who hold seats in the national legislature and are essentially the leadership of the party.

partition The political remedy of dividing a territory among two or more antagonistic communities without much likelihood of satisfying any of the parties.

party discipline The efforts political parties make to get their own legislators to support the party line on various issues, to guarantee both party solidarity and party support for the individual members at election time.

party whips Legislators who work between the party leadership and the rank-and-file members; whips must ensure that on any parliamentary issue, all members will be present and voting, and they must try to persuade members to support the party's position.

party-state A one-party system where the party dominates all state and social institutions. The state is simply an agency of the party to implement party programs and agendas.

plurality Simply the largest number of votes cast, which need not be a majority, for a candidate in an election.

polis The city-state form of government that Plato and Aristotle regarded as the optimal political arrangement for conducting human affairs.

political crimes Acts that demonstrate opposition to a regime's policies or that clamor for change.

political implosion The collapse of a political system from within, usually caused by a breakdown in public confidence in the economic and political institutions.

political trauma A severe or devastating shock to a national society as the result of war, unprecedented economic hardship, accelerated and violent civil strife, or a combination of these factors.

positive law The philosophy that law is what a particular society decides it is for itself alone, not an absolute.

pragmatism A practical approach to politics and diplomacy as opposed to an ideological style. Pragmatists often experiment to see what works and what doesn't.

professional interest group An organization that strives to lobby for and reflect the values and preferences of career professionals such as lawyers or physicians.

proletariat The class of workers who produce goods and, therefore, profits.

proportional representation (PR) An electoral system that allots legislative seats to political parties on the basis of each party's percentage of the total popular vote.

R

Red Brigades Founded in 1970, the Red Brigades became the most notorious left wing terrorist group in Italy. Its most notorious activity was carried out in 1978 when it kidnapped and murdered a former Italian prime minister. Popular support quickly diminished following this event.

referendum A legal provision that allows the entire electorate in a region or a country to vote yes or no on an issue. The outcome becomes law without requiring legislative action.

regional or separatist political party A political movement with an appeal in a precise geographical part of the country or to a particular segment of the national population.

reign of terror Arbitrary violence institutionalized by a newly installed revolutionary regime that is both insecure and ideologically driven.

religious constituency A voting group politically defined largely by its predominant religious affiliation.

religious party A political organization with a religious agenda that calls for laws and lifestyles to be consistent with scriptural doctrine.

right A common reference to ideologies that tend to be conservative in nature.

rotten boroughs British electoral districts in which only one person owned enough land to be able to vote or stand for office. The candidate faced no opposition, simply voted for himself in parliamentary elections, and declared himself the winning candidate.

S

Sharia Islamic law that provides a code of rules for correct moral behavior.

shock therapy The sudden and rapid dismantling of a collectivized economy and maximized state control, replaced with a free market and minimal government supervision.

single-issue interest group An organization that seeks to influence policy according to a usually uncompromising point of view on a particular issue, such as abortion or capital punishment.

single-member (SM) district A region in which the constituency elects one representative, usually the individual who receives a plurality of the votes cast.

social contract An arrangement Thomas Hobbes and John Locke proposed for the establishment of a civil society under a sovereign government.

Speaker of the House The presiding leader of the lower legislative chamber. The Speaker has substantial powers when it comes to setting legislative agendas, recognizing members, and maintaining order. This term is used in the English-speaking democracies.

state The institutional structure of a political society that contains sovereignty, a governing apparatus, and a population that, while contained within designated geographical boundaries, may or may not be characterized by ethnic, linguistic, or religious homogeneity.

statutory law Law based on parliamentary or congressional legislation.

supranationalism A phenomenon in which several countries in a region pool their resources and agree to be monitored by the same institutions. Some believe supranationalism will succeed nationalism in global politics.

T

targeted killings For decades, Israel has pursued a policy of assassinating leaders of terrorist groups to demonstrate that no one is immune from retaliation. Targeted killings have become a favorite method of counterterrorism that has also been adopted by the United States in Afghanistan and Iraq.

theocracy A political system where religious considerations dominate the legal and judicial process.

Third World A term traditionally used to denote the 150 or so countries, whose populations include four-fifths of the human race, considered lacking in comprehensive economic modernization.

threshold A requirement that a political party receive a minimal percentage of the popular votes cast in order to receive parliamentary seats. In Germany, the threshold is 5 percent; in other countries, such as Israel, the percentage can be lower.

"tiger cubs" Relatively large countries in East Asia and Latin America attempting to modernize their economies. Chile is a successful example of this characterization.

tribal democracy A society that is democratic but extends democracy only to citizens who possess certain ethnic or religious characteristics.

tribalism Refers to a form of political loyalty that is more restricted than the familiar one normally reserved for the state. Tribal political loyalty is often focused on marital and blood ties.

Truman Doctrine Promulgated in 1947, this plan provided a strategy for containing Soviet communist expansion in southeastern Europe and the Near East. Later it was extended to Western Europe through NATO.

U

unipolarity An international situation in which a single superpower has unchallenged global supremacy, commanding a disproportionate share of military force and economic dominance.

universal nation A collection of diverse peoples from throughout the world who have migrated to one country and made a place for themselves and their descendants. The United States is the first (and at present, only) universal nation.

V

vote of (no) confidence A device often used by the legislative opposition in a parliamentary system to embarrass or bring down the government. The government must win every vote of confidence; if it doesn't, it no longer controls the legislative majority, and a new government is formed.

W

Wahhabi Islam An extremist form of Islam established by ibn Abd al-Wahhab, (1703–1792). Wahhabism is Islam's most rigid and puritanical branch, totally and violently opposed to any breach of what it considers to be orthodox Islamic doctrine.

warlords Political or military leaders who take control of small territories and populations when national order and the central government break down.

Z

zero-population growth (ZPG) A policy that promotes a controlled birth rate, encouraging no more than two offspring per set of parents. Germans and Italians, for example, are barely replacing themselves and are only modestly increasing their populations because of immigration.

Page numbers in italics identify an illustration. An italic *n* next to a page number (e.g., *177n*) indicates information that appears in an endnote. An italic *t* next to a page number (e.g., *177t*) indicates information that appears in a table.